D1565768

# Mirabeau

Barbara Luttrell

Southern Illinois University Press
Carbondale and Edwardsville

Published in the United States,
its dependencies, and Canada by
Southern Illinois University Press,
P.O. Box 3697,
Carbondale. IL 62902-3697

First published 1990 by
Harvester Wheatsheaf
66 Wood Lane End, Hemel Hempstead
Hertfordshire, HP2 4RG
A division of
Simon & Schuster International Group

Typeset, printed and bound in Great Britain

---

*Library of Congress Cataloging-in-Publication Data*

Luttrell, Barbara.
   Mirabeau/Barbara Luttrell.
    p.  cm.
   Includes bibliographical references and index.
   1. Mirabeau, Honoré-Gabriel de Riquetti, comte de, 1749 – 1791—
Political and social views.  2.Revolutionaries—France—Biography,
3. France–History—Revolution, 1789 – 1791.  I. Title.
DC146.M7L95   1990
944.04'1'092—dc20
(B)                              90-39621
   ISBN 0 – 8093 – 1705 – 2                  CIP

*To*
*Richard Henry Phillips*
*belatedly*

# Contents

# Acknowledgements

I have received valuable assistance from Mlle Trouillet, *Conservateur* of the Musée Arbaud, Aix-en-Provence; from the staff of the British Library; and also from the staff of the Bibliothèque Nationale, Paris, and the Bibliothèque Publique et Universitaire, Geneva. I thank Lord Lansdowne for permission to quote from unpublished letters in the Bowood archives. My thanks also to Dr C.A. Luttrell for many helpful discussions in the course of preparing this book.

# Introduction

The opening years – 1789 to 1791 – of the French Revolution, which saw the demolition of the *ancien régime*, the Declaration of Rights, and the foundation of a more equitable society, were the years of the Constituent Assembly. They were also the years of Gabriel-Honoré Mirabeau, who dominated the Assembly from its earliest days, and whose reputation as statesman and orator was matched by his national popularity. To ordinary people he was 'the Father of Liberty'. His fellow Provençal, Adolphe Thiers, noted that he had the 'unique honour, when all popularity ends in the revulsion of the people, of having his own cede only to death'. Moderates in the Assembly came to believe that he alone could handle the extremism, of both the right and left, which threatened to undo the achievements of the Revolution; that without him any hope of conciliating the monarchy and the Revolution, and so of creating future political stability, was gone. His death in 1791 was regarded as a calamity. He became a symbol of liberal values, of resistance to state tyranny, to be remembered as Jacobin dictatorship was succeeded by Napoleonic repression, and that in turn by a resumption of reactionist Bourbon rule. Thirty years after his death he had been turned – at any rate, by the apolitical – into a legend.

But was his reputation justified? What did he contribute to the Revolution? Who was right, those who rallied to him as a patriot or those who said he was nothing but an opportunist? Were his policies well reasoned or did he hinder the Revolution from following its inevitable course? None of the other revolutionary leaders has proved more controversial than Mirabeau. As the enemy of privilege and social divisions he belonged with the left. As the advocate of an active executive he put himself apparently in the same camp as the right. As the defender of 'law and order' he reassured the bourgeois spirit of the Assembly. As the champion of the ignored masses he alarmed it. He wanted a monarchy but had little regard for monarchs. He was a pre-Revolution republican; the Revolution created Republicans.

The judgement of historians and critics at different periods has reflected these paradoxes and conflicts. In France his reputation has been at its best at moments of democratic optimism, when Louis XVIII granted a liberal constitution, and when Louis-Philippe first came to the throne; at its lowest in the authoritarian atmosphere of the Second Empire, when reminders of past challenges to the established order were unwelcome. (However, the first Napoleon had admired him sufficiently to have his bust at the Tuileries, apparently unaware that he had condemned military dictatorships as the worst form of government.) Any conclusions about him as a politician and revolutionary leader have always been complicated by questions about the man. Unfortunately for Mirabeau, his most memorable character references were supplied by his political enemies, who called him unprincipled, self-seeking, venal, treacherous, a monster of depravity. His image to this day owes something to the propaganda of both royalists and Jacobins, handed down and authoritatively repeated so often that it has acquired the respectability of fact.

The first historians of the Revolution were royalists for whom the event and the actors were wholly evil, Mirabeau as much as the directors of the Terror, for he, they said, had made possible the later violence. These histories, and the flood of memoirs by monarchist survivors of the Revolution, established a picture of him – the demagogue who had undermined the monarchy and wished to destroy religion – which 'right-wing' opinion accepted throughout the nineteenth century and into the twentieth. Mignet and Thiers were the first historians to make rounded, objective studies of the Revolution, and in Thiers' *Histoire de la Révolution française* (1823–7), a more tolerant picture emerges, of a political moderate who 'did his duty *par raison, par génie*', and not 'for a little gold thrown to his passions'. Etienne Dumont, whose *Souvenirs sur Mirabeau* appeared posthumously in 1832, had followed his career in the Assembly and had provided a number of passages and perorations for his speeches. His book, while falling into the 'I knew Mirabeau' category, is more interesting than most, though the author's Genevan standpoint has to be kept in mind.

The Revolution of 1830 saw something of a Mirabeau cult in a new generation of revolutionaries: in 1831 four plays celebrating his memory were running simultaneously in Paris theatres. Right wing writers continued to attack him. It was Victor Hugo, in 1834, who appreciated that he could not be given a political label, that he was neither monarchist nor Republican nor tied to any sectarian point of view, and that this was why he had become a national symbol, as those identified with régimes and parties never could: 'His work is not the Republic, it is the Revolution'. Hugo's study – which possibly inspired Carlyle's warm portrait – appeared as a preface to *Mémoires biographiques, littéraires, et politiques de Mirabeau*, Lucas de Montigny's reply to all the earlier scandalmongering literature about his father. Despite its filial piety, this work served a useful purpose by reproducing unprinted political material and speeches, as well as extracts from his early writings. Many questions were still unanswered, however: the important Notes in which he tried to convert Louis XVI into a 'king of the Revolution', which explained an ambivalent area of his activities, were not published until 1851. Before then Michelet's assessment of his career and character appeared: an admirer but to the left of Montigny, Michelet regarded him as a Republican in the making, and rejected the vague charge of treason which left-wing ideologues brought against him. Like Hugo he saw him as being forever identified in the nation's imagination with the spirit of the Revolution.

In England it was natural that there should be both greater prejudice about him and greater objectivity. For Burke he was 'the Grand Anarch', the embodiment of that active ability which he saw as posing a constant threat to orderly society. Whig historians admired him as a parliamentarian and champion of personal and political freedom; they did not care for his democratic sympathies, or his character as they understood it. 'Resembling Wilkes in the lower and grosser parts of his character, he had, in his higher qualities, some affinity to Chatham', noted Macaulay after reading Dumont's book; while at the end of the century Lord Acton described him in the same breath as 'odious' and as 'the supreme figure of the time'.

The questions whether he was a patriot, and whether his was a true or a false voice, with their ideological overtone, had first been put by his fellow Jacobins. A century after his death they were asked again by the Sorbonne professor, Alphonse Aulard, a Dantonist and a Republican, whose work on the political history of the Revolution was much admired by Acton. Aulard's Republicanism was that of the revolutionaries who had declared the first Republic in 1792 and who had regarded this act as akin to the Creation. Although when Mirabeau defended the monarchy nearly everybody, future Republicans included, still wanted a king, and although he had died before the advent of the Republic, he was still an apostate to Aulard, whose pronouncements that he lacked revolutionary faith and that his speeches had to be seen in the light of his being paid by the Court, had a lasting effect. He has generally been looked at askance by historians of the left. Aulard's pupil, Mathiez (who became a Robespierrist), called him 'the Machiavellian champion of the people'. While Marx himself had respected him as the one revolutionary leader who was economically literate, Marxists were, and are, suspicious of a revolutionary who wanted a revolutionary king. The exception to the received view was provided by Jean Jaurès, whose *Histoire socialiste* first appeared in 1901. Jaurès saw him as the driving force of the Revolution, 'the great revolutionary', who understood the people, and who had already recognised that they could use their labour as a political weapon. In his opinion, if Mirabeau had succeeded in winning Louis XVI over to the Revolution it would have saved France from both Napoleonic despotism and the bourgeois empire of Louis-Philippe. There is a certain irony in the fact that among the bridges of Paris, with their names recalling Napoleon's battles, there is now a pont Mirabeau.

In recent years there has been a revival of political emphasis in the historiography of the Revolution. The earlier preoccupation with social themes, with 1793 instead of 1789, had the effect of making the Constituent Assembly period, with its concentration on political and constitutional matters, seem extraneous to the Revolution proper. Georges Lefebvre, the inspirer of the history-from-below movement, depicted Mirabeau in his *La Révolution française* as a superficial figure, eloquent, corrupt – 'the Court could buy him at will' – who did not deserve his reputation for statesmanship. Similarly Albert Soboul, in *Précis d'histoire de la Révolution française*, states that he sold his services to the Court; and conveys the impression that subversion was his main activity. Another generally accepted view brackets him with Danton as being a 'physical' type of revolutionary, in contrast with the 'thinking' type represented by Robespierre and Saint-Just, a hypothesis which ignores the existence of Mirabeau's corpus of serious political writing. The recent trend in French Revolution studies, however, has resulted in a revalidation of the aims and achievements of the first Assembly, and as part of this process Mirabeau's ideas have been reassessed, in particular by François Furet, the editor of his speeches.

Jaurès said of him that because he was the only revolutionary leader who did not go to the scaffold his work possessed a particular value. Put another way, he had no part, as the later leaders had, in those stages of the Revolution when normal reasoning gave way to the jargon of dictatorship, and decisions based on the need to retain power became morally right; because of this his views have a certain integrity and independence. Because of this they deserve, perhaps, to be heard again.

A quick gallop like this through various authorities answers none of the questions about Mirabeau, but serves to show the diversity of opinions on him. In this present book an attempt is made to sort out the conflicting evidence about his revolutionary role, to show the range of his ideas, and to see to what extent he deserved his reputation, good or bad. It does not attempt to chronicle in full every aspect of his life: his marriage and relationships with women make compelling reading but the story has been told many times, and scenes from the private life of a revolutionary would have distracted from the account of his political career. Indeed, he was often criticised by his fellow revolutionaries for having a private life. His family background and intellectual apprenticeship have been covered in some detail, however, for they are essential to an understanding of his political philosophy, and the nature of his personal commitment to the Revolution.

# 1

—❧—

# The Family Mould

In 1760, nearly thirty years before the Revolution, the windows of the *ancien régime* were rudely broken; not, on this occasion, by rioters but by a well-aimed book. From its title it sounded respectable, even pedantic – *Théorie de l'impôt*, Theory of taxation – which increased the shock effect of its opening lines, addressed to the king himself:

> Your majesty has twenty million men, more or less . . . their services cannot be obtained without money, and there is no money. In plain language that means that your people are withdrawing from you, though they are still loyal to your person . . . your power exists only because they will it; it follows that the severance of that will cuts the nerve of your power.

Taxation was only one topic in the book, which examined the plight of Louis XV's oppressed subjects and their growing restlessness, and culminated with an attack on the all-powerful tax-farmers whose commission for their services amounted to a right to drain the national revenues. The author of this brave – or seditious – outburst was Mirabeau's father, the marquis de Mirabeau. Written at the height of the Seven Years War when France was crippled and demoralised, it seemed to be an incitement to rebellion, at least to those in government. The marquis went to prison for it.

At this time Mme de Pompadour, who had herself been married to the nephew of a tax-farmer before her promotion, encountered the marquis's brother, the chevalier de Mirabeau, another outspoken critic of the regime. 'What a pity it is that the Mirabeaus are all so wrongheaded', she remarked. 'True, this is the sign of legitimacy in our family', he replied, 'but when the right heads are responsible for so many disasters it might not be a bad idea to try the wrong ones.'[1]

The chevalier knew very well what Pompadour meant by wrongheadedness. However, the Mirabeaus were not a docile breed of courtiers. The family came from Provence, that turbulent, sun-brazed land in the south, which still did not feel that it was part of France though formally united with her for nearly three hundred years. The Provençaux carried the spirit of rebellion in their genes. Their strength of character – so the marquis de Mirabeau told Rousseau – came from the violent climate in the region, the sun and wind, drought and floods, with which the Provençaux had to contend; this, he said, was responsible for the fortitude of his own line, was why they were so unsubduable and tenacious, so passionate in their loves, hates and convictions.

The Mirabeaus' southern background affected their political views – they were opposed to centralised government and the domination of Paris – but their reflex antipathy towards the Court, the king's advisers, and all those who directed or supported the system as it stood, reflected in the marquis's denunciation of tax-farmers and his brother's riposte to the royal mistress, had a different explanation. Their personal philosophy was rooted in feudalism, in the feudal code they had inherited. The very word suggests a regressive, unenlightened cast of mind. Paradoxically, it was their 'feudal' view of the monarch's role which put the marquis and the chevalier ahead of many of their contemporaries; it was a 'feudal' resistance to royal despotism which set them against the absolute monarchy of their own day and the kind of system it produced. When the marquis declared in his *Théorie de l'impôt* that no one could be taxed without his consent, he was not anticipating a modern democratic principle but reiterating a feudal one.[2] (Taking lessons from French history – as the Mirabeaus did constantly – was highly unusual at this time when an educated man knew all about the Roman Republic but nothing about the Valois.) The chevalier dated the decline of the monarchy from the reign of Louis XI, when the struggle for power between the king and the great nobles began, which ended in royal absolutism and political impotence for the nobility. To the Mirabeaus the upset in the power balance between the throne and the nobility had caused a functional degeneration to set in which had gradually paralysed the governing process. In their own time the proper purpose of kingship had been forgotten, first by Louis XIV who gathered all power in his own hands, then by Louis XV who debased his role and neglected his people. The historical purpose of the nobility, to oppose despotic kings, had also been forgotten. Fiefs with their attendant titles and privileges could be bought by anyone wealthy

*Mirabeau*

enough; nobility had become a business transaction between the king and his subject, and so the ranks of the nobility were filled with men whose only concern was to protect their investment. It was the moral rot of their own caste that the Mirabeaus found most despicable in the general decay of principles. The key words in their own vocabulary were duty and integrity. Disinterested public service was their ideal. In this they typified the traditional nobility. The concept of virtue, which influenced so much of the debate during the Revolution, was rooted in historical noble perceptions just as strongly as it was in the civic humanism which inspired Rousseau's republic of virtue.

Gabriel-Honoré de Mirabeau, son of the marquis and nephew of the chevalier, inherited the family's independent views and code of service. In 1774, when he was twenty-five, he began a history of the Mirabeaus that he was writing for the benefit of his infant son with these words:

> Ever since I can remember I have heard my father and uncle recalling and honouring the memory of our forebears, several of whom were distinguished, not because of success at Court or rewards for servility, but by reason of their uprightness and the services they rendered to their fellow citizens.[3]

Possessing an ancient name was not a virtue in itself, he explained; its lustre derived from the moral qualities of those who had borne it. Therefore it was not his purpose to compile a family tree, since there was little merit in something which so many others possessed as well. Of course, he did insert the family tree into his narrative; the Mirabeaus set just as much store by their lineage as the rest of the nobility; and in an age of proliferating nobles, most of whom would not have rated as much as a passing sneer from Saint-Simon, it was vital to establish one's place in the hierarchy. But there was nothing hypocritical about his homage to moral virtues. It reflected the uneasiness of the enlightened minority of nobles who realised that the aristocracy's assumptions about its preeminence no longer held in a world that was questioning all assumptions. Possessing fiefs and the privileges that went with them, the Mirabeaus untypically did not take those privileges for granted. Even the marquis de Mirabeau, who was not given to soul-searching, believed that privileges should be earned. His brother (in 1771) went further, saying: 'All privileges attached to sacerdotal, noble, or any position whatsoever, are abusive'.[4] This was heresy. Take away the fiscal and other privileges enjoyed by the first two orders and the essential, tangible difference between them and the rest of society was gone. The existence of privileges allowed the infiltrators into the ranks of the old nobility to arrogate the prestige of antiquity implicit in their possession. These people needed their privileges to confirm their identity. They were the ones who would protest the loudest about the loss of them during the Revolution. First and last they were profiteers, unconcerned with either the philosophy or the principles of nobility.

The Mirabeaus despised them as a species. Perhaps Gabriel de Mirabeau's invocation of his ancestors' moral credentials was also an act of disassociation from the shallow values of a society that fed on its own fantasies. Moral worth was the only justification for possessing the privileges of nobility that could be reconciled with a social conscience.

Although the Mirabeaus occupied a prominent position in Provençal society they did not belong to the truly old nobility. The marquisate of Mirabeau was only registered in 1685. Like many other leading families in the province they came of *roturier* stock and their advancement had been helped by money. No less than the others, they boasted of their ancient lineage. To hear Mirabeau's comment (in his family history) on the exotic origins claimed by other noble families – 'The value one can place on these games of human vanity is well known' – one would never suspect that the very same games had been played by his own ancestors. Their deception had long since imposed itself on their descendants; hence he could, and did, believe in the Mirabeaus' exalted origins, though in fact they were the invention of a seventeenth-century genealogist.

The family name was Riqueti.[5] It first occurs in written records in 1346, as that of a municipal officer at Seyne, a village near Digne, high among the peaks and ravines of north-eastern Provence. Early in the sixteenth century Honoré Riqueti moved to Marseille and laid the foundations of the family's commercial fortunes, which expanded rapidly. Honoré's son, Jehan or Jean, was described by Nostradamus as one of the richest traders in Marseille; he married a Glandevès and acquired valuable land and property in the city, as well as the estates of Beaumont and Mirabeau near Aix. In 1562, as chief consul of Marseille, he prevented the city from falling into the hands of the Huguenots, who had already seized Rouen and Orléans in that year which marked the beginning of the prolonged religious wars in France. It was the beginning also of a family tradition of political awareness; successive generations of Riquetis held high civic offices and ceremonially opened the gates of Marseille to successive monarchs. In the 1630s four of Jean's grandsons were entered as Chevaliers of the Order of Malta, a feat requiring not only unlimited capital but also proof of noble descent. Who concocted the necessary pedigree at the time is unknown, but sixty years later an obliging genealogist[6] stated that the Riquetis were descended from one Azzo Arrighetti of Florence, who had fled from there during the feuds between the Guelphs and

Ghibellines. In his history of the family Mirabeau noted that Azzo's son, Pierre, married 'Sibille de Fos, of the house of the Counts of Provence, of whose talents and beauty so many troubadours have sung'. Sadly there is no trace of Sibille in the troubadour poetry of the late thirteenth century. Her existence was vital to the Riquetis since their claim to noble antecedents depended on it, but she is as insubstantial as the pedigree which they adopted.

Mirabeau's grandfather, Jean-Antoine de Mirabeau, was a distinguished soldier and man of granite character, who went through life wearing a silver collar after his neck had been partially severed at the battle of Cassano in 1705. He had a caustic tongue which he curbed for no one: on his first and last visit to Versailles he told Louis XIV that if he had spent his time uselessly as a courtier, instead of fighting, he might have been treated with more appreciation by his sovereign. Late in life he married the daughter of an ancient Provençal family, Françoise de Castellane, by whom he had seven children. Three sons survived him, to whom he was an object of awe and terror: Victor (Gabriel de Mirabeau's father), Jean-Antoine-Joseph-Charles-Elzéar (the chevalier), and Alexandre-Louis.

Like his father, the eldest son, Victor, went into the army; unlike him he did not distinguish himself, and after Jean-Antoine's death in 1737 he took little further part in campaigns. Finding himself marquis de Mirabeau at the age of twenty-one, with 16,000 livres a year, his first act was to move to Paris and into the path of immediate high office, as he thought. To his friend and fellow officer, the writer Vauvenargues, he wrote when he was twenty-three: 'I am devoured by ambition, but of a strange sort. It is not honours I crave, or money, or favours; but a name, to be somebody'.[7] He struck those who knew him as brilliant but undisciplined. 'What genius is in that head', said Montesquieu on first meeting him in 1739, 'and what a pity he cannot harness it.'[8] At this time Victor de Mirabeau was wondering whether he would have been wiser to stay in the army; he told Vauvenargues that one day he expected to pay dearly for his folly in leaving. In a very literal sense that day had already arrived, for in 1740 he bought – or, rather, was sold – an estate at Bignon near Nemours. Set in the fertile countryside of the Gâtinais, within reach of Paris, it was, he persuaded himself, a sound investment, though he admitted that the land was in a severe state of deterioration, and he had to borrow heavily to buy it at the price asked, 112,000 livres. He also bought, for 100,000 livres, a mansion in the rue Bergère in Paris, a corpse of a house as he came to call it, for it decayed more rapidly than repairs could be made; three years later, the roof still leaking, he sold it at a loss and bought a smaller place in the rue des Saints-Pères, at the corner of the rue de Seine, for a mere 50,000 livres.

It was a lifelong characteristic of his that he did not learn from his mistakes. As stubborn as he was impressionable, he prided himself on his ability to remain unflinching in the face of disaster, not realising that the disasters which beset him were usually of his own making. His impulsive speculations in property and taste for the fashionable pursuits of Paris led to the rapid depletion of his fortune. The accepted remedy was a judicious marriage, and in 1743 he pledged himself to a seventeen year old heiress from the Limousin, Marie-Geneviève de Vassan,[9] without even meeting her, so attractive were her expectations; the go-between, ominously, being the same friend who had advised him to buy his house and estate. Too late he found out that although Mlle de Vassan would inherit 300,000 livres a year from her mother, she had a meagre 4,000 meanwhile and little else to recommend her.

He never forgave his wife for the mistake he had made in marrying her. His deepest resentment stemmed from the social mortification he suffered on taking his uncultivated, provincial bride into the exclusive circle he moved in himself. Pride demanded that he should allow no comment on his choice, and it was years before his brother, breaching the wall of silence, told him that his wife was the reason he had been turned down for a post in the diplomatic corps. For her part Geneviève de Mirabeau loved her husband with an abandonment he found indecent in the context of marriage. Expected to play a role beyond her capacity, she made an effort at first to meet his exacting standards, but eventually she grew discouraged, or rebelled, and in his last scathing picture of her she appears hunched over her sewing in 'bedraggled skirts and a bedjacket, taking no notice of time, domestic order, her husband's repugnance', 'falling asleep as soon as she has supped, legs obscenely open'.[10] He was later to describe his marriage as twenty years of renal colic. Nevertheless, there was a long period of relative harmony, during which eleven children were born and the marquis flung himself into vast schemes for improving his estate. He loved Bignon, the moated Renaissance château surrounded by lakes and woods. A little vegetable basket, he called it, and the phrase conjures up something of what Bignon stood for in his mind: a symbol of honest virtue, of thrift and order, man and nature in fruitful partnership. Armies of workmen were brought in to clear the land and repair farm buildings. The role of seigneur, caring for his people, with the entire neighbourhood dependent on him for work and shelter, was one he took to as naturally as his ancestors had done at Mirabeau. The cost of the projects he embarked on was crippling, the returns poor, and while he indulged in risky agricultural experiments at Bignon his estates in Provence, from which he drew his income, suffered from lack of investment. He never returned to Mirabeau, perhaps because the shade of his father still occupied it, preferring instead to cultivate a romantic memory of his birthplace and the untameable landscape which had moulded his race.[11]

His letters suggest certain other reasons for his self-imposed exile. He had little use for Aixois society, which combined the frivolity of Paris with its own kind of inbred amorality: his son was to say that the nobility of Provence was the most corrupt, parasitical, and reactionary in the country. But, equally, he was at odds with the Provençal character as history had formed it, at least when he came up against it in his seigneurial role. He was, as Tocqueville and more recently Furet have remarked, both ahead of and behind his time, and his flight from Provence may be seen as a response to the two conflicting sides of his character, the progressive and the conservative. The liberal intellectual could not endure the superficial minds of the Aixois nobility; the powerful landowner, entrenched behind his proprietorial rights, could not stand the truculent behaviour of his villagers at Beaumont and Mirabeau. When he encountered the ungovernable Provençal spirit on his own doorstep his liberal instincts vanished. At Bignon, on the other hand, where the local population had not yet lost its innocence to an awareness of its potential political power, the arrogant overlord was quiescent. He could pursue new ideas and preserve old values. The traditionalist and the enlightened aspects of his character both found expression and he was satisfied.

A military career was the only one open to a nobleman of the marquis de Mirabeau's generation. His impatience with that convention, and decision to become a writer, was both a personal revolution and a reflection of the growing restlessness of the century; at the time, however, he had no idea that his latest impulse would bring him the fame he craved. The War of the Austrian Succession had ended in 1748, leaving France exhausted and starving. During the war the Paris *parlement* had sanctioned a new tax on the understanding that it was only a temporary measure, but when an attempt was made to impose a new and permanent tax in 1750 the *parlement* refused to register the edict, and the new tax was forcibly imposed. The riots that followed did not seem especially significant to most people, but the marquis sensed an ominous change in the national mood and foresaw open rebellion sooner or later. On the spur of the moment he wrote a book suggesting that provincial assemblies should be established, which would improve the administration of the regions, deal with grievances at source, and so avoid the build-up of pressure. By enabling the nation to participate at least in local government this proposal would have been a step in the direction of constitutional monarchy. Scant notice was taken of *Des assemblées provinciales* at the time; the ideas in it conflicted totally with the principle of centralised authority which the monarchy believed to be indispensable; yet it was one of those books which are seen afterwards to have been extraordinarily prophetic. Twenty-five years later Turgot tried to reintroduce the idea of administrative autonomy in the regions, and Necker took it up after him; in 1779 two provincial assemblies were established; and in 1787 Calonne included a general plan for them among the reforms which he presented to the Assembly of Notables. The Notables rejected them, Calonne fell, and his successor Brienne presented his reforms again: this time the Notables gave their assent to provincial assemblies, and in 1788 twenty had been set up. The marquis had to wait until the end of his life for any action to be taken on provincial assemblies, but he then had the satisfaction of reminding people that he had fathered the idea of them. Another idea, advocated in *Des assemblées provinciales* and not given a second thought in 1750, was that the representation of the third estate in assemblies should be doubled, since it was the people who bore the heaviest burden. The voice of 1789 could be heard, in a most unexpected quarter, long before anyone was bothering to listen.

When the marquis began to write political revolution was not yet in men's minds, but the intellectual revolution that was preparing the way was everywhere in evidence. The year 1751 saw the publication of the first volume of the *Encyclopédie* which, after initial suppression, resumed its assault on all the old institutions and old orthodoxies which maintained the existing system. In 1755 Rousseau published his *Discours sur l'origine et les fondements de l'inégalité parmi les hommes*, in which he struck a blow at the very base of the social system with a denunciation of private property. It was not this limited work of protest, however, but one as eloquent and of much wider scope which really seized the public imagination. Entitled *L'Ami des hommes*, this now forgotten work was read and admired throughout Europe; its influence on Rousseau is apparent in both *Emile* and the *Contrat social*. When it appeared in 1756 it simultaneously made the name of its author and confiscated it: henceforth the world knew the marquis de Mirabeau as *l'ami des hommes*.

The sub-title, 'A treatise on population', does nothing to explain its popularity. Books on population and agriculture, taxation and government, were published all the time, following the fashion set by Montesquieu's *L'Esprit des lois*; most of them were unreadable. Now this lively, unprofessional, almost chatty book appeared, its author full of new ideas and vivid images which gripped his readers. He had the knack of saying things which they had always thought themselves or which they realised they should have thought about before, and which were all the more striking in the context of the depression the country was in. He spoke of a nation which gave priority to wealth as being an assembly of civilised brigands; of the false sense of values which made people despise working on the land and led them to seek an easier life in the towns, only to create new poverty there; of the dignity of labour; of the sterility of money; and of the damage that was done when the land was concentrated in the possession of a single owner – 'the big pike depopulates the pool, the big owners stamp out the little ones'. At the time of writing that he was in the process of adding still further to his own extensive estates but the contradiction between theory and practice did not trouble him. His original intention had simply been to draw attention to what he saw as the country's most serious economic problem: the decay of agriculture, leading to depopulation, leading to further decay. Instead he had written not a treatise on population or economics – indeed, he declared that he knew as much about economics as his cat – but a kind of tract for the times, containing lessons which could be learned by all men.

The success of *L'Ami des hommes* led to a meeting with the economist, François Quesnay;[12] it was the turning point in his life for the marquis, who became Quesnay's most ardent disciple. The group of thinkers he had joined still went by their original name – the *Economistes* – but eventually they coined the word 'Physiocrat' to describe themselves. They claimed to have invented a system of government and administration which conformed to the laws of nature: which, very roughly, meant a system which allowed the individual the maximum personal liberty provided he did not invade the natural rights of others. In their own day they were regarded as being either gurus or cranks, and French historians of the nineteenth century, assessing their influence on their time, were as sharply divided in their opinion of them. For Tocqueville they were dangerous disseminators of revolution, ready to sacrifice all private rights. Historians of the left, equally critical, said that their doctrines were false since they put individualism before fraternity, and that the Physiocratic principle of *laissez faire et laissez passer* would leave society at the mercy of private interests. Quesnay was credited in one quarter with being the first to define a proper code of social ethics; in another he and his colleagues were accused of being concerned with nothing but material benefits, indifferent to whether they received them from an absolute monarch or the sovereign people, from a monarchy or a republic. Their doctrine was summed up as security, freedom, ownership; these three words, it was contemptuously said, formed the social trinity of the Physiocrats.[13]

Physiocrats were not primarily concerned with economics but sought to bring about radical changes in social attitudes and morality. They held that natural law – the *ordre physique* – was the base to which all social, moral, and political laws were related, and that man possessed natural rights, conferred by the *ordre physique*, which were not subject to arbitrary and variable legislation, these being the right to freedom, to the ownership of land, and to the fruits of his own labour. It was the first time in France, or in Europe, that a group of men had attempted to reorganise society according to a systematic plan based entirely on their particular interpretation of natural law. Their concept of absolute natural rights went beyond any previously held views. For Montesquieu and Locke man's natural rights were inevitably restrained by the rights of society as a whole. Rousseau echoed this view in his *Contrat social*, basing his contract on the alienation of individual rights in return for rights possessed in common with the community. Quesnay, on the other hand, held that man's natural rights were based on what he called *justice par essence*, absolute justice, and could not be overruled by society.

The moral doctrine of the Physiocrats may be summarised thus: first, the natural aim of man is his own well-being; second, his natural duty is to attain this; and third, no man should attain his own ends at the cost of another's, and all men must try to procure the well-being of others as well as his own. (This was where Jeremy Bentham got his precept that everyone, while pursuing his own interest, should help to produce as much good fortune for as many others as possible; Utilitarianism was the offspring of Physiocracy.) The marquis de Mirabeau answered the frequent charge that the Physiocrats subordinated the moral to the physical too much, by saying that 'anyone who was dying of hunger would eat his own father, and one must never speak to men of moral virtues before physical necessities have been attended to'.[14] The first moral virtue, he continued, was justice, and the first exercise of justice was the equitable distribution of the parts. (The physical and moral were therefore synonymous, or would be in a perfect Physiocratic world.) In one of his later works, *Les Economiques*, he wrote that the aim of economic science was to demonstrate that there was no situation in which the most honest and just course was not also the most profitable. According to this argument even the most self-interested man could not avoid being virtuous, which was not what he meant. Physiocrats harboured no illusions about being able to change the basic nature of man. Accepting self-interest as unalterable, conceding that if not enlightened in its form it was the cause of discord, they saw their greatest task, according to the marquis as enlightening the public on the nature of this personal interest, on the principles which establish it, on its effects in relation to other interests, and in consequence to the general interest, and finally on the meeting point at which all human interests converge.[15]

Enlightened self-interest, he believed, could lead to the end of poverty, the source of most human unhappiness.

Physiocracy, with its insistence on the right to work and the abolition of all unearned privileges, its call to develop the inherent wealth of the land without exploiting nature, and its ethos of fair shares for all, became an international movement. During the 1760s and early 1770s the marquis de Mirabeau was its figurehead, writing tirelessly on its theories, and it was the personal fame of *l'ami des hommes* that brought the young economists and future policy makers of Europe to hear the teachings of the master at his Tuesday dinners. 'The political revolution of nations is brewing visibly', he reported to his brother in 1769. The one period when Physiocratic policies were adopted by the French government was under Turgot; they were blamed for the grain shortages of his administration, and his downfall in 1776 brought to an end any hope of their being tried again. It was the extinction of all the marquis had lived for, and even those who thought the Physiocrats were slightly mad shared the blow of their failure. Everyone, said Voltaire, would mourn the loss of the golden age that they had been promised.

One man who drew the line at the wilder flights of Physiocracy, though he revered the marquis from the depths of his being, was his brother. The chevalier Jean-Antoine de Mirabeau was the conscience of the family. The marquis, who rejected criticism from everyone else, nearly always accepted it from him, while protesting humorously 'Jean-Antoine's volcano is erupting again!'. His nephew said afterwards that he had all the qualities of a hero, the loyalty, fortitude, and integrity which the Romans termed collectively *virtus*. Gabriel de Mirabeau was deeply attached to him, and his own character, as it was expressed in the causes he espoused in his political career, revealed the humane influence of his uncle whose good opinion he valued as much as that of his father.

As a younger son, the chevalier had had no fortune or estates awaiting him. At the age of twelve, in 1729, he entered the navy and spent the next twenty years almost entirely at sea, with classical authors his only consolation. Governor of Guadeloupe in the early 1750s, he improved conditions for the slaves on the sugar plantations and enforced the law against the planters: until he arrived the murder of a slave had gone unpunished. In one of his letters to his brother, he ended a description of the creoles, who spent their time 'getting drunk, whipping slaves, and begetting bastards', with the remark that in his experience the character of the black man was superior to that of the white. Complaints about his interfering reforms reached Versailles, but it was yellow fever and not the planters which eventually forced his return to France. In his next job, as Inspector-General of the Coastguard, which coincided with the start of the Seven Years War, he made a nuisance of himself by exposing the negligence of the government department responsible for maintaining the coastal defences. His friends expected him to be the next Minister for the Navy; but their candidate's refusal to campaign for himself – due to an aversion, half feudal, half republican, which he had for the servile role of courtier – lost him the post. He had spent years in preparatory study, in the hope that he would be able to restore the French navy to its former glory. (Of the five navy ministers appointed during this period only one had ever been to sea.) The possibility of his appointment had probably filled the department concerned with dismay.

The thousands of letters exchanged by the marquis de Mirabeau and his brother during the forty years that preceded the Revolution provide a unique commentary on what was happening as it appeared to two shrewd and informed observers. Everything interested them, philosophy, religion, classical literature, history, as well as politics and the manifold social and economic problems that engulfed the country. Their characters speak on every page: the marquis intellectually inflated, rash, a prey to his own weaknesses and yet strictly honourable; his brother always cooler and sounder in his judgements, terse, agnostic, compassionate, self deprecating, a survivor from another age; both of them instinctive republicans,[16] and pessimistic about the future. The chevalier, especially, displayed in his letters the same gift of prophetic insight that his nephew was to possess, making it a kind of family attribute. As early as 1745, in an unedited *mémoire*, he declared that nothing could prevent the downfall of the monarchy; the wealth of national resources might delay it but no more.[17] He lived long enough to see his bleak prediction come true. The marquis died the day before the fall of the Bastille, his life fitting precisely into the space between one historic watershed, the death of Louis XIV, and another. The century, he said, had been given over to fools; he was not sorry to leave the rest of it to them and to his son.

That son, who led the final demolition of the *ancien régime*, had the good luck to be born into a family that was not only enlightened, but politically articulate and politically mature. Intellect, strength of will, vision, and personal charisma all went to the making of Mirabeau, but his greatest asset as a revolutionary lay in that early conditioning.

## NOTES

1. *Lettres originales*, II, 317.
2. Staël (1820–21: XII–XIV, 24–5), contrasting contemporary royal absolutism with the limited power of medieval kings, which was limited by the power of the nobles, wrote: 'It is liberty which is old, and despotism which is modern'.
3. *Mémoires biographiques*, I, 83. Mirabeau's history, which Montigny reproduced in full, was entitled *Vie de Jean-Antoine de Riqueti, Marquis de Mirabeau, et Notice sur sa maison, rédigées par l'aîné de ses petits-fils, d'après les notes de son fils*.
4. Loménie (1879–91: II, 381).
5. In sixteenth-century documents the name is spelled Riquet. Mirabeau's father always wrote Riquetty, except in his will (1789) in which in his own hand he wrote Riqueti. Mirabeau himself wrote Riquety or Riqueti. The variant Riquetti appears in various histories and memoirs.
6. *Nobiliare de Provence* (1693) by the abbé Robert is dedicated to Jean-Antoine de Mirabeau, and as this work provides the family with a genealogical alibi it may be assumed that they paid for its publication. Charles d'Hozier, Court genealogist in the reign of Louis XV, did not accept the Mirabeau claims, but his nephew Louis d'Hozier included an article on the family, written by the marquis de Mirabeau, in his *Armorial de France*, which was published in 1764.
7. Loménie (1879–91: I, 403).
8. Ibid. I, 406.
9. Marie-Geneviève de Vassan was born on 3 December 1725. In 1737 she married her maternal cousin, Jean-François de Ferrières, marquis de Saulvebeuf, who died in 1738 before the marriage was consummated. Her father, the marquis de Vassan, died in 1756, her mother, Anne-Thérèse de Ferrières de Saulvebeuf, died on 4 November 1770.
10. Loménie (1879–91: II, 452–4).
11. Describing it in a letter to Rousseau, dated 27 October 1766, he wrote: 'Mirabeau is the house of my fathers and the domain which providence has especially entrusted to me. It is exposed to the burning sky and extreme climate of Provence: wild in aspect, arid tracks, rocks, birds of prey, raging rivers, torrents either dried up or in flood, the trees only those that survive and produce, the men strong, hard, independent, and restive' (Rousseau, 1978: XXXI, 72f., letter 5496).
12. François Quesnay (1694–1774) held the post of surgeon to the king. His first writings were on medical subjects. He then turned to economics, contributing articles on farmers and grain to the *Encyclopédie*. His economic theories, which formed the basis for Physiocracy, appeared first in *Tableau économique*, which was published in 1758.
13. For further reading on the Physiocrats see Weulersse (1910), Fox-Genovese (1976) and Ripert (1901).
14. Mirabeau (1780: 324).
15. Mirabeau (1769: IV, 498).
16. See Aulard (1910: I, 90f). As Aulard points out, a republican, in the sense used by writers before the Revolution, was not someone who wanted a republic, but anyone who was concerned with the common weal (*res publica*), who hated

despotism, discussed the nature of sovereign power, and wished to reform the monarchy.

The chevalier de Mirabeau illustrated the bad and the good meanings of the word 'republican' – as he understood it – in a letter dated 30 June 1759 to his brother, in which he described Parisians as 'republican by insolence and, at the same time, unworthy of being republican by virtue' (Loménie, 1879–91: II, 363).

17. Loménie (1879–91: II, 354).

# 2

## Father and Son

### (1749-1772)

Gabriel-Honoré Riqueti de Mirabeau was born at Bignon on 9 March 1749. Of his parents' four previous children only two daughters still survived, Marie-Anne-Jeanne and Caroline-Elisabeth. Their first son had died at the age of three, after drinking ink which his mother, according to the marquis, had left within reach. There was great rejoicing at the birth of a second son, an enormous infant with teeth already formed, which was taken to be a sure sign of future greatness. Other indications, however, were less auspicious. From the beginning he looked so unlike the Mirabeaus that his father said he would have believed him to be a bastard, had he not been born in a place where there were no visitors. He had the features of his maternal relations, the Vassans, while his younger brother, Boniface, born five years later, looked every inch a Mirabeau: this physical difference coloured the marquis's assessment of his sons' characters throughout their formative years.

When he was three Gabriel had smallpox which left him severely scarred. Although his friend, Vauvenargues, had been similarly disfigured a few years earlier, the marquis had neglected to have his children inoculated out of deference to his mother, who saw it as an attempt to flout the will of God, and only when his son was attacked did he take steps to protect the others. In a family noted for its physical beauty Gabriel's ravaged face was regarded by his father almost as a deliberate affront. The child learned early how to defend himself against the unfeeling comments of both his parents; he was eight years old when his father wrote to his friend, the comtesse de Rochefort:

My son, whose body grows, whose chatter increases, and whose face is becoming amazingly ugly, actually chooses and prefers to be ugly. Yesterday his
mother made him a sort of refusal as from his future wife; he replied that he
hoped she would not judge him by his face. His mother asked innocently,
'Where do you want her to look at you?' and everybody laughed. He retorted,
'What's below will help what's above', and we laughed even more. Even so,
such a sally from an infant makes one think.[1]

His intelligence was the talk of Paris by the time he was five, according to his father, whose letters abound with references to his
'breathtaking' memory and 'phenomenal' mind. But these reports
were prompted more by egotism than love; only by becoming a prodigy could Gabriel hope to atone for the sin of his physical imperfec-
tion. When he fell seriously ill at the age of ten, it was the fear of losing
the prodigy, and not the child, that made his father cry out: 'We shall
have to make another, and where the devil is another piece of material
like this to be found?'

Ready to praise his son, the marquis almost always qualified his
remarks: 'few vices, but little depth of feeling', 'willing and quick, but
the sort of quickness that turns to idleness'. So seriously did he view
these symptoms of what he took to be incurable legerity of character
that when the time came to put him into the hands of a tutor he gave
instructions that he was to be dealt with rigorously at all times. '*M. le
comte* never emerges from his round of punishments', he wrote in 1756.
'I serve as an extra weapon for Poisson [the tutor] because when he has
promised remission I enable him to cancel it, without breaking his
word, and so I keep a tight rein.'[2]

This implacable attitude, all the more disturbing in a man who
treated his other children with doting fondness, did not genuinely
reflect his feelings. In his handling of his elder son he was strongly
influenced by his mother, the widow of the inflexible Jean-Antoine,
who lived with him, and for whom he had such a great reverence that
in his fifties he still knelt before her every night to receive her blessing.
The old lady had not been consulted over her son's marriage. She
hated her daugher-in-law, and much of the marquis's prejudice against
the Vassans, and horror of Gabriel's supposedly Vassan characteristics,
is traceable to her vindictive ill will. Exerting almost as strong an
influence over him was the spirit of Jean-Antoine himself; his austere
treatment of Gabriel, a careful emulation of the way his father had
treated him, was perhaps a subconscious atonement for his filial im-
piety in not being, or wishing to be, a soldier like the hero of Cassano.

The constant struggle between his mind and his heart, his natural
opinions and those implanted by others, is reflected in his remarks
about his heir, whom he appeared to value one moment and despise

the next. To take one year alone, in the summer of 1761 Gabriel 'does not have the vices which are attributed to him'; two months later he still 'promises to be a most likeable person'; in November 'he is wilful, quick-tempered, clumsy, with a drift to evil before knowing about it or being capable of it'; in the same month he has 'a noble heart', only to be an example of 'unparalleled baseness' four days later.[3] At this time the marquis had many domestic problems, which would account for some of his irritability, but the violent swings from pride to detestation point to the presence of an *agent provocateur*. What damaged the victim of his moods most was not his anger itself, but the injustices into which it led him. In later life Mirabeau reproached his father bitterly for the excessive punishments he had been subjected to as a child. While many of the charges laid by him against his father are exaggerated, and sometimes deliberate lies, this one of unjustified harshness stands, all the graver because the marquis allowed his attitude to be dictated by others, and would never acknowledge the fact, all the sadder because this obduracy led to a permanent lack of understanding between father and son.

It never occurred to him that his approach was unduly harsh. He regarded himself as the most just and reasonable of men, and, indeed, in his treatment of his tenants at Bignon and in his written works he was. He abhorred tyranny, declaring that 'coercion invariably produces the opposite effect on men to the one intended'. At heart he was a sentimentalist. In one of his letters to Rousseau he recommended the therapeutic effect of weeping, confessing that he would often read his favourite author, Richardson, until the tears came.

Gabriel was eleven when the marquis was arrested for writing *Théorie de l'impôt* and sent to the prison of Vincennes. The detention of *l'ami des hommes* caused a public outcry, and within a week the 'martyr to the public weal' (as his son derisively described him afterwards) was released and ordered to retire to his estates. Three months later he was free to come and go again, and to enjoy his ever increasing fame. The *Théorie* ran to eighteen editions; surprisingly, it was never banned.

The marquis departed for Bignon at the beginning of 1761, leaving his sons and the dowager marquise behind in Paris. His daughters, Marie, Caroline, and Louise,[4] were being educated at this time at a convent in Montargis. However, the tedium of exile was alleviated for him by the presence of a certain Mme de Pailly, whose company, he assured his friends, was welcomed as much by his wife as by himself. Born Marie de Malvieux in 1731 in Switzerland, and married to an army officer who obligingly stayed out of her life, Mme de Pailly rapidly became indispensable to the marquis. It was now eighteen years since his marriage, during which time his wife had turned from a boisterous girl into a confirmed slattern with a passion for gambling. Too urbane to comment directly on her shortcomings, he made dry references in his letters to arguments at table, and menus consisting of goose claws for *entrée*, cauliflower in water for vegetable, and mouldy grapes for dessert. A man to whom fastidiousness was a mark of caste, he was constantly irritated by her slovenly habits; disorderliness, he warned his daughters later, was the mark of a prostitute.

Among his friends Mme de Pailly was known as the black hen. No one, knowing the acrimonious relationship he had with his wife, was in any doubt about her true position, though outwardly their conduct was scrupulous, and remained so: in Paris she never slept under his roof, even after knowing him for thirty years. In so far as she was on good terms with many influential people, and could promote his interests, she was very useful to him. If she had been content to deploy herself in Paris all would have continued smoothly, but it soon became apparent that she regarded Bignon as her rightful territory as well. In March 1762 Mme de Mirabeau went to visit her mother in the Limousin. The letter she wrote to her husband the day after her arrival gives no indication that they were estranged: she looked forward to his joining her, as something already decided on; yet when he eventually journeyed into the Limousin several months later it was in order to inform her that he wanted a separation, and would pay her a pension of 6,000 livres to stay where she was and never return. She refused.

The circumstances make it look as if the idea of separation only entered his mind when his wife was already in the Limousin – otherwise it has to be assumed that he arranged her trip deliberately as a way of removing her from the marital home. All the evidence shows, however, that such a course was out of character. Four years earlier he had decided to end sexual relations, saying that after eleven children it was time to stop, but he stated plainly that this did not constitute a separation, that if his wife wanted one he could not leave Bignon in his mother's lifetime, but that after her death he would be prepared to leave her in possession of Bignon while he lived as a bachelor elsewhere. One thing he did not question was his wife's right to continued occupancy of the marital residence, and this is what makes his behaviour in 1762 seem to be directed by others. Almost as if he had been told that the only way to force a separation on his own terms was to provide evidence of her wrongdoing, towards the end of 1762 he came into possession of a paper, signed by his wife, in which she testified to the sexual prowess of a certain officer in the Dauphin regiment. Mme de Mirabeau did not deny that she had signed such a paper, but protested that it had only been 'a party joke'; in a bitter, rambling letter, dated 3 February 1763, she agreed to accept the pension and stay where she was, confident that her family would not believe the accusations that had been brought against her. Mme de Mirabeau has been condemned for her apparent willingness to give up her children, which, it is argued, would not have been her attitude had she been innocent; but her maternal concern is evident in this same letter. Having heard that her eldest daughter was about to become a nun, she demanded to see her in order to judge whether she had a true vocation. Marie de Mirabeau suffered from intermittent insanity, and her mother rightly doubted her ability to make decisions. She guessed, too, that it was Mme de Pailly's work, and it must have increased her resentment to think that another woman, a Protestant moreover, should dispose of her daughter in this way.

She was not allowed to see Marie. Nor was she allowed to attend the wedding of her second daughter, Caroline, which took place in 1763, though the marquis du Saillant, her son-in-law, belonged to a Limousin family and she had arranged the match herself. The marquis was so grateful to Mme de Pailly for bringing peace into his life that he gave way to her over everything short of applying for a *lettre de cachet* for his wife. He wished to avoid scandal, and also not to alienate his mother-in-law whose fortune his wife would inherit. Letters exchanged at this time between Mme de Pailly and the marquis's friend, Mme de Rochefort, leave no doubt that she was behind the conspiracy against the Marquise. She not only wanted her out of the way but also wanted Mme de Mirabeau's inheritance to go instead to her children. She was furious when Mme de Vassan refused to change her will and the marquis even agreed to increase his wife's pension. 'What afflicts me most is seeing how distressed he is', she told Mme de Rochefort. 'I would like to see him able to study the situation coldly and to act in consequence.'[5] By that she meant going above the law: if the marquis obtained a *lettre de cachet* his wife would lose all her civil rights, and he would be free to enjoy her fortune; but she could not persuade him to follow her advice in this matter.

His financial straits, which he blamed on his wife's extravagance, were essentially his own fault. Not content with grandiose schemes at Bignon, he had also bought the estate of Roquelaure from the Rohan family, borrowing 450,000 livres for the purpose. Roquelaure was a duchy, and he hoped to have the title confirmed by the king, but his creditors would not wait, and in the end he had to sell his investment at a heavy loss. He had to borrow another 80,000 livres for his daughter's dowry, in addition to which he had paid 150,000 livres in 1762 to purchase for his brother the post of General of the Galleys in the Order of Malta. This last, in fact, was the only sensible investment he made in his life. Had he been less infatuated with Mme de Pailly he might have seen the folly of antagonising his wife before her inheritance was in his pocket. Indeed, had it not been for this seductive Iago they would probably never have separated.

His children hated her. Gabriel, who was fourteen when his parents separated, vented his feelings by composing a crude satire on Mme de Pailly. Following this he was sent away to school, to the abbé Choquart's academy in Paris, noted for its military discipline, where he was enrolled as Pierre Buffière (the name of one of his mother's estates), as his father declared he did not wish the distinguished name of Mirabeau to be seen on the benches of a reformatory.[6] He exaggerated – the establishment run by the abbé enjoyed an international reputation. The curriculum, which included modern as well as ancient languages, history, mathematics, music, dancing, horsemanship and, apparently, economics (a course in which was prepared for the pupils by the marquis), being much wider than that usually offered in schools for the sons of the aristocracy. Thanks to Mme de Pailly's desire to be rid of him Gabriel received an excellent education. Reformatory or not, the atmosphere at abbé Choquart's was positively sympathetic compared with home, and, as always, and to his father's affected surprise, he won over his teachers completely. Perhaps the other boys found him rather less engaging. Two brothers who attended the school remembered him as an impossible character, forever boasting; but they were English. Self-glorification was instinctive with him; years of paternal fault-finding were to blame.

With Gabriel away there was illusory peace at Bignon. The marquis was able to complete his *Philosophie rurale*, a further study of Physiocratic doctrines, and to write numerous articles for the *Ephémérides du citoyen*, the official organ of the Physiocrats, of which he was the shadow editor. This period, when his reputation was at its height and his domestic problems were temporarily solved, was the happiest in his life. His letters abound with good humour. Two of his servants marry and he honours the occasion by leading the bride out in a minuet: she does not know the steps, and he finds himself being taught how to perform a country dance instead. On another occasion he returns to Bignon after a day's absence to find that Mme de Pailly has decided to give him a delightful surprise: his study has been turned into a boudoir with bows and ribbons everywhere, and his books have all been dumped in a corner. Even this fails to annoy him. Now that his wife was gone his mother was mistress of Bignon, but in practice Mme de Pailly presided. The old lady waged a futile war against the intruder, whom she hated as much because she was a Protestant as on moral grounds, but this was one issue on which the marquis refused to defer to his mother's wishes.

Another permanent resident at Bignon was the comtesse Julie de
Mirabeau, the widow of the marquis's youngest brother who had died
in 1761, and with her Mme de Pailly got on well, being of the same age
and religion. Like the black hen, she enjoyed a state pension obtained
for her by the marquis; she had no children and remained at Bignon
until her death in 1772.[7]

While the marquis was happy with his new domestic arrangements,
Mme de Pailly began to suffer from fits of depression. Mme de Mirabeau was gambling more than her pension away in the Limousin, and
her mother, with whom she lived, was paying her debts. They had to
be separated. Mme de Vassan moved in with her married granddaugh-
ter, Caroline du Saillant, and Mme de Mirabeau, who was not invited,
had to become a paying guest in a convent at Limoges. It was an
opportune moment for a fresh attempt to obtain a *lettre de cachet* for her.
This time the marquis was told that she had compromised herself with
a grenadier. He was sufficiently angered to seek a *lettre de cachet* confining her to the convent, but no sooner had it been granted than he
opted to reach a settlement by some other means, and so his wife
escaped the net once again.

Contrary to the popular view that the marquis de Mirabeau was a
maniac who spent his life obtaining *lettres de cachet* for his family – at
one time his son estimated that twenty-seven had been issued – this
was the first occasion on which he resorted to them, and the speed with
which he sought a cancellation suggests that he had been led into
acting and had then thought better of it. Personally, he viewed the
*lettre de cachet* system with abhorrence, not only, he said, because im-
prisonment without trial was a denial of human rights, but also because
it facilitated private vengeance and generated a climate of corruption
which damaged all the institutions of society. Only a few years earlier,
in correspondence with his brother, he had rejected the idea of using
them in any circumstances as evil, and there is no reason to suppose
that he had revised his opinion. His acquiescence when urged to employ one was all the more reprehensible in view of his known principles; his change of mind was the act of a man unable to subdue his
conscience.

In 1767 Pierre Buffière graduated from the abbé Choquart's academy,
his prize-winning oration being greeted by a press comment that the
young eagle promised to fly higher than his father; but, despite his
pride in his performance, the marquis was not yet ready to relent, and
declaring that it was his right and duty to be severe, he sent his son into
the army as a sub-lieutenant in the Berri cavalry regiment, the commander of which, the marquis de Lambert, was a rigid disciplinarian.

Before leaving Gabriel had a memorable encounter. Rousseau, newly returned from England and still a fugitive, had accepted the marquis's invitation to stay at his country house at Fleury-sous-Meudon. As the son of *l'ami des hommes*, Gabriel had read the *Discours sur l'origine et les fondements de l'inégalité parmi les hommes* and the *Contrat social* as a matter of course, and he placed *Emile* among the masterpieces of the century; meeting Rousseau himself – 'the god of eloquence, the apostle of virtue, always commanding our adoration' – was therefore a momentous experience.[8] It must have been while Rousseau was at Fleury that he read or heard readings from his *Confessions*, much of which had been written in England; he referred to it nine years later as a work he was already familiar with, although it was not published until 1779, after the author's death.

Gabriel's army career was short and unglamorous, much of it spent in confinement for various misdemeanours. An offer of marriage to a local girl at Saintes, where he was stationed, was the signal for his father to obtain a *lettre de cachet* for his detention, and he was taken from the house of his godfather, the duc de Nivernais,[9] where he had sought refuge, to the Ile de Ré off La Rochelle. His fate might have been even worse. His father's first intention had been to ship him off to the East Indies, and he was only prevented from doing so by his brother, who advised him to

> see whether the wretch's excesses deserve his permanent exclusion from society, in which case the best thing of all is to send him to the Dutch colonies. You are sure then of never seeing this unfortunate on the horizon again, whose fate is to be the sorrow of his parents and the shame of his race.[10]

The commandant of the Ile de Ré persuaded the marquis to give his son another chance, and in the summer of 1769 Gabriel found himself seconded to the Lorraine regiment en route for Corsica to subdue the rebellion of the patriot Paoli. This expedition wrought a decisive change in him, thanks partly to a more understanding commanding officer, and partly to the island itself: he was deeply stirred by the Corsicans and their struggle for independence. By the time he left Ajaccio a year later the schoolboy had become a young man. At that moment he wanted to stay in the army, having decided that he had a talent for soldiering, but his father refused to purchase the commission he wanted. It would have been inconsistent for the marquis, who once said that an army career was as outmoded as tourneys, to have encouraged this particular ambition. He did write to Choiseul, enquiring after a captaincy, but the one offered was in a different regiment, a cavalry regiment moreover, and he felt that the glamour of it, and the sense of freedom his son would have among strangers, would

undo all his reformatory efforts. 'Does he think I have the money to
provide him with battles like Harlequin and Scaramouche?' he demanded, and on this sour note Gabriel's military career came to an
end.

He spent the next four months on probation at Mirabeau with his
uncle, who had been given the task of assessing him before he was
allowed back under the paternal roof. The good chevalier had not seen
his nephew for ten years. Expecting to meet the hardened delinquent
of his brother's letters, he was pleasantly surprised and instantly sympathetic: he knew what it was like to be on the receiving end of his
brother's autocratic edicts. In his own case, following his failure to
become Minister for the Navy, the marquis had ordained that he
should enter the Order of Malta. (By family custom he had been
enrolled as a Chevalier of the Order in infancy; it was a kind of insurance policy which enabled impecunious younger sons, if necessary, to
enter the Order formally later on and to benefit from one of its lucrative posts.) In 1761, the year Mme de Pailly began making decisions
for him, the marquis purchased the post of General of the Galleys for
the chevalier and he took the permanent vows of the Order of Malta.[11]
There is no evidence that his own wishes were taken into account,
though he was on the point of marrying at the time, and no trace of
resistance on his part beyond the remark, in a letter to his brother, that
he had never expected to be the first of his family to become a martyr
to chastity. In 1766, when he was about to become Grand Master of the
Order, the marquis again intervened, ordering him to take on the
stewardship of Mirabeau, and again he obeyed. This extraordinary
submissiveness to his brother as head of the family was part of his
feudal code; he saw their relationship as that of lord and vassal, but this
did not prevent him from bluntly criticising his brother's attitude towards his children.

His first report on Gabriel was enthusiastic. Behind the smallpox
scars he had discovered 'intelligence, grace, and an air of nobility', and
he prophesied: 'if he doesn't turn out to be worse than Nero he will be
better than Marcus Aurelius, for I have never met such an intellect; my
poor head was quite overwhelmed.' His nephew had written a history
of Corsica and its people. 'I assure you', he told his brother, 'that you
didn't do as much at twenty-one.'[12]

'He may have won over his uncle, he won't recapture his father as
easily', commented the marquis when he told his daughter what his
brother had written. He gave instructions that his son should occupy
himself, while he was at Mirabeau, with collecting material for an
agricultural survey of Périgord and the Limousin, using the same
methods as in his work on Corsica. In his next letter his brother

reported that Pierre Buffière was writing volumes and was the most prolific writer he had ever seen, having used up half a year's stock of paper in one week. His energy was astounding. 'He is working like a galley slave, getting the lands of Mirabeau into his head. He lets nothing distract him or interfere with his work. I have never seen a gypsy who was less afraid of sun and wind, rain or hail.' To which his brother grudgingly replied: 'Resistance to work is what is wrong with France.'[13]

Letters praising Gabriel continued to arrive. He had excellent qualities, a good heart, but was young for his age: his immaturity contrasting strangely, his uncle thought, with thoughts that might have come from Locke. Lockeian thoughts were all very well; what the marquis wanted was to see his son follow in his own footsteps, and so the order went out that he was to read *Les Economiques* and the *Ephémérides*. With the order went a catechism on economics, with this egotistical explanation:

> It is essential for him to know my science in depth if he wishes to bear my name, since almost everywhere he will find himself a rallying point for men suffocated by the prejudices which surround them, and his ignorance if he did not know it would either calumniate me or make him appear contemptible.[14]

The catechism was intended for his brother as well as his son, though whether either of them treated it with proper reverence is open to doubt. Gabriel began to read his father's works, but for the time being he was far more interested in his uncle's views on history and feudalism:

> Your son considers, as I do, that only the feudal régime can prevent a monarchy from being oriental despotism, because he feels, as I do, that only a group possessing respect as a sort of tribe can hold a king in check; that is to say, a man who has been continuously convinced of his omnipotence by the vilest portion of humanity.[15]

There was no trace as yet of the man who would one day rebel against the aristocratic tribe and revile oligarchic government.

The marquis still showed no eagerness to see his son again, not wanting him to think he could forget his shortcomings; inhibited, also, from taking a step which involved some lowering of his pride. Only his brother could fully appreciate his difficulty, and when he finally relented the chevalier hid his own jubilation and wrote apologetically:

> You may not find him very strong in the field of the economist. But with all due deference I wish you would receive him as a man for whom I have gone bail; and that you would unbend a little, without giving yourself away, and find out his aspirations; so that he may feel that you are his friend and take a great interest in him.[16]

And so, aged twenty-one, Mirabeau returned to his father's house, ending his formative years not with a fatted calf, but at least on a note of hope.

The year 1770–71, which Mirabeau spent with his father, had a lasting effect on him. Following their reconciliation, prejudice was replaced by mutual admiration, one consequence of which was Mirabeau's partial conversion to Physiocracy. The scorn he poured on his father's ideas and writings in the course of their later feuds makes it easy to overlook the extent to which he absorbed his teachings, and to turn for the sources of his moral and political philosophy to the figures he paid homage to as a young man: Montesquieu, Locke, Newton, Bacon, and Rousseau; but the abiding, synthesising influence was that of his father. This is apparent in both his written works and his political life. Mirabeau in the Constituent Assembly, attacking speculators, contemptuous of metaphysics, assigning a working role to the monarchy, putting pragmatism and personal liberty before Utopian dreams and ideological dogma, was putting into practice the elemental Physiocracy he had acquired twenty years before.

At the time of their reunion the marquis was at the zenith of his glory. His published works multiplied year by year, studies on the grain trade and the legal order in 1768, *Les Economiques* in 1769, *Leçons économiques* in 1770. Stylistically they were more tangled than ever, causing his brother the bailli (as he was now known) to remark, on finishing the latest, that he had had to guess at his meaning more often than he could understand it. Anyone who has tried to follow *l'ami des hommes* through the undergrowth of Physiocratic doctrine has had the same experience. As his son Mirabeau was expected to be word perfect, and judging by the fun he had later on with such sacred Physiocratic terms as *produit net*, that is precisely what he became. In *Les Economiques* he learned that the *produit net*, the residue left after subtracting the cost of land cultivation, was the nation's only true source of wealth. It was the landowner's duty to distribute the *produit net* fairly, and to increase the size of it; his position was not to be compared with that of financiers with their *jouissance oisive*, unearned privileges. Duty was a favourite word with the Physiocrats. The marquis wrote a whole book dealing with the duties of different members of the society; landowners who carried out their duties faithfully he deemed to be the country's foremost citizens and the king's natural advisers on finance and taxation. They proved his equation between profit and justice. To him there was a rightness about the connection which gave it a spiritual significance: religious ethics satisfied only privileged souls, he wrote in *Les Economiques*, while the ethics of the *produit net*, assuring man's well-being, also led him towards God.

It was when *l'ami des hommes* started talking about the spiritual significance of profit-making that his son's eyes, like the bailli's, started to glaze. The same mixture of conscience, self-righteousness, and conviction which marked his Physiocratic analyses was present when he was talking about himself. In a letter to his brother, dated 18 February 1771, he wrote:

> Everywhere in history I have only found the triumph of ignorance, of prejudice and of error. Accordingly I have followed the law given by God to nature regarding subsistence, in trying to form the true idea of the essence of *just* and *unjust*, which leads to understanding of the distinction between wrongdoing, duty, and virtue. The security of soul, rectitude of heart and ease of conscience, which this understanding promotes, should not make us confident that we will escape the traps of egotism in everything which concerns our personal interest.[17]

This reflection from a man whose every act was dictated by his ego explains the remorselessness which the marquis showed towards his wife and son. It was his alibi for the inconsistency between his private life and his public principles.

Mirabeau was desperately anxious to please his father, and he made up for his failure to appreciate the arcane side of Physiocracy by his more practical talents. In November 1770 Mme de Vassan died and the marquis came into possession of her estates in the Limousin at a time when famine had produced serious unrest among the people there. He had previously criticised his son's ability to get on with people – 'flabby, vulgar familiarity towards the lower classes, which puts them at their ease' – but now it proved useful. Sent to Aigueperse to deputise for him, Mirabeau exhibited administrative powers which surprised his father, organising famine relief and setting up a court of *prud'hommes* to deal with complaints. The punitive name of Pierre Buffière was dropped and replaced jocularly by *monsieur ouragan* (hurricane); and on his return the marquis bore him off to Paris, though he had sworn, with memories of his own reckless youth, that none of his children should go there before the age of twenty-five. Mirabeau's *début* at Versailles was a great success. 'For five hundred years they have suffered from the Mirabeaus who have never been made like the rest', his father commented triumphantly, 'and they will suffer again from this one, who, I promise, will not let the name down.'[18] But the highest mark of his approval appeared in the report he sent to the *Ephémérides* on the court of *prud'hommes*: 'The young man accomplished this unimaginably difficult task with wisdom and success'.[19] He could not have given his son greater proof of his love than this public tribute in the journal of the enlightened.

When her daughter's marriage contract was drawn up, Mme de Vassan had reserved the right to make her a legacy that would not be subject to it, and in her will she left Mme de Mirabeau an estate in Brie worth 8,000 livres in rents. It came as a shock to the marquis to find that, in addition to paying his wife her increased pension, he would also forfeit a sizeable part of his expectations from his mother-in-law. He responded to the will by refusing to raise his wife's pension as agreed, calculating that she would make no difficulties since she lacked the means to seek legal redress. As Molière's Scapin observes, it takes money to go to law. But he erred fatally in his tactics; the marquise's desire for revenge was intensified and she now had grounds for complaint. When Mirabeau was sent to reason with her she expressed her feelings quite plainly by trying to shoot him. The pistol misfired. His father hoped that this experience would open his eyes to his mother's true nature, but although he was shaken by it the encounter failed to extinguish a lingering sympathy: he referred to her afterwards as 'my poor mother'.

At Bignon he and his father continued to live on the best of terms. In June 1771 he returned to the Limousin, hoping to take over the management of Mme de Vassan's estates, but his plans were crushed, perhaps because it was feared he might form an alliance with his mother. It is possible – and Mirabeau's son, Lucas de Montigny, suspected this – that Mme de Pailly encouraged the marquis to send him to the Limousin in the hope that he *would* form such an alliance, and so destroy the trust that was building between father and son. By November he was back at Bignon where a new mission was waiting for him, to deal with the growing unrest of the tenants at Mirabeau, and on 2 December he set off for Provence. His behaviour on ancestral soil showed that he still identified himself first and foremost as the son of a seigneur. The problem this time required sensitive handling: the marquis had annulled a two hundred year old regulation which allowed the people of Mirabeau and Beaumont to cut wood and graze their flocks on land in the neighbourhood. The villagers were determined to recover their ancient rights; the marquis was determined they should submit. Mirabeau, who knew none of the facts, willingly tried to browbeat the protesters his father had depicted as insolent vassals. Ten years later he would have been fighting on their behalf against seigneurial despotism, but at twenty-two his liberalism was still soft and half-formed. The case went to court and the marquis lost. He blamed his son.

But there was another reason for the stay in Provence. After studying him for a year the marquis had decided that his son was fit to marry. The bailli, who had found a husband for his niece, Louise, in 1770, had already picked out a likely bride, Emilie de Covet de Marignane, the only child of the immensely powerful marquis de Marignane, and one of the richest heiresses in Provence. The bailli's first venture into marriage broking had been disastrous: intelligent, vivacious Louise de Mirabeau had gone straight from her convent to wed the unstable marquis de Cabris, who already exhibited signs of the insanity which was known to run in his family. However, no such skeletons threatened to blight the present project. Mlle de Marignane was eighteen, rather plain, and with bad teeth, but she had wit and youthful spirit, could sing prettily, and was a talented actress; 'essentially an attractive character', as the bailli reported optimistically.

Essentially, in its superficiality, mental inertia, and self-absorption, her character reflected that of the society in which she had grown up, a society which existed in its own micro-world, modelled on that of Paris and the Court. It too had its Versailles, the Château de Tourves near Aix, where Emilie de Marignane played the leading role in amateur theatricals; and its Court, a Court of Love inspired by the one which flourished at Les Baux during the golden age of Provence. Nothing conveys better the total indifference of Aixois society to what was happening in the real world than that Court of Love, where the aristocracy of the province distracted itself, as the Revolution approached, with endless elegant games; killing time, the bailli said, as a revenge on time for killing them. No two people were less suited to each other than Mirabeau and the Queen of the Court of Love. The only fitting match the marquis could think of for a man with his son's mental and physical appetites was the Empress of Russia; he viewed the prospect of being connected to the imperial family of Provence without obvious excitement. Telling Mme de Rochefort the news, he added:

> I have this quirk about wishing to be an honest man in the conduct of my affairs. It was necessary, therefore, to spare my conscience future remorse for having offered such a character to become the father of a family; and so I have loudly protested that we neither know what he's doing nor offer him, and that I have left him at Aix, a town as big as a snuffbox, in order that they can decide. If they want him I will give him.[20]

Mirabeau's courtship was a rude affair. Mlle de Marignane was already intended for the marquis de La Valette when he arrived in Aix, and he had to be seen one morning at her bedroom window before Marignane would give his consent. When he married on 22 June 1772 neither his father nor his uncle were present: the occasion could have been embarrassing for them in view of the scandal he had caused; and his mother was not there either, having refused to have anything to do with the son she felt had deserted her. But if the marquis lacked evident warmth he behaved handsomely in the provision he made for his son, who received rents worth 6,000 livres, rising annually by 500 to 8,500 livres. The estate of Mirabeau was also entailed on him, which represented a real sacrifice on his father's part, since in registering the nomination he made it impossible for himself to touch the property, and he did this at a time when his resources were severely strained. The new comtesse de Mirabeau, though heiress to more than half a million, had no money of her own when she married. Marignane gave them an allowance of 3,000 livres, a calculated snub. Mirabeau soon realised that he had made enemies of an entire society. His marriage had considerably outraged the Court of Love, he remarked; but he underestimated the tinsel courtiers' capacity for revenge. The wedding at Aix marked the beginning of a war between him and them which would finally be fought out during the Revolution itself.

## NOTES

1. *Mémoires biographiques*, I, 303. Letter of 5 October 1757.
2. Ibid., I, 301. Letter of 10 October 1756.
3. Ibid., I, 306–7.
4. Marie-Louise-Elisabeth, born 4 September 1752, married Jean-Paul Clapier, marquis de Cabris, in 1769.
5. Loménie (1879–91: II, 526). Letter of 30 August 1763.
6. Chaussinand-Nogaret (1982: 42) contends that the marquis did not intend the alias to be a humiliation, as generally supposed, because the name Pierre Buffière was flattering, being associated with the premier barony of the Limousin. But in the circumstances he was hardly likely to have selected the name because of the lustre it would confer on his son. Most probably Gabriel had been behaving in a particularly Vassan way and his incensed father announced that his name, accordingly, should come from the same source.
7. Julie-Dorothée-Sylvie, comtesse de Kunsberg, was the second wife of Alexandre-Louis de Mirabeau, who had been grand chamberlain to the margrave of Brandenburg-Bayreuth. His first wife was an actress who, according to Lucas de Montigny, 'had escaped from the harem of the maréchal de Saxe'. Marmontel, another of her lovers, says in his *Mémoires* that the couple were pursued to Avignon by *l'ami des hommes* who wanted to have them arrested, and that she died in childbirth, terrified by the arrival of the police.
8. *Lettres originales*, IV, 237. Letter of 17 July 1780 to Mme de Monnier. In the same letter he wrote: 'It's not this extraordinary man's great talents that I envy, but his virtue, which was the source of his eloquence and the essence of his works. I knew him, and know several people who also did. He was always the same, full of integrity, frank and unassuming, without any kind of ostentation, or the art of concealing faults and displaying virtues.'
9. Louis-Jules-Babon Mancini, duc de Nivernais (1716–98). Poet, minister, and member of the Académie, he was one of the marquis de Mirabeau's closest

friends. He married the long-widowed comtesse de Rochefort as his second wife in 1782, a fortnight before her death.

10. Letter of 10 September 1768. Musée Arbaud, fonds Mirabeau, registre 27, fol. 475. The chevalier's sarcasm and imitation of Mme de Pailly's cliché-ridden epistolary style were intended to convey to the marquis that he guessed that the idea had originated with her.

11. In 1763 the chevalier became a *grand-croix* of the Order of Malta, and took the title of bailli. In subsequent chapters he will be referred to, as he was by the family, as the bailli.

12. *Mémoires biographiques*, II, 11. Letter of 21 May 1770.

13. Ibid. Letter of 30 May 1770.

14. Ibid. II, 25. Letter of 1 June 1770.

15. Ibid. II, 25f. Letter of 23 August 1770.

16. Ibid. II, 29.

17. Loménie (1879–91: II, 384).

18. *Mémoires biographiques*, II, 58. Letter of 20 March 1771.

19. *Ephémérides*, Paris, 1771, III, 110–94.

20. *Mémoires biographiques*, II, 76. Letter of 1 May 1772.

# 3

—❀—

# Rake's Progress

## (1772-1783)

In the first six months of his marriage Mirabeau amassed debts equal to more than seven years' income. Some of them he had contracted as a bachelor; some had been forced on him – Marignane left all the expenses of the wedding to him; the remainder were simply the result of the discrepancy between his income and the lifestyle appropriate to a young seigneur. He spent 20,000 livres on gilding and panelling a single room at Mirabeau, which the bailli had vacated on his marriage, and nearly 25,000 on clothes and jewels for Emilie. As he was still a minor (the age of majority in Provence being twenty-five) he was unable to obtain bills of exchange from moneylenders unless they were endorsed by a third party. A cousin performed this service for him.

By November 1773, when his son Victor was born, his creditors were pressing him so hard that he turned in desperation to his father-in-law. He stood to inherit 300,000 livres from Marignane, who, in fact, survived him by twelve years, and 60,000 livres on the death of Emilie's grandmother. Marignane offered to advance him this 60,000 livres but his father refused permission, probably because he had his grandson's future in mind, and also because what was proposed would not cure his son's extravagance. Marignane, writing to the marquis with his offer, said that his son-in-law had told him he was ready to ask his father to get a *lettre de cachet* against him in order to save him from his creditors. This request is interesting in view of the picture Mirabeau liked to draw of his father hounding him with *lettres de cachet*. Certainly some form of evading action was necessary, as his creditors were only waiting

36

for his next birthday, when he would cease to be a minor, to have him arrested. To spare him the humiliation of having this happen in front of his tenants at Mirabeau, the marquis sent him to Manosque, a village ten miles away, while Emilie sought refuge with her family at Aix.

His twenty-fifth birthday came a few weeks later, and immediately his father took the only step that would save him from arrest, by having him declared a bankrupt. Mirabeau always protested that this was an unnecessary move. His debts amounted to 180,680 livres, three quarters of that being in letters of exchange from usurers, and he argued that these could be discounted as unreclaimable since usury was illegal. Theoretically he was right, but there remained his other debts, the interest on which already exceeded his income. Marignane's 60,000 livres would merely have postponed the day of reckoning, and meanwhile there was the real risk that the estate of Mirabeau would be seized by his creditors. Appearing in court at Manosque on 9 May, he admitted that his conduct had been foolish and tried to explain the pressures which had brought him to his present state. His language was restrained, very different from that used in the account he wrote in 1778 of the same events, which was published after his death.[1] His original statement was also more honest, though he lied about his income, saying that he had only 1,000 livres from his father and 5,000 from his wife, in the hope that what was hers would not be confiscated by the judges of the Châtelet in Paris who were to decide his case; but it made no difference. They left him 3,000 livres to cover all his expenses, while the remainder went to his creditors. Had he been prepared to live frugally for a few years he could have discharged his bankruptcy; only a year later, Emilie's grandmother dying, he was able to pay some of his debts; but the recklessness with money which he had inherited from both his parents could not be eliminated from his blood. He remained an undischarged bankrupt, of his own choice, for the rest of his life, finding that, although the state had been forced on him, it had its advantages.

His bankruptcy put an end to the *entente cordiale* between himself and his father, and set in motion a chain of actions and reactions on both sides which was self-perpetuating. Good relations might have survived the crisis brought about by Mirabeau's creditors, however, had the marquis not discovered that his son was party to a plot against himself dreamed up by his estranged wife and his daughter Louise, now Mme de Cabris. The marquise had taken legal action regarding her pension and the estate left to her by Mme de Vassan, and in consequence he was ordered to pay her the revenues of the estate and 4,000 livres in lieu of further pension. The worst part of it was the discovery that Louise had given her the money to litigate against him. The marquise was determined to seek a separation *de corps et de biens* from her husband, which would have the effect of restoring to her everything that he had received under her marriage contract (including the value of properties sold with her consent). If she succeeded he would be ruined.

It was Louise's idea in the first place. Mirabeau said afterwards that without his sister urging her on his mother would have calmed down; but at the time he was quite ready to stir the pot. To Louise must also go the credit for inflaming him against his father. Lyrical accounts have been written, on too literally interpreted evidence, of the supposedly incestuous relationship which existed between Mirabeau and his younger sister; her influence over him can be explained much more mundanely. It grew from a basis of shared grudges and was helped by the similarity of their characters: they were both egotistical and impetuous, with the histrionic streak which one recognises from the marquis's descriptions of his wife's behaviour as being peculiarly Vassan. They also had a common bond in their marriages, neither of which was happy. And so an alliance was formed, which led Mirabeau into family treacheries he should have avoided and further along the route to his own involuntary destruction.

In the spring of 1774 he was outraged to discover that Emilie had been unfaithful to him. He ordered her to write a farewell letter to her lover, a letter which he later retrieved and kept. According to his own version of what happened next, hearing that the lover's forthcoming marriage was now in jeopardy, he broke the ban ordering him not to leave Manosque and rode to Grasse, in order to reassure the parents of the prospective bride that the young man had not behaved dishonourably. The only certain facts are that on the road between Manosque and Grasse he encountered the Baron de Villeneuve-Moans who had spoken slightingly of Louise de Cabris, that he knocked him down, and that the Baron lodged a charge against him of attempted murder.

Threatened with imminent arrest, he sent Emilie to enlist his father's help. On 13 September she wrote from Bignon to tell him that the marquis had obtained a *lettre de cachet* for his detention in the Château d'If. It turned out that the ministers had heard, even before his father, of the Manosque incident, and that they had wanted to have him arrested. By acting as he did the marquis had saved his son from becoming a state prisoner, and one of his first acts was to send his son-in-law, Saillant, to arbitrate with Mirabeau's creditors; but these were irrelevant points as far as the culprit was concerned.

Mirabeau entered the Château d'If on 23 August 1774. His father told Marignane:

He is where he deserves to be, and there he will remain. Supposing a miracle, and that the commandant is satisfied, I shall send him to some secure place, where he will have to prove his repentance. Supposing another miracle brings him through this second test, I shall have other ways of testing his capacity as a husband and father.[2]

Writing to his son's father-in-law he had to show a proper degree of indignation, but privately he told the bailli that Villeneuve-Moans had got what he deserved.

Emilie wrote to tell her husband that she was ready to fly to his side the moment he called. She remained at Bignon. The Court of Love had ill prepared her for the real world, and whatever attractions Mirabeau may have had as a suitor he had none as a jealous, bankrupt, imprisoned husband. She sent him no news of their son, left behind at Manosque, whom Mirabeau, in fact, never saw again. He soon realised that, far from doing all she could to press for his early release, she would be happy to have him out of her way forever. The only other person he could turn to was the bailli, who thought that his brother had acted unwisely in assuming a custodial role which would inevitably make him the target of his son's resentment. He warned:

Take care. You are regarded as being a little hard towards your son. He is considered to be guilty only with regard to his debts; and to tell the truth, youngsters have adopted strange habits in this respect, and if all the young men with debts were shut up one would see only greybeards in the streets.[3]

Written in April 1775, this letter reached the marquis when he had already had his son transferred from the Château d'If. His new prison was the Château de Joux on the frontier of Franche-Comté, where, said his father, 'he will be less restricted'.

During his eight months in the Château d'If Mirabeau wrote his first book, *Essai sur le despotisme*. He described it as a declaration of faith, and for this reason it is interesting to compare it with the early pieces written by other future revolutionaries in the years before the Revolution. At once the dearth of anything comparable is apparent. Thinking about certain principles did not simply lead the author of the *Essai* into Utopian theorising as it did most of his contemporaries; he already rejected the self-indulgence of protest unaccompanied by relevant remedies. And he showed a marked capacity for thinking ahead. Generally the revolutionaries went in for hindsight more than prescience. Some, like Lameth and Barnave, committed their political philosophy to paper either when the Revolution was over, or over for them; others, like Sieyès, Malouet, Mounier, and Clavière, wrote nothing until the very brink of the Revolution; and Clavière's *Foi publique* was really a publicity stunt, designed to give him an eligible political image. Among those who began to write earlier, Robespierre published an essay in 1784, when he was twenty-six, on a particular legal problem, which showed him to be neither a radical as yet, nor with a sound grasp of the principles he was invoking. Brissot, five years younger than Mirabeau, began with a pamphlet, *Testament politique de l'Angleterre*, when he was twenty-three, in which he prophesied England's downfall and warned the French Foreign Minister to avoid wars of conquest. A few years later the expert on English politics was generalising on philosophy in *De la vérité*, and looking for 'the good of humanity', which was no more than what most men aspired to do at his age. Marat, six years older than Mirabeau, went from fiction to *belles lettres*, and produced his first political work in 1774 when he was thirty-one. *Chains of Slavery*, written in English and published in London, was aimed at the English electorate. It therefore falls outside the mainstream of works by future revolutionaries, but is the only one of sufficient weight to be compared with the *Essai sur le despotisme*. Written in the same year, by an odd coincidence it had a similar theme: Marat declared in his sub-title that his work revealed the 'villainous attempts of princes to ruin liberty' and disclosed 'the dreadful scenes of despotism'. Like Mirabeau's book, it was partly historical and partly political; unlike his, it turned every argument into a diatribe. As to the effectiveness of the two works, *Chains of Slavery* did not sell; *Essai sur le despotisme* ran through two editions in six weeks.

Mirabeau began the *Essai* by imitating Rousseau, looking at man and contrasting his natural state with that in an ordered society; he asked, particularly, whether man was inclined to despotism, and answered that in a natural state he was not, and that in a social state he was. He asked whether man was good in his social state, and answered that he was, whatever Rousseau had said. Continuing his study of man in society, he came to the *autorité tutélaire*, the guardian authority which men accepted in their own interest, and which led in turn to the idea of a king. Men gave themselves leaders, and then found that the greatest stability lay in hereditary leadership. But a king was never intended to be a master: men 'have forgotten that the right of sovereignty resides uniquely and inalienably in the people, the sovereign being the first magistrate of the people and only that'.[4]

So far he was another Rousseauist. But when he discussed natural law he revealed his debt to Physiocracy, declaring that man's rights and duties all derived from this law which was 'obligatory for all, ineffaceable despite the most frenzied prejudice, imprescriptible whatever contradictions they encounter in human legislation'.[5] His vision of a monarch's relationship with his people, based on natural law and at risk when men, forgetting this, deprived him of his proper function, was also Physiocratic. The king, he said, fulfilling his role in accordance with natural law, would not become despotic; he recognised that he had been given power by the people only in order to carry out his mandate. Despots were those who thought that power was theirs by right. But since it had already been demonstrated that man in his social state was despotically inclined, what defence was there against misuse of power by the king? The answer lay in education:

> Education and liberty are the bases of all social harmony and all human rights. I could say education alone, for liberty depends on it absolutely, universal education being the invincible enemy of despots.

When kings and their subjects were enlightened through education, despotism would be eradicated, he continued. Kings would exercise their authority more carefully; citizens would submit only out of ignorance or because they had forgotten their rights.[6]

Mirabeau went on to address the monarch directly – the *Essai* was, in effect, a manual on kingship for the inexperienced Louis XVI who had just succeeded to the throne:

> O prince, to whom nature has given no more organs or faculties than to any other man, your people and you are only joined by the thin tie of utility. If you break it you compromise your existence; whether society confiscates the power which has brought only oppression and misery in place of protection and prosperity, or whether you succeed in wearing out your subjects with servitude, and in ruining their country with the ravages of despotism; for your exaggerated power will suffer the same fate as the state which, drained of resources, collapses at the first threat.

And if, as king,

> you overturn the hierarchy of which you are the head, if you make men conscious of their chains, if you insanely devour the riches your insatiable tyranny has seized from them, they will remember that they are stronger and more numerous than you, and that you only have as much power as they choose to give you.[7]

Writing this, he did not pretend that only kings could act despotically. He insisted that laws were for the protection of the king against conspiring factions as much as for the protection of the people against their rulers. He regarded those who used force to impose their own views, who invested themselves with sovereign authority, as potentially greater despots than the one they had replaced. Better one despot than a thousand – this was also Voltaire's view.

Licence, said Mirabeau, brought as much misery to society as tyranny. So, for the good of society, all men should be aware of both their duties and their rights.

But where are the philosophers capable of rebuking the great and defending all men? Courage in battle is common; courage in principles, in conduct and morals, is very rare. We dare not think differently from the rest when it is dangerous to go against general opinion; we do not even know how to think differently when social institutions have filled us with prejudices which are carefully nourished by the ambitious and those in power. The imitative spirit, cleverly worked on by them, becomes universal. Passive obedience becomes fashionable, as love of liberty was the commonest virtue in happier times and under less arbitrary governments.[8]

In his first book, despite its debt to his father's writings, the young Mirabeau appears already equipped with all the verbal and intellectual gifts which he deployed in the Revolution, and with his own distinctive turn of mind. He is sceptical of theories that take no account of reality. Historical facts, the evidence of experience, are for him the only basis for a viable political philosophy. While his fellow revolutionaries are influenced by ideologues, he is more inclined to consider problems in the light of history: the author most quoted in the *Essai* is Tacitus. He is prepared to contradict the accepted masters: Rousseau insisted on man's natural goodness, but one only had to see an infant howling in a cradle to know that the germ of despotism exists in everyone. The desire for power of some sort, said Mirabeau, is the most active passion in the human heart, and statesmanship is required to control and distribute this explosive force. This understanding of statesmanship apropos of despotism, a subject the revolutionaries viewed with the eyes of rhetoricians, is another instance of his divergence from the norm.

So, too, in the age of enlightenment, is his defence of feudalism. 'Under this much maligned feudal system', he wrote, 'there was at least a constant maxim that no man could be taxed without his consent. This principle embodies the foremost guarantee of liberty.'[9] And again, writing about modern absolutism:

Under feudal governments the monarchy was regarded as a military office, not as a proprietary one. There was no country in Europe, no matter what despotic tyrants had invaded it, that was not administered in those barbaric times by a legal and limited government.[10]

If this was the bailli speaking it was the marquis who dictated his comments on the tribunals which 'the detestable Maupeou' had set up in 1770 in place of the *parlements*. As defenders of liberty and critics of the *parlements* with their entrenched self-interest, Mirabeau *fils* and the marquis might have been expected to hail Maupeou's reform. The passage has been taken as proof that Mirabeau, at this time, identified fully with the nobility who controlled the former *parlements* and who had been replaced. This misses the point of his attack. He was not condoning the former corruption but denouncing ministerial dictatorship. Reactionary though the *parlements* were, they offered the only resistance to the despotism of the crown. Maupeou's coup, still recent when he wrote the *Essai*, showed how easily liberty could be confiscated even in an age of heightened awareness.

When the marquis spoke of his son being less restricted at Joux he was telling the truth, for Mirabeau was free to come and go as he pleased, to lodge in the neighbouring town of Pontarlier, even to take a trip into Switzerland to see a publisher. He went to Neuchâtel, ostensibly in order to deliver the manuscript of a work he had written on the salt marshes of Franche-Comté, but taking with him the *Essai sur le despotisme*, which would never have passed the French censor. The publisher, Fauche, paid him 1,500 livres for the *Essai* – the first money he had earned with his pen – with a promise of 1,000 crowns a year for any future writings. His life in Pontarlier continued agreeably for several months, until a local bookseller went to the governor of Joux with a bill of exchange drawn up by Fauche, which Mirabeau had offered in payment of his account. As a bankrupt he was not allowed to contract fresh debts, but he took the governor's order confining him in future to the fortress as an unforgivable affront, and responded by absconding. That, in itself, would have had serious repercussions, though not as far-reaching as those which were about to ensue in consequence of another matter.

The leading citizen of Pontarlier was the marquis de Monnier, a retired president of the Exchequer Court at Dôle, who had a young wife. When Sophie de Ruffey[11] was barely fifteen her father had offered her in marriage to the naturalist Buffon, a widower of sixty-two, who was shocked at the idea. Soon, however, another widower had appeared, five years older than Buffon but possessing a title and fortune. 'I did not know that M. de Monnier was a marriageable young man', wrote Voltaire to Ruffey when he heard of the wedding, 'I think he is very fortunate to wed your daughter. I wish both of them all possible felicity.'[12] It was well known that the bridegroom was motivated by something less excusable than lechery: Monnier was marrying out of spite. His daughter having eloped and then having successfully sued him for her dowry, he intended to punish her by begetting a son. Mirabeau arrived when Sophie had been married for four years. He became a frequent visitor at the Monnier house,[13] while provincial Pontarlier watched and whispered. Reading all the relevant correspondence, it seems clear that what he, at least, regarded as a passing affair became a grand passion obligatorily as the result of family interference. After vanishing from Pontarlier he surfaced in Dijon, where he was seen by Mme Ruffey, and placed under house arrest by the provost pending further instructions from the authorities. Sophie herself, who had returned to her parents in Dijon a defiant sinner, was under guard in her own home. The agitation he had created in the bourgeois Ruffey family afforded Mirabeau considerable amusement, but his presence in Dijon had an inconvenient effect on Mme de Monnier, who saw it as proof of an immortal attachment, and who was quite prepared to be a martyr to love. Her infatuation was an added complication at a time when he had already prejudiced his future by absconding. He was greatly relieved when she was persuaded by her parents to return to her husband; but his own affairs went from bad to worse. Commissioners investigating his case decided that he should be kept in detention until the Villeneuve-Moans lawsuit was settled; his new prison was to be the fortress of Doullens in Picardy. When he heard this he appealed to Malesherbes, the Minister of the Household and his mother's acquaintance. There was no answer. A fortnight later all his hopes collapsed on hearing that Turgot had been dismissed and that Malesherbes had fallen with him. According to his mother the minister's last advice had been that he should go abroad and there obtain promotion – which may have been a suggestion that he should go to America, as so many Frenchmen were doing, to fight for the colonists in their war against George III.

He had always rejected the idea of becoming a fugitive. It seemed to set the seal on his guilt, would sever him from his past and from his family, and would end all possibility of reconciliation with his wife. He wrote to her at this time. She did not reply. With Malesherbes gone his last avenue of appeal was closed; all he could do was to follow his parting advice. On 25 May 1776 he left Dijon secretly and headed for Switzerland.

When the marquis de Mirabeau heard of his son's escape he assumed that it was his intention to join his mother and aid her in her legal battle against himself. Advised by his friends not to pursue him, he hesitated, but 'finally the cry of conscience, consulted in the silence of the night', prevailed, and two detectives, Muron and Brugnière, set off on Mirabeau's trail. They discovered that for part of the time since his disappearance he had joined forces with his sister Louise and her lover. The lover, Briançon, handed over a paper listing Mirabeau's future movements which he was supposed to pass on to Mme de Monnier; but even with this information the detectives failed to find their quarry, and after a month they gave up. Mirabeau wrote four letters to Mme de Monnier via Briançon during his wanderings. The first, which was opened by Briançon, contained a boast by Mirabeau that he had had an incestuous relationship with Louise.[14] Mme de Monnier never saw it, but the others, which reached her, were in a similar vein: in one he accused her of having been seduced by her brother, in another he doubted her fidelity only to glory in his own promiscuity. By these crude tactics he may have hoped to cure her of her infatuation for him, and so make things easier for himself, but they only produced fresh avowals of devotion. In August he turned up in Turin, and from there he headed northwards through the Valais to Les Verrières, a few miles from Pontarlier on the Swiss side of the frontier. A note to Mme de Monnier to let her know where he was brought back a cry for help; she threatened suicide if she did not join him. Knowing that he had forfeited his future, he sent two men to conduct her to Les Verrières. While Monnier lingered over supper that evening his wife changed into men's clothes, climbed over the garden wall, and out of his life for ever.

Mirabeau and Mme de Monnier went to Amsterdam. Calling himself the comte de Saint-Mathieu, Mirabeau applied to the bookseller, Marc-Michel Rey, for work as a translator, describing himself as the author of the *Essai sur le despotisme*. Rey knew that this work was by someone with a different name, and Mirabeau had to ask Fauche to confirm that he was indeed the author of the *Essai*. Fauche obliged, but passed on his address to the police.

Working for Rey was a form of slavery, as Rousseau had also found; Mirabeau earned a louis a day as a hack journalist. The strident tone of pamphlets such as *Avis aux Hessois*, which denounced the Landgrave of Hesse Cassel's promise to send troops to fight for England in America, and *Le Lecteur y mettra le titre*, a protest against government destruction of the arts, led to his being approached by members of the Dutch patriot party who saw in him a useful propagandist for their cause. Their interest was flattering, and he gave them his enthusiastic and vocal support. For the first time in his life he had the satisfaction of working for his daily bread, and the optimism this induced helped to blind him to the magnitude of the encumbrance he had taken on: when his mother wrote, begging him to send Mme de Monnier back to her husband, he replied that honour and duty forbade it.[15] He was moved by her devotion to him, contrasting as it did with his wife's indifference. She was not beautiful, she lacked Emilie's polish, but she had an independence of mind which outweighed all else. He later wrote:

> I could never have felt deep love for an unintelligent woman because I want to discuss things with my companion. A limited mind bores me. I have so few

of the usual prejudices that a silly little woman, full of trivialities and a slave
to convention, would never have suited me.[16]

The Dutch idyll lasted eight months. His father hoped that now he
was out of the country he would trouble them no more. He had enough
vexation already from the marquise, who was making ever greater
claims against him as her debts and her lawyer's fees mounted, and
who now took advantage of the backlash against the Physiocrats which
had followed Turgot's downfall to start a campaign of public abuse
against him. She was joined in this exercise by her son. In December
the Marquis came across a biting attack on himself in the *Gazette
littéraire*, under the initials S-M (Saint-Mathieu), and a few weeks later
a *mémoire* supporting the marquise de Mirabeau, in which he recognised 'the style of that rogue in Holland', appeared in Paris. Put together by the marquise's lawyer from letters and material supplied by
Mirabeau, it was a crude but effective bit of character assassination
which he later repudiated, saying that he had not corrected the draft, as
though the libels it contained were simply printer's errors. All this only
encouraged his father to leave him where he was in Holland. Early in
1777, however, Monnier started proceedings against him, and this was
the signal for Vergennes, the Foreign Minister, to order his arrest. At
the same time the Ruffeys sent the detective Brugnière to Amsterdam
to arrest their daughter. On 10 May the court at Pontarlier judged
Mirabeau in his absence and condemned him to be beheaded in effigy,
to pay a fine of 5,000 livres to the king, and 40,000 livres to the marquis
de Monnier for the crime of *rapt et séduction*. Mme de Monnier was to
be confined during her husband's lifetime and branded as a prostitute;
her civil rights were cancelled, and her dowry was confiscated.

At the time of their arrest she was three months' pregnant. In view
of this, on reaching Paris she was not sent, as previously ordered, to the
notorious Saint-Pélagie prison, but to another place, just short of the
horror of Saint-Pélagie, a house of detention for prostitutes and luna-
tics in the rue de Charonne. Mirabeau's destination was Vincennes,
the prison his father had briefly graced in 1760. At the time they began
their sentences Sophie was twenty-two and he was twenty-seven.

In his book *Des lettres de cachet et des prisons d'état*, Mirabeau described
the forbidding interior of the *donjon* of Vincennes: the towers entered
through triple doors so strong that only cannon could force them, the
prisoners' cells within the towers, each with three doors and each door
with triple bolts, the perpetual darkness broken by a feeble ray of light
from a barred window high above the ground, the guards making their
rounds every half-hour day and night, the surly turnkeys who were

forbidden to speak to the inmates. The *donjon* was surrounded by two moats. Only two prisoners had ever succeeded in escaping.

Mirabeau was held under a *lettre de cachet* which his father could have revoked at a future date, but which Marignane, Villeneuve-Moans, or Monnier might then seek to have renewed, since they all had cause for grievance. It was no consolation to the victim of arbitrary arrest, but had his father not acted first he would have been imprisoned by a *lettre de cachet* originating from an even more hostile source. How long his detention would last he did not know. He was allowed to write to his wife and father, and, on matters relative to his case, to police headquarters and government ministers. The man who decided what he could and could not do was Jean Lenoir,[17] the head of the Paris police, and it was thanks to his leniency that he was able to correspond with Mme de Monnier, although their letters had to be censored first. They both played consciously on the sympathy of the police clerk, Gabriel Boucher, 'the good angel' whose job it was to examine their letters. Undoubtedly there was an element of calculation in Mme de Monnier's hints of suicide, and in Mirabeau's detailed recapitulations of what he had suffered at the hands of his father, for Lenoir might be sufficiently concerned to recommend his early release.

Mme de Monnier's situation was pitied by everyone. The matron of the reformatory, a Mlle Douay, retired whore, put her in a room with only three other women, but could not protect her from the vermin or the sound of screaming and brawling. As the date of her confinement drew near she was taken to a midwife's house in the rue de Bellefonds, where, on 7 January, she gave birth to a girl. In a disingenuous note written a few days earlier, Mirabeau told her to register the baby not in his name but Monnier's, saying that he wished to safeguard it by giving it a name which would bring it legal rights:

> If I die destitute you have nothing to leave him; he will at least have a plank to cling to in the wreckage, and the fear of litigation will persuade the Valdahons [Monnier's daughter and her husband] to sacrifice a little in order to save a lot.[18]

Mme de Monnier believed him, but the fact was that he wanted to be able to deny his paternity in law. The baby was put in the care of a foster mother. Officialdom did its best: Mlle Douay, anticipating Maupassant, went into the country to visit her, and Lenoir had her sketched for her parents, but he was unable to save Mme de Monnier from being sent six months later to a convent at Gien, ninety miles away. The move completed her isolation and broke her mentally.

After a year in prison Mirabeau's health had deteriorated; he had symptoms which he thought were those of a kidney stone and suffered the first of the attacks of opthalmia which eventually almost destroyed his sight. His affairs seemed further than ever from solution, and the news that his mother and sister were now also confined by *lettres de cachet* increased his gloom.[19] In March 1778 he completed a *mémoire*, 37,000 words long, addressed to his father but obviously designed to be read by others, in which he went through the whole history of his marriage and debts. Basically it was the same document he had prepared for the judges at his bankruptcy hearing, but carefully worked over, a brilliant piece of self-justification, seemingly frank but bearing the same relation to the truth as Rousseau's *Confessions*. He hoped it would force his father's hand, but the marquis had not forgotten his wife's *mémoire* and his son's contribution to it. His private life had been made public at the very moment when his reputation was discredited by the political failure of Physiocratic theories; the marquise's *mémoire*, appearing within weeks of Turgot's fall, had purposely poured salt into the wound.[20] The judgement of the fashionable world had never counted for much with the marquis, who once observed that people with rooms decorated in pink and grey invariably had minds to match; but the rejection of Physiocracy was a terrible, personal defeat, and he was not ready yet to show generosity towards the son who had derided him. In the end it was not his son's self-justificatory arguments, nor his promises of good behaviour, but a completely unforeseen event, which caused *l'ami des hommes* to change his mind about keeping him in prison indefinitely.

Mirabeau had not seen his son since the day of his arrest at Manosque, and had had no news of him from Emilie, who had resumed her life at the Court of Love. She was performing in a play on 8 October 1778 when Victor, who had been unwell for a few days, suddenly died. 'The last hope of our name', groaned his grandfather. Mirabeau's sisters were convinced he had been poisoned; he was surrounded by collateral heirs to his mother's fortune, and there had even been anonymous letters warning the family that his life was in danger.

Following his death it was popularly felt that Mirabeau and his wife should be reunited. The marquis was in a dilemma, urged on one hand by what the bailli called his posteromania, held back on the other by his promise to his daughter-in-law not to act against her wishes. In order not to appear personally involved he sent his friend and disciple, Samuel Dupont,[21] to persuade his son to seek a reconciliation. Mirabeau doubted whether he could persuade the woman who hated him that they could be happy together; nevertheless, he composed the necessary letter. In her reply Emilie told him that she found his references to her in his *mémoire* offensive. Therefore she could not assist in making him happy, but would be charmed to learn that he had become so.[22]

Mirabeau had now been in solitary confinement for two years and four months. Dupont continued to visit him, but the end of 1779 found him more depressed than at any time since his captivity began. His only constant support was Mme de Monnier, who wrote to him several times a week. She still believed, despite his overture to his wife, that one day they would escape to some Rousseau-like Eden where they would live together, Julie and Saint-Preux, in eternal happiness. Mirabeau was partly responsible for encouraging these fantasies – out of kindness and, doubtless, because it was difficult to admit the truth that for him their affair was now an unfortunate episode which he wanted to terminate as soon as honour and decency permitted. Five months later fate intervened: their daughter, Sophie-Gabrielle, died of convulsions while teething. While she lived there had always been the fear that he and Mme de Monnier might elope again. Now there was no obstacle, apart from her aversion, to prevent her from returning to her husband, and with a callousness born of his own desperation he urged the grief-stricken mother to use this opportunity to settle her affairs. As for his own, they were progressing better than he knew. Negotiations with the most pressing of his creditors were proceeding, and some agreement with Villeneuve-Moans seemed to have been reached, for he ceased to be a threat. The marquis de Mirabeau had decided to set his son free despite and because of his daughter-in-law's desire to have him permanently incarcerated. The same honourable scruples which obliged him to punish his son also ensured that he would not keep him in prison on the whim of a fickle wife. A letter from Marignane, telling him that his son was plotting to murder him, sealed his contempt for Emilie and her family.

On 13 December 1780 Mirabeau was released from Vincennes. He was to live with Boucher, the police clerk, until he had proven to his father's satisfaction that he had truly turned over a new leaf, but his brother-in-law, Saillant, was already impressed by his changed attitude, and reported to his father-in-law that Dupont must have used a hammer to produce such a transformation. The marquis replied with a certain pride:

> I would rather put it down to the effect of bolts and gaolers. Forty-two months alone in a gloomy vault, with only the sound of howling in the underground passages to keep him company at night, is a medicine that would alter anyone.[23]

During his years in prison Mirabeau read extensively: history ancient and modern, economics, political philosophy, law. Although his intellectual apprenticeship had already been completed under his father, this long solitude allowed his ideas to mature and crystallise,

accounting for that consistent sense of direction, unaffected by immediate events, which afterwards marked his thinking during the
Revolution.

When he was not reading he wrote. Much of his output was pretty
ephemeral, catchpenny novels like *Ma conversion*,[24] translations of
Tibullus and the *Decameron* and Ovid's *Metamorphoses*; and Pope's *Il-
iad*, which he considered a great improvement on Homer's original,
'whatever fanatical admirers of antiquity may say'.[25] Even his letters to
Mme de Monnier, sighing pastiches of *La Nouvelle Héloïse* which once
inspired a whole school of drama and romantic fiction, are no longer
read.

The same nineteenth-century editors who found the verbal mastur-
bation of some of the letters to Mme de Monnier embarrassing, were
disgusted to find him discussing with her a work he had written, in
which he had taken 'the most scabrous subjects' from the Bible and
antiquity, and made them 'sufficiently philosophical' for puritans to
read. Lucas de Montigny cringed when he mentioned *Errotika biblion*,
saying that his father could only have written it out of dire necessity; it
took Baudelaire to observe that the Revolution of 1789 was as much
the work of 'libertine' (the French word also means free-thinking)
writers as of the *Encyclopédistes*, and that Mirabeau, along with Nerciat
and Laclos, provided the best documentary evidence of the spirit of
the nobility at that time.

In its own way *Errotika biblion* is as much a philosophical commentary on the age as *Les Liaisons dangereuses*. It studied the moral progress of mankind. Surveying the vices of the ancients, modern man
might see, by his revulsion, how far humanity had advanced. If de-
basing practices still continued, and morals had not kept pace with
the human spirit as it moved from darkness to light, it was because
the same institutions which kept people in political and social subjection also subjected them morally. To make his point Mirabeau invented a Utopian city, situated in the ring of Saturn; *L'Anagogie*, his
tale of an ideal civilisation in outer space, which forms the opening
chapter of the book, is a fable of man's perfectibility in a free society.
(By making it a fable he also indicated what he thought of social
Utopists.) His choice of a Saturnian setting would not have been lost
on readers of Ovid's *Metamorphoses*: the golden age there described,
in which men did what was right without being compelled, and lived
in peace without the need for armies, was the age of Saturn. Mirabeau's Saturnians knew nothing of war or superstition. Their intelligence and sciences were highly advanced; they had consequently
attained a state of cognitive perfection which allowed ideas and
knowledge to circulate freely through the air, resulting in universal

harmony. There was no private ownership. Ethereal socialists, they felt that without it there was little ground for disputes. Politically there was perfect equality; if indeed, their creator added, 'such beings might be supposed to have needed a political system'.

*L'Anagogie* was an evocation of the happy state which would ensue for humanity when it had escaped from the despotism of ignorance, perpetuated by the censorship of the press, and superstition, perpetuated by the Church. If the readers of *Errotika biblion* sought or found only what was licentious in it they unwittingly testified to the truth of Mirabeau's argument. Master of irony, he moralised in the very act of pandering to immorality. Erotic writing for him, as for other writers on the eve of the Revolution, was a political weapon; the flouting in print of sexual taboos hastened the demolition of the old order, by demonstrating that the dictatorship of the Church in moral matters was at an end; and the fact that all forms of licence were now condemned more loudly than before showed that the political nature of the assault on orthodox morality was well understood. In the days when the monarchy and the Church occupied unassailable positions, sexual licence, at least aristocratic sexual licence, caused no unease. Only twenty years earlier a marquis de Sade would not have been imprisoned for perversion.[26] Fear breeds conformity, and society in 1780, bereft of its old sense of certainty, sought reassurance that its world was as secure as ever by instinctively adopting less liberal moral attitudes.

*Errotika biblion* was one of two important political statements which Mirabeau made in Vincennes. The other was a development of his youthful *Essai sur le despotisme*. Early in 1779 he completed *Des Lettres de cachet et des prisons d'état*, an indictment of state tyranny which his father later described, not without admiration, as 'seditious, rampaging insanity'. Seditious it certainly was, to examine *lettres de cachet* as an inseparable part of the whole system of absolutism, and to analyse by contrast the principles of liberty and good government; to denounce the forces of arbitrary power while at the mercy of those forces required the sort of courage that passes for insanity. Mirabeau had lifted the lid of a Pandora's box, exposing not only the injustice of the *lettre de cachet* system but the moral corruption it engendered, which permeated every public institution and vitiated the national conscience. A lot of his material came from the *Essai sur le despotisme*, but there was a new awareness. Whereas before he had focused on the nobility as historical resisters to royal despotism, now he saw the nobles as its born defenders, and included himself, as an aristocrat, among the guilty: 'Slaves by condition, by prejudice, by ignorance, and proud of it, we have done more to further despotism than all the other bodies together, and it is by us that it sustains itself'.[27] Absolute monarchies and arbitrary power were the cemetery of liberty, but it was not enough to realise this.

> I know, and I declare unequivocally, that the law, in order to be just, legitimate, obligatory, in effect truly *law*, must have the seal of general consent. Any state where the citizens do not participate in the legislative power, by delegating representatives freely elected by the majority of the nation, does not have, and cannot have, public liberty.[28]

*Des lettres de cachet*, with this prophetic challenge, was published in 1782 in Neuchâtel. Even so, they took the precaution of describing it as a posthumous work. The first edition sold overnight. It was read and discussed openly, even at Versailles, and the pressure of opinion built up by it eventually forced the government to act: five years before the fall of the Bastille the *donjon* of Vincennes, equally grim symbol of oppression, was evacuated.

Mirabeau spent the first months after his release negotiating with his mother's lawyers in an attempt to modify the terms of her case against the marquis. He was still waiting for his father to receive him. One day they nearly collided on a doorstep; he flattened himself against the wall to let his father pass. Neither spoke. It was the first time in nine years that they had seen each other. In the end their reunion was precipitated by the disaster that struck in May, when the marquise finally won her case, leaving her husband financially ruined. Mirabeau hastened to Bignon and an emotional reconciliation with *l'ami des hommes*, who reported that he was the same as he used to be: 'the greatest possible intelligence, an incredible talent for seizing the surface but nothing underneath . . . good at heart all the same'.[29]

Before he could resume a normal life he had to get his head replaced on his shoulders, as his father put it, by contesting the Pontarlier judgement; and after that he had to remind the comtesse de Mirabeau, in the courts if necessary, that they were still legally man and wife. But first he went to Gien to see Mme de Monnier. Eyewitnesses reported that their last meeting was acrimonious; artless Sophie, who once thought that they were reliving *La Nouvelle Héloïse*, could not forgive him for being less perfect than Saint-Preux, and his promise that he would fight for the restoration of her rights at Pontarlier was no compensation for a future without him. The rest of the year he spent at Bignon alone with his father while he prepared for his encounter with the Pontarlier judges. His brother was serving with the French forces in America,[30] and Mme de Pailly had gone to visit her relatives in Switzerland. His lawyer was of the opinion that the case which had been proved against him at Pontarlier was unassailable, and the marquis thought it would be safer to seek a royal pardon, but Mirabeau was determined to proceed. The following February he went to Pontarlier to confront his judges, all of them related in some way to Monnier, and had himself arrested as a voluntary act in order to force their attention. Six months and three sensational *mémoires* later, he triumphed: his sentence was quashed and his civil rights restored; Mme de Monnier was granted a separation from her husband, her dowry was restored, and she received a pension; in return she had to remain in the convent until Monnier's death. As it turned out this condition made little difference; her own sad life was already over though she had seven more years to live.[31]

After Pontarlier, Aix. Mirabeau said of his return there in October 1782 that it created as much terror as the arrival of a ghost at the height of a party. Emilie told her sister-in-law that the moment he arrived he had demanded her return in a most arrogant way, apparently thinking that after 'dictating the law' at Pontarlier he was invincible. For her part she wanted a divorce, and her father, she said, would spare neither money nor means to save her from a man who was so uncontrolled. She was sure that her father-in-law would not support him in his proposed action.

She misjudged the marquis's militant pride. For him, as for the bailli, the matter was not one of a wife being reclaimed but of family honour being defended. The bailli was pessimistic about his nephew's chances as he faced the closed ranks of Aixois society. He reported that Marignane had retained twenty-three lawyers to defend his daughter, an unintentional tribute to Mirabeau's forensic power. More serious was the news that he intended to publish the marquis de Mirabeau's letters, containing his promise never to let his son approach the comtesse without permission. Thinking to seal his son-in-law's fate, Marignane also denounced *Des lettres de cachet* (the identity of the anonymous author being no secret) to the public prosecutor. Mirabeau replied with an injunction for his wife to return to him within three days, which she answered by applying for a separation.

The Mirabeau case opened in the great chamber of the Aix *parlement* on 20 March 1783, before an audience drawn there by the prospect of high drama from places as far away as Grenoble and Lyon. Emilie was supported by the most powerful families of the province; Mirabeau was alone, the only counsel he had to assist him being a young man named Pellenc who had never been on a case before. Yet verbally and psychologically he dominated his opponents from the start. Both sides relied on *mémoires* to sway public opinion in their favour. Marignane accused his son-in-law, among other crimes, of being a gambler, an outlaw, and a murderer; Mirabeau published Emilie's letters written during his detention in the Château d'If, and maintained that the love expressed in them had never lessened, and that only her interfering father kept them apart. Though his argument was somewhat weakened by the sight of his wife sitting with her lover in the courtroom, his *mémoires* won him strong public support; and when he produced the letter she wrote in 1774, admitting infidelity, her lawyers were thrown into confusion, and suggested that she should spend two years in a convent if he, in return, would deny that she had been guilty of misconduct. This concern for her reputation might seem odd in view of her open liaison with another man, but Provençal society had its own rules, one of which defined adultery as a relationship to which the husband objected.

On 17 June an enormous crowd gathered to hear Mirabeau's closing speech in which he was expected to exonerate his wife. Among his hearers was the Archduke Ferdinand, the Queen's brother, who had come to see this orator at Aix whom everyone was talking about. The effect of the atmosphere on Mirabeau was like adrenalin: 'The lion roared and shouted until his mane was white with foam', reported the bailli. It was soon apparent, however, that exoneration was the last thing he intended, as he asked the court to witness his grief at having to reveal his domestic secrets:

> Oh God, what would I not give to be able to bury them in oblivion! Why did she want to extract from me all these frightful truths? I offer Mme de Mirabeau honour and peace; I forget her faults, I even forgive her calumnies. Only reunion can remove the slur cast on her honour, only reunion can remove her imprudence from memory.[32]

On 5 July the judges granted Emilie de Mirabeau an absolute separation, basing their decision on a minor point of law, that a husband who made accusations had no right to demand a reunion. The scales were tipped by the *avocat général* of the *parlement*, an old friend of Marignane's, who browbeat half the judges into agreeing with him and then announced that the customary unanimous vote would not be necessary. When he heard the verdict Mirabeau promptly challenged Emilie's lover to a duel, and wounded him in the arm. There was nearly a riot at Aix, where the people equated his cause with their own struggle against vested privilege. In a letter to the journalist, Jacques-Pierre Brissot, Mirabeau commented:

> The ancients were right to deify the art of oratory. The public, always prone to extremes, sided with me to the point of idolatry. I have ended by becoming the demagogue, as it were, of Provence; the winner of the case is in flight and the loser is proclaimed the illustrious victim. You may well imagine that these melancholy successes do not turn my head, especially as an insurrection never amounts to anything in France.[33]

He had cause to feel melancholy. Ten years after a marriage that promised him a brilliant future he had no money, no position, no prospects, an invidious reputation. If he was not an outlaw, as Marignane had said, he was now an outsider from the world of privilege, with nothing to help him beyond the talent that adversity had stimulated.

## NOTES

1. Mirabeau's statement to the court at Manosque is reproduced in *Mémoires biographiques*, II, 92–8. The 1778 version was published in *Lettres originales*, I, 325f.
2. *Mémoire à consulter pour la comtesse de Mirabeau*, Aix-en-Provence, Mouret, 1783. Letter of 11 October 1774.
3. *Mémoires biographiques*, II, 120. Letter of 24 April 1775.
4. *Essai*, 24.
5. Ibid., 47.
6. Ibid., 60.
7. Ibid., 67 and 88.
8. Ibid., 116.
9. Ibid., 201.
10. Ibid., 101.
11. Marie-Thérèse-Sophie Richard de Ruffey was the sixth and youngest child of Gilles-Germain Richard de Ruffey, president of the Exchequer Court at Dijon, and his wife Anne-Claude de la Fôret.
12. Voltaire (1962, 174).
13. The Monnier house still exists. Originally a single-storey building in a large garden, at the corner of what was then called the Grande-rue and the rue des Trois-sols, it is now the Hôtel de la Poste.
14. This letter has been printed in Meunier (1914, 128–31). Mirabeau's letters to Mme de Monnier were published by Cottin in 1903. In 1981 *Lettres d'amour à Sophie* was issued by Les Editions d'aujourd'hui, based on the 1875 Edition Garnier text which was edited by Mario Proth. The 1875 text was a brief selection of letters from *Lettres originales*, which Manuel published in 1792. The reader of the 1981 reprint, who did not know otherwise, would assume that this was the complete Mirabeau–Monnier correspondence.
15. Mirabeau always maintained that he had 'sacrificed himself' only out of compassion for Mme de Monnier; 'All the rest was forced, all the rest was duty' (*Lettres originales*, I, 369). In a letter to Sophie, written while he was on the run, he uses more ardent language to describe his feelings: 'sacrificed all for love' (Montigny, 1834–36: II, 186); but it has to be remembered that this letter was one of a number which fell into the hands of Louise de Cabris and Briançon, who threatened to publish them, and who may have 'improved' the contents in order to compromise him. He had to buy the letters back.
16. *Lettres originales*, I, 25. Letter to his father of 2 August 1777.
17. Jean Lenoir succeeded his father as head of the Paris police in 1755. Turgot dismissed him at the time of the grain riots in 1775, but when Turgot fell he was reinstated, and held his post until 1785. In 1771 he was sent to Provence to

superintend the setting up of a Maupeou tribunal there. An account of his administration, *La Police de Paris dévoilée*, was written by Pierre Manuel, the same man who published Mirabeau's letters from Vincennes.

18. *Lettres originales*, I, 268. The baby was baptised on 8 January by the *curé* of Saint-Pierre-de-Montmartre, who registered her as the daughter of *dame* Thérèse-Sophie Richard de Ruffey, wife of M. Claude-François de Monnier, *chevalier*. Monnier was not actually named as the father.

19. The marquise, accompanied by two lawyers, had staged a sit-in at her husband's house, and had finally been arrested for disorderly conduct as she harangued the crowd outside. She was held in the convent of the Dames de Saint Michel. Louise de Cabris, who had published a libellous *mémoire* against her father, was held in a convent at Sisteron.

20. The passage in the *mémoire* which seems to have cut the marquis most deeply, for he quoted it in a letter to his brother, was one in which she twisted the phrase *produit net*, often used by him in connection with Physiocratic economics: 'The marquis de Mirabeau came to Paris in 1741 to seek a cure which he had been unable to find at Bordeaux and Montpellier for those maladies which are guaranteed to have a *produit net*.'

21. Pierre-Samuel Dupont (1739–1817), economist, the Dupont de Nemours of the Revolution. After the Revolution he emigrated to America where he founded the DuPont empire.

22. Emilie de Mirabeau's letters are printed in Meunier (1908).

23. *Mémoires biographiques*, III, 259. Letter of 20 December 1780.

24. *Ma conversion* reappeared as *Le Libertin de qualité, ou confidences d'un prisonnier au château de Vincennes*, Stamboul, de l'imprimerie des Odalisques, 1784. *Le Libertin de qualité* was reissued by the Cercle du Livre Précieux in 1962.

25. *Lettres originales*, II, 88. Undated letter.

26. The marquis de Sade was a prisoner in Vincennes at the same time as Mirabeau. The two families were distantly related: in 1493 Girard de Sade married the widow of Raimond de Glandevès, and in 1564 Marguerite de Glandevès married Jean Riqueti. This tenuous connection scarcely justifies the significance which some writers attach to Mirabeau's erotic writings on the strength of his kinship with Sade. The assumption that they were cousins may have its origin in the statement, by several historians, that the maiden name of Mirabeau's mother was Caraman, which might be confused with Carman, the name of Sade's mother.

27. *Des lettres de cachet*, quoted by Chaussinand-Nogaret (1982: 78).

28. Ibid., quoted by Chaussinand-Nogaret (1982: 79).

29. Loménie (1879–91: II. 639). Letter to marquis de Longo, 4 September 1761.

30. The Vicomte André-Boniface-Louis de Mirabeau (born 30 November 1754) fought at Yorktown under La Fayette and Rochambeau, and at St Eustatius under Bouillé. Returning wounded to France in 1782, he was made colonel of the Touraine regiment. He went back to America and served there for the rest of the war.

31. Following Monnier's death, seven months after the Pontarlier settlement, Mme de Monnier lived in a house attached to the convent at Gien. In September 1789 she committed suicide. In 1792, the year after Mirabeau's death, a novel was published with the title *La Morale des sens ou l'Homme du siècle*, by M. de M., which exactly described his last visit to Mme de Monnier. In it a young man climbs into a convent to visit a nun named Sainte Sophie and stays with her undetected, hiding in a cupboard. A potboiler written by

Mirabeau in his impecunious days, as has been suggested? More probably it was the work of his brother, who wrote various facetious pieces, and who was led by curiosity to visit Gien, where the locals all knew about this secret escapade. Mirabeau could be callous, but his former mistresses always enjoyed a sentimental prestige in his mind.

32. Mirabeau's speech was printed in full in *Observations du comte de Mirabeau sur une partie de sa cause*, Aix-en-Provence, 1783.
33. Brissot (1912:69).

# 4

## The English Lesson

## (1784-1785)

Before making his fateful journey to Aix, Mirabeau passed some time in Neuchâtel, where he had gone to deliver the manuscript of *Des lettres de cachet* to Fauche. This placid town, under Prussian sovereignty and a convenient asylum for refugees from France and Geneva, had become a hive of revolutionary thought with the arrival there of two of the chief conspirators in the recent insurrection at Geneva, Clavière and Duroveray,[1] together with the journalist, Jacques-Pierre Brissot.[2] Mirabeau's meeting with these men at an unsettled moment in his life, and in a highly charged atmosphere – he was staying in the house of Rousseau's friend, du Peyroux – acted as a catalyst on his undefined ambitions. For the first time in his life he was among political activists, and communicating his ideas verbally instead of on paper. The confirmation of his own weight in argument made it a heady experience.

Geneva, sanctified for a generation of Frenchmen by its associations with Rousseau, had been a political hot spot for twenty years, ever since the ruling Senate condemned *Emile* and sparked off a feud between the executive power and the democrats. Work began on a new constitution in 1768 with the setting up of a Code Commission under the direction of Clavière and Duroveray, then an ambitious young law student of twenty-one, but ten years later it was still unfinished, and fresh trouble broke out with the democrats when the Council of Two Hundred, the seat of legislative power, refused the Code Commission further time for its work. France exerted an overriding influence on Genevois affairs and in 1780 Duroveray and Clavière went to Paris in an unsuccessful attempt to get Necker, the Director-General and a fellow Genevois, to end French interference. A year later, on French orders, the Senate deprived Duroveray of his civic rights. In 1782 its refusal to improve the conditions of unenfranchised citizens as promised led to the overthrow of the government, and the setting up of a dictatorial Commission de Sûreté by Duroveray, Clavière and Marat, the brother of the more famous Jean-Paul. The April revolution was finally quelled in July by France, with the support of neighbouring states, all of them anxious to stamp out an infection that might take hold in their own territories if ignored. Clavière and Duroveray were banished and fled to Neuchâtel.

Mirabeau, encountering a revolution in the raw through its leaders, and when he had his own denunciation of governmental tyranny in his luggage, was readily caught up in a cause that seemed to present itself so neatly in terms of black and white. For their part, Clavière and Duroveray saw his arrival as heaven-sent. 'Clavière liked Mirabeau best of all his friends', wrote Brissot rather jealously later, 'The cause of this attachment, if I am not mistaken, lay in the irrepressible urge which carried the Genevois towards revolutions and towards those who could engineer them'.[3] With this in mind they proceeded to play on his vanity. Clavière was to remember him saying, in what seemed like a fit of vainglorious dreaming at the time, that one day France would have an assembly, and he would be a deputy in it and would free Geneva from the oligarchy which ruled it. Already nearly fifty when he met Mirabeau, Clavière had a dream of his own, which was that he would succeed Necker as the minister in charge of French finances. He possessed an entrepreneurial vision: Brissot described him as an inexhaustible mine of rough diamonds; but he needed someone to set them, and in Mirabeau he saw the right man. Duroveray's character was more that of an intellectual revolutionary, uncompromising, arrogant, secretive, sarcastic in argument; he did not like Mirabeau, but was prepared to employ him so long as he was useful and did not forget his place.

Evidence of his usefulness was soon forthcoming. While at Neuchâtel he wrote a vigorous defence of the exiled Genevois leaders which he sent to the Foreign Minister, Vergennes, advising him that the withdrawal of French troops was the necessary preliminary to peace in this troubled area. His closely reasoned *mémoire*, with its criticism of government policy (a copy of which in the Geneva archives in Duroveray's handwriting has led to a supposition that he was the author), was doubly bold coming from a man already unpopular with the establishment, whose own position could only be jeopardised by his association with men marked down as agitators. As a precaution against reprisals after *Lettres de cachet* was published, he sought Vergennes' protection on the pretence that his father was seeking a fresh warrant against him. In return for the minister's protection he offered him his analysis of Genevois affairs, as 'the first evidence of my gratitude'.

By the autumn of 1782 the Prussian authorities at Neuchâtel had tightened up on dissidents. Clavière and Duroveray went to join Brissot in England, and became naturalised subjects of George III; Mirabeau went to Provence. They parted with mutual illusions: Duroveray thought he had found a political puppet who would caper to order, Mirabeau thought he had found disinterested friends. Later, when he entered public life, the Genevois connection was the cause of greater prejudice against him than anything else.

The idea that he also might go to England was not planted in his head until the following summer, when he received an offer of help from Hugh Elliot, the British Minister Plenipotentiary at Copenhagen, who had once been a schoolfriend of his at the abbé Choquart's academy. Although the sensation produced by *Lettres de cachet* had something to do with Elliot's renewed interest in its author, it was a meeting with Brissot, who described the current state of Mirabeau's affairs, which led him to make his offer. From the garbled account which reached him, Mirabeau understood that Elliot had a post in the diplomatic service for him; he was bitterly disappointed when he learned that the minister's message had been intended to express nothing more precise than his willingness to extend such protection to a former friend as might be within his power. For the time being he put it out of his mind. A year later, in 1784, however, when all his attempts to appeal against the Aix judgement had failed and he found himself threatened with a *lettre de cachet* by Marignane, he thought of Elliot again, and wrote to remind him of his offer. There was no time to wait for a reply. Convinced that his life depended on his leaving France at once, he fled to Dieppe, chartered a vessel, and set sail for England.

As befitted the man his father declared knew everything better than anyone else, Mirabeau's ideas about England and the English were firmly fixed before he went, and the impressions he gained during the seven months he spent there acted merely as a codicil to his existing views. The bailli said: 'I have come to regard the English as the enemies of the human race, and particularly of France',[4] and everything he had read inclined his nephew to agree with him. The only moments when he came near to being an anglophile were in Brighton, where, he said, he had the best beef he had ever eaten, and on the journey to London by post-chaise, when the beauty and neatness of the countryside told its own story.

These domineering people are first and foremost farmers at heart. I was profoundly moved travelling through these luxuriant and prosperous regions and asked myself, why this new emotion? . . . Everywhere in our country there are handsome buildings, examples of sumptuous workmanship, great public enterprises ; one sees only a scattering here, and yet I am much more enchanted by the scenes here than by the impressive sights at home. It is because here nature is improved and not forced, because this admirable cultivation shows a respect for ownership, because this universal care and neatness is an eloquent symptom of well-being; because all this richness does not reveal excessive inequality of fortune, as do our magnificent buildings surrounded by hovels. Everything tells me that here the people count, that here every man is able to develop his faculties and to make free use of them, in fact that here I am in a different order of things.[5]

He had brought with him the manuscript of a work he hoped to publish, and a companion, Henriette-Amélie de Nehra. There had been a succession of affairs in recent years, among them the fleeting epistolary romance with Julie Dauvers which came to nothing,[6] and an interlude with the wife of the sculptor, Lucas de Montigny, which left him with a son, Coco.[7] Mme de Nehra, Yet-Lie as he called her, was a natural daughter of the Dutch poet and statesman, Willem van Haren: her name was an anagram of her father's. Although only nineteen when they met, and by all accounts of dove-like appearance, there was nothing timid about her character. When his *mémoire*, which had been suppressed by the Keeper of Seals, was published in Holland, she helped him to smuggle copies of it into Paris; its arrival in the book-shops there precipitated their flight to England.[8]

Only a few weeks in London convinced Mirabeau that the at-mosphere of opportunity he had sensed on his arrival was an illusion. The English calculated everything, he told the writer, Chamfort, even talent; most of their writers had literally died of hunger: 'As for anyone who does not belong to their nation!' He had expected England to offer him something more than the seedy existence of a literary hack. The letter he wrote to Elliot heralding his arrival implied that little short of a royal progress would be in order for the hero of the battle of Aix, but Elliot had returned to Copenhagen before it arrived, and his absence altered everything. The lodgings they had taken in Pall Mall had to be vacated, and he, Mme de Nehra, her maid, her dog, and Hardy, his valet-secretary, installed themselves in cheaper ones in Hatton Street off Holborn, an area heavily populated by French refugees.

Despite their numbers he came into contact with few of his country-men. Brissot, after launching a journal in London which slowly sank, had been arrested for debt, and on his release had returned to Paris, where he was charged with circulating libels against the queen and sent to the Bastille. Clavière, whose banking interests took first place in his life, had returned to France in the autumn of 1783 when the Caisse d'Escompte, in which he held many shares, entered a profitable phase; together with Duroveray and the patriot writer, François d'Ivernois, he had hoped to start a colony near Waterford, based on the Genevois clock and watch industry, but the scheme had foundered for want of funds from the British government. The Genevois remaining in London took Mirabeau under their wing and introduced him to their circle of sympathisers, among them the radical Benjamin Vaughan, who had taken part in the peace negotiations with the Americans in 1782, Richard Price, the nonconformist clergyman and writer of radical tracts, and Samuel Romilly, then at the start of a legal career which was to take him to the post of Solicitor General in Fox's administration of 1806, and already noted for his interest in legal reform. Seeing England through their dissenting, reformist eyes, all Mirabeau's pre-conceived theories about her as a nation seemed to be confirmed; the perfidious Albion syndrome in his thinking, inherited from his revered uncle, came to the fore and found forceful expression. That his opinions were often exaggerated, and led to arguments with his new friends, can be deduced from the remark in one of his letters that 'one has to be English to criticise their nation'. His overbearing manner put off many people he met. The unfortunate man he mistook for Gibbon, and castigated for writing in praise of an empire of despots, was understandably rendered speechless by the onslaught. On another occasion, reported by Romilly, he attacked John Wilkes:

> The conversation turned upon the English criminal law, its severity, and the frequency of its public executions. Wilkes defended the system with much wit and good humour, but with very bad arguments . . . Mirabeau was not content with having the best of the argument and with triumphantly refuting his opponent; he was determined to crush him with his eloquence. He declaimed with vehemence, talked of Wilkes's profound immorality, and with a man less cool, less indifferent about the truth, and less skilled in avoiding any personal quarrel than Wilkes, the dispute would probably have been attended with very serious consequences.[9]

Romilly was one man who not only made allowances for his excitability but genuinely liked him. A Huguenot by descent, he was linked to the Genevois through his sister, who was married to the pastor of the Genevois church in London. He was sufficiently impressed by the manuscript of Mirabeau's work on Cincinnatus, which he had brought from Paris, to undertake an English translation; not a relaxing exercise, for 'the Count was difficult enough to please . . . He went over every part of the translation with me; observed on every passage in which justice was not done to the thought, or the force of the expression was lost'.[10] Mirabeau wanted to publish them simultaneously, but owing to printing delays Romilly's translation (intended to help Mirabeau financially) did not appear until after his return to France. The work was published in its French version, however, on 20 September by John Johnson of St Paul's Churchyard, quite a feat considering its length – over 300 pages – and the fact that Mirabeau had only arrived in England at the end of August. It was the first of his works to appear under his name (though, in fact, he could not claim sole authorship, Chamfort and the lawyer, Target, having both contributed to it) and he told Chamfort that in future he would sign everything, in order to avoid having all 'the anonymous muck that pullulates in London' laid at his door.

*Considérations sur l'Ordre de Cincinnatus* had its beginning in a pamphlet which Benjamin Franklin had asked him to translate for him when they met in Paris. The Association of Cincinnati had been formed by American officers in 1783; its purpose was to perpetuate the memory of the War of Independence, and its statutes stipulated that the right to membership would be hereditary. Mirabeau's brother was one of those chosen by Washington to belong to it. The whole idea struck a shockingly undemocratic note in the ears of fundamentalist patriots, who saw in the birth of the new American nation the victory of equality and virtue over privilege and corruption, and who feared that old-style European despotism would follow the sanctioning of privileged groups. Reading Franklin's pamphlet in the heat of his personal battle against the forces of inherited privilege, Mirabeau realised its possibilities; the topic was American but he could use it as a springboard to attack all those symbols of corruption and despotism which the celebrated Franklin abhorred, and which Frenchmen still had to endure. In *Cincinnatus* he delivered his most merciless strictures to date on his own caste, the resentment born of his own experience sharpening the barbs that acute perception had already made lethal. The result: well, however justified, the result was going to find few readers in England outside a small circle of extreme radicals. In order to give it wider appeal supplementary material was added: a tract of Price's on civil liberty, translated by Mirabeau for the occasion, and a piece on aeronautics by the duc de Chaulnes, but it only added to the rushed and makeshift air of the whole production. Ironically, before it appeared the Association of Cincinnatus had already yielded to public opinion, and dropped the hereditary format which had started the rumpus.

Following *Cincinnatus*, Mirabeau cast around for further ways of making money. The cost of living in London was shocking; it was impossible to live there, he said, on less than £350 a year. He thought at first of starting a journal with himself as sole contributor, analysing the latest books and political ideas, but was unable to find an enterprising publisher. Then Ivernois offered an outlet for his unemployed mental energy: he had completed the first volume of a history of the revolutionary movement in Geneva, and asked him to collaborate on the rest of the work. Mirabeau agreed that Ivernois should have full credit as the author. A later addition to the Genevois clan, Etienne Dumont, wrote afterwards that the reason he made this concession was because he calculated that Ivernois would be regarded merely as the mason employed on the building, while he, Mirabeau, would be hailed as the architect. Whether Ivernois suspected this, or whether it was just one of Dumont's feline comments, one cannot know, but when, a week later, Mirabeau presented him with a resumé of the remaining volume, he decided to cancel the undertaking, giving as his reasons Mirabeau's inaccuracy, and his bad reputation which would have offended the public. (This last seems to have been an afterthought, perhaps of Dumont's, for if Ivernois had really been worried about the adverse effect of Mirabeau's reputation he would not have approached him in the first place.)

London and Londoners gave him plenty both to criticise and to admire. He was amazed by the riotous tendencies of its citizens, by the licence of the press and theatre, by the scurrilous nature of the political cartoons, and impressed by these proofs of liberty. He found the English sabbath repellent. He admired the Thames, though he thought the scenic possibilities of its banks had been neglected, and the pavements, but not the other pedestrians: Englishmen were cold, mercenary, and hostile to foreigners. As the weeks passed and Mme de Nehra's savings dwindled his jocular comment, that the best way to die of hunger in London was to be a French writer, looked more and more like a statement of fact. There were, of course, some Frenchmen who did very well: those who supplied the pornographic book trade, and journalists who also acted as government informers; men like Linguet, the editor of *Annales politiques*, or the notorious Théveneau de Morande of the *Courrier de l'Europe* whom Mirabeau called a hired spy. He was certain that Frenchmen were as much under the scrutiny of the Paris police in London as they were in their own country. By November his financial straits forced him to turn to the wealthiest man with whom he could claim acquaintance. Sir Gilbert Elliot was Hugh Elliot's elder brother, a Member of Parliament and one of the commissioners appointed under the India Bill of 1783 to manage the affairs of the East India Company. Sir Gilbert reported to his brother that when he went round to Hatton Street he found Mirabeau just as 'overbearing in his conversation, as awkward in his graces, as ugly and misshapen in his face and person, as dirty in his dress, and withal as perfectly *suffisant'*, as he had been twenty years before at school. Even so, he added, 'His courage, his energy, his talents, his application, and above all his misfortunes and his sufferings, should increase rather than diminish our affection for him.'[11]

Elliot took him down to Bath to meet Lady Elliot, staying overnight on the way with Edmund Burke at Beaconsfield, to whom he had explained beforehand that the comte de Mirabeau was the son of *l'ami des hommes*, and a much better writer and man than his father. The meeting with Burke, which apparently went off very well apart from language difficulties, led Mirabeau to take an interest in Burke's campaign to end corruption in the administration of Indian territories. The following January he was present at the re-opening of Parliament, where he saw Mrs Warren Hastings, and that evening he sent Elliot a note, with a passage from Pliny describing the appearance of Lollius's niece, decked with the riches her uncle had snatched from the provinces under his sway. Elliot passed it on, and Burke used this passage at the trial of Warren Hastings. He never forgot that Mirabeau had once been his house guest. During the Revolution, expecting a visit from the abbé Maury, he warned him that the comte de Mirabeau had stayed in the house, but promised to have it purified and exorcised before his arrival.

Mirabeau was enchanted by the hospitality he received in Bath, quite unaware that for the Elliots it had been a traumatic experience. Elliot told his brother:

> I took him with me the other day to Bath, where he made such hasty love to Harriet [their sister] whom he had little doubt of subduing in a week, and where he so totally silenced my John Bull of a wife, who understands a Frenchman no better than Molly Housemaid, where he so scared my little boy with caressing him, so completely disposed of me from breakfast to supper, and so astonished all our friends, that I could hardly keep the peace in his favour; and if he had not unexpectedly been called to town this morning I am sure my wife's endurance, for I cannot call it civility, would not have held out another day.[12]

Lady Elliot refused ever to have him under her roof again. Sir Gilbert, a long-suffering but dutiful friend, continued to show the unwitting offender what courtesies he could, introducing him to his friends, lending him money, even appearing at the Old Bailey to testify to his character. This last service was occasioned by Mirabeau's valet, Hardy, whom his employer had accused of stealing his linen and some private papers, apparently copies of letters between Voltaire and d'Alembert. At his trial Hardy was charged with the theft, among other things, of twenty-seven shirts and a book of court scandal, the *Journal de Monsieur*, valued at two shillings – the book was later found in Hardy's luggage and he was acquitted for lack of evidence. Romilly and Elliot printed a full account of the trial in the *Public Advertiser*, for they foresaw that Mirabeau's enemies would use the story to his disadvantage, and they were right: Morande and Linguet were both present at the proceedings, and Linguet published a libellous pamphlet by Hardy against Mirabeau which was widely circulated. If Mirabeau had indeed brought a manuscript copy of the Voltaire–d'Alembert correspondence to England it was doubtless with the intention of publishing it; hence his embarrassment when it disappeared – it was not mentioned specifically at the trial – and his determination to catch Hardy, whose connection with its disappearence may be deduced from the fact that Linguet came to know about it.[13]

In December a Charing Cross bookseller published *Doutes sur la liberté de l'Escaut, reclamée par l'Empereur,* Mirabeau's second work to appear during his stay in England. The controversy over the navigation of the Scheldt was caused by the fact that the upper reaches of the river were in Austrian territory while below Antwerp it was controlled by the Dutch, and had been closed to navigation since the drawing up of the Treaty of Westphalia in 1648. Determined to open up the Austrian Netherlands to sea trade, the Emperor Joseph had attacked Dutch forts on the river and sent Austrian troops to the Netherlands. The danger of a local issue turning into a European war was considerable, for Austria was backed by Russia and Holland could be expected to call for aid from England. Mirabeau defended the Dutch cause, though not to please Mme de Nehra, and to the surprise of his friends, who assumed that as a believer in free trade he would side with the Emperor. In a recent letter to him Clavière had written in favour of Joseph, but he lacked Mirabeau's understanding of French affairs. The crisis in the Netherlands put France in a delicate position: on one hand she was allied to Austria and the Emperor was Marie-Antoinette's brother, on the other Vergennes' policy was aimed at strengthening relations with Holland in order to lure her away from her traditional alliance with England. A split already existed in Holland between the Stadholder's pro-English party and the burghers who sought commercial ties with France. From the French point of view there were significant advantages to be gained by supporting the Dutch; not to do so would allow Joseph to advance Austria's sphere of influence still further across the map of Europe.

Had Mirabeau wanted to placate his own government, *Doutes sur la liberté de l'Escaut* might have been expected to assist his purpose, but he damaged his own cause by directing a violent attack on the Emperor in its pages. It was a stupid thing to do in the circumstances, and yet in his disregard for the retribution his language invited he exhibited that courage of opinon which makes up for many of his personal and literary faults. It may be that he was encouraged to overstate the Dutch view by others: Romilly said that Benjamin Vaughan wrote the book, and with his polemicist's preference for seeing every issue as a simple fight between the wicked and the virtuous Vaughan would certainly have sympathised with the Dutch. Mirabeau may have incorporated material from a tract by Vaughan in his book, in the same way as he utilised some of the arguments put by Clavière and which he proceeded to contradict, but the statesmanlike content, the concern with long-term effects, and the understanding of both French and European needs, could only have come from him. The clash of disparate minds in the book gave it the appearance of a literary transvestite, serious theories decked out in polemical frills, and he seemed to acknowledge this, telling his readers that he intended they should find the author both provocative and sagacious. Sagacity apart, his probable reason for writing it lay in his desire to score against Linguet, who had just published a work on the same subject, supporting the Emperor (who rewarded him handsomely). It was later believed that Linguet had written his book in answer to Mirabeau's, but the existence, and success, of this prior work by the man who wanted to destroy his reputation was what really stimulated him in his undertaking. His only fear, having produced something that would get him noticed in France, was that Clavière might take too much of the credit. Serving as an assistant to Ivernois had been a wounding experience. Just as hunger taught parrots to talk, so it had forced him into being a hack, he told his friend Vitry, and 'to work at the dictation of others, expressing the mind of others, is not a good occupation for anyone with intelligence, but necessity is a law against which one has no protection'.[14]

On its appearance in Paris *Doutes sur la liberté de l'Escaut* succeeded even better than he had expected in being provocative: it annoyed everyone, from Vergennes who was making conciliatory gestures in Vienna, to the queen who was offended by the assault on her brother. It sold well, but delays over the English edition left him once more without money, and he had to borrow another sixty pounds from Elliot. Hardy's acquittal in February, and the damaging lies in his subsequent pamphlet, made him fear a vendetta by Linguet and Morande, and after the trial Mme de Nehra travelled to Paris to see whether it was safe for him to return. Thanks to her persistence the Minister of the Household, Breteuil, promised that he would not be molested by the authorities, and by 1 April he was back in Paris. Elliot, who had borne the expense of the trial, and who paid for his ticket, was left to settle his bills and the arrears on the lodgings in Hatton Street and Pall Mall. A few weeks later a letter came, asking him to forward Mme de Nehra's dog which had been left behind in the rush. Strangely, one item which Mirabeau never sought to retrieve was a packet of papers which he had deposited with Elliot for safekeeping. It remained un-opened in the Elliot family archives until 1848, when it was acquired by Mirabeau's son, Lucas de Montigny, and found to contain letters relating to Mirabeau's marriage. They were eventually published in 1889 by Charles de Loménie.

Mirabeau was not as ungrateful as he appeared. In the preface to his book on the Caisse d'Escompte, published in 1785, he wrote that England was a country he could not love, but one nevertheless 'where I have found the truest and most devoted friends on earth'.

What ideas did he bring away with him from England which might have influenced him later in the National Assembly? Very few. His political ideas and ideals were formed long before his visit to England; and although he shared the Montesquieurian belief in the virtues of the English governmental system, which was part of the accepted thinking of his age, he never made the mistake of also thinking, as the *monarchiens* did, that a pudding made to an English recipe would taste the same in France. Even the critical comments on English institutions in his letters were not prompted by any new-found disillusionment. He had become critical years before, studying Blackstone's *Commentaries on the Laws of England* in his cell in Vincennes, and reading English newspapers. His letters to Mme de Monnier and passages in *Lettres de cachet* reveal his familiarity with political events of the Grafton and North administrations of 1770 onwards, a period when inter-ference by the Crown in the affairs of Parliament, and wholesale cor-ruption in the disposal of parliamentary seats, brought demands for reforms to a head. He was certainly familiar with the anti-government *Letters of Junius*, which were reprinted in the *Public Advertiser* at that time; he referred to them in Vincennes, and in 1785 a quotation from Junius headed his letter indicting the Controller-General, Calonne.

One of the delights of studying English journals in prison had been the discovery that the institutions which he had grown up envying were so seriously flawed. Mirabeau wanted to find grounds for despis-ing the English as a nation; he paid intellectual homage to their institu-tions, but it was as a Frenchman, rather than objectively as a reformer, that he criticised them. Nationality played a part also in his interpreta-tion of abuses by the Crown. George III's role in the American War of Independence sufficed for Frenchmen generally to damn him as a tyrant; English affairs were studied more closely in France following

French intervention in the war, and he became permanently typecast in French minds when evidence appeared of his apparent unpopularity with his own subjects. For students of the French monarchy, like Mirabeau, the temptation to judge his actions as they would have judged them had he been king of France was inevitable. In this respect his judgements on the British monarchy in practice were based on a false analogy between a constitutional and an absolute monarch.

He came to England ready primed with ideas of English royal tyranny and constitutional malpractice, and with Gilbert Elliot as his guide, a Foxite and entrenched representative of the Whig establishment, his views remained one-sided. Being a foreigner, he tended to over simplify his equations, and because the Whigs opposed the Tories (or supporters of royal despotism) they were seen by him as the equivalent of European 'patriots'. He was probably unaware that Elliot had begun his parliamentary career by supporting North. The most distinguished political figure he met in England was Shelburne, whose premiership saw the conclusion of the peace treaty with America – the most accomplished minister of the eighteenth century, according to Disraeli, but unlucky in his colleagues, several of whom resigned on his appointment, while Fox, prepared to go to any length to get rid of him, formed a coalition with North to bring him down. Sabotage of this sort, engaged in for personal motives regardless of the wider interest, was something which Mirabeau would also experience. Like him, Shelburne (created marquis of Lansdowne in 1784) outshone the men who defeated him. Like him, Shelburne was a subtle, imaginative statesman with a European vision; an opponent of royal influence, who nevertheless defended the royal prerogative against the attacks of those who ignored the constitutional purpose of prerogative; a champion of administrative reform. His enemies accused him, as Mirabeau's were to accuse him also, of being devious. Like Mirabeau, he did not conceal his contempt for some of his colleagues. They were so similar in outlook and ability that it is surprising that Mirabeau did not mention his visit to Bowood in his letters. Priestley, Price, Romilly, and Jeremy Bentham all enjoyed Shelburne's patronage, and Mirabeau's name was not forgotten by the Maecenas of Lansdowne House. In 1789 Bentham, who was then working for Shelburne, sent Mirabeau (whom he had not met personally) several papers he had written on political tactics, which he hoped would be useful to the newly formed National Assembly.[15]

On the strength of this alone it is tempting, but insular, to look for English influences behind Mirabeau's political thinking. The only direct evidence of it was his attempt to introduce the House of Commons rulebook to the National Assembly. His 'English' stand on the question of a powerful but legally limited royal authority was reached without the example of British constitutional practice to guide him. In all matters relating to the French constitution he drew on his knowledge of French circumstances and temperament to decide what was best. Over and over in his letters and political writings he said that a system of government had to be an indigenous growth in order to work and be acceptable. The strongest disincentive, in French eyes, to modelling their own institutions on British ones lay in the very fact that the models were British: the procedural rules of the House of Commons were rejected for this reason. Nationalistic prejudice apart, Mirabeau pointed out one all-important factor which weighed against the establishment in France, at least for some time, of democracy along English lines. It was not just a matter of achieving representative government. The independent character and civic maturity of the ordinary Englishman, fundamental to the survival of democracy, was itself the creation of liberties enjoyed for generations. His French counterpart not only had yet to attain the same liberties but had to be educated in understanding how to use them: this understanding, for people who had never had any public voice, could only come gradually, but Mirabeau realised that it was as important for the future of France as the liberties themselves.

He never doubted the educability of the people, but that of the French aristocracy was another matter. In *Cincinnatus* he had commented acidly on the difference of character between the English nobility, whose ranks were renewed by 'men of merit', and the French, recruited as it was from 'satellite friends of the monarch or from scribes and publicans', a guarantee of self-seeking compliance. The scribes and publicans were the wealthy bourgeois who had bought their way in ever increasing numbers into the nobility in the eighteenth century. Their power and influence, based on money, had almost replaced that of the old nobility, which often had nothing beyond ancient lineage to support it, while its claim to represent traditional values carried little weight without the persuasion of visible power. The division between the new and old nobility was thus also a division between the powerful and the no longer powerful. When Mirabeau reviled his own caste as time-servers and vampires he was thinking of that part of it which now wielded the real power, not of the old nobility in which he included his own once bourgeois family. His accusations were founded on truth. The bitterness with which he made them reflected the resentment of a displaced élite, an internecine resentment as intense as that which the third estate felt for the aristocracy as a whole.

One of his friends during the Revolution, La Marck, wrote in his memoirs that Mirabeau 'greatly admired the English form of government, and found every guarantee of sound liberty in that balance which a powerful but moderate aristocracy maintained between the royal power and the enthusiasm of the people'.[16] Anxious to rehabilitate him posthumously in the eyes of conservatives horrified by the excesses of the Revolution, La Marck failed to make clear that when Mirabeau spoke of liberty being guaranteed by a moderate aristocracy he was thinking simply of England. And, though Parliament had its aristocratic second chamber, that was insufficient justification in his opinion for the establishment of a Gallic House of Lords. Mirabeau expressed himself plainly on this subject: the value of a second chamber in checking excessive power was incontestable, but its members had to be seen as not being in league with the Crown for their constitutional function to be tolerated. The French nobility, he often said, was inescapably linked in the mind of the French people with the worst aspects of absolute monarchy; the hatred which the nobility had earned guaranteed that a second chamber of nobles would be seen by the people as a perpetuation of detested abuses; and until that feeling had been moderated by the passage of time a bicameral system in France could only be a source of discord. In saying this Mirabeau put his finger on the greatest obstacle to government *à l'anglais*. The question of who would have been eligible to form an upper chamber, since there was no clearly defined French peerage, is irrelevant to this argument. The essential point, as Mirabeau saw it, was the psychological unacceptability of an upper chamber to the French people.

If he brought anything away with him from England it was the conviction that stability was the fundamental requirement for any nation, stability based on civil liberty. Because of this underlying stability a riot in London, he remarked, was a greater proof of good health than the quiescence of those who lived in subjugated societies. The by-product of stability and civil liberty was the sense of national superiority which he commented on so furiously in the letters he wrote to Chamfort from England, but which, at the same time, made him reflect on the conditions which gave rise to it:

> But what is liberty when a particle of it contained in one or two good laws can raise a people so little favoured by nature to the front rank? What can a constitution not achieve when this one, though incomplete and defective, saves and will continue to save for some time yet, the most corrupt people on earth from their own corruption? How great is the influence of a few favourable gifts on the human species when this ignorant, superstitious, obstinate, acquisitive, untrustworthy nation is worth more than most other nations, just because it has civil liberty?[17]

He had asked the same question, in almost the same words, in *Lettres adressées à un ancien magistrat*, a work written in 1783 in the course of his proceedings against his wife, and had answered it then himself:

But the English have a *patrie*! And that is why the most fanatic, most ignorant, most corrupt people on earth have a public spirit, civic virtues, incredible successes even in the midst of their excesses; that is why, despite nature, they have acquired the first rank among nations'.[18]

This idea of a *patrie*, which he borrowed from Montesquieu, and the strength that arose from a sense of nationhood, he returned to again and again in his writing. It came from a feeling of unity, he said, of common identity as citizens, which Frenchmen, fragmented by social, regional, and linguistic divides, had yet to acquire. The foundation of this strength was civil liberty, although it was not the sole source of it. And obtaining constitutional liberty was only the beginning. The end he looked for would not arrive until his countrymen had been educated by the possession of their civil liberties and had confidence in them. Only then would they have the foundation for that intangible, invincible oneness which he chose to call a sense of *patrie*. For a moment in 1789 Frenchmen would come near to the unity and sense of nationhood which Mirabeau envisaged. It was not constitutional liberty, however, but the war of 1792 which finally made the *patrie* a reality.

## NOTES

1. Etienne Clavière (Minister of Finance in 1792) was born on 15 January 1735 in Geneva, the son of a wealthy linen merchant who came originally from Dauphiné. He spent his early years working in his father's firm before turning to banking, and a lifelong career in speculation which brought him several fortunes.

   Jacques-Antoine Duroveray, born in 1747 in Geneva, grew up in a professional family. He became a lawyer in 1771, having already figured from the age of nineteen in Genevois politics. He was a member of the Council of Two Hundred in 1775, and *procureur général* of the Republic of Geneva in 1780.
2. Brissot was born in 1754 at Ouarville, the son of a prosperous innkeeper. Pamphleteer, journalist, employed for a time by Swinton, the English publisher of the *Courrier de l'Europe*, and also by the duc d'Orléans. He was taken up by Clavière, with whom he formed a close friendship and political alliance. Like Mirabeau, he avoided the French censor by publishing a book in Neuchâtel: *De la vérité* appeared at the same time as *Lettres de cachet*.
3. Brissot (1911: II, 30).
4. Loménie (1879–91: I, 250).
5. Montigny (1934–36: V, 127f).
6. His letters to Mlle Dauvers were edited by D. Meunier and G. Leloir, *Lettres à Julie*, Paris, 1903.
7. Jean-Marie-Nicolas Lucas de Montigny, 'Coco', was born on 10 February 1782 in Paris; his mother, Edmée-Adélaïde Bagnières, was the wife of the sculptor

Jean-Nicolas Lucas de Montigny, and sister of Dr Bagnières, Mirabeau's physician. Bénétruy oddly asserts in Dumont (1851: 299) that the identity of Coco's mother was unknown and that she could have been one of various women with whom Mirabeau was supposed (according to the ever fertile Dauphin Meunier) to have had affairs in 1781. Coco's legal surname is the strongest proof that his mother was Mme Lucas de Montigny: her husband had no reason to give his name to Mirabeau's child by another woman.

At his death Mirabeau left his son to the care of Mme du Saillant, who ignored her brother's wishes in this respect, and he was befriended by Nicolas Frochot, prefect of the department of the Seine under the Empire, who employed him in his office. There he remained throughout his working life, rising through the ranks of the civil service to become president of the council of the prefecture of the Seine, until he was dismissed in 1848. Apart from his official duties he had one consuming passion: to collect every document and letter pertaining to Mirabeau, to consult every archive, and interview every person who had known his idol. The inexhaustible energy he put into his researches, and the mass of detail he accumulated in his *Mémoires biographiques* (1834–36), reveal him to have been very much the son of his father.

8. *Mémoire du comte de Mirabeau supprimé par ordre de M. le Garde des Sceaux et réimprimé avec une conversation de M. le Garde des Sceaux et du comte de Mirabeau* was published in Maastricht in 1784.

9. Romilly (1841: I, 83–4).

10. Ibid., 78–9.

11. Kynynmound (1874: 285–6).

12. Ibid.

13. How Mirabeau came to see the Voltaire–d'Alembert correspondence, if he was the actual copyist, is a mystery. Meunier (1926) points out that Chamfort was private secretary to the prince de Condé, who owned the original letters. Chamfort may have shown them to Mirabeau, or may have copied them himself, and publication in England may have been their joint idea.

For details of the trial see Old Bailey Sessions Papers, 1784–85, pp. 388–9 and 395–6.

14. *Mémoires biographiques*, V, 260. Letter of 14 February 1785.

15. For Bentham's influence on Mirabeau, see Chapter 7.

16. *Correspondance entre Mirabeau et La Marck*, I, 110.

17. *Mémoires biographiques*, V, 129–30. Letter of 10 November 1784.

18. Ibid., V, 130n.; and VIII, 104.

# 5

~≈~

# The Cause of Truth

## (1785-1788)

Of all the professions open to talented but impecunious young men who wanted to be noticed by the establishment, journalism was the most inviting and the most hazardous, a means which might bring esteem and advancement, but which could also create suspicion commensurate with the strength of talent displayed. For four years, following his return from England in the spring of 1785, Mirabeau made his living from journalism, exposing the financial malaise which was killing the state invisibly. The probability of an explosion from political and social causes was understood by most thinking people; the need for reforms was glaringly obvious. Less apparent was the triangular nature of the crisis. The explosion that finally took place was precipitated by the financial situation, the critical causal factor without which it might have been postponed, but which, acting in conjunction with political and social issues, gave them their irreversible momentum.

The terrible significance of the financial crisis had not yet dawned on the general public, or even on the government. In 1781 Necker, the Director-General, produced his *Compte rendu de l'état des finances*, a financial report to the nation, which revealed such a crisis in the economy that his opponents were able to force his resignation; but his attempt to shock the government into a sense of reality was ignored, and after his departure the deterioration proceeded at an ever increasing rate. France was on the verge of bankruptcy, thanks largely to her commitments in the American War, to raise money for which the government had been forced to borrow enormous sums. Government

stock, however, was less attractive to investors than the shares issued
by various private enterprises which sprang up at the time, encouraging speculation on a scale not seen since the days of John Law and his
Compagnie d'Occident early in the century. The first of these private
institutions was the Caisse d'Escompte, a government-sponsored discount bank which opened for business in 1776 in the final weeks of
Turgot's ministry, under the direction of the Genevois banker, Isaac
Panchaud. All went well for the Caisse d'Escompte until 1783, when
the bank found that it did not have enough specie to meet the growing
demand. A government decree, authorising payment in letters of exchange instead, caused a crisis on the Bourse, and the first action of the
next Controller-General, Calonne, on taking office in November, was
to take measures to restore confidence in the Caisse d'Escompte. In
1784 Panchaud successfully fended off attempts to oust foreigners
from the board of directors, investors recovered from their panic, and
speculation in discount bank shares became more frenzied than ever.
Between November 1784 and the spring of 1785, when Mirabeau
returned to Paris, shares rose in price from their original 3,000 livres to
8,000 livres. At the height of the boom Panchaud and Clavière, two
heavy investors, made fortunes by selling their shares, but many
people remained who had invested every penny they possessed, and
who had no inkling of what was to come.

The Caisse d'Escompte did at least have the merit of stimulating
the circulation of currency and so of benefiting business. The Banque
de Saint-Charles, founded in Madrid in 1782 by Cabarrus, the father of
the future Mme Tallien, benefited no one except its powerful directors. It had the privilege of exchanging its own notes for those of the
realm, and controlled a number of monopolies, including the Compagnie des Philippines. The French government, though anxious to divert
the flow of capital back from foreign-controlled banks into government
stock, could not afford to offend its own chief creditors. The only
alternative it had to dealing with the Caisse d'Escompte and the Banque de Saint-Charles was to impose new taxes. Necker's successor,
Fleury, did get one new tax law accepted by the Paris *parlement*, but his
general incompetence led to his dismissal. Ormesson, who followed
him, was an honest man who tried to curb the practice whereby a
number of families in the queen's favour had their debts paid by the
exchequer; the families in question got rid of him in seven months.
The rapid turnover in controllers-general reflected both the growing
panic of the government and the throttling power of Court factions
which opposed any reforms prejudicial to their own interests. Where
Turgot and Necker had failed it seemed unlikely that Ormesson's
successor, Calonne, would succeed. Talleyrand wrote:

M. de Calonne had a facile and brilliant mind, he had the gift of embellishing what he knew and of brushing aside what he did not know. He was capable of affection and loyalty to his friends, but his mind chose them rather than his heart. To obtain his ministry he had compromised, or, at least, neglected his reputation.[1]

Diverting as it is to see Talleyrand deploring another man's lack of principles, this is a fair picture. Calonne tried to carry out a programme of reforms but damaged his credibility at the start by sanctioning the purchase of Saint-Cloud for the queen and Rambouillet for the king, while millions of livres went to the king's brothers and to members of the queen's cabal; fresh loans raised the total of those already crippling the country to more than 800 million livres. He can either be viewed as a spendthrift political charlatan, the Court's poodle, or as an astute politician, buying the time he needed to stabilise the economy. Believing in free trade and fiscal reform – the marquis de Mirabeau's disciple, Dupont, was his adviser – he also evinced all the Physiocratic horror of speculation and unproductive capital. In January 1785, to halt the continued buying of Caisse d'Escompte shares and return money to government stock, he forbade the bank to increase its dividends. As prices fell public indignation against foreign bankers mounted, and the wily Clavière decided to get himself an alibi by assisting the campaign to discredit the discount banks. He invited Mirabeau to write against the Caisse d'Escompte, knowing that he would regard an attack on speculation as a welcome duty. According to Brissot, Clavière only asked Mirabeau for the use of his name, because that name, 'in view of his bizarre adventures and daring character, always attracted attention' and it was a 'sound speculation to buy it'.[2] Professional jealousy would not allow Brissot to admit that Mirabeau's name was known because of his literary achievements; he claimed that six of the chapters in *De la Caisse d'Escompte* were written by Clavière, one by Dupont and two by himself.

On the book's appearance in May, Caisse d'Escompte shares suffered, though not as much as had been hoped. Mirabeau told his friends in England that he had written it 'to save Calonne and avert bankruptcy'. In his enthusiasm for his patriotic mission he never doubted that Clavière and Panchaud and their circle were as committed as he was himself to stamping out speculation, and for the same altruistic reasons. It seems not to have occurred to him that the two Genevois were motivated by political expediency. The French distrust of Genevois financiers was focused mainly on Necker; it would have been better reserved for Panchaud, the spider at the heart of an international banking web, who not only escaped unscathed from the Caisse d'Escompte affair, but continued to control the country's credit in his position of banker to the Crown. Calonne tried to distance himself from the speculating world in the course of 1785 by breaking with both Clavière and Panchaud. It was an insincere and futile gesture, for he could not break with Geneva: when he tried to rejuvenate French trade by resurrecting the Compagnie des Indes the project was backed by Panchaud's associates. Unable to disentangle himself, Calonne could appreciate, better than anybody, Necker's observation that Court bankers were for unsuspecting finance ministers what the praetorian guard had been for the Caesars – they served them for a time and then overthrew them.

It was a letter from Mirabeau about the Compagnie des Indes, and how to prevent it from becoming a monopoly, that first brought him to Calonne's notice. The Controller-General was interested in what he had to say. He asked Clavière, who was preparing an attack on the Banque de Saint-Charles, to let Mirabeau take over. He, Calonne, would pay the costs. (Mirabeau was to state on several occasions that the only money he received from the minister was for printing the book.) Again Brissot had his own bitter version of what happened: after Mirabeau's death, when he was leader of the Girondins and Clavière was his ally, he said that 'Mirabeau had the honour of it and kept the money, while Clavière paid the expenses'; which overlooked the fact that at the time he and Clavière were quite willing to let Mirabeau be the scapegoat if necessary.

The book caused Saint-Charles shares to plunge overnight, but Calonne's delight turned to consternation when the Spanish ambassador lodged a complaint. The French agent of the bank, Le Couteulx de la Noraye, whom Mirabeau had attacked in the book, wrote a philippic of his own against Mirabeau, which the latter duly returned in kind. In order to avert a serious diplomatic incident, Calonne proceeded to have the work he had sponsored suppressed. Mirabeau was incensed by this hypocrisy, and particularly by the wording of the decree condemning his book, which described it as the work of 'one of those individuals who dare to write on important matters about which they are not sufficiently informed to provide useful knowledge'. Only capitals could express the magnitude, for him, of the insult: 'I, ILL INFORMED!' he exclaimed in his letters.[3] If he had not known it before he knew now what the response would be to the truth. And the establishment knew what kind of man they were dealing with. It should have been apparent already, from his book on the Emperor's invasion of the Netherlands, that here was no venal mind, vacant and for rent.

'The book by the ill-informed man', he told his father, 'had no sooner been suppressed by a decree of Council than the Minister of

Finance asked him to do another one on loans'. (This was true, as the
Austrian ambassador, Mercy-Argenteau, confirmed.) Calonne certainly
wished to retain the services of a brilliant publicist, but Mirabeau was
aware that accepting the commission now would compromise his integrity, and he left the bait dangling.

He spent much of his time at Panchaud's. As the director of Calonne's
atelier of economic advisers, the banker was the patron saint of the
politically ambitious. Besides Clavière, Dupont, and Brissot, many of
Mirabeau's other friends were his disciples: Chamfort, the comte de
Narbonne, who would become War Minister in 1792, the comte
d'Antraigues, an early associate of Rousseau's and confidant of the king's
brother, the comte de Provence, the duc de Lauzun,[4] and the Abbé de
Périgord, the future Talleyrand.[5] In his open-hearted way Mirabeau
listed Lauzun, the abbé, Panchaud, and Mme de Nehra as the four
people he held most dear in the world. His enthusiasm for Panchaud
does not seem to have been returned in the same degree, judging by
Panchaud's remark (snapped up by Brissot) that no one could talk better
about things he knew nothing about than Mirabeau. This dismissive
comment expressed a common view, the subconscious wishful thinking
of many of Mirabeau's associates. To a Brissot, working his way up from
humble beginnings, there was something intensely irritating in his combination of inborn advantages and ability. In his memoirs Brissot tried to
depict Mirabeau as a fraud, declaring that the bailli wrote *Lettres de cachet*,
and that the translation of Tibullus – which Mirabeau made in Vincennes – was the work of his tutor's son. He provoked a similar defen-
siveness in Clavière and his compatriots so consistently that it might be
called the Genevois reaction; but with these industrious, professional,
self-esteeming men Calvinistic rectitude substituted for envy. The latent malice he aroused would be unimportant, were it not for the fact
that it contributed to the later construction by his enemies of a particular
image of him, the image that appealed both to the prejudiced and the
principled, of Mirabeau as the man with a bad reputation.

Inclined always to see his friends in the best light, he did not notice
snide behaviour until it became unmistakable. But when he encountered rank prejudice towards himself, in his professional role, from the
ranks of the Establishment, he was furious. The man with a bad reputation was a propaganda ploy also used by the government, alienated by
the sight of a nobleman who demeaned himself to follow the most
disreputable of professions, journalism, and totally unwilling to concede that such a person could have disinterested motives or anything
valuable to say. Later in 1785 Mirabeau wrote in desperation to
Montmorin, a liberal-minded minister, about the wilful folly of this
attitude to journalists.

The English more than value us. There is not a man of ability, a public figure of established talent, among them who has not written for periodicals, these ephemeral sheets that our ignorance disdains, and which, everywhere, have produced great changes, great revolutions in ideas, great effects on men. I do not feel humiliated doing what the élite of England have always done, and still do; and I do not believe I have been useless to my country if the example of a man, inferior neither in name nor talent, destroys this unreasonable and damaging prejudice.[6]

Determined to continue attacking speculation – after all, the government had declared that speculation was a social evil – he turned his attention to the Compagnie des Eaux de Paris, which had been set up to finance a scheme for piping water from the springs at Chaillot to every house in Paris. Backing had been provided by Beaumarchais, one of the directors and a principal shareholder. The value of the shares had risen rapidly in 1785, from 1,200 livres to more than 4,000 livres, assisted by the government's purchase of many shares; Calonne was known to have extensive holdings. In October a pamphlet was published in London under Mirabeau's name, in which the directors of the company were accused of defrauding the investors; it was a scarcely veiled attack on Beaumarchais himself. Mirabeau could say, in all honesty, that he was performing a public service in exposing fraud. At the same time he took a particular satisfaction in discrediting Beaumarchais, the social upstart and successful operator, whose advice was sought by government ministers while his own was publicly devalued. Beaumarchais, who could afford to be complacent – *The Marriage of Figaro* had been performed at Court that summer – replied smoothly to his heckler: 'Formerly, when criticisms were extremely harsh, they were called "philippics". Perhaps one day some wit will grace them with the name of "Mirabelles", after the comte de Mirabeau who *mirabiliar fecit*.' Everyone who read this knew that a mirabelle was a very small plum with a very strong smell.

If this taunt were not enough Mirabeau learned that Calonne himself had encouraged Beaumarchais to attack him in print. He immediately produced a *Réponse à l'écrivain des administrateurs de la Compagnie des Eaux de Paris*, 116 pages of mirabelles, which was published in Brussels on 10 December. He then sat down to write a long, indicting letter to Calonne, detailing his experiences as a citizen wanting to further the public good, at the hands of a government that supported the very abuses it professed to condemn. He heard no more from Beaumarchais, but his reply to him brought a warning from Calonne which Lauzun delivered. This was the last straw. His letter to the Controller-General was nearly finished and he proceeded to quote in it what Lauzun had been ordered to say:

That the king is very annoyed with me because of my *mémoire* on the Eaux de Paris. That everyone at Court is very annoyed with me. That this last pamphlet has caused feeling against me to reach its highest pitch. That you now learn that the investors are about to charge me, or perhaps have already charged me, to undertake a study of your whole administration; that I have couched it, or will couch it, in the most damaging and inflammatory language; that I could do so at my own risk, but that if I gave the slightest annoyance to the government in future you would have me punished as severely as possible.[7]

The finished composition (he called it a letter, but at 300 pages it was really a book) he entrusted to Dupont. His one-time mentor could read it and speak to Calonne on his behalf, and the minister could either support his writings on important issues, and vindicate himself in the process, or he could ignore him and face disgrace when the letter was published. As soon as it had been delivered to Dupont, Mirabeau and Mme de Nehra left Paris for Germany, to escape the possibility of arrest.

Three years later, replying to his father who had made remarks about his venal pen, he submitted a detailed account of his activities in 1785. He had never been paid by Calonne for his writings. The only payment Calonne had made was to the printer of the book on the Saint-Charles bank. He himself had never had anything to do with speculation – 'I have lived by my pen and with help from my friends' – and had never received 'a sou' by way of a bribe. He and Calonne, he told his father, had been on good terms prior to his pamphlet on the Eaux de Paris. Calonne had taken no part in speculation before then, the leader of the speculators was Le Couteulx de la Noraye; but later, he continued, Calonne had gone over to the speculators, and had unleashed '*ce saltimbanque de Beaumarchais*' against him. He concluded:

I consummated a rupture that was already public by writing a letter to M. de Calonne such as no receiver of a bribe ever addressed to his purchaser. If you read this letter, which Dupont will show you, you will not doubt that I voiced my own opinions, and not those basely accepted in exchange for a degrading retainer.[8]

It was Mirabeau's wild intention to punish the French government for their treatment of him by offering his services to Frederick the Great. He had an audience at Sans-Souci, but his hints were courteously ignored. However, the king's brother, Prince Henry, took an instant liking to him, and he found another ally in the Foreign Minister, Hertzberg; and he was warmly welcomed by the Germans themselves, especially by that section of middle-class society, liberal, intellectual, predominantly Jewish, which gave to German culture of the time much of its vitality. The philosopher Christian von Dohm introduced him to contemporary literature and criticism, in particular to the writings of Lessing, Nicolai, and the Jewish philosopher, Moses Mendelssohn, who had died only a fortnight before his arrival. The following year Mirabeau published an essay on Mendelssohn, *Sur Moses Mendelssohn, sur la réforme politique des Juifs*. Forgotten in the welter of his polemical works, this soberly reasoned plea for racial tolerance is one of the best pieces he ever wrote; it also had the honour of being the first of his writings to earn his father's approval.

Another piece, which also shows him in this new light, reflective instead of contentious, was an essay on Cagliostro and Lavater, which was published in Berlin during his stay. In effect it was a sermon on the dangers of fanaticism. Cagliostro at that moment was in the Bastille for his part in the affair of the queen's necklace, but before his luck ran out he was the most successful swindler of the day, who had made a fortune in England and France with his so-called Order of Egyptian Masonry. Belonging to the same venerable profession as peddlers of the elixir of life and the philosopher's stone, he offered his own century, intent on pulling down old altars and erecting new ones, an escape from rationalism into a world of arcane beliefs. Even after his frauds were exposed many serious-minded people remained convinced that the occult powers he claimed were genuine. One of these believers was the Swiss pastor poet, Lavater, a figure revered in the Germany of the *Aufklärung*, whose work on physiognomy had swept Europe. Lavater, mystic and fanatic, believer in exorcism and the raising of the dead, constituted with Cagliostro two sides of the same coin.

Whilst announcing himself as the born enemy of charlatans, it was not Mirabeau's aim simply to denounce Cagliostro; the credulity of Lavater, whose sincerity he recognised, the credulity of all dupes, had to be examined. He was concerned with the larger issue, the danger which lay in the usurpation of minds and the deployment of the power thus gained for ulterior purposes. To this end he used the relationship between Cagliostro and Lavater as a parable, by means of which he drew attention to the spread in Germany of what he aptly called philosophico-cabalistic Christianity. The allusion to the sect of free thinkers known as the Illuminati was clear enough, and with it his main reason for writing. Among the converts to *illuminisme* at Frederick's Court was his nephew and heir, the mentally inert Frederick-William, who spent much of his time attending mystic rites with his entourage of sycophantic advisers. The prospect for the future did not inspire confidence. Princes, wrote Mirabeau, especially absolute princes, were already sufficiently surrounded by illusions regarding themselves, illusions harmful for the people whose fate was in their hands.

The message would not have been lost on Frederick, but if he hoped to disarm the king with his sagacity he was doomed to disappointment.

There was no news from Lauzun or the abbé de Périgord about Calonne's reaction to his letter. He had imagined they would be soliciting the Controller-General on his behalf, as he would have done for a friend: he cannot have understood the abbé's character very well. In May, to everyone's horror, he turned up in Paris. Calonne was preparing a series of fiscal and trade reforms to revitalise the economy; he did not want the comte de Mirabeau around, threatening the peace and his own popularity with compromising *mémoires*. It was arranged that he should return to Berlin in the role of secret correspondent to the French government. Everyone could breathe again and Mirabeau had a position at last, albeit one not worthy of his talents. The knowledge that it had been fabricated in order to get him out of the way mortified his pride: he wrote bitterly afterwards of having been muzzled.

How much did it cost the government to exile its most effective critic? He told his father:

> When they asked me what reimbursement I wished, I replied, 'I shall only spend on your behalf, therefore you will pay what I shall spend'. Anyway, this was the start of the rumour that M. de Calonne was paying me. In effect the king paid me. I spent 42,000 francs on his behalf in eight and a half months, which is accounted for by secret expenses, various journeys and two secretaries, clothes for the northern Courts, horses, journeys into the interior of Germany acquiring material for *La Monarchie prussienne*. Of these 42,000 francs the king owes me 12,000 which I shall probably never see. If you add that I did not predict any event which did not occur, and that no event occurred which I did not predict, I doubt whether you will find that I cost more than I was worth.[9]

Mirabeau's secret reports from Berlin, sixty-six in all, written between 13 July 1786 and 19 January 1787, covered a vital period in Franco-Prussian relations. Frederick the Great died on 17 August. His successor Frederick-William was antagonistic to France, which already occupied a weak position in Europe, while Prussia could boast a full treasury and the best-trained army in Europe. An offensive and defensive pact with Prussia, to counterbalance the Austro-Russian *entente*, was essential for France. It was Mirabeau's job to win the support of the new king's advisers, but the secrecy of his role – ostensibly he was just a private citizen – halved its effectiveness, and he also had to contend with the French ambassador, Esterno, who resented his presence and, even more, his friendship with Prince Henry. To Esterno's satisfaction Mirabeau almost wrecked his favourable position soon after his arrival. On the day of Frederick's death he sent Frederick-William a long essay on kingship and the modern state, in which he set forth with passionate eloquence his duties towards his people, above all his duty to ensure civil liberty, religious toleration, freedom of the press and of movement, justice, and public education.[10] It was not the sort of address a Prussian monarch received from his ministers, let alone a private individual, a foreigner as well. But for Prince Henry he might have been ordered out of the country.

The men naturally placed to advise the new king were the ministers and generals who had been formed by Frederick the Great and by the circumstances of the age, itself formed by him as an extension of his own ego. Instruments of the late king's power, they now became, under his feeble successor, depositaries of power themselves. Mirabeau guessed that Hertzberg, Frederick's foreign minister for thirty years, was trying to turn the king against a French alliance by telling him that he could either be a Frenchman, in which case he would be a pallid imitation of his uncle, or that he could reject French pressure and become entirely German, adored as such by his people, and worthy in his own right of being called the Great. The king's faith in supernatural voices was helping Hertzberg to tip the scales against the French. His life was dominated by a Rosicrucian named Wöllner, whose talents included the ability to conjure up spirits: at séances attended by the king he had produced the shades of Julius Caesar, Marcus Aurelius, and Leibnitz, all of them well informed on current affairs, who saluted Frederick-William as the saviour of Prussia. The reign of superstition, predicted by Mirabeau, had indeed begun.

Apart from Hertzberg, the two in the strongest position round the throne were Prince Henry and the duke of Brunswick. Prince Henry, said Mirabeau, was ambitious and unscrupulous in his methods; the duke concealed his ambition. Neither of them could be trusted. His failure to pin them down was a blow to his *amour propre*, and as the months passed he grew increasingly bitter and impatient. In France important matters were taking shape; his friends all had active parts to play: Lauzun, for instance, had gone to London to represent Calonne at the drawing up of the Anglo-French commercial treaty. Yet when he suggested an active role for himself (the Princess of Orange wanted him to arbitrate in the Dutch patriots' uprising against the Stadholder) he was ignored. He wrote;

> Only the most immediate usefulness could make me endure much longer the extreme indecency of the double existence to which I have been committed. If I can do nothing I am costing too much. If I deserve to do something, after I have tackled thousands of obstacles unassisted, developed some knowledge of men, some wisdom, not to mention the precious facts reported in my letters, I owe it to myself to demand and obtain a position.[11]

Those letters, deciphered and censored by the abbé de Périgord before being passed on, had made next to no impression. When Chateaubriand came to read them he could only say: 'I have been struck by one thing, that is the shallowness, the incompetence of a government which saw the correspondence of such a man and did not perceive what he was'.[12] At the end of the year Mirabeau's spirits rose when he heard that Calonne had decided to call an assembly of Notables in a final attempt to solve the financial difficulties of his ministry. 'The idea was entirely mine', he told his friend, Mauvillon, but despite this he did not expect any recognition: 'I cannot believe that our government has reached such a degree of enlightenment that it could wish to have me in an assembly of Notables, still less in the place reserved for me by public demand, that of secretary'.[13]

Mirabeau said nothing more about his claim to have thought up the idea of an assembly of Notables. He may have recommended such a step in letters to Calonne, or it may have figured in the essay on provincial administration which he sent to Calonne from Berlin, an essay which turned out to be an unpublished work of Turgot's, reworked by Dupont. (Dupont duly claimed it as his own work, telling Calonne that he had lent it to Mirabeau when he was in Vincennes, and that he must have made a copy of it.) But that was not the whole story. Brissot recounts in his *Mémoires* (II, 36) that Clavière gave him a copy of an unpublished work on provincial administration by Turgot, and that he, Brissot, was about to publish it when Mirabeau threatened him with a *lettre de cachet* if he went ahead. (Mirabeau 'was then all powerful with Calonne', Brissot explains.) Clavière also warned him not to publish. Brissot goes on to state as fact that Mirabeau had sold the Turgot piece to Calonne as his own work. He was afraid of being found out, hence his anxiety to stop Brissot publishing. Brissot economises with the truth: Mirabeau passed off the Turgot/Dupont work as his own in order to impress Calonne but he did not sell it to him for money. Nor did he publish it later under his own name, as alleged. How Brissot himself came to be publishing the manuscript without permission is not explained.

Mirabeau was right about not being appreciated by the government. On reaching Paris he learned that the position had been given to Dupont. Worse, he heard that when Calonne was warned against giving him cause for resentment he had replied: 'I shall arrange all that with money'. These words, said Mirabeau, 'not only released me from all obligations towards him but provided every justification for crossing to the opposition'.[14]

The Assembly of Notables opened at Versailles on 22 February. On 26 February, Mirabeau published *Dénonciation de l'agiotage au roi et à l'assemblée des notables*, the unanswerable indictment of ministerial mismanagement which delivered the *coup de grâce* to Calonne's administration.

The decision to call the Assembly of Notables was taken some months before the public announcement. Meanwhile, the government still had to find the money to pay the interest on its debts, and Calonne had turned to the Caisse d'Escompte. The share capital of the bank was increased by 80 million francs, of which 70 million were advanced to the government, which proceeded to purchase futures on the stock market through two companies, dealing in shares of the Compagnie des Indes and the Compagnie des Eaux de Paris. The shares were deposited with the bank and funds were advanced on the strength of them. The idea, the brainchild of the abbé de Périgord, ended disastrously for the government when it fell victim itself to the kind of arch speculator against whom it had officially inveighed. The truth leaked out towards the end of 1786 when the operations of a highly successful speculator, the abbé d'Espagnac, began to attract attention. He was the Vicar-General of Sens (like the abbé de Périgord, he had a greater vocation for finance than for the Church) and he had been selling shares in the Compagnie des Indes to the government, knowing that it could not pay for its acquisitions, and engaging in forward purchases of them at enormous profit to himself. He eventually held more shares in the company than existed on the market, and the government could do nothing to stop him without revealing its own involvement. Mirabeau learned about Espagnac's 'villainous enterprise' on his return from Berlin, and in three weeks the *Dénonciation de l'agiotage* was written.

'The book has had a prodigious success', he reported to Mauvillon. 'Most of the Notables, official people, and decent men of all classes have congratulated me and thanked me.'[15] To the Controller-General's colleagues who regarded the Assembly of Notables simply as an expedient to solve his current problems, any criticism of him at that moment was wilful sabotage; but Mirabeau saw it as a stepping-stone to a more democratic France, a unique opportunity for public debate which might be lost if the minister were allowed to censor the evidence. He did not deny Calonne's 'courage and skill' in convening the Assembly, but 'the man is the greatest obstacle to the *chose*'.

According to the marquis de Mirabeau, Calonne attempted to get the most damaging passages in the book removed. He told the bailli:

It was his friend, the abbé de Périgord, a great intriguer, who showed the manuscript to the minister. The minister said 'There are some good things in it and some that must be cut out. I know the secret; he needs money. Here is a promissory note for 3,600 livres which will stop him.' The abbé went to his house and found him gone to Orléans to get his piece printed, having failed to receive an answer quickly enough.[16]

If this were true one of Mirabeau's aims in writing was to extort money. He had many enemies who would have been prepared to circulate such a story, even the abbé himself. But had money been his object he would not have rushed off prematurely; again, if his only interest was personal vengeance he could have published his 1785 letter to Calonne, without alteration; the facts in it were the same as in *Dénonciation de l'agiotage*. His resentment was real enough, but it took second place to concern for the public good. Calonne, in fact, is only mentioned once in the book, and then flatteringly. The savage quotation from Junius which headed the 1785 letter – 'I would pursue him through life, and try with the last exertion of my abilities to preserve the perishable infamy of his name, and make it immortal' – is replaced by more detached lines from Voltaire:

> Pensais-tu qu'un instant ma vertu démentie
> Mettrait dans la balance un homme et la patrie?

It remained an indictment, but one to be read thoughtfully. The speculation of the title was really but a side-effect of a chaotic administrative system, and it was this wider theme which Mirabeau developed. The Notables, he said, summoned in consequence of the crisis as it stood, should realise that the crisis would remain insolvable while the interests of the nation as a whole were subjugated to those of the capital, and while Paris continued to suck wealth from the provinces which otherwise could have been put to productive use. (Speculation drained the country but only benefited the sterile Paris market.) The solution to the problem – or, at least, a step in the right direction – lay in the establishment of provincial assemblies, responsible for the regions, answerable to the centre. It might have been the marquis writing:

> As long as the kingdom is not organised with a regulating constitution we will only be a society of different, discordant orders, a people without any social links, an aggregation of provinces united under one head, but almost alien to each other.[17]

Provincial assemblies had another purpose besides administration: that of public instruction, 'in which the duties of a citizen, a member of a large family, will form the foundation of all other duties'.[18] The importance which he attached to public instruction, well understood and utilised later by the Jacobins, was lost on the Notables, intent only on the exercise of their own power. Provincial assemblies, however, as instruments of power if not instruction, were something they could readily agree with. La Fayette went further and proposed the convocation of a national assembly. 'The Notables are behaving wonderfully', wrote Mirabeau. 'They are showing energy and wisdom, breadth and foresight. This epoch will stand as a glorious one for the king and a beneficial one for the nation.'[19]

But the atmosphere deteriorated when Calonne announced an annual deficit of 80 million livres. Under pressure he admitted that the true figure was 112 million livres, and he laid the blame on Necker, who had borrowed from foreign banks at exorbitant rates of interest. A public dispute ensued when Necker published a pamphlet denying his own mismanagement and attacking Calonne. Mirabeau joined the fray, aware that if Calonne fell his place might well be filled by the Genevois banker, with all that his species stood for in French eyes. On 19 March he published *Première lettre du comte de Mirabeau sur l'administration de M. Necker* to counteract the swing in opinion. The next day Dupont and the abbé de Périgord told him that Espagnac and another leading speculator had been ordered to leave Paris, and that his own arrest would follow. Probably Necker had denounced him to the Keeper of the Seals. Raging at the fact that he was being punished along with the swindlers he had exposed, he retreated to Liège, until Calonne obtained permission for him to return.

He was not unappreciative. In the middle of April Calonne was dismissed and retired to London, where he wrote a book in answer to Necker's accusations; and on 1 May Mirabeau issued a second letter against Necker, in which he dismissed the latter's charges that Calonne had deliberately falsified his accounts. One could not make a mistake of 500 million livres even if one wanted to, he argued reasonably; clearly there was a disagreement between the two ministers over the definition of items which should be included in the government's accounts, but this was a difference of interpretation, not of fraud on the part of Calonne.

The discredited Controller-General was succeeded by Loménie de Brienne, the relentlessly ambitious Archbishop of Toulouse, whereupon the Notables proceeded to endorse all Calonne's proposed reforms, with the exception of the tax on land. They were dismissed on 25 May, leaving widespread feelings of dissatisfaction over what they had failed to achieve, but also some hope for the future. Mirabeau left Paris again, a precautionary move until he saw which way the wind would blow under Brienne. He spent the summer in Brunswick, completing *De la monarchie prussienne sous Frédéric le Grand*, which he had been working on for two years in collaboration with Jakob Mauvillon.[20] From Brunswick he watched the latest developments in France, where Brienne was engaged in a battle of wills with the Paris *parlement* over the registration of edicts approved by the Notables. Edicts for internal free trade, the establishment of provincial assemblies, and the redemption of the *corvée*, were registered in June without argument, but when it came to the land tax, which the Notables had rejected, and a new stamp tax, the *parlement* refused to co-operate. One of the counsellors, the abbé Sabatier, declared that perpetual edicts could only be registered by the Estates General. The suggestion was fantastical – the

Estates General had last met in 1614 – but the counsellors warmed to
the idea when they realised that, by acting on it, they would avoid
registering taxes that they would have to pay themselves. On 30 July
the *parlement* rejected the land and stamp taxes, and demanded that
the king should summon the Estates General.

Immense excitement greeted this challenge to royal authority. The
king's only recourse was to hold a *lit de justice*, at which the edicts were
registered as the law ordained they had to be, and afterwards he exiled
the *parlement* to Troyes. Mirabeau described this inept decision as an
absurd horror; it only increased the popularity of the *parlement* and led
to humiliation for the king when, inevitably, he had to back down. In
September the exiled counsellors registered an edict levying two *ving-
tièmes* on all property (a drop in the bucket compared with what was
needed) and returned in triumph to Paris.

Also back, Mirabeau received an invitation to work for the government from Brienne, who doubtless had learned a lesson from Calonne's mistake; but, having no faith in the present ministry, he did not
want to be identified with it. He replied:

> Leave me to my obscurity; I say my obscurity because my intention is to
> remain out of sight until an orderly state of affairs emerges from the tumult
> we are in now, and until some great revolution compels every honest respons-
> ible citizen to raise his voice. This revolution cannot be delayed. The strait in
> which the ship of state has to manoeuvre is both narrow and difficult. A skilful
> pilot could, no doubt, bring her through to the open sea, and once there she is
> safe; but he could only do it with the help of the crew.[21]

And few sailors, he added, would volunteer to join the crew in question
at that particular moment. Nevertheless, he went to see Montmorin,
Vergennes's successor as Foreign Minister, hoping to obtain employment on his own terms: these were that it should be 'executive rather
than speculative', and abroad – 'Warsaw, St Petersburg, Constantinople, Alexandria, they are all the same to me, provided I can be usefully
occupied'.[22] But nothing further happened, and he sat back to watch
the progress of events.

At a *lit de justice* in November, Brienne presented an edict to raise 420
million livres, promising that the Estates General would meet in 1792.
On this occasion the duc d'Orléans protested that enforced registration
was illegal, and the king committed another tactical error by exiling his
royal cousin to his estates. The following day the *parlement* rejected the
edict, whereupon Mirabeau wrote to Montmorin in the hope that his
advice would be passed on: the deadlock could be resolved by promising
that the Estates General would meet very soon, in 1789 instead of 1792;
the *parlement* would then be willing to register fiscal edicts without the
need for suicidal loans, and the people's respect for the king would be

restored. But the government still believed that there was no need to summon the Estates General, and that it was only being driven to do so by the obduracy of the *parlement*, which ought to be subjugated. It saw Mirabeau as just the man to turn public opinion against the *parlements* and so shatter their power. However, when Montmorin suggested it in April 1788, Mirabeau refused. Not, he said, because he realised that the government's main desire was to save its own skin, nor because he was afraid of drawing the hatred of the *parlements* on himself, nor even because it would be a psychological mistake to attack them at the height of their popularity, but because a war on the *parlements* must only be waged when the nation was witness to it:

> Only in the presence of the nation should they be, can they be, reduced to their role of simple ministers of justice . . . If the nation is deprived of the phantom which it has long regarded as the guardian of its rights, without being called on to supervise the conservation of those rights, it will not believe that one is destroying in order to construct . . . it will believe that we are heading for absolute despotism. It would be a brave man who could say that such circumstances, aggravated by public suspicion, would not lead to insurrection.[23]

His refusal to write either for the government or against the *parlements* was part of a decision he had made on his return to Paris not to become involved with a ministry and a regime that were doomed. Instead, at Panchaud's request, he wrote the *Suite de la dénonciation de l'agiotage*, in which he once again attacked speculation and called for a constitution as the only base for economic stability, and he joined with Clavière and Brissot to found a journal analysing English newspapers. His only other publication at this time was the *Adresse aux Bataves*, his response to repeated demands from the Dutch patriots for his support. The news that he had written a book admiring Prussia had caused consternation in the Netherlands: the Hague had been occupied by Prussian troops just as he returned to Paris, and the patriots had written to him in October, asking him to publicise their cause. It would give him an opportunity, they added, to confound his enemies, who were saying that he had abandoned truth and justice in order to genuflect before the Prussian monarch. What they wanted was a denunciation of Prussian interference in the Netherlands, which would have angered Frederick William and also damaged French interests. For this reason Mirabeau would not be drawn. He had personal considerations as well: he was arranging with Fauche (the son of his publisher in Neuchâtel) in Hamburg to publish *De la monarchie prussienne*, and Fauche might have second thoughts about associating with a dangerous author.[24] The *Adresse aux Bataves* therefore had to be postponed. When it appeared in April 1788 it bore all the marks of having been tossed off under an irksome sense of obligation.[25]

His refusal to write in defence of the *parlements* exasperated his friends. He told his collaborator, Mauvillon:

> I have been criticised by everyone because I do not echo the fanaticism for the *parlements*. In fact I have not written anything for the other side either; I have always believed that between the king and the *parlements* there is a poor, obscure little party called the nation, to which sensible, honest men should belong.[26]

Thanks to Brienne's mishandling, the Paris *parlement* was able to parade as the only remaining guardian of liberty. In May, when Brienne had two counsellors, Goislard de Monsabert and Esprémenil, arrested during a session of *parlement*, they became instant martyrs. Two days later the *parlements* were suppressed, and a tumult of support for them, and resentment against royal authority, swept the country.

At this moment Mirabeau abandoned his neutrality, albeit anonymously. In *Réponse aux alarmes des bons citoyens*, he reassured those who feared that the Estates General would weaken the power of the monarchy, and dismissed the illusion that the *parlements* were the defenders of the people's interests. Frenchmen seeking liberty, he said, had to look beyond the *parlements*, in which they would never have any voice, to the Estates General, which alone could implement the will of the people. His friends, emotionally whipped up by the arrest of the counsellors, were furious. Although he justified his stand in a letter to Lauzun, who led the attack against him, he was not forgiven for putting reason before partisan passion.

Brienne's suppression of the *parlements* was hailed as illegal by *parlements* throughout the country. At Grenoble the order to exile the local counsellors caused a riot, and the nobles of Dauphiné demanded both the restoration of their *parlement* and the convocation of their provincial assembly, warning that they would assemble anyway, and that if their rights were ignored Dauphiné would seek its former independence, and the son of the sovereign would no longer be known as the dauphin. The author of these words, a young lawyer named Jean-Joseph Mounier, became a national hero. In July the Assembly met as it had threatened. On 8 August the king suspended the *cour plénière* which had replaced the *parlements*, and announced that the Estates General would meet at Versailles on 1 May 1789.

'In twenty-four hours the nation has stepped forward a hundred years', wrote Mirabeau exultingly to Mauvillon. 'Ah, my friend, you will see what sort of nation this is the day the Assembly is constituted, the day when talent will come into its own.' The first Estates General would be 'tumultuous', he warned another friend, the second would consolidate the progress made by the first, the third would achieve a constitution. They must not undertake too much at first. 'National consent on taxes and loans, civil liberty, regular assemblies: these are the three points which depend on a precise declaration of national rights; the rest will follow.' As for his own views, they were those he had always held: the defence of liberty, the end of absolutism, consensus between the king and his people. 'War to the privileged and to privileges, that is my motto. The privileged are useful against kings, but they are detestable against nations.' Liberty depended on a constitution and on the monarchy. 'That is why we must remain, and why I personally shall remain, very monarchist.'[27]

## NOTES

1. Paul Léon (1953: 101).
2. Brissot (1911: II, 30).
3. *Mémoires biographiques*, V, 181.
4. Armand-Louis de Gontaut, duc de Lauzun, afterwards duc de Biron (1747–93) fought in the American War of Independence. 'Handsome, brave, generous and intelligent' according to Talleyrand, he belonged to the radical chic set at Court which gathered round the duc d'Orléans. He shared Mirabeau's interest in the constitution and Anglo-French relations, and, like him, wanted to have a commercial treaty with England. In 1793 he commanded the army of the Republic which was sent to repress the counter-revolutionary rebellion in the Vendée, but was replaced when suspicion fell on officers who were former aristocrats, and guillotined.
5. Five years younger than Mirabeau, Charles-Maurice de Talleyrand-Périgord became Agent-General for ecclesiastical affairs at the age of twenty-six, in which position he candidly admitted he made a fortune. One of Mirabeau's most attractive characteristics was his willingness to help his friends: he recommended the abbé to Calonne as the right man to reorganise the Caisse d'Escompte, pointing out that besides being able to keep a secret he exerted a great influence over Panchaud, which would be to his employer's advantage. The abbé got the job.
6. *Mémoires biographiques*, V, 190f. Letter of 25 November 1785.
7. Ibid., V, 208–9. Mirabeau's letter to Calonne, from which this passage is taken, fills sixty-two printed pages. It deserves to be read in its entirety as a masterpiece of forensic eloquence, and also because it illuminates and justifies his seemingly provocative purpose in attacking the Controller-General.
8. Ibid., V, 165, Letter of 4 October 1788.
9. *Mémoires biographiques*, V, 293–4.
10. *Lettre remise à Frédéric-Guillaume II*. Etienne Dumont asserted that Clavière supplied the material for this work, but the only passage which might owe anything to him is one in which Mirabeau condemns lotteries. In a letter to the abbé de Périgord, dated 2 August 1786, he wrote, 'I have asked Clavière for his views on lotteries in relation to morals and religion' (Welschinger, 1900: 158). If Mirabeau had used footnotes in his works to acknowledge even the most generalised borrowings, he would have avoided accusations of plagiarism, and

frustrated the pretensions of those who afterwards claimed to have written, *in toto*, some of his works.

11. *Histoire secrète*, II, 248.
12. Cited by Castries (1960: 242).
13. *Lettres amicales*, 178.
14. Ibid. Letter of 24 March 1787.
15. Ibid., 203.
16. Loménie (1879–91: III, 661n).
17. *Dénonciation*, 129.
18. In *Essai*, 60, Mirabeau had already stressed the importance of instructing the public: 'Education and liberty are the bases of all social harmony and all human rights. I could say education alone, for liberty depends on it absolutely, universal education being the impregnable enemy of despots; or rather, when society has reached a stage of universal enlightenment despotism will become a state of mind, impossible to realise'.
19. *Mémoires biographiques*, VI, 28. Letter of 19 March 1787.
20. Jacob Mauvillon (1745–94) was a Prussian major in the engineer corps and professor of tactics at the Carolinum, whose family came originally from Provence. He published German translations of various French works, among them the letters of Mme de Sevigné, and wrote a work on the influence of gunpowder in modern warfare.

    *La Monarchie prussienne* suffered from having collaborators with different aims. Mirabeau explained his clearly (*Lettres amicales*, 171): 'Works of this nature should emulate Tacitus, who criticised Rome by implication when he wrote about the morals of the Germans. It is France that I see, and wish others to see, in Prussia'. Mauvillon's contribution, consisting of deserts of statistical tables, of ephemeral value, obscured the real purpose of the book.
21. *Mémoires biographiques*, VI, 67. Letter to Brienne's secretary, Soufflot, 4 October 1787.
22. Ibid., VI, 70–72. Letter of 12 October 1787.
23. Ibid., VI, 90–91. Letter to Montmorin, 22 April 1788.
24. In the eventual contract which Mirabeau signed in November four names appear: Fauche, Desenne, Volland, and Le Jay. It was his association with Le Jay's wife, Anne Marais Le Jay (1764–1844), which Mme de Nehra gave as her reason for leaving him in the summer of 1788.
25. Often cited as one of Mirabeau's great patriotic declarations, the *Adresse aux Bataves* (real title: *Aux Bataves sur le Stathouderat*, 1788) really belongs to the school of Mirabeau. He supplied the oratorical passages, which were strung together by two collaborators: Bourges, the son of a former administrator at Besançon, and Louis-Henri Marron, pastor of the reformed church in Paris. The reply which Mirabeau originally sent to Van Kussel, the leader of the Dutch patriots, supporting their cause in principle and, at the same time, teaching them about *realpolitik*, is printed in *Mémoires biographiques*, VI, 110–15.
26. *Lettres amicales*, 374. Letter of 21 August 1788.
27. *Mémoires de Tilly*, Paris, 1828, III, 128–31. Letter to Levrault, 16 August 1788.

# 6

The Campaign in Provence

## (1789)

Mirabeau's *Réponse aux alarmes des bons citoyens* awakened the public, still either apathetic or cynical, to the real significance of the Estates General and the decisive role which awaited the third estate. It appeared months before Carra, Cerutti, Sieyès, and other pamphleteers published their views on the eve of the Estates General, and set the tone for the most extreme of them in its denunciation of privileged castes. As so often happened, he said what others would say later, but then went further: other revolutionaries joined him in reminding the king that the source of his power lay with the people, but he then set the cat among the pigeons ideologically by stating that the king and the people were natural allies against the privileged in the cause of liberty and justice. This conflicted with the thinking of radicals who did not wish the king to exercise any redeeming role, and also with that of the conservative middle classes who looked to the king to defend their interests against the people. From the first announcement of the Estates General Mirabeau was thus identified as a radical who was a monarchist, and as a monarchist who was a democrat, in either case a dangerous enigma.

In the run-up to the Estates General the Paris *parlement* emerged in its true colours as the self-interested 'black aristocracy' Mirabeau had always proclaimed it to be. Determined to safeguard its privileges and to prevent the third estate from taking an active part in the Estates General, the *parlement* called for the composition and procedure of the Estates General to be the same as of the last assembly in 1614: voting

by order, not head (ensuring that the third estate would be constantly
outvoted), nobles to possess a fief, and the clergy a benefice. The
*parlements* only wanted to render the Estates General useless, Mirabeau commented in a letter to Mauvillon; if they insisted on the prece-
dents of 1614 it would mean that one part of the nation would still be
able to oppress the other. 'But in the end this other part will be
conscious of its grievances', he warned, 'and will measure its rights by
its real power'.

The crucial decisions about the voting power of the three orders in
the Estates General, which would determine whether the nation's
hopes were to be fulfilled or mocked, would be made by Necker,
whom the king had recalled to office when Brienne resigned in August.
This time, though still Director, not Controller-General, the aloof,
powerful Genevois had a seat at the Council table. 'Here is M. Necker,
king of France at last', announced Mirabeau, who thought, like the
abbé de Périgord, that his talents and character were unequal to the
task confronting him. Everything Necker had done in the past, his
financial mismanagement, his complacency, his compromises, pointed
to a man blinded by his own vanity and essentially weak. He was easy
to hate, a foreigner who ran the affairs of France, a commoner in
aristocratic circles, a Protestant among Catholics, a man who had made
8 million livres in eight years on the stock market, whose daughter,
Mme de Staël, had ranked in the marriage stakes as highly as a princess. He was also ostentatiously virtuous. All this tended to obscure the
fact that his instincts were strongly democratic. He despised the system he served. But much as he personally wished for changes, he saw
the Estates General, first and foremost, in terms of the financial problems he had to solve. They were his responsibility; constitutional reforms were the responsibility of Frenchmen; and, as an outsider, he
would have preferred to remain detached.

The Paris *parlement* having voted for the pattern of 1614, Necker
recalled the Notables in November, in order to hear their views. They
agreed with the *parlement*, except for one committee headed by the
comte de Provence, which voted to give the third estate parity by
means of double representation. Mirabeau had spent every moment
since the *parlement*'s decision looking for a fief in order to make himself
eligible for election. At this stage he took it for granted that nobles
elected to the Estates General would represent the nobility rather than
the third estate. He started by asking his father if he might represent
him at the Estates General, borrowing, as it were, the fief of Mirabeau.
Unmoved by the recent dedication of *La Monarchie prussienne* to himself,[1] the marquis replied that *he* intended to occupy the seat to which
his fiefs entitled him and that his son was not going to usurp his place.

It was the touchy reaction of an old man who knew that the world regarded him, in his own words, as 'finished and buried', and who saw in his son's suggestion another attempt at premature interment. Cut off and alienated from his family by Mme de Pailly, whose true nature the bailli vainly pointed out to him, he took her opinion for his own without realising it. Still, his view of his son was not too Paillycised for him to tell his brother:

They won't have seen such a head in Provence for a long time. The brazen voice is muted: I have proved it myself in conversations and letters; I have truly witnessed genius. His exhaustive work and innate pride, added to intelligence, have made him a figure in the banking, and, above all, in the modern political world.[2]

The fief, however, was not bestowed. Mirabeau also failed to obtain one in Alsace and in Dauphiné. He tried to borrow 4,800 livres from Lauzun, his friend and Necker's colleague, to buy the Dauphiné fief; the stone wall he met everywhere made him believe that there was a conspiracy afoot to keep him out of the Estates General, that this was Necker's revenge for his attacks on him. He appealed repeatedly to Lauzun to speak to Montmorin on his behalf: 'As it matters a great deal to me in my appalling uncertainty to know where I stand, I beg you to tell me'.[3] Gripping with his finger tips to the ledge which would lead him to fulfilment, he saw his friends prepared to let him fall rather than compromise their own political futures by helping the man their leader had proscribed. The idea of a pressure group working to frustrate him was not pure paranoia on his part. The counsellors of the Paris *parlement* had no particular reason to assist a critic of their corps. His failure to write in their support in 1787 when they refused to register Brienne's land tax edict (a tax they themselves would have had to pay) had caused much ill feeling at the time. He met them socially at the *Société des trente*, which he had helped to found in November 1788, and which gathered at the house of Adrien Duport, one of the leading counsellors and an outspoken critic of Calonne. Brought together by their desire for a national constitution, the members of the *Société* were dominated in their proceedings by the *parlement* faction. While the rest wanted the king to have some constitutional authority they were intent on destroying it while maintaining their own. To diminish their influence Mirabeau had urged a change of venue: 'We have to escape from parliamentary tyranny', he told Lauzun, 'and those of us who thought to form a group of good citizens, and not a reserve corps of parliamentarians, must unite to stop a very dangerous tendency'.[4]

The powerful *parlement* faction, ministry acolytes, Necker himself, all found him a thorn in the flesh. Still without a fief at the end of December, he turned in desperation to Montmorin:

The man of whom all are thinking, the *god* of the moment, has too many reasons to hate, perhaps to fear me, for my absence not to be preferred during the first moments of public effervescence. It would be better to let him return to the stature of an ordinary mortal, which I am sure will not take long. Meanwhile, you love the king and are bound to him as a man and as a minister. For my part, as a citizen, I tremble for the royal authority, which is more necessary than ever at this moment. Never was the coalition of the privileged more daunting to the king, or more threatening for the people; never did a national assembly promise to be as stormy as that which is about to decide the fate of the monarchy.

However, is the minister considering what means there are of avoiding the danger of falling under the Assembly's control, or rather, of turning its assistance to good account? Has he a fixed and solid plan which the representatives of the nation will have only to sanction? Well, I have such a plan. It is linked to that of a constitution which could save us from aristocratic conspiracies, from democratic excesses, and from the utter anarchy into which authority, by wishing to be absolute, has plunged it and us. Do you wish to see it? Do you wish to show it to the king? Will you have the courage to appoint a faithful subject, a brave man, and an intrepid defender of justice and truth, to his post of citizen? Without the support – the secret support at least – of the government I cannot get into the Estates General. I have already realised that one of your colleagues will shut all doors against me. If we come to an understanding it would be easy for me to overcome obstacles; and, indeed, there is not more than three months in which to get ready, to draw up one's policy, and to show oneself a worthy and influential defender of the throne and of the common weal.[5]

Such a letter was unanswerable. Montmorin would have had to admit that the government had no solid plan, had not even considered the possibility of a challenge to ministerial supremacy. In the last days of December Necker's long-awaited rulings on the Estates General were published, and all Mirabeau's fears about his indecisiveness were confirmed. The third estate was to have double representation, but the question of whether voting was to be by order or by head was left unanswered, and, as a counterbalance to the concession to the third estate, the nobles and clergy would not require fiefs or benefices in order to vote. On reflection it was apparent that neither the third estate nor the king would gain from this arrangement. Doubling their numbers would not help the third estate if the privileged orders elected representatives of dominating quality. And while the king could normally have counted on the support of the nobles and clergy, the waiving of the condition regarding fiefs ensured the presence of a sizeable body of nobles, unfettered by caste loyalty, whose voting pattern would not be determined by a need to preserve the status quo. In itself that was promising, but whether these freelance nobles would have an effective voice depended on Necker. The suspicion that, for all his democratic parade, he would still capitulate to pressure was strengthened by his declaration on 29 December that money backed by loans from the Caisse d'Escompte would continue in circulation. To economists this enforced currency gave as much food for thought as the clauses of the *loi électorale*.

At this point Mirabeau flung all caution aside in his determination to hammer home the truth. In the first week of January 1789 he made a searing attack on Necker in a pamphlet entitled *Correspondance entre M. C—— et le comte de Mirabeau, sur le Rapport de M. Necker, et sur l'arrêt du Conseil du 29 décembre.*[6] Necker's financial methods, he declared, were no better than those of his discredited predecessor; he was incapable, muddle-headed, negligent. The Director-General, he added, wanted to exclude him from the Estates General, but whatever happened he desired passionately to be present. He told his readers:

> I do not think that I would be useless there. But I would make no headway without the force of public opinion to assist me, that force which I have valiantly raised to confront all who try to stop us. I have no one to fear therefore, and no one of sincerity need fear me.[7]

The force of public opinion, which no minister could ignore with impunity, was to be his weapon. Having delivered his challenge he set off for Provence on 8 January to begin his electoral campaign.

Under her ancient constitution Provence enjoyed a form of local government unique among the *pays d'état*, an assembly of commoners, called the *Assemblée des communautés*. For 150 years after the suppression of provincial assemblies it took over the administration of the affairs of Provence, elected representatives of the third estate meeting once a year under the presidency of the Archbishop of Aix, assisted by four magistrates and two *procureurs du pays*. They authorised the taxes, including the annual *don gratuit* to the king, and provincial taxes, which were divided among the dioceses of the province. When the Assembly of Notables recommended the re-establishment of provincial assemblies the nobles of Provence decided to regard the *Assemblée des communautés* as their provincial assembly, and took their right as fief holders to sit in it, with the result that the third estate became a minority, and the *Assemblée* became the instrument of privileged interests.

The third estate wanted the return of a provincial assembly no less than the nobles. As tax payers and property owners they resented the fact that much of the land belonging to the privileged orders was exempt from taxation, and, while they were outnumbered by the intruding fief holders in the *Assemblée des communautés*, they counted on being able, in the provincial assembly, to obtain equality in land taxation for all citizens. Their spokesman was Pascalis, one of the lawyers in Mirabeau's divorce case. He drew up a plan for modernising the old provincial assembly which allowed for sixteen bishops to represent the clergy, thirty nobles with fiefs, and forty-six representatives of the third estate; this plan was submitted to the king, but the riots of 1788 in Provence, sparked off by Mounier's action in Dauphiné, intervened before it was put into operation. The decree of 27 December, finalising the conditions for election to the Estates General, only heightened the conflict between the reactionary and progressive elements in the province, between the unyielding privileged orders and an activated third estate with its supporters, the nobles who were not fief holders. At the beginning of January the town council of Aix called a meeting of all citizens, at which it was agreed that an assembly of delegates of the three orders should meet to elect representatives to the Estates General. The meeting was boycotted by the nobles with fiefs and the clergy. In this way they not only registered their opposition to the equal representation of the third estate allowed by the decree of 27 December, but affirmed that in Provence they ruled, and royal decrees were an impertinent irrelevance.

Until Mirabeau arrived in Aix on 13 January, the opposition to their dictatorship had been too diffuse to constitute a threat, but suddenly his presence concentrated it into a force that was real, immediate, and dangerous. The tumultuous welcome he received from the people roused fears that the electors of the third estate would turn to him for leadership, and that he would become a demagogue, another Mounier. To prevent this happening the oligarchy decided that when the assembly of electors met on 21 January all three orders should sit together, instead of separately, calculating that when Mirabeau confessed his desire to become a deputy for the nobility the third estate would be disillusioned, and desert him. As for Mirabeau, far from encouraging his partisans, he reported to his sister that they were only adding to his difficulties:

> The third's demonstrations of confidence and enthusiasm for me do not help their own cause, for it increases the rage of the nobles, which reminds one of the convulsions of the dying Turnus. I have never seen nobles more ignorant, covetous, and insolent. These characters will make me become a tribune of the people despite myself if I don't guard my reactions carefully . . . If they refuse me my place in the assembly, on the pretext of proofs [of a fief] not being submitted in time, it is because they are as cowardly as they are insolent, and want to muffle my public spirit, and, above all, to make me an object of distrust.[8]

In the same letter he commented on his sister's suggestion that the time was now right to patch up his differences with his wife. Mme du Saillant was thinking of Emilie's wealth, but her idea that the ashes of his marriage might yet be coaxed into flame was too ludicrous for him to give it a second thought:

> As to what you call the object of my desire, we have too much masculine business on hand to have time for women's affairs. All the same, your erstwhile

sister-in-law thinks it ridiculous that they have demanded my proofs for the assembly.

The opening meeting of the three orders was preceded by a procession through the centre of Aix, headed by the comte de Caraman, the governor of Provence, and the Archbishop of Aix; followed by bishops and nobles who held fiefs; at the rear the third estate and nobles without fiefs. Watching them pass was the son of Portalis, another of Mirabeau's adversaries in his divorce proceedings. He recalled that Mirabeau marched alone, 'somehow between the nobility and the third estate', and from this symbolic position

> his piercing eyes ranged over the crowd, and he seemed to be questioning them with his challenging gaze. There was something imposing about his ugliness, and his face, scarred by smallpox, expressed strength of will and a temperament quick to passion.[9]

The non-fief-holders at the back of the procession could not be ignored; their grouping there with the third estate was also symbolic. Not bound by self-interest to their own caste, their way to political influence lay in supporting the cause of the third estate. Their numbers and the certainty that they would win the popular vote made their tactical elimination a necessity if the nobles with fiefs were to keep their position of absolute power. The latter unearthed a decree of 1620 which stipulated that all nobles seeking a seat in provincial assemblies must possess a fief. On 23 January, in the nobles' assembly, Mirabeau challenged this ruling, pointing out that a large part of the Provençal nobility would be disenfranchised, enjoying neither the rights of the third estate nor the privileges of their own order. His motion was defeated. The privileged orders insisted that the *loi électorale* should be rejected as an interference in the affairs of Provence, and Caraman and Latour, the president of the Aix *parlement*, were given the job of persuading the representatives of the third to agree. At this crucial point, on 30 January, Mirabeau addressed the nobles again.

It was one of the key speeches of his life. In the course of it the son of *l'ami des hommes* emerged in his own colours as a social democrat, committed to universal suffrage, rejecting as divisive the idea of a property qualification:[10]

> When a nation is too populous to meet in a single assembly several are formed, and the members of each assembly give to one the right to vote for them. All representatives are, in consequence, elected; collectively they are the Nation, and all those who are not representatives must have been electors by reason of the fact that they are represented. The first principle in this system is that of personal representation. I know that several nations have limited this principle by according the right of election only to property owners, but it is already a great step towards political inequality.

The word 'nation' exerted a double appeal here because Provence spoke of itself as the nation of Provence. Continuing his speech, he denounced their system of restricting representation in the privileged orders to fief-holding nobles and bishops as illegal, and condemned the discriminatory representation of the third estate: only thirty-five towns had deputies in the assembly, and most of those deputies were associated by self-interest with the privileged orders:

> Three orders are in the *états*, but the nation is not there, if those who call themselves its representatives have not been chosen in free and individual elections, if the representatives of groups equal in importance are not equal numerically and in voting power. When shall we see no distinctions in assemblies of citizens? I ask if it is just that the two orders which are not the nation should prevail over the nation.[11]

His speech ended in uproar, the nobles refusing to put it to the vote. Three days later it appeared in print. By taking the facts out into the marketplace he enraged them still further; he was denounced as an enemy of the peace, and refused permission to answer the charge against him; but on 5 February he replied in print again:

> What have I done which is so culpable? I have desired that my order should be wise enough to give today what will certainly be seized tomorrow; I have desired for them the glory of convoking the assembly of the three orders . . . that is the crime of *the enemy of the peace*! But I am more guilty than is supposed, for I believe that the people who complain always have reason, that their tireless patience waits for the last degree of oppression before deciding on resistance; that they never resist long enough to obtain the reparation of all their grievances. Take care, do not disdain the people who are the producers of everything, who have only to remain immobile to become formidable. The most innocent and most invincible power is that of inertia. That is what I think; punish the enemy of the peace!

He added a final warning to this ultimatum with its early grasp of strike action as a weapon:

> In all countries, in all ages, the aristocrats have pursued the champions of the people implacably, and if, by some combination of fortune, one of the latter has risen in their midst, they have attacked him above all. Thus perished the last of the Gracchi at the hand of the patricians, but, mortally wounded, he threw dust skywards, calling on the avenging gods; and from that dust was born Marius, Marius less great for having exterminated the Cimbri than for having brought down the aristocracy of Rome.[12]

On 8 February he was summoned to the nobles' assembly. He wrote to his secretary, Comps:

> I am going against the advice of all my friends, so high is their opinion of these characters. I always believe that one has to fulfil public duties, and 180 men who are cowardly enough to join together to insult one man lack

sufficient courage to assassinate him. And to tell you the truth, my obsequies might be accompanied by bloodshed![13]

His fate, as he learned on appearing before his fellow nobles, was to take the form of expulsion from their assembly, on the grounds that he was only the tenant of a fief, and not the possessor of one. Delivering their verdict, the marquis de La Fare, first consul of Aix, triumphantly disposed of Marius and his pretensions, unaware that the allegory had a hidden twist: this Marius, who now became their implacable enemy, was the only man who might have saved them from their own impending fate.

Within hours of leaving the nobles' assembly, Mirabeau had written his manifesto, *A la nation provençale*.[14] By comparison with his preceding pamphlets it was soberly expressed, though the phrase '*nation provençale*' was in itself highly political and inflammatory. In it he described himself as 'a gentleman possessing a fief', who hoped he would be regarded as the fellow citizen of all good citizens. The allusion to his birth was not gratuitous; in all his writings and speeches the self-focusing had a purpose, and in this instance he was seeking to kindle a similar sense of personal worth in his readers, as the necessary preliminary to their political education. Guard your privileges, he advised them,

> for privileges, although despicable when weighed against the nation, are useful against ministerial despotism. Guard them, but only so long as France lacks a constitution; that unifying, stable, and lasting constitution, for which it will be in everyone's interest to exchange their local pretensions and rights.[15]

It was still not certain that he would be elected to the Estates General, even by the third estate. Events in Paris in the middle of January threatened to ruin everything. Besides the Cerutti letters he had left another manuscript with the printers before departing for Aix, his confidential letters written while he was in Berlin. Published anonymously, as *Histoire secrète de la cour de Berlin*, they caused a major scandal, all the more so since Prince Henry, whom he had depicted so unflatteringly in them, was visiting Paris at the time. He told Comps:

> You have no idea of the horrors these two works have unleashed here. I am nothing less than a mad dog in whom the Provençaux can place no trust. I answer this by saying 'I'm glad I'm a mad dog, for despotism and privilege will die from my bites'.

Still, he issued a public denial of his authorship, and took a hasty trip to Paris to make his peace with the authorities. Prince Henry, who had most cause to be offended, was highly amused by the book, but the abbé de Périgord, whose name appeared in it, thinly disguised by initials, refused to speak to him again. It was said that he had published the secret letters from Berlin in order to get money to buy a fief, but it was already too late for that.[16] His friends blamed Mme Le Jay. Mirabeau's publisher, Le Jay, was going bankrupt, and his grasping mistress, they said, had persuaded him to save the firm by letting her use his copies of the confidential correspondence. There was also a rumour that while he was in Berlin Mme de Nehra had had an affair with the abbé de Périgord, and that he had influenced her into leaving Mirabeau in the summer of 1788: if true, he had a score to settle.

The Paris *parlement* ordered *Histoire secrète* to be burned, but the *lettre de cachet* which Mirabeau feared on account of the Cerutti letters did not materialise. The situation in Provence had completely changed in his absence, for Necker had moved to enforce the *loi électorale*: the elections in Provence were to be by a freely elected convocation of the three orders in each *sénéchaussée*. For Mirabeau all the obstacles to his election had miraculously vanished. He returned to Provence in March, already the people's hero. He reported to Comps that at Lambesc, five leagues from Aix, his carriage was engulfed by villagers bearing branches of laurel and shouting '*Vive le comte de Mirabeau, vive le père de la patrie*', while men unharnessed the horses and took their places for the remainder of the journey. This joyful abasement filled him with emotion and sadness: 'I can understand how men become slaves, tyranny grows from gratitude.' Headed by drums and galoubets, the three-holed flutes of Provence, the procession reached Aix at nightfall. Outside his lodging the crowd sang and cheered in the light of torches; he addressed them from the balcony, advising them that if they hated oppression as much as they loved their friends they would never be oppressed. He could have said anything and they would still have hung on his words; in fact, the theme he chose had a familiar ring, he had made the same speech before, but then it had been Batavians instead of Aixois who heard his undemagogic warning:

> If some extraordinary citizen renders you important services, even if he saves you from slavery, respect his character, admire him, but, above all, fear his talents. Misfortune attends grateful people. They yield all their rights to him who has restored a single one of their rights to them. They forget their own chains. By their gratitude they corrupt a great man whom they would have honoured by their ingratitude.[17]

Among those who heard the jubilant noise in the place des Prêcheurs that night was Emilie de Mirabeau, as easily carried away by fashionable crazes as ever, who now found that she had married a hero. 'Mme la comtesse longs to return to the arms of her dear and glorious husband despite the opposition of her family', Mirabeau told his sister. A reconciliation would also have delighted the townsfolk of Aix, but sentimentality had never influenced his judgement in the past and would not now, when his future hung in the balance. He trusted nothing to luck. For this reason, though almost certain of election at Aix, he also offered himself to Marseille, and published a manifesto entitled *Lettre d'un citoyen de Marseille sur M. de Mirabeau et l'abbé Raynal*, in which, under cover of praising Raynal, celebrated for his opposition to tyranny, he lauded a still greater defender of liberty, whose works would prove as enduring as bronze: 'Provence was enslaved; the comte de Mirabeau arrives and restores her freedom . . . the most eloquent man of the century . . . his courage astonishes as much as his talents . . . no human power can make him abandon a principle.'[18]

Overstated? Mirabeau knew his Provençaux. On 18 March, when he rode into Marseille to the hosannas of the citizens, he was met by civic dignitaries and saw flags flying in his honour from every masthead in the harbour.

> Imagine, 120,000 people in the streets of Marseille, an entire industrial city brought to a standstill for the day; the carriage of the man who only wished for equality covered with branches of palm, laurel, and olive; the people kissing its wheels, women offering him their infants to kiss . . .[19]

The next day saw the same scenes as he was escorted back to Aix by 300 carriages and 500 of the 'most distinguished young men'.

Afterwards the electors of Marseille voted unanimously in favour of a proposal that they should bear eternal hatred towards the enemies of their *héros bourgeois*.[20] The language of the barricades was heard more and more in Provence as the primary elections approached, in which every citizen possessing the franchise could take part. Inevitably the most vocal and radical candidates would win the votes in a province stricken by famine, where prices were soaring, and no proper organisation of food supplies existed. More than forty riots occurred between 15 March and 15 April; at Riez and Toulon the episcopal palaces were attacked, and at Manosque the peasants nearly killed the Bishop of Sisteron, who was one of Mirabeau's bitterest opponents. On 23 March, the eve of the election, a mob invaded the town hall of Marseille, demanding that the price of bread and meat should be lowered at once. The counsellors agreed and news to this effect was circulated in an attempt to avert further violence. The governor of Provence, Caraman, arrived from Aix and addressed the rioters, threatening that order would be restored by force if necessary, but as soon as he left rioting recommenced and the citizens sent an urgent message to Mirabeau to come to their assistance.

With Caraman's permission he set off at once, and arrived to find the city in an ugly mood. Troublemakers had been inciting fresh riots, and groups of men – some of the 500 who had attended his royal progress – had formed themselves into companies of vigilantes. He welcomed their goodwill but knew that it would take more than well-spoken amateurs to control a city as tough as this one. Accordingly, he appealed to the dockers, and within hours had organised a civil militia. There were two infantry regiments and one of cavalry in the area, but troops had not been seen inside Marseille in living memory, and their introduction, as he pointed out to Caraman, would only have inflamed the situation. His body of citizen soldiers was the first of its kind in France. He later justly claimed in the National Assembly that he had had the honour of anticipating the establishment of a national militia.

The prevention of violence was the first essential, the removal of causes of discontent the next. The following day the *Avis de Mirabeau au peuple de Marseille* was distributed throughout the city; it explained in simple terms the causes of the situation and what had to be done to resolve it. Better than any of his speeches, this circular enables the reader to divine what it was that gave him his particular hold over his audiences. Here is neither a rhetorician nor a seigneur exerting his authority – the particle was deliberately omitted from his name in the heading; instead it is the voice of the local *curé*, sensible and patient, reassuring his flock:

> My good friends, I have come to tell you what I think about what has been happening these three days in your proud city. Listen to me; I only want to be of use to you, and I do not want to deceive you. Every one of you desires only what is good because you are all honest men, but individually you do not know what needs to be done. Often one makes mistakes, even about one's own interest. Let us first consider bread. Two things are needed for bread; first, that there should be some, and then that it should not cost too much.

And he continued in the same vein, assuring them that there was enough grain in the city at that moment to last three months. It came from many parts of the world; sometimes, therefore, it would be delayed, or it would cost more if there were wars going on. It was not just the good people of Marseille who had to pay more when that happened, but everyone else in France as well, and their good king in Paris would do his best to help all his children.

The first question an aggrieved peasant would ask after everything had been explained would still be why bread cost so much, and so he continued:

> You ask again why bread costs three and a half sous: I will tell you why. Marseille, like all other towns, pays something towards the expenses of the kingdom and for the maintenance of our good king. The money comes partly from here, partly from there. In the villages they pay the *taille*; in the big towns the *taille* is not sufficient. Up till now it has been supplemented by a tax on meat and bread. The tax on bread is called the *piquet*; it amounts to six livres on each charge,[21] and that is why bread costs three and a half sous.

These ways of covering expenses are certainly not the best; it will all be changed, but we know that changes cannot all be made in a day.

However, as corn is already very dear and everyone must be prepared to put up with bad times, it seems reasonable to me that for the present one should not pay more than thirty-four deniers for a pound of bread, not counting tax; and be sure, my good friends, this is the best that can be done.

I hope, therefore, that you will tell everyone that this price is fair and necessary. Each of you will stay calm in order that others should be as well, and your example will bring peace everywhere.[22]

His homily had a decisive effect. Three days later, with the city tranquil again, he could feel that he had acquitted himself in line with family tradition, and that Jean Riqueti, who had quelled the uprising at the time of the League, would have been pleased with his performance.[23] But while he was pacifying the Marseillais, riots were breaking out at Aix, where on 25 March citizens going to vote for their delegates to the assembly found the roads blocked by crowds of the un-enfranchised, calling for prices to be lowered and the *piquet* abolished. Watching the scene from the steps of the town hall was the first consul, La Fare; witnesses said that he insulted a woman who clutched at him demanding bread, that he aimed a gun at the crowd and fled indoors under a hail of stones. Troops arrived who fired into the crowd; several people were shot, and the cry went up: 'If Mirabeau were here we would get justice and not be killed'. In vain La Fare ordered bread prices to be lowered. As the violence continued the authorities, panicking, unlocked the municipal grain stores, which were then sacked by the rioters.

At this point Caraman sent for Mirabeau. The disturbances at Marseille had barely been brought under control, and he could not leave until he had been to every district of the city to check that the civil guards were up to strength. He reached Aix at three in the morning. The rioters, who had been firing shops, had finally dispersed, and Caraman, not expecting him to arrive before six, had gone to bed. Leaving him to sleep, Mirabeau went off to round up a group of responsible citizens to act as peace officers. The day about to dawn was market day, and there was a rumour that the rioters intended to stage an insurrection, helped by the presence of bigger crowds. With only a few hours to go he organised preparations, posting a strong guard at the town gates, meeting the leading agitators to hear their views, forming vigilante patrols. His popularity made his task easier. At half past five he woke Caraman with the news that the troops assembled in the town would not be needed, and by eight they had been withdrawn, grain was back in circulation, and the citizens of Aix were going about their business as on any normal market day. Columns of peasants flocking in to fight alongside the townsfolk were persuaded by Mirabeau to return to their villages. He wrote to a friend at Marseille:

But do you know what happened then? Hardly was calm restored when the nobles, who hadn't been seen for thirty-six hours, reappeared armed and arrogant, crying: 'It is M. de Mirabeau who has created all the trouble!' Strange logic, that of hatred. But it is nothing to the vengeance they are preparing to take. They will demand hangings for this little performance. That's the human heart for you. Human nature fills me with horror.[24]

The outcome of the election was a foregone conclusion, despite all the efforts of the nobility to pin the blame for the riots on Mirabeau. He won 290 votes out of a total of 344.[25] He was still savouring his success when he learned that he had been elected at Marseille as well. It was an honour he had to decline, though assuring that city of his constant support, and, indeed, in the National Assembly the affairs of Marseille prompted some of his most vigorous speeches. But there was no doubt as to which place he wanted to represent: his triumph at Aix symbolised too much for him to relinquish it.

The nobles there were infuriated by his double victory. Unable to do anything about his election at Aix, they tried to annul that at Marseille by propagating the rumour that he had manoeuvred it by dishonest means: Peuchet and other historians stated this as a fact after his death, and Etienne Dumont, supposedly his friend, said that he accepted the Aix nomination because he knew that that at Marseille was invalid. Alexandre de Lameth, an open enemy, recounted a conversation with Duport and Barnave in which they told him that Mirabeau had arranged for a partisan of his to stand behind a doubtful election speaker, with instructions to shoot him if he took the wrong line.[26] According to another story he set himself up as a shopkeeper in Marseille prior to the election, in order to win the popular vote. Despite its absurdity it was repeated by all his early biographers, one of whom asserted that he bought the shop with 300,000 francs paid to him by Brienne in return for his promise not to publish *La Monarchie prussienne*: actually Brienne resigned months before it appeared, and this tale was one of the many invented by those who wanted to destroy him by labelling him as venal. Of all the stories circulated by his enemies the shopkeeper one was the most malicious, designed to let him know that his fellow nobles still remembered the merchant origins of the Mirabeaus, but it failed entirely in its object of making him look ridiculous to the citizens of Marseille. Shortly after his election he paid them a farewell visit and received the freedom of the city. His return to Aix was a repeat of the first triumphant procession, with hundreds of horsemen escorting his carriage; it was late at night and his valet, Legrain, recalled that the torches they carried lit up the countryside, making it as bright as day, and that when they reached Aix the whole town was waiting to greet them. Noisy crowds remained outside his lodging, making it impossible for him either to sleep or to have food brought in. He planned to leave unnoticed for Paris in the middle of the night, but when the post horses were brought round his adorers were waiting, and, with pipes and tabors playing, they followed him for miles. Later, as his carriage rolled northwards, at every village along the way, to the border of Provence and beyond it into Dauphiné, every time he stopped to change horses he was mobbed by excited crowds. He might be the representative for Aix; to them he was 'the Friend of the People', the name given to him by the third estate of Mirabeau in their *cahier*: he represented them all.

## NOTES

1. Mirabeau dedicated it to the *philosophe patriote*, with a rather wistful explanation: 'You may have desired to have a son more worthy of you; I have tried to be so by this undertaking to which I have devoted my feeble talent'. Writing to his disciple, the marquis de Longo, on 15 December 1788, the marquis de Mirabeau described the work as a masterpiece, and his son as 'the rarest man of his century, and perhaps one of the rarest ever produced by nature' (*Mémoires biographiques*, VI, 138). *La Monarchie prussienne* made amends for Mirabeau's transgression seven months earlier when a new edition of *Lettre remise à Frédéric-Guillaume II* appeared, to which had been added *Conseils à un jeune prince qui sent la nécessité de refaire son éducation*: an adaptation of a work by the marquis de Mirabeau, made without his permission.
2. Letter to the bailli, October 1788, cited by Vallentin (1948), *Mirabeau*, 282.
3. *Mémoires biographiques*, VII, 206n. Letter of 24 November 1788.
4. Ibid., VII, 204.
5. Letter of 28 December 1788. *Correspondance entre Mirabeau et La Marck*, I, 237.
6. Generally known as the *Lettres à Cerutti*. Joseph-Antoine-Joachim Cerutti (1758–92), who protested to the press that the correspondence was spurious, was a former Jesuit, editor of a journal *La feuille villageoise*. He became a member of the Legislative Assembly in 1791.
7. *Lettres à Cerutti*, 9.
8. *Mémoires biographiques*, VII, 241. Letter to Mme du Saillant, 20 January 1789.
9. Portalis (1848).
10. See Jaurès (1901–08: I, 406) 'Although brought up by his father in the system of the Physiocrats, he set no store by landed property, nor even by property in general as the measure of all social value. Going far beyond Turgot and even Condorcet, who, in their projects on municipal and provincial assemblies, only gave the right to vote to property owners, he held for universal suffrage.'
11. *Discours sur la représentation illégale . . .* (1789, 11).
12. *Réponse aux protestations . . .* (1789, 12–17). Mirabeau used the parable of Marius several times in the course of his career. Mont Sainte-Victoire near Aix was the site of Marius's battle with the Cimbri; it was this detail, taken in conjunction with Marius's later achievements as consul, that gave his words their particular bite.

Lucas de Montigny, in his role of expurgator, thought fit to omit from his quoted version of this speech the lines which gave the greatest offence: 'How could they halt him in his civic course, he who was the first Frenchman to express his opinions aloud on national affairs, at a time when circumstances were less urgent and the task more perilous! No, outrages will not affect my determination. I have been, I am, I shall be until I die the defender of public freedom and the constitution. Woe to the privileged orders; better to be one of the people than one of the nobles, for privileges are doomed but the people are eternal.'

13. *Mémoires biographiques*, VII, 265. Letter of 9 February 1789. Comps was the son of an old but impoverished Provençal family, who became Mirabeau's secretary in 1788. He tried to commit suicide when Mirabeau died but survived. After the Revolution he joined the diplomatic corps, was dismissed in 1798, and then worked for the Dutch patriot and Grand Pensioner, Schimmel-Penninck.

14. This was his third pamphlet in eleven days. His printers, Gibelin and Emeric David, who risked arrest by publishing them, deserve their own small place in the history of free speech.

15. *A la nation provençale*, 34.

16. The acquisition of a fief had to be registered within a certain period or the transaction became null and void. Time was already running short when Mirabeau tried to borrow money from Lauzun in November for the Dauphiné fief. At the time he was still waiting to be paid for *La Monarchie prussienne*, and also for *Sur la liberté de la presse*, based on Milton's *Areopagitica*, which was published in December.

17. *Adresse aux Bataves*, 26. (See also note 25, Chapter 5.)

18. G.-T.-F. Raynal (1713–96), political writer and contributor to the *Encyclopédie*. His most influential work, *Histoire philosophique et politique des établissements et du commerce des Européens dans les deux Indes*, was condemned as a threat to the sovereign authority and burned in 1781: 'the last notable book', said Carlyle, 'that had such fire-beatitude'.

19. *Lettre de M. le comte de Caraman, commandant en Provence, à M. le comte de Mirabeau et la réponse*, published 30 March 1789. See Montigny VII, 282.

20. Whilst he was in Marseille Mirabeau had attended a performance of *Le Bourgeois Gentilhomme*, at which he had been hailed as 'le gentilhomme bourgeois'.

21. A charge of corn weighed 245 lb.

22. *Avis de Mirabeau au peuple de Marseille*, 25 March 1789. See Montigny VII, 301.

23. Jean Riqueti's actions were the subject of a play entitled *Liberté, ou Marseille sauvé*, by a Provençal dramatist named Le Blanc, which was staged in Paris two months after Mirabeau restored order to Marseille.

24. Letter of 27 March 1789 to Bremond-Julien.

25. The two representatives of the nobility elected at Aix were Antoine-Balthazar-Joseph d'André de Bellevue (1759–1825), a non-fief-holder and counsellor in the Aix *parlement*, and his cousin, Louis de Clapiers-Collonges. The fief-holding nobles refused to take part in the reformed election process; however, they elected their own representatives – this illegal deputation was turned away from the Estates General. The undying resentment of the Provençal nobility was summed up in the attitude of Mirabeau's old adversary, Portalis, invited to stand at Toulon, who refused to represent any part of Provence because 'a *sénéchaussée* there has so misunderstood its interests as to elect the comte de Mirabeau'. (Letter cited by Guibal, 1889.)

26. Lameth (1828–29: I, 181).

# 7

## The National Assembly

### (May-June 1789)

In Provence it was the people, far removed from the circles of social and political power, who idolised him. In Paris it was the people again who took him to their hearts with a warmth they would show to none of the other revolutionary figures. Our little mother Mirabeau, the market women called him. He, it was remembered, had defended the water carriers of Paris when their livelihood was threatened by the projects of the Compagnie des Eaux de Paris. He was seen as the one who would side with the powerless against the powerful, and who was not afraid to speak out. The man in the crowd was more inclined to pin his hopes for a better future on an actual champion than on the prospectuses of political theorists. As Mirabeau would remind the Assembly, the nation was interested in action, not metaphysics; and the devotion which he inspired until the end of his life was the measure of the general public's continuing image of him as the leader who acted as he spoke, and who understood how people lived. His street popularity had little to do with politics, certainly not with the high politics of the Assembly: a reason why the sustained political attacks on him by the press and by public orators, which influenced the politically minded, failed to touch it.

In sharp contrast to Mirabeau's popularity outside the Assembly was the dislike and suspicion with which he was viewed from the start by so many of his Assembly colleagues. Inevitably, his birth and much publicised activities, and the idolatry he inspired in Provence, alienated a number of deputies, who felt that such a sensational character would not share their own deep seriousness about the Assembly's work, and would also expect to monopolise the proceedings. There were other sources of resentment: his polemical writings, which offended supporters of the government; his attacks on his own order in Provence, which many besides the nobility saw as breaking the code of decent behaviour; his conscious intellectual superiority. All reasons for envy or indignation or coldness. Hence the tone of much of the commentary by his contemporaries on his politics and character. That said, there is one accusation which they made against him which cannot be ignored. His admirer, Victor Hugo, might have been thinking of him when he wrote in *Les Misérables* that what is said about men often has as much influence on their lives, and especially on their destinies, as what they do. In Mirabeau's case it was the charge of venality which cast a shadow over his career, robbing him of trust and consequently of political allies at crucial moments, creating a weapon for anyone to turn against him, making it easier to devalue and ignore his ideas. 'Venal' would become the stock adjective used by historians to describe him. But to what extent was the charge of venality justified?

The dictionary definition is precise and blunt: 'venal' means for sale, to be bought or bought over, corruptly mercenary. It was the word chosen by the marquis, who criticised his son's 'venal pen' when referring to the books which Mirabeau wrote in 1785 – at the invitation of the Controller-General Calonne – against the Caisse d'Escompte and the Banque de Saint-Charles, as part of a campaign to halt the speculation which was destabilising the economy (see above, Chapter 5). He might have been expected to approve of these works; after all, the Physiocrats condemned stock market speculation as a sterile use of money. But the public storm over the books was highly distasteful to him, as were his son's links with figures in the financial world like Clavière, the abbé de Périgord and Calonne himself. It made no difference that he received no personal payment from Calonne for the books, and was writing on a subject he felt deeply about – to his father his involvement in any politically motivated enterprise was faintly sordid, venal. At the time he reported that his son was 'now in the hands of the speculators', which suggests that he regarded him as being more gullible than wicked, and Calonne and his assistants as the real villains.

Mirabeau continued his exposure of speculation in his book on the Compagnie des Eaux de Paris. This time the Controller-General had not invited him to write. It led to the row with Calonne, who was himself speculating in the Compagnie's shares; and this in turn prompted him to compose the frank letter on the minister's conduct which he left with Calonne's adviser, Dupont, before fleeing to Germany at the end of 1785. For Calonne the fear was not so much that he would publish the letter but that further *mémoires* similar to the Eaux de Paris book might appear. The appointment as secret correspondent in Berlin, which followed in May 1786, was intended to prevent that happening. Mirabeau's letter to his father, in which he explained the salary arrangements that went with the Berlin job, has already been quoted (page 82). Significantly, in it he says that his salary 'was the start of the rumour that M. de Calonne was paying me'. The image of the venal Mirabeau was manufactured in the office of the Controller-General. Outside the circle of Calonne, Vergennes, Dupont, Lauzun, and Périgord, his real purpose in Berlin was not known at the time; nor, therefore, the reason for his salary, the payment of which soon leaked out. His hands were tied. He could not break the seal of secrecy about his job. At the same time, Calonne was free to explain the salary payments in any way which suited him. The minister could hardly announce that it was his own activities which had made him decide to get rid of Mirabeau by sending him abroad on a fabricated mission. Instead he depicted him as a calculating scrounger, safe in the knowledge that he would be backed up by Lauzun and Périgord, his fellow speculators. Even the principled Dupont would raise no objections since it was all important to guard against any damage to Calonne's image in the run-up to the Assembly of Notables. He could persuade himself that removing Mirabeau to Berlin was in the national interest.

And so the assumption grew that Mirabeau had been paid to neutralise him; indeed, that he had demanded money in return for withholding further *mémoires*. If he had been wealthy enough to accept the Berlin job without any salary the suggestion of venality could not have been made. It was his acceptance of that salary for work not publicly identified that gave Calonne his opportunity to discredit him, and in doing so to render him unimportant as a critic of the government. He refused to take him seriously. Early in 1787, when Périgord showed him the text of the *Dénonciation de l'agiotage*, Calonne flippantly affected to believe that he had only to bribe the author for the book to be withheld: 'It can all be settled with money'. The publication of the *Dénonciation* proved otherwise.

Once in circulation, however, the rumour of Mirabeau's venality all too easily became an assumption. It made useful propaganda in government and Court circles opposed to reforms and the Revolution, where he was feared as a voice of destruction. Already in 1787 he had made plain his aims for the future, demanding in his *Analyses des papiers anglais* the liberalisation of the regime and the control of power by the nation. Reactionaries had no compunction about denigrating such a man in order to turn opinion against him. There was also the prejudice harboured by the nobility against a nobleman who demeaned himself by working for his living, especially in the disreputable profession of journalism – a polemical journalist. This was one of the reasons why Mirabeau was looked at askance by his fellow nobles and not, say, the abbé de Périgord, the future Talleyrand, whose actions were unprincipled but who never made the mistake of publishing his opinions.

The charge of venality, explicit or implicit, brought against him before the Revolution could not be sustained. But an image had been created. During the Revolution the same charge would crop up again, amid rumours that he was advising the king, and accusations that he was sold to the Court and secretly helping to destroy the Revolution. A venal reputation, the weapon first used against him by the government, would be used again and with lasting effect by the political left; and statements in his defence by friends and political colleagues only appeared after his death. 'Those who believe that he suffered himself to be bribed to do what his own heart and judgement condemned . . . do him, in my opinion, very great injustice', wrote Samuel Romilly after hearing him slandered at London dinner tables.[1] La Fayette, who worked as hard as anyone to make the charge of venality stick, withdrew it in his old age, though his wording indicates his reluctance to admit that his original opinion was wrong: 'Mirabeau was not inaccessible to money; but for no sum would he have upheld views which destroyed liberty and dishonoured himself.'[2]

At the end of April 1789, with the deputies already gathering in Paris, the fate of the Estates General still hung in the balance.

In the decree announcing the opening date, Louis XVI had declared his readiness to accept the will of the people, and had invited them 'to reinstate the nation in the complete exercise of all the rights belonging to it'. The conciliatory tone was an illusion. Acceptance did not imply welcome. And the rights that belonged to the nation were left undefined, suggesting a reluctance to be committed. The vagueness of language was a refuge: if the general rejoicing over the Estates General persuaded Louis that he had made a wise decision, the warnings of his advisers, civil unrest, and radical doctrines put out by the press all helped to undermine his resolution. From the moment the Estates General was announced the Court had been trying to abort it and intriguing to replace Necker and his liberal colleagues with a right-wing ministry. Necker's failure to pronounce on whether voting would be by head or by order was the result of this Court pressure; had he insisted on voting by head his own would certainly have fallen.

During April the witch hunt against the Director-General grew more frenzied, fed by evidence of national determination to sweep away the old world of privileges, which was revealed daily in the *cahiers* of local grievances that the arriving deputies brought with them. Not only the *cahiers* of the third estate but many of the nobility's carried the same message: abolition of all distinctions, constitutional liberty, refusal of all subsidies until the constitution was completed. A rival sovereign will had loomed into view, threatening the foundations of the monarchy itself, and Necker was held responsible. On 27 April the marquis de Ferrières wrote:

> You cannot imagine the frightful outburst unleashed by the privileged, the financiers, the *parlements*, against Necker. His enemies are redoubling their furious efforts to oust him before the opening of the Estates General. They say the comte d'Artois has spoken most forcibly to the king, telling him that his crown, even his life, are in danger, that Necker is a second Cromwell.[3]

Artois also called him a fornicating foreign bastard. Usually impassive, Necker was shaken by the hostility and only his sense of duty prevented him from resigning. The cabals working against him managed to get the opening date of the Estates General postponed, but ministerial authority prevailed and a new date, 5 May, was announced; a temporary victory for the Director-General, and for Louis the lasting fear that his mentors might be right, that he had just taken the step which would carry them all into the abyss.

On 2 May the king received the deputies of the three orders separately at Versailles. Despite Necker's advice in his *Rapport au roi* that tribal marks which could only offend and humiliate the third estate should be abandoned, strict rules had been issued regarding costume which underlined the determination of the privileged orders to maintain symbolic distinctions: embroidered coats, gold-bordered cloaks, and plumed hats in the style of Henri IV for the nobility, and for the third plain black capes, coats, and knee-breeches. The deputies of the third, who had been ordered in their *cahiers* to concede no distinctions, were consequently in a belligerent mood from the very beginning. On Sunday 4 May, the king and queen and all the deputies walked in procession to the church of Saint-Louis, where the liberal Bishop of Nancy preached a sermon on the sufferings of the poor: fighting broke out in the church as members of the third estate tried to occupy seats which had been reserved for the nobles, and they punctuated the sermon with loud applause. 'Never', said Mirabeau in disgust, 'has so great an occasion been so completely ruined.'[4]

The procession brought thousands of sightseers out from Paris; they lined the route in the spring sunshine and watched with more curiosity than enthusiasm as it went by. Few of the deputies of the third estate, walking past in a sombre phalanx, were known outside their own regions – Mounier, the hero of Dauphiné, was an exception, as was Mirabeau, identified by his immense head of hair and air of rough-hewn strength, 'strength appropriate to a tribune of the people', wrote Necker's daughter[5] – and the majority of them had served no kind of apprenticeship to public affairs. They included eighteen mayors and intendants, experienced in local administration, that is, *ancien régime* administration, sixteen doctors, nearly 200 merchants and landowners, present because they exerted the most influence in their home towns, sixty-two magistrates, 152 lawyers. The preponderance of lawyers, mostly young, all bent on stunning their colleagues with their oratorical powers, was to set the tone of the National Assembly's proceedings. Some deputies had been elected for their personal distinction: Dupont, elected at Nemours; Lanjuinais, the professor of law, at Rennes; the intendant Malouet, at Riom; Rabaut de Saint-Etienne, the champion of the Protestants, at Nîmes. Others, still lost in the anonymous mass, would eventually emerge to set their mark on the Revolution: there was Robespierre, the deputy for Arras, Pétion from Chartres, Barère from Toulouse, Le Chapelier from Nantes, Barnave from Grenoble. The largest delegation, twenty strong, was that of Paris, but, the elections in the capital still being incomplete, the Paris deputies were not present at the opening. Headed by Bailly, the academician and writer on astronomy, they included the lawyers, Camus and Tronchet; Dr Guillotin, the future inventor of a machine for painless killing; and Sieyès, celebrated for his pamphlet, *Qu'est-ce que le Tiers Etat?*, who nearly failed to get into the Estates General, having been rejected by his own order, the clergy.

Mirabeau's political support was already being solicited. However, he did not want to be identified with any particular group or faction, not caring for the premature certainties and narrow vision that such bandings together proclaimed. He realised that the third estate would never be able to act effectively in the Assembly while its voice was divided. The great advantage of the first two orders lay in their unity as defenders of the established state; the third would need to be backed by the full force of public opinion if it were not to be dismissed as irresponsible and dangerous. The most powerful moulder of opinion being the press, he decided to take direct action, and the opening of the Estates General saw the appearance of a new periodical, the *Journal des Etats-Généraux*. The first issue was dated 2 and 4 May. The influence exerted by the man who thus became the public voice of the third estate was a good reason in itself for turning editor, but there was also a fundamental principle involved: the freedom of the press, though approved in theory, did not exist for political periodicals other than those licensed by the government. The alternative to waiting for the censorship laws to be changed was to challenge them and see what happened.

On 5 May the king and Necker addressed the Estates General. In the morning the deputies filed into the Salle des Menus Plaisirs, watched by thousands of spectators in the galleries. The deputies of the third estate were the last to enter, having been kept waiting for hours before being let in by a side door, the tradesmen's entrance in effect. The ceremonial of 1614 had required the spokesman for the third estate to address the king on his knees, but to avoid trouble it was decided he should not speak at all. The highlight was Necker's report on the finances. He told them that when he resumed office the previous August only 250,000 francs had remained in the treasury; he had organised loans and restored confidence: public funds had risen an unprecedented 30 per cent in one morning; and though there was still a deficit of 56 million livres it could be covered by increases in taxation. They were there to restore the finances, but also to achieve a constitution which would recognise, besides the royal power, the power of the French people, and guarantee their liberties under the king's authority. There was no suggestion in his three-hour speech that taxation required consensus, no mention of the crucial questions of whether the orders would sit together or separately, or whether voting would be by head or by order. In the second issue of his journal Mirabeau poured all his scorn on the idol of France, whose speech had shown him to possess neither 'the resourcefulness of a statesman, nor even the expediency of a financier', and who thought he could be 'not only the moderator but the legislator of France'.[6]

'Thanks to the blows Mirabeau rains on him, the man and the speech have been torn to pieces in Paris', wrote the writer Marmontel, a friend of Necker's. The Director-General reacted by having the *Journal des Etats-Généraux* banned, which was possibly just what Mirabeau wanted him to do, foreseeing the outcry it would cause. In Paris the electors of the third estate passed a nearly unanimous vote of censure on the suppression. Only Marmontel objected, and forfeited his chance of being elected as one of the Paris deputies. In Versailles the deputies already elected gazed at the cause of the storm with new respect. The deputy for hell, as he was called in Neckerite papers, got round the proscription of his journal by reissuing it under a new name as *Lettres du comte de Mirabeau à ses commettans* – no one could deny a deputy his right to correspond with his constituents. In his first editorial he adopted the tactic which he was to follow consistently, of differentiating between the king and his ministers, between his good intentions and the despotic actions of those who served him:

> It is fortunate that these proscriptions, which the circumstances render yet more criminal, cannot be imputed to the monarch. No one today is unaware that the decrees of the Council are eternal falsifications to which the ministers

do not hesitate to put the king's name. Twenty-five million votes demand the liberty of the press. The nation and the king unanimously seek the collaboration of all enlightened men. And at this moment a ministry claiming to be popular has the effrontery to place our thoughts under seal.[7]

Nine days later the Keeper of the Seals announced that journalists could report what went on in the Estates General, provided they abstained from comment. Mirabeau had scored. Necker, smarting at being described as 'a good sort of man unjustly accused of possessing talent and depth of thought', had the added annoyance of hearing his own belief in the natural alliance of the king and the people being promoted by his opponent. Mirabeau wrote piously:

> Let us hope that the Minister for Finance will understand that the time for manoeuvres has passed, that it is impossible to resist the current of public opinion . . . that the cabals will perish if he is faithful to principles and will soon beat him if he abandons them.[8]

There was a bitter truth in these words. By trying to placate all parties Necker had created general discontent. The nobility, bored with the whole business of the Estates General, said that it need never have been convoked since the minister was apparently managing the finances so well, and the third estate, at his feet a week before, were already listening like fickle sheep to a new leader.

In certain quarters Mirabeau's election to the Estates General had a special significance. To the Genevois exiles he had met in Neuchâtel in 1782 it seemed that his promise to them about liberating Geneva would soon be fulfilled. Their leader, Duroveray, was already in Paris when he arrived from Provence, having come to see Necker in connection with an amnesty which the General Council of Geneva had just offered to the exiles of 1782, apart from himself. He wanted Necker to intervene, but the Director-General had attracted enough suspicion already without taking up the cause of a republican activist, who was also rumoured to be a spy in the pay of the British government. Mirabeau's arrival at this point gave Duroveray new hope, and he lost no time in seeking him out, seeing him as the stepping-stone to the fruition of his political ambitions.

Duroveray had with him his acolyte and fellow countryman, Etienne Dumont.[9] The previous year, meeting Mirabeau for the first time during a visit to France with Samuel Romilly, Dumont had been captivated by his warmth and interest. Twelve months later Mirabeau showed him the same genuine interest, but Duroveray's influence had now put Dumont on the defensive: 'It was a positive *ranz des vaches*', he wrote bitterly in his *Souvenirs* recalling that taurine advance upon his virgin personality, which he was convinced had been a calculated manoeuvre. Had Mirabeau been as calculating in his friendships as Dumont alleged he might have been more cautious about accepting the two Genevois, whose overtures at the start of his public life were nothing if not calculated. In the coming months it was this connection, more than anything else, which was held against him both by his enemies and his friends.

Mirabeau's English friends had also heard of his metamorphosis into the deputy for Aix. One member of that English circle, who knew him only through a one-sided correspondence, was the jurist, Jeremy Bentham. The convocation of the Estates General, and the promise of an exciting constitutional experiment which could hold lessons for the whole of Europe, distracted Bentham completely from his own work; his studies on the reshaping of the legal system in line with his Principle of Utility were laid aside as he considered what advice he could offer on the problems which would beset an assembly last in operation in 1614. The frustration he had experienced in making converts to his ideas would soon be over, it seemed, if he could gain for himself the distinction of having contributed by his advice to the reconstruction of France. Romilly, his fellow jurist, suggested that he should ask Mirabeau to find a French publisher for his writings. (Bentham's *Defence of Usury* had just appeared, and Mirabeau had told Romilly that he wanted to translate it; hence, probably, Romilly's choice of him as agent.[10]) Bentham shared Romilly's high opinion of Mirabeau as a political writer; accordingly in September 1788 he sent him the first of a projected series of papers on French affairs, but had no reply, Mirabeau at the time being preoccupied with his election to the Estates General. In February 1789 Bentham sent the unfinished sixth essay of his *Political Tactics* to the abbé Morellet, asking him to get it published and also to retrieve the paper he had sent to Mirabeau. Morellet was not very helpful: publishers were inundated with works on the Estates General, and he could have nothing to do with Mirabeau 'because he is such a violent enemy of M. Necker and has just offered him so violent an indignity' – a reference to the Cerutti letters. Undiscouraged, Bentham forwarded the rest of his sixth essay on *Political Tactics* and his *Introduction to the Principles of Morals and Legislation*. It seems that, despite his opinion of Mirabeau, Morellet passed on to him all these writings, for in a letter to Bentham, probably written in May, Dumont reported that Mirabeau was interested in all his works on French affairs which he already possessed, and that he was eager to see the next instalments as soon as they were completed.

Bentham's hopes that through Mirabeau, whom he called 'my Translator and Preserver', he might make his voice heard in France, were doomed to disappointment. Six of his principles of debating from the *Political Tactics* appeared in an early issue of Mirabeau's journal, but three articles on finance, which he sent to him the following October, were never printed. But while he failed in his attempts to exercise a direct influence on the organisation of the Estates General, his influence on Mirabeau may be seen in Mirabeau's own attempts to guide the Assembly's thinking on various matters – as when he tried to get the procedural rules of the House of Commons accepted by the Assembly, and again when he argued against giving priority to the drawing up of an American-style Declaration of Rights: Bentham thought that all the verbalism about natural rights was irrelevant, since the laws which were supposed to defend them could always be broken, and in France those laws had yet to be written when the deputies decided that a Declaration of Rights took precedence over everything else. Mirabeau's debt to Bentham is also apparent in his insistence that the Assembly should make regular reports to the electorate – Bentham held that political representatives should always be answerable to their constituents. But as for the closer collaboration which Bentham hoped for, 'the honour of having M. de Mirabeau for my editor', it came to nothing. The position of editor to Bentham would eventually be claimed by Dumont. Because of this, and because he worked in Mirabeau's *atelier* from June 1789 to January 1790, it is natural to suppose that Dumont could have been instrumental in bringing Bentham's ideas to Mirabeau's knowledge. In reality Mirabeau owed nothing to him in this respect. And, though corresponding with Bentham from 1789, Dumont did not start working on his manuscripts until 1793, after Mirabeau's death.[11] Such works of Bentham's as Mirabeau studied were in his possession before he met Dumont. Slight though his influence may have been, however, the inventor of Utilitarianism has to be included among the political philosophers who contributed to Mirabeau's understanding of his subject.

On 6 May the deputies of the third estate gathered in the Salle des Menus Plaisirs which had been assigned to them; the nobles and clergy went to their own meeting places. But while the first two orders proceeded to verify their mandates and form committees, the third sat tight and waited for the others to join them. Even the preliminary task of verifying mandates was postponed on the ground that conducting any business by themselves would constitute acceptance of the separation of the three orders. A motion by La Fayette in the nobles' assembly that the three orders should verify their mandates together was massively defeated, but the clergy rejected a similar motion by a narrower margin, and this indication of support by its humbler members encouraged the third to resist all pressure. The daily scenes in the Salle des Menus Plaisirs were emotional and noisy, with more than 500 deputies clamouring for precedence. Mirabeau tried to get the seats rearranged as in an amphitheatre, saying that if they only heard the loudest voices they would miss the best brains, but the same people who resented his ascendancy thought that this would enable him to rivet attention on himself even more commandingly; he had already imposed the idea of passive resistance to separate verification upon the third and there was a movement to reduce his influence. Duquesnoy, deputy for Bar-le-Duc, who loathed him, noted in his journal on 8 May, after a ruling had been voted despite Mirabeau's opposition, that 'a little skill by men of wisdom has diminished his credit; I believe that he will damage himself.'[12]

Opinion was divided as to the wisdom, or legality even, of remaining in a state of deliberate inactivity. Malouet and Mounier recommended that a means of reconciliation should be sought with the other two orders, but the majority believed that immobility, 'the omnipotence of inertia', would bring victory in the end. On 11 May the nobles, in a move designed to make the third estate appear intransigent, announced that they were constituted and ready. Mirabeau warned that if they capitulated now they would be conceding that the nobles had a right to impose their will on the rest, and his logic prevailed. 'The privileged orders say that it is my insidious and deadly eloquence which drives them on', he told his Brunswick friend Mauvillon, 'in the commons they say that the cause will be lost through my excessive zeal'.[13] On 13 May the clergy showed willingness to accept the principle, at least, of consensus, proposing that commissioners from all three orders should try to settle the deadlock. Rabaut de Saint-Etienne thought that the third estate should confer with commissioners from both the clergy and the nobles, but the Breton, Le Chapelier, went to the other extreme, demanding that the other orders should be summoned to unite with the third and condemned as defaulters if they refused. Mirabeau made his first speech on 18 May, when he intervened in this dispute. Taking the role of mediator, he pointed out that nothing was easier than to grab at easy solutions. Rabaut condoned the nobles' behaviour, Le Chapelier wished to pass a decree before the third estate had any legal existence. They should avoid these two extremes and respond to the clergy's commissioners, while continuing to ignore the nobles, who were consenting to commissioners only after making an arrogant, unilateral declaration that they themselves were legally constituted. 'Isn't that joining derision to despotism?' Rabaut asked. The nobles wished to dictate. Let them. The longer they continued the more united the commons would become, 'the more our public spirit will form, and from that will derive our irresistible power, our glorious and lasting success'.[14]

Rabaut's motion was adopted, on condition that the discussions were limited to the verification of powers. But to all the suggestions put by the commissioners of the third estate the nobles' commissioners only replied: we will not unite to judge common mandates. To which Mirabeau replied: we want to verify mandates in common. On his proposal a deputation was sent to gain the clergy's support against the nobles, and at this point Necker invited the commissioners of the three orders to continue their discussions in the presence of the Keeper of the Seals and other ministers. The signs of a growing bond between the third estate and the lesser clergy had created panic in the Artois camp, which was pressuring the king to replace Necker with a minister who would compel the third either to submit, or to face the dissolution of the Estates General. For Necker the discussions with the Keeper of the Seals offered him an escape from responsibility. For Mirabeau it was a trap. A trap whether they accepted it or not, he told the third estate on 28 May, for if they agreed it would all end with a decree drawn up by ministers unanimously in favour of voting by order, and if they refused they would be regarded as rebels, bent only on destroying the king's authority. As a course which would avoid both these rocks he proposed an address to the king, in which they would explain that feeling was for one assembly, that mandates could only be verified in an assembly of all three orders, and that, without abandoning these fundamental principles, the commons would do everything to bring about a return of amity between the different orders. But the third decided that the commissioners should meet with the ministers as directed.

'Mirabeau is not yet listened to, though he speaks a lot', commented the vicomte de Mirabeau maliciously in *La Lanterne magique*, the journal he had started in imitation of his brother.[15] The vicomte, elected by the nobility of the Limousin, belittled him every time he spoke in the nobles' assembly, but there was truth in this particular gibe. Although he had gained ground with his speeches, Mirabeau still did not command the same deference as the scholarly Bailly, or the old hand at administration, Malouet, or the dogmatic Sieyès. The enormous success of his journal prompted suspicion that publicity was all he aimed at, and his visible contempt at times for his fellow deputies was resented.

Then there were his associates. He was shadowed everywhere by the Genevois, Duroveray and Dumont. In the tense atmosphere of 1789 this foreign entourage was enough to start rumours about his loyalty, though Dumont was harmless enough, lacking the sharp wits necessary for an intriguer. The two Genevois regularly attended the sessions of the third estate, and Dumont's letters to his employer, Lord Lansdowne, recorded Mirabeau's growing influence. At first he had been 'convinced that he will govern everything'; he had been able to block Malouet's plans, 'but soon saw that he had the power to destroy but not to govern'. Since then he had changed his tactics and his moderation had won over many people. If he went on like this, Dumont wrote, 'he will gain a great ascendancy and will perform outstanding public service'.[16] Duroveray's presence in the assembly excited much suspicion. He could be seen whispering and passing notes to Mirabeau, until one day a deputy named Madier de Montjau demanded that outsiders should be made to leave; in particular, he said, he denounced 'a foreigner proscribed by his own country, with a pension from the king of England'. Mirabeau managed to calm the storm but his association with the Genevois continued, and his enemies made the most of it.

The commissioners' conferences with the Keeper of the Seals ended in total failure on 9 June. Dissolution by the king now seemed certain, but the third estate had won the support of the public by their long resistance, and knew that they had the tacit sympathy of the majority in the clergy's assembly. On 10 June the third agreed that the other two orders should be summoned to join them for the verification of powers. If they refused the nation would be witness to their contempt, they would have renounced their right to take part in a national assembly. An address was sent to the king, explaining the action of the third estate, but they heard that he was out hunting and had not received it. In fact the government could not decide how to respond to the third's challenge; whether to act punitively, or whether to do nothing and risk further loss to the king's authority. The danger was that under pressure from his colleagues, and in order to compensate for his previous vacillation, Necker would yield to reactionary opinion and allow the king to play a despotic role, to pronounce the immediate dissolution of the Estates General. He had to be persuaded that moderation was the best course for the king; that far from menacing legitimate authority by its action, the third offered the government its surest hope of survival, since in return for a policy of regeneration it could count on the assembly's co-operation.

This was the message that Mirabeau wanted to give to Necker. Being Necker, he would not welcome advice; he had his supporters in the third estate, and was too blinded by prejudice to realise that the polemicist had now become the statesman. For these reasons the ground had to be prepared before he could hope to discuss future policies with the minister. He went to see Malouet, Necker's ally, who confessed to being deeply suspicious before the meeting. According to Malouet, Mirabeau amazed him by saying:

> I have wanted to have a talk with you because I recognise in your moderation a friend of liberty, and because I am perhaps more frightened than you by the stirring up of minds, and the misfortune that can result from it. I am not a man who sells himself to despotism like a coward; I want a free constitution, but with a monarchy. I have no wish to shake the monarchy.

Malouet goes on to record their conversation word for word. Reconstructions of this sort by memoirists years after the event have little value, and only the fundamental point needs to be noted. Malouet's surprise that Mirabeau was peaceful and moderate, and not intent on bringing down the monarchy. The royalist press depicted him as a dangerous demagogue, consumed with ambition and prepared to destroy the state itself; and this image had been accepted not only by Malouet but by all the Malouets in the Assembly, cautious men who wanted reforms but within strict limitations. This broad conservative cross-section had as its priority the preservation of what it saw as rightful authority. Questions about the nature of authority did not form part of its thinking; it was concerned only to safeguard law and order from the threat of those it classified as extremists. In their conversation Mirabeau allegedly told Malouet that there were 'so many obsessed and misguided minds in the assembly', and 'such stubbornness in the first two orders', that he feared terrible upheavals, even whether the monarchy would survive. He asked what Necker and Montmorin intended to do. If they had a reasonable plan he would support it, and use all his influence to 'halt the invasion of democracy which is advancing towards us'.

This, of course, is Malouet paraphrasing Mirabeau's words with hindsight after the Revolution. However, he quite probably did refer to the 'invasion of democracy'. In doing so he was not denying his lifelong advocacy of democratic, representative government and social equality; he diplomatically used 'democracy' in the sense Malouet understood it, to mean a state of disorder, akin to anarchy. As it was, Malouet was so relieved to find that Mirabeau was not an anarchist that he urged Necker to see him, pointing out that he could win over opinion both in the assembly and outside. Necker was incapable of rising above personal animosity in the national interest. To his mind there was only one reason why Mirabeau was approaching him: to sell his patriotism, to demand money in return for vague promises of support. (He had heard stories from Calonne's former assistants, now his.) Confident that he had judged his character correctly, he opened the interview by asking Mirabeau what his proposition was, in such a way that there was no doubt what he was thinking. Mirabeau retorted that his proposition was to bid the minister good day. 'Your man is a fool', he told Malouet, 'he will be hearing from me.'[17]

The reality which the government refused to confront was now advancing inexorably. On 12 June Bailly, the first deputy for Paris, was elected provisional president in the third's assembly and the roll-call commenced, *bailliage* by *bailliage*. On 13 June three *curés* from Poitou defied their bishops and joined the third estate amid loud applause. Others followed the next day. On 15 June the debate opened on the name which the assembly was to adopt. For three days the arguments continued, the passions roused by the significance and derivation of a few nouns and adjectives exceeding anything seen before. Some of the names put forward were stupefying in their pompous complexity: Sieyès proposed the 'Assembly of known and verified representatives of the French nation', and Mounier the 'Legitimate Assembly of the major part of the nation in the absence of the minor part'. Imagine being asked your job, said Mirabeau, and having to say that you were a deputy for the major part of the nation in the absence of the minor part. He had been suffering from fever and jaundice since the opening of the Estates General, and when he rose to speak he apologised for not being in a fit state to discuss an important question. Nevertheless, Arthur Young wrote:

> Mons. de Mirabeau spoke without notes, for nearly an hour, with a warmth, animation, and eloquence, that entitles him to the reputation of an undoubted orator. He opposed the words *known* and *verified*, in the proposition of Abbé Sieyès, with great force and reasoning; and proposed, in lieu, that they should declare themselves simply *représentants du peuple français*; that no *veto* should exist against their resolves in any other assembly; that all taxes are illegal, but should be granted during the present session of the [Estates General], and no longer; that the debt of the King should become the debt of the nation, and be secured on funds accordingly. Mons. de Mirabeau was well heard, and his proposition much applauded.[18]

Careful thought had gone into his choice of the title 'representatives of the French people'. He wanted to avoid any name which could be challenged as implying that the deputies had wider powers than those actually accorded, one that could become the excuse for royal sanctions against them. The fear that they might be dismissed arbitrarily was not far fetched.

This was the reason for his reminder that the king had the power to veto their decisions. However, his words were taken the wrong way, drawing angry protests at the existence of any limitations on the power of the legislature. Rousseauist deputies could quote from the *Contrat social*: 'The legislative power belongs, and can only belong, to

the people'. Mirabeau agreed. But as the debate continued an argument developed over the relative authority of the legislative and
executive powers. Rousseau also said in the *Contrat social* that in the
body politic nothing should be done without the concurrence of both
powers, the executive and the legislative.[19] This would always be
Mirabeau's view. In the present debate he defended the idea of a
single-chamber legislature and the right of veto for the king. It roused both the conservatives who wanted a two-chamber system as in
England, and those who wanted to strip the monarch of power. Mirabeau argued that a royal veto was necessary to prevent democracy
turning into dictatorship. If they had an upper chamber the privileged orders would possess a right of veto which would be used for
their own ends. If, on the other hand, the king retained his power of
veto, he would be cautious about using it, since his greatest strength
lay in the support of his people, and wrongful use of his veto would
quickly erode it. (Rousseau disagreed with the theory that kings
would always be guided by the desire to win the love of their people.)
Finally, Mirabeau warned that if they insisted on stripping the king
of his authority in this respect he would prorogue the assembly, the
sequel to which would be 'hideous anarchy, which always brings a
return of despotism'.

Barnave accused him of trying to terrify them with his eloquence.
Others joined in. Young said he saw a hundred deputies on their feet,
all shouting at once while Bailly tried vainly to restore order. The
attack was led by Thouret who said, with a lawyer's cleverness, that he
had not told them whether he took the word 'people' in his proposed
title to signify *plebs* – which would mean that he approved the division
of orders – or *populus* – which would go beyond the intentions of the
commons. The next day, replying to his opponents, Mirabeau was
sarcastic regarding Thouret's red herring; he thought he had expressed
his views clearly on the separation of orders, yet he was accused of
favouring it; he thought he had presented resolutions which demonstrated the dignity of the people, and he was informed that he had
given this word a base connotation. Turning Thouret's show of erudi-
tion back on him, he continued: 'It has even been feared that this word
only signifies what the Romans called *vulgus*, what the English term
*mob*, what aristocrats and roturiers refer to insolently as the *canaille*'. In
America and England the word 'people' figured in the language of
liberty; was a usage he had learned in that school, he asked, likely to be
suspect?

Addressing the Rousseauist deputy, who had declared that there was
no place for a royal veto once the people had spoken, he defended it
again.

I believe the King's veto to be so necessary that I would rather live in Constantinople if he did not have it: I know of nothing more terrible than the sovereign aristocracy of six hundred persons, who could render themselves irremovable tomorrow, and hereditary the day after. But, gentlemen, since my motion has been so misunderstood I must defend it with reasons rather than recriminations.

And he recapitulated what he had said the previous day. The advantage of 'people' lay precisely in its many interpretations.

Yes, it is because the name of people is not enough respected in France . . . because it is pronounced with contempt in aristocratic circles, that we should choose it, seeing it as the most precious opportunity to serve the people, these people who are everything, whom we represent, whose rights we defend, and from whom we have received ours, yet whose name apparently it is shameful to borrow.

His finale was withering:

Representatives of the people, are you going to say to your constituents that you have rejected this name of people? That you need a title more splendid than that they have conferred on you? Do you not see that the name of representatives of the people is necessary to you, because it joins you to the people, that imposing mass without which you would only be individuals, frail reeds that could be broken one by one? Do you not see that this name will tell the people that we have linked our fate to theirs, and that they can place their trust in us?[20]

The end of his speech was nearly lost in the fury that surrounded him. The deputies of the third estate, exalted in their own eyes, and already distanced from the people who were their justification for being where they were, did not like criticism. The previous day a deputy named Legrand had suggested that they should call themselves the *assemblée nationale*, the name already in common use. Sieyès now proposed this title, the National Assembly, in place of his original one, and the next day it was adopted, by 491 votes to 90.

Mirabeau had wanted a name that was not provocative. The word 'national', suggesting all three estates, in the chosen title produced the very reaction he hoped to avoid: the infuriated nobles pressed the king to take punitive action against the third estate. 'I would not be surprised if civil war was the result of their fine decree', he told Dumont. In a letter to Mauvillon in Brunswick he described the hostility he had stirred up with his speech:

They thought they could get rid of me, and circulated the rumour that I am the government's man. I am supposed to have sold myself to so many people that I cannot understand why I do not yet rule the universe. They are irritated by my moderate views, but I am so convinced that there is a vast difference between studying an atlas and actually travelling; so convinced that our constituents are very little interested in our metaphysical discussions, important though they are, and that we could not really count on their support when things get hot; so convinced that the best way to make the revolution miscarry is to demand too much, that I shall invite being reproached as a moderate for a long time.[21]

This was the same man Mme de Staël accused of proclaiming 'the most destructive principles' and of having but one aim: to use his demagogic force to place himself at the head of government.

He called for the reunion of all the powers in a single assembly, although he knew perfectly well that such a political organisation was disruptive of all good; but he persuaded himself that France would be in his hand, and that having precipitated her into confusion he could direct her at his will.[22]

Mme de Staël echoed her father's views; this is how Necker saw Mirabeau. Reason and moderation would find no recognition here.

As its first act the new National Assembly, accepting Mirabeau's proposal, declared all taxes illegal but granted them for the duration of the session (an insurance against summary dissolution), and agreed to have debates on the national debt and famine relief at the earliest opportunity. On 19 June the clergy voted to join the third estate, together with a minority of the nobles. Meanwhile the king and Privy Council had been discussing their next move, and on 20 June it was announced that a *séance royale* would be held on Monday 22 June.

The news was half anticipated, the manner of imparting it stupidly provocative: the third estate only learned about the royal session when they found soldiers guarding the doors of the Salle des Menus Plaisirs, who told them that the hall was being prepared for the king's visit. The angry deputies moved to the Jeu-de-Paume, the tennis court, which was the nearest large hall, and there, at Mounier's urging, they took an oath never to be dissolved except by their own consent, but to continue with the business of the National Assembly no matter what happened. Mirabeau, with a report to prepare for his next letter to his constituents, went to see Clavière, who staggered him when he mentioned the *séance royale*, by saying that it had been Duroveray's idea. Apparently he had written to Necker, suggesting that the king should command the three orders to unite, and Necker, seeing this as a way by which the third estate would get what they wanted while the king got the credit for it, had agreed. Mirabeau was furious. Duroveray may have thought that he could ingratiate himself with Necker by tendering advice – very different from Mirabeau's motives when he offered advice to the Director-General – but his idea revealed the shallowness of his political understanding. Far from presenting the king as a benevolent peacemaker, a *séance royale* was the last resort of an absolute monarch, determined to impose his authority. (It could be that Du-roveray, a committed republican, advised it in the hope of alienating the king from the National Assembly, in which case his double role *vis-à-vis* Mirabeau becomes even more apparent.) Psychologically a *séance royale* would be a catastrophe. Dumont never forgot Mirabeau's comment: 'This is the way kings are led to the scaffold.'

A meeting of the Privy Council lasted till midnight on 21 June, and with another meeting planned for the morrow, the *séance royale* was postponed for twenty-four hours. A blanket of secrecy lay over the proceedings but the news leaked out that Necker had offered his resignation to the king, who refused to accept it. This, and the increasing number of troops in the town of Versailles, created an atmosphere of fear and drama. It was widely believed that the leading deputies of the third estate were about to be arrested and sent to the Bastille. On 22 June the commons returned to the Jeu-de-Paume only to find it also shut to them on the pretext that the comte d'Artois wanted it for a game of tennis. They went on to the church of Saint-Louis. While they were in session two nobles, three bishops, and 150 lesser clergy joined them, cheered by the crowd both inside and outside the church.

On 23 June the *séance royale* took place. The commons were kept waiting in the rain for a long time, and when the doors were finally opened they found the privileged orders already seated. Several regiments of troops lined the streets and in the hall itself armed guards stood at every entrance, heightening the impression that violent scenes were expected. A platform had been built for the throne, but one seat was conspicuously vacant: Necker had stayed away. That empty seat testified to the struggle which had been going on at the meetings of the Privy Council, between Necker and Montmorin, who wanted the king to use the *séance royale* to make concessions on liberty and the power of the legislature, and the other ministers, subjugated by Artois, who wanted him to act like Louis XIV, to cancel all the third's insubordinate decrees, and imperiously proclaim that the *ancien régime* was sacrosanct and eternal. On 22 June the queen added her voice to Artois' and Necker was defeated. Louis had been taken hostage by his destroyers.

As the king made his speech he sounded to the shocked and incredulous deputies almost like a parody of an absolute monarch. The distinction between the three orders was to be preserved, with the deputies keeping their three separate assemblies. The deliberations of the third estate up till that moment were declared null and void. Freedom of admission to public employment was refused. All property was to be respected, including all tithes, rents, feudal rights, and all privileges attached to lands or fiefs. ('At the reading of this article some of the nobles had the indecency to applaud', reported Mirabeau in the thirteenth letter to his constituents. 'Only by cries calling them to order were they induced to restrain themselves.') There was no mention of the responsibility of ministers, or of participation by the Assembly in the legislative power, and nothing about fiscal equality beyond a bland hope that the privileged orders would accept it. The king spoke of his strong desire to obtain the public good. 'If you abandon me in this enterprise I shall work alone for the good of my people. I shall consider myself their only true representative . . . and I shall proceed to the end I desire with courage and firmness.' He ended on a note of menace: 'Reflect, gentlemen, that none of your projects, none of your dispositions, can have the force of law without my personal approbation'.[23]

'Seeing his majesty's good intentions, the ministers' last resort was to persuade him that he needs no one but himself to put them into operation', Mirabeau told his constituents. 'Today, when there is a legislative assembly, by what right do they usurp the faculty of making laws, which cannot and should not belong to them?' Such a speech could only shake the people's trust in the sovereign, 'and the courtiers have dared to advise a good king to use this approach with the nation he needed to convoke!'[24]

After his speech the king departed, followed by the senior clergy and the nobles, visibly savouring their triumph. The stunned deputies of the third estate stayed in their seats. Eventually the royal master of ceremonies, the marquis de Dreux-Brézé, a young man of twenty-seven whose *hauteur* made him instantly dislikeable to anyone his senior in age, entered and asked Bailly if they had heard the king's commands. The mild-mannered president replied that the Assembly adjourned after the *séance royale* and he could not dismiss it without discussion. Into the moment of silence broke another voice, Mirabeau's:

> Yes, we have heard the king's suggested intentions; and you who have no right to be his mouthpiece in the National Assembly, who have no place here, no right to speak, you are not qualified to remind us of his words. However, in order to avoid all equivocation and delay, I declare that if you have been ordered to make us leave you must seek orders to employ force, for we shall not leave except by the force of bayonets.

'I only recognise M. de Mirabeau as the deputy for the *sénéchaussée* of Aix and not as the spokesman for the Assembly', retorted Dreux-Brézé, but Mirabeau's words had had an alchemic, transmuting effect on his hearers; suddenly they were no longer powerless and uncertain; they, at that moment, in that place, they were the Revolution, and they joined their defiance to his, shouting: 'That is the will of the Assembly'.[25]

As Dreux-Brézé left Bailly said rebukingly to Mirabeau that there had never been any question of bayonets, but he insisted that they must safeguard their work by declaring the inviolability of all deputies, adding, when Bailly protested that this was surely unnecessary, that sixty deputies and Bailly with them could be arrested that night. His motion was passed by 493 votes to 34. Bayonets might have been welcomed by wishful martyrs; they were not what Mirabeau wanted, nor a solution that the king was prepared to sanction. His show of force at the *séance royale* had been imposed on him, and on hearing that the commons refused to be moved his only reaction was a fatalistic, 'They want to stay; then let them get on with it'.

The day following the *séance royale* Paris was in a ferment. In the cafés and grounds of the Palais-Royal, always the centre for popular demonstrations, speakers denounced the ministerial criminals and called for death to all aristocrats. Pamphlets which had poured off the radical presses overnight strengthened the rumours that the king was about to use force against the Assembly, that massacres were planned: why else were there 30,000 soldiers encamped round the capital and Versailles? On 24 and 25 June more of the clergy joined the commons, among them the abbé de Périgord, now Bishop of Autun. In his case the move was not dictated by any latent egalitarianism; essentially patrician, he believed that benefits were something to be bestowed, not to be demanded as a right; but noting the public mood he concluded that it was wiser to join the third estate than to be marked down as one who had held back.

With every passing day the king's position was becoming more untenable. Bread riots were expected in Paris; if they were dealt with by force further damage would be done to his public image, already harmed enough by the *séance royale* which had identified the monarch with aristocratic self-interest. Anxious to prevent this fatal identification from becoming fixed in the public imagination, Mirabeau proposed an address to the people, which the Assembly authorised him to prepare. In it he excused the king, whose own feelings, he said, were not reflected by his commands of the 23 June, and denounced the privileged orders who used him for their own ends as enemies of both throne and people. He called for calm, an avoidance of disorders which would only serve the counter-revolutionaries, and restraint:

> How glorious it will be for France, for us, if this great revolution costs human-
> ity neither penalties nor tears . . . All too often history has related only the
> actions of wild beasts; we at least can hope that we are beginning the history
> of humanity'.[26]

On 25 June forty-seven nobles joined the third estate, headed by

Orléans, the king's cousin. Two days later Louis conceded defeat, and ordered 'his faithful clergy and faithful nobles' to unite with the commons. The National Assembly was victorious. Paris celebrated with fireworks and a new slogan appeared on the walls: *'Pas d'impôts, vive les Etats'*. Rumours that the army would be used to subjugate the Assembly still persisted; the defeated nobles wanted vengeance, but the king lacked their appetite for civil war. The truth had to be faced: two sovereign powers now existed and a *modus vivendi* had to be found. 'It will be our constant resolve to work together with our king', Mirabeau declared on 30 June, 'not for fleeting benefits but for the very constitution of the kingdom.' The man who had fought for the Assembly's recognition now offered peace terms. The king's authority was not being usurped. The Assembly hoped for concord, though it was unwilling to buy it with the sacrifice of the people's rights. It looked forward to seeing 'all the children of this immense nation' reunited and prosperous, 'cherishing the common father whose reign will have been the epoch of France's regeneration'.[27]

*Vive le roi. Vive les Etats.*

# NOTES

1. Romilly (1841: I, 109).
2. La Fayette (1837–38: IV, 151–2).
3. Ferrières (1932: 29). Letter of 24 April 1789.
4. *Journal des Etats Généraux*, no. 1.
5. Staël (1820–21: XII, 182).
6. *Journal des Etats Généraux*, no. 2.
7. *Lettres du comte de Mirabeau à ses commettans*, 10 May 1789.
8. Ibid.
9. Etienne-Louis Dumont (1759–1829), born in Geneva, became a pastor in 1783. His first sermon, a Savonarola-like denunciation of sin, was censured by his superiors; offended, he went to St Petersburg, but left a year later on the pretext that his congregation did not justify his efforts. He went to London and joined the circle of Genevois exiles headed by Duroveray. He was tutor to Lord Lansdowne's younger son in 1786–89. This employment led to his first meeting with Jeremy Bentham, some of whose works he translated for publication in French in the first quarter of the nineteenth century. After being briefly involved in Genevois politics in 1792 he lived mostly in England, but returned to Geneva in 1814.
10. *Apologie de l'usure* was published in 1790 by Le Jay, Mirabeau's publisher. The name of the translator is not given. As Mirabeau's main motive in studying this work was to glean material to use in his attacks on speculators he probably translated only those letters (it is composed of letters, not chapters) which he found most applicable. Possibly Dumont – afterwards

Bentham's translator – was responsible for the footnotes to the French edition, and for the translation of the superfluous Letter 13. Untypically, Dumont made no claims with regard to this work, and Bentham never acknowledged that he had a part in it.

*Apologie de l'usure* appeared at a moment when Le Jay, Mirabeau, and the two Genevois, Duroveray and Dumont, were engaged in a bitter quarrel. The fact that Mirabeau's name did not appear as translator may point to a bargain struck between him and Dumont, whose contribution did not justify the title of co-translator which he may have desired.

11. The assumption that Dumont was already working on Bentham's papers in 1789 has been disproved by Blount (1952) and Mack (1962).

12. Duquesnoy (1894: I, 9).

13. *Mémoires biographiques*, VIII, 177. The commons, *communes*, the term used here by Mirabeau, which had been adopted by the third estate to describe themselves, had a long history in France in connection with resistance to the despotism of the Crown.

14. *Discours*, 30–34.

15. The vicomte left serious political comment to his brother. *La Lanterne magique* entertained the beau monde with irreverent pictures of the currently famous, the figure most often projected on its mocking screen being that of the deputy for Aix: 'See how the people cheer him, it is the great comte de Mirabeau; admire his coiffure, the most elaborate one there; he smiles at his backers, he will repay them in Assembly motions for the benefits they heap on him.'

16. Dumont to Lord Lansdowne, 3 June 1789. Bowood Archives.

17. Malouet (1874: I, 276f).

18. Young (1929: 143). Mirabeau's style of speaking was described by many of his contemporaries. Mme de Staël, Barnave, and Vergniaud all said that he began slowly; as though he needed to fire the furnace, said Vergniaud, who added that as he proceeded 'the vaults of the temple resounded with his voice, he filled the tribune with his majesty, he was the god of it.' Barnave found that although his delivery seemed too studied at first this came to sound natural, with an attractiveness of its own. Dumont was struck by the care with which he selected his words, so that meaning was never sacrificed to emotional effect: 'He had a great contempt for French volubility and the affected passion which he called the thunder and storms of the opera. He never lost the gravity of a senator' (*Souvenirs*, 157). Ferrières said that his style was 'hard, rocky, expressive . . . comparable to a hammer in the hands of a skilful mason, shaping men at his will, not by persuasion but by subjection'.

19. Rousseau (1968: Book III, ch. 1).

20. *Discours*, 54–62. The previous day, when Mirabeau made his speech on the title of the Assembly, Dumont was sitting in the gallery with Lord Elgin. Dumont scribbled 'a sort of apostrophe or peroration' on a piece of paper and passed it to Elgin who liked it. Mirabeau decided to add it to his speech of 16 June; the final sentence is Dumont's, yet on the strength of this Stern (*Das Leben Mirabeaus*, 1889) and Aulard (1914) ascribe the whole speech to Dumont. Stern, Aulard, and Bénétruy (who edited Dumont, 1951), accepted unquestioningly Dumont's claims regarding Mirabeau's speeches.

21. *Lettres amicales*, 467. Mirabeau alludes in this letter to the words he used in his speech of 16 June, when he described the difference between the theorist's (Sieyès) and the pragmatist's approach to problems: 'It is this essential difference between the metaphysician who, in the seclusion of his study, grasps

the truth in its intense purity, and the statesman, who is obliged to take into account antecedents, difficulties, obstacles . . . The metaphysician voyaging on a map conquers mountains, deserts, rivers, without effort, but we must remember that we are travelling on earth and not in an ideal world' (*Discours*, 52).

It is hardly necessary but should be stressed that Mirabeau was *not* against the concept of the sovereignty of the people when he spoke on the Assembly's title. He was not against the assumption of national sovereignty by the third estate, merely anxious about the consequences of using the word 'national' – the definition of which might be contested – in the title.

22. Staël (1820–21: XII, 249).
23. *Lettres à ses commettans*, no. 13, 8.
24. Ibid.
25. *Discours*, 63–64.
26. *Mémoires biographiques*, VIII, 231 f.
27. Ibid.

# 8

Reason and Circumstance

## (July-September 1789)

'Only violence could endanger or even destroy that liberty which reason assures us': in his address to the French people Mirabeau appealed for calm in the face of mounting tension.

'Liberty', the word used constantly by the revolutionaries, could have many definitions, but what writers and political thinkers of the time principally meant by the term was political liberty, in keeping with humanist tradition which analysed it as the right to self-determination. In his *Discorsi* Machiavelli equated liberty with independence from external aggression and tyranny, and with the power of free people to govern themselves. This was the ideal of liberty pursued by the men of 1789. Their education in humanist civics had also taught them that the chief threat to liberty came from disunity, an idea that went back to the Aristotelian belief in a direct relationship between factions and tyranny, leading to violence and the loss of liberty.

As Mirabeau was writing, all the theories about liberty and the dangers facing it were becoming manifest. From the opening of the Estates General the implicit threat of violence had been ever present, in the soldiers barring the doors of the Salle des Menus Plaisirs, the increasing number of troops in Versailles, the army lying in wait outside Paris. There was growing fear that force was intended against the Assembly, against the populace who supported it. The 400 electors of the Paris deputies had formed themselves into a commune rivalling the authority of the *hôtel de ville*, and were calling for a militia to defend the citizens against the assault by the army that seemed imminent.

Paris was a volcano, its sixty districts seething with political fumaroles. The arrest of some local *gardes françaises*, and their rescue by a sympathetic crowd, played into the hands of those who wanted to read the onset of chaos into everything that had happened since the start of the Estates General. The Assembly had helped to feed their prejudice. Not wanting to forfeit public goodwill it sent a deputation to the king, who agreed to pardon the *gardes* but warned the deputies that their insubordinate behaviour might lead to a changed estimation of the value of their labours.

Following this incident the king ordered in a further ten regiments, mostly of foreign mercenaries. (It was the use of mercenaries which political writers historically cited as one of the greatest threats to liberty.) Camps were set up in the Champ-de-Mars, at Sèvres and Saint-Denis; at Versailles Swiss and German regiments were stationed in the gardens of the palace which their commander, the baron de Besenval, used as his headquarters. All this menacing preparation increased the tension in Paris, where there was already fear about a shortage of bread.

On 6 July Mirabeau raised the question of food supplies to Paris in the Assembly. The matter gave him an opportunity – which he never missed – to deflect criticism from the king to his advisers, since Necker was ultimately responsible for provisioning the city. He asked whether the Subsistence Committee knew that the American Minister in Paris, Jefferson, had offered to have food sent from America to relieve the situation in Paris, and that Necker had declined the offer. It was something of a bombshell. Jefferson consulted La Fayette, who, on the strength of his favoured relationship with Washington was regarded by the American government as its best authority on French affairs, and they decided that Jefferson should issue a denial for the Assembly's records. Jefferson told La Fayette that a probable confusion existed over an American merchant who had offered supplies to Necker, but this was not mentioned in his formal denial, which he made in order to save Necker from embarrassment. La Fayette asked Mirabeau to retract his error in the Assembly, which he did to the extent of retracting one word, 'propositions', from his statement; the rest, he said, was essentially correct. The Assembly remained suspicious that the minister was attempting a cover-up. Jefferson and La Fayette tried to minimise Mirabeau's criticism of Necker by publishing the letter of denial, but the damage had been done.[1]

La Fayette was ruffled by the episode for he had an obsessive need for popularity and the ministers were annoyed with him because of Mirabeau's unsatisfactory retraction. Equally he had a compulsion to be on the winning side, and so when, on 7 July, the Assembly demanded a translation of Jefferson's letter, he supported Mirabeau, declaring that further readings were unnecessary. However, the appearance of cordial relations between them was an illusion. Outside the Assembly La Fayette regarded Mirabeau as a cunning demagogue. Mirabeau regarded La Fayette as a conceited fool. The man who had been handed the trappings of glory ready-made at the age of twenty, when he was singled out by George Washington, may have been the idol of Paris society, but his political understanding left doubts. From the radical Brissot, who said that La Fayette loved liberty as a eunuch loves women, to the conservative Gouverneur Morris, the comments were deflationary. Mirabeau – rather too harshly – saw him as a megalomaniac; though a letter from La Fayette to his mistress, the comtesse de Simiane, on 19 June supports this impression, for after telling her how he had long worked to bring 'the liberty of men and the destruction of despotism' to France, he declared that he 'had tried everything but civil war, which I could have started; but I did not because I dreaded its horror'.[2] Only an exaggerated ego could talk of being able, godlike, to start at will a civil war.

By 7 July the atmosphere in Paris was critical. At a private meeting in the Salle des Menus Plaisirs La Fayette, Mounier, Mirabeau, and some others decided that the Assembly must demand the withdrawal of the troops. The next morning Mirabeau interrupted the order of the day. The Court, he said, was leading on a king too good to wish for evil, too weak to resist it. Did they not see that their actions would threaten the throne itself?

> Have they never studied history and seen how revolutions start, or observed how a fatal chain of circumstances sweeps the soundest minds beyond the limits of moderation, how people are precipitated by some terrible impulse into excesses they would earlier have shuddered at?

The Assembly appointed him to prepare an address to the king on the withdrawal of the troops, and a deputation of twenty-four deputies, including himself, presented it on 10 July. Throughout the reading of it Louis watched him fixedly. Possibly he was thinking of that earlier king, Charles I, whose history he knew by heart, and wondering if the face before him was that of another Pym. He refused to order a withdrawal, suggesting that if the military precautions alarmed them the Assembly could move to Noyons or Soissons. Mirabeau told the Assembly the next day:

> We demanded the withdrawal of the troops. We did not ask to flee from the troops, only that they should be withdrawn some distance from the capital. And we asked this not for ourselves, and certainly not out of fear, but in the general interest. Despite the troublemakers we must bring about peace, and

we must therefore stand firm, and insist unremittingly on the withdrawal of the troops.[3]

Ever since his denunciation of them on 8 July the counter-revolutionary intriguers at Court had been preparing for their final victory, and on 11 July they played their trump card: Necker was dismissed by the king and ordered to leave Paris at once. Montmorin, Puységur, and all the moderate ministers were also dismissed, and a new counter-revolutionary ministry, headed by Breteuil, took their place. The Assembly learned of Necker's dismissal on the morning of 12 July; Paris heard the news in the afternoon. At the Palais-Royal speakers urged the crowd to take arms (the threat of violence by the army had set an example) and the busts of Necker and Orléans were carried through the streets at the head of a vast crowd. Looting and rioting continued through the night. The next morning the electors of Paris set about forming the National Guard of Paris; 12,000 men were enrolled in the course of the day, and while the citizens were organizing their own defence force Besenval and his troops in the Champ-de-Mars prepared to deal with any confrontation. A deputation from the Assembly went again to ask for the troops' withdrawal. Again the king refused.

Mirabeau was not at the Assembly on the day of the Paris riots. The previous evening the marquis de Mirabeau had died at the age of seventy-three. In one of his last letters to his brother he delivered his final verdict on his son:

> Everything he has done is bad; even now, in attacking abuses he is clearly tending towards the destruction of the established order, and evil will come of it. Like all men fundamentally lacking in morals he will reap what he has sown; he will never win confidence though he wishes to merit it; he will have partisans, admirers even, when it suits them, but never friends.[4]

Announcing his father's death in his nineteenth letter to his constituents, Mirabeau declared that this loss must put all the citizens of the world into mourning. A futile hope: *l'ami des hommes* had long been relegated to the catacombs of demoted idols. Yet there was one, the bailli, to whom his death brought utter desolation and silence, as the correspondence finally closed which began fifty years before, when they were young and the Revolution still an abstraction that they never believed would become a reality in their own lifetime.[5]

The marquis was buried at Argenteuil on 13 July. That day the electors of Paris took over municipal power and decided on the formation of a civil militia. Hearing that the king still refused to withdraw the troops, the National Assembly formally declared that the ministers and their military agents were responsible for all enterprises contrary to the decrees of the Assembly, and that the current ministry was 'personally responsible for the present troubles and all those that might follow'. Mirabeau returned to the Assembly, picking up a report on the way that he, Sieyès, La Fayette, Le Chapelier, and Lameth were to be arrested, whereupon the deputies decided to stay overnight in the Assembly chamber as it was unlikely that they would be seized in what the outraged press would call the temple of liberty. On 14 July the deputies waited in fear and confusion for news from Paris. Late in the afternoon they heard of the fall of the Bastille, and of the deaths of the governor, Delaunay, and the provost of merchants, Flesselles, on the steps of the *hôtel de ville*. They heard, too, that whilst this was happening the queen and Artois were entertaining the foreign regiments at Versailles to a banquet. This act of fraternisation between the royal family and the foreign troops, who were widely seen as a force of imported terrorists, there to silence the free political voice of the French people, infuriated the deputies. They voted to demand the instant withdrawal of the troops. Mirabeau declared that they should tell the king that such feasting in a royal palace had been the prelude to the massacre of St Bartholomew. Let the king remember 'that his ancestor Henri IV, of blessed memory, carried food to a rebellious Paris, and that his own savage advisers had refused it to a Paris that was faithful and starving'.

The message was never sent; Louis came to the Assembly the same day to announce that the troops would be withdrawn. He was rewarded with delirious cheers from the deputies, who escorted him back to the palace, but he and they were equally aware that a transformation of roles had taken place; no longer was it the king who commanded and the Assembly which received his orders; now it was a defeated monarch who came on foot to appease his conquerors, and who knew that the Assembly's ultimatum over the military presence would lead to others. In his response to the king, Bailly had renewed the declaration of 13 July which stated that the dismissal of the ministers had been the principal cause of the trouble. On 16 July there were calls for the dismissal of Breteuil, and Barnave proposed that they should also demand the recall of Necker. Mounier, rigid exponent of the separation of powers, said that they had no right to intervene. He condemned the principle of ministerial responsibility, declaring that England had been lost as a result of it.

'England is lost. Good God, what sinister news', Mirabeau answered drily. Ministerial responsibility would never be exercised if they could not initiate it by accusation, he pointed out. Those who wished to deny the legislature any control over the executive forgot that the people were 'the source of all the powers', and that 'even the power of the monarch could be suspended if he failed to agree with the representatives of the people'. ('The power of the people must be greater than that of the monarch', he had written in the fourth letter to his constituents.) Just as he would always insist on the right of the executive power to restrain the legislature so the legislative power must be able to bring pressure on the executive. They were 'not trying to make or unmake ministers by decree', only to manifest the opinion of their constituents. 'Public opinion', he concluded, 'is the incorruptible sentinel of the *patrie*'.[6]

In this intervention Mirabeau deems public opinion to be 'incorruptible' in the same way that Rousseau deems the general will to be 'incorruptible'. Rousseau rarely uses the term 'public opinion'. In the *Contrat social*, he says: 'The greater the harmony that reigns in public assemblies, the nearer, in other words, that public opinion comes to unanimity, the more the general will is dominant [my translation].' But this is not the same as Mirabeau's 'public opinion'. Rousseau is only talking about those who have been elected to assemblies; they are the representatives of the 'sovereign people', they express 'the general will'. The people always want what is good for the people. Therefore the general will, by definition, is rightful and good. Criticism or alternative viewpoints, if not forbidden, are not to be encouraged, for they detract from the idea of rightfulness and unity which is synonymous with the general will. 'Long debates, dissension, and disturbances bespeak the ascendance of particular interests and the decline of the state', Rousseau continues. This passage in the *Contrat social*[7] had the effect in practice of legitimating intolerance in Assembly debates and, as the Revolution progressed, in the Jacobin Club, where unanimity became the badge of revolutionary integrity and disagreement was made to seem subversive.

Rousseau was not concerned with public opinion in the sense of the man in the street, *vox populi*, or even – as Mirabeau mentions here – 'constituents', those people represented by a member of the Assembly. For Rousseau that external, wider assortment of voices, dignified with the name of public opinion, expressed only what he termed 'particular interests', those of individuals or groups. Particular interests obstructed the general will. Mirabeau's insistence on the answerability of ministers to the Assembly he would have endorsed but not his insistence on the answerability of deputies when that involved being influenced by particular interests. Perhaps most unacceptable to unreserved Rousseauists who heard him was Mirabeau's stress on the incorruptibility of public opinion: it implied that the Assembly did not have the monopoly of virtue.

The king anticipated the Assembly's demands by announcing that the ministers had resigned and that Necker was to be recalled. Hearing that the electors of Paris had nominated Bailly as mayor and La Fayette as commander of the newly formed National Guard, he further announced that he would go to Paris himself the following day. Perhaps he recognised that this was the only way to counter the psychological advantage which the Assembly and the capital now held. At the *hôtel de ville* he endorsed the symbols of the city's new power, the municipality and civil guard, and accepted a cockade for his hat: not the green one first adopted by the revolutionaries as it had been pointed out that Artois' livery was green, but one of red and white – which lovers of coincidence realised were Orléans's colours. In Bailly's ambiguous words, Paris had achieved the reconquest of its king.

Mirabeau's friends urged him to stand for mayor against Bailly. Whether his influence would have altered the progress of events, however, as they afterwards believed, is open to doubt. Enjoying official access to the king, he would have had the opportunity to offer sound advice, but his very popularity with the public would have been a barrier to gaining the king's confidence. As mayor he would have controlled the militant districts much more successfully than the timorous Bailly, but what would Marat have said in his *Ami du peuple* about the defender of liberty who now resisted the people's will? Accepting the office of mayor of an insurgent city would have fixed him in the king's mind as a demagogue, would have led to his being blamed for all future unrest there, and strengthened belief that he was part of the Palais-Royal network.[8] For all these reasons the post would have been a trap. Apart from that, his ambitions went higher than local government, and he rightly saw himself playing a more valuable role in the National Assembly.

His performance in the Assembly so far had been studied with particular interest by a deputy for the nobility of Quesnoy. The comte de La Marck,[9] Belgian by birth, French by allegiance, trusted by the queen, and devoted to the monarchy, was struck by his reasoned defence of royal prerogative, as opposed to royal privilege, in debates; but found it difficult to believe that this leader of the popular party was not playing a double game. When they first met at a dinner in Versailles, La Marck's initial reaction was one of horror at the vulgar size of Mirabeau's coat buttons, but all was forgiven when the conversation turned to politics: 'one was only aware of the fertility and rightness of his ideas, and he captivated everyone with his brilliant and energetic manner of explaining'. Several times since then La Marck had included him among his guests, but after the Assembly triumphed over the king at the end of June he invited him by himself. Over dinner he asked what he hoped to achieve with the inflammatory line he had adopted in the Assembly. 'France's fate is decided', Mirabeau told him. 'There is no solution now without a government more or less similar to that of England.' La Marck was inclined to agree. But why was he using his eloquence to increase the government's difficulties? 'The day the king's ministers consent to talk sensibly with me they will find me devoted to the royal cause and to the salvation of the monarchy.' Where did he think the present course would end?

> In the ruin of France, and if they wish to save her there's no time to be lost. The way they are going on is mad. They leave the Assembly to its own devices, and flatter themselves that they can either suppress it by force, as the aristocratic party would like, or bring it to heel with Necker's empty and redundant phrases; whereas what is needed is for the government to form a party within the Assembly through the agency of men who have the power to influence it, lead it, and calm it.[10]

La Marck was not yet sufficiently convinced of his sincerity to become his sponsor, and for the time being he decided to watch and wait. When Mirabeau visited the Bastille a few days after its fall, and was showered with flowers by the crowd, his scepticism grew. Mirabeau's colleagues in the Assembly who were certain never to receive floral tributes, called him a demagogue, and his enemies said that he was whipping up feeling in Paris in order to overturn Bailly and make himself mayor. In fact, he had been doing what he did in Marseille during the disturbances there, making the rounds of the districts, especially the Oratoire district where he had an apartment, exerting his verbal skill to prevent further outbreaks of violence. Despite the presence of the National Guard, Paris was still in a state of ferment, fearing martial reprisals and the onset of famine. Bailly was attempting to restore calm by selling bread below cost but his influence was negligible. Parisians were on the verge of that kind of 'terrible impulse' which Mirabeau had warned against in his speech of 8 July.

On the 22nd July Foulon, one of Breteuil's ministers who had made a fortune from the grain shortage, and his son-in-law, the intendant of Paris, were murdered outside the *Hôtel de Ville*. In the Assembly Mirabeau tried to maintain a sense of proportion: these acts of vengeance, horrible as they were, did not reflect the true spirit of the citizens; they did not compare with the acts of ministerial vengeance carried out in the dungeons of Vincennes and the Bastille. The people had meted out summary punishment; it was inevitable, but for the health of the revolution it must not become a precedent, for by acting outside the law people encouraged anarchy, and prepared the way for a rebirth of despotism. However, when he urged that those deputies who lived in Paris should use their influence in their own districts to enforce order, he met with suspicious opposition. He was untypical in having apartments both in Versailles and Paris, and although he had lived there for years before the Revolution the fact that he himself was not a deputy for Paris was enough to persuade his hearers that his only aim was to gain power for himself. They recalled the old adage that he who ruled Paris ruled the kingdom. A motion forbidding any deputy to enter any Paris district unless on a special mission was applauded, and only defeated after he had challenged the rightness of preventing deputies who lived in Paris from carrying out their duties. Reason for once prevailed over prejudice.

The tension in the capital eased temporarily with Necker's return from exile. The day he was received by the municipality his popularity reached its zenith. Taking advantage of the euphoria of the occasion he appealed for a general amnesty, to include the hated Besenval, who had been placed in protective custody by the municipality, and who faced summary execution like Foulon if the people insisted on vengeance. Possibly with his altruism went an awareness that a plea for the general, who was the king's friend, was a good way of improving his own relations with the Court. When he begged them to spare Besenval the crowd roared its assent; it was Necker's hour of glory. But by the next morning the emotions roused by his visit had already subsided. Deputations from the districts of Blancs-Manteaux and Oratoire reported to the Assembly that the amnesty was illegal and would lead to disorders. In the ensuing debate even those who applauded the amnesty as a generous gesture thought that the minister had overreached his authority – Duquesnoy regretted that he had not thought it necessary to consult the Assembly's Research Committee which investigated alleged crimes. Barnave, Robespierre, and Mirabeau all protested against Necker's abuse of power. The Assembly finally voted to send Besenval for trial if and when he was recaptured. In due course he appeared before the Châtelet and was acquitted, despite the public demand for his blood.

The amnesty debate polarised opinion in the Assembly: monarchists and nobles were indignant at the campaign against Besenval, an officer only performing his duty, they said; the left denounced ministerial interference. Duquesnoy, a moderate right-winger, blamed the intrusive influence of Paris and thought it would be better if they moved fifty miles away, where they could concentrate on their main task of making the constitution, undistracted by the affairs of the capital. The sense of noble purpose with which they had started out had already been replaced with factional preoccupations; bureaucracy was growing, and with it an apparent desire to curtail liberty rather than to defend it. The Research Committee was a case in point. It had been set up to receive denunciations against agents and councillors of the king, anyone who had acted against the interests of the people during the events of 14 July, or who might be suspected of doing so in future. The deputies of the left who sponsored it told the Assembly that if they did not punish those who had planned the people's ruin the people would dispense their own justice, and so the Research Committee, prototype of so many like it, was established. It was kept busy during July when the leaders of the Court party, headed by Artois, left the country. The National Guard, ordered to detain counter-revolutionaries, stopped anyone who looked like an aristocrat; it was in this way that the French ambassador at Geneva was arrested, and his letters opened and forwarded to the Research Committee. On 25 July an angry debate on the inviolability of letters took place, in which Mirabeau clashed with Robespierre.

'Of course letters are inviolable', said Robespierre, 'but when a whole nation is in danger, when there is plotting against liberty, what is a crime at another time becomes a praiseworthy action'.

'Is it believed that plots are transmitted by the ordinary post?' Mirabeau asked, always pungent when he found expediency dissembling as virtue. Opening private letters was inexcusable:

> It would be said that in France, on the pretext of public security, citizens are deprived of all rights over their letters by those very men whom the nation has appointed to secure those rights. Those very men have decided that the most private communications may be turned into depositions; that citizens, friends, sons, fathers, may thus become each other's judges without knowing whether one day they could be causing each other's death.[11]

(This was true, but in his indignation he ignored the fact that the interception of letters was also part of the *ancien régime*'s surveillance system. Acting on information received was not a new practice.)

On opposite sides on this occasion, Mirabeau and Robespierre generally voted the same. Malouet noted in his memoirs that there were only two men on the left of the Assembly who were not demagogues – Robespierre and Mirabeau – adding that they were the only two who followed their own views, irrespective of public pressure. At this stage of the Revolution they had much in common: a hatred of royal and ministerial despotism, antipathy to the new aristocracy of wealth that was emerging, anxiety about an external war. Over a range of issues – slavery, liberty of the press, rights for minorities, passive citizens, clerical marriage – Robespierre echoed Mirabeau's views in debates; outside the Assembly the lawyer from Arras followed him about so attentively that he was known as Mirabeau's monkey. Later in the Revolution it was inconvenient for Robespierre to acknowledge this early admiration. Whether he believed the royalist propaganda about Mirabeau's character at the time he passed for his monkey is not known. If he did a man of his conscious rectitude might have been expected to avoid being seen in his company. On the other hand, a privately ambitious, self-contained, thinking man might believe the stories and still want to learn what he could from the dominant leader of the day. For political leaders have to have successors. Mirabeau belonged to the moderate left, Robespierre to the radical left, but in the early summer of 1789 the ideological gap was not marked. They both believed passionately in the sovereignty of the people, in abolishing all forms of privilege, in the need for constant vigilance against counterrevolution. The difficult business of converting revolutionary ideals into reality still lay ahead. In the long run the bitterest battles in the Assembly would not be between those who cheered the Revolution on and the rearguard of nobles who detested it, but between the hard left and the soft left, the ideologues and the pragmatists. The ascendancy of the ideologues was already visible in the letters debate, in Robespierre's justification of extreme measures when liberty was in danger. Mirabeau would have said that liberty was in danger because of the extreme measures.

The debate on the inviolability of letters took place as outbreaks of arson and violence spread in rural areas. Reports of attacks on property, and of rents and taxes not being paid, profoundly disturbed an Assembly dedicated to an egalitarian society, but one, nevertheless, rooted in the principle of property. For weeks the deputies had been wrangling over the phraseology of the Declaration of Rights. On 3 August, when Salomon of the Assembly's Reports Committee read out its report on the peasant revolt, it was as if the windows of the hall had been flung open, changing the muffled sounds of the world outside into a terrifying roar; they were jolted back to earth, and into realising that their intellectual revolution had been superseded by one based not on ideas but on direct physical expression, ungovernable, unauthorised. Anarchy seemed inevitable if the disorders continued; the disorders would continue until grievances were put right. The Assembly was torn between its desire for law and order and its sense of justice.

On the next day Target, doyen of the Paris *parlement*, refused to compromise: the sacred right of property was under attack, rents and dues must be paid as before; but the decision to force the Assembly into making immediate concessions had already been taken overnight by a large number of deputies, united by the Breton Club which also secured the election of a sympathetic president, Le Chapelier. That day, 4 August, saw the demolition of the feudal system. Fired by speeches from the duc d'Aiguillon and the vicomte de Noailles, one a wealthy landowner, the other landless, the Assembly voted to abolish feudal rights, then the rights connected with the game laws and copyhold system, then the tithes paid to the Church.

They were carried away by 'that kind of noble drunkenness which accompanies a burst of generosity', commented the *Courrier de Provence*, adding that though a more methodical procedure could have been followed the results should not have been different.[12] Right-wingers called it an orgy; rather it was a massive moral recantation, an act of atonement which those involved hoped would propitiate an angry nation. But the grand gesture was made without any regard for the consequences and without any constitutional means available as yet to deal with them. As Mirabeau pointed out, the people were told that all feudal dues and tithes had been abolished, but they were not told that taxes would have to take their place, that taxes were a political necessity. Instead of restoring peace the Assembly's flood of resolutions could only add to the confusion, and to the disillusionment which people were beginning to feel for the Assembly itself.

Mirabeau was not present on 4 August. Knowing in advance what tactics the Breton Club were going to use, he avoided a situation in which his own style of objective reasoning would have been inopportune.[13] The time for guidance would come during the subsequent debates as the Assembly converted the declarations of that day into decrees, and in the process had to resolve the contradictions between what it had willed emotionally and its fundamental belief in the principle of property. There was no going back on the decisions that had been taken. It was a question of choosing between expropriation, which the course decided on that day amounted to, and redemption of those rights which might be legally regarded as personal property.

The problem presented itself most sharply six days later on 10 August, when the Assembly debated the redemption of tithes. Sieyès, vehement opposer of aristocratic privilege, was compelled by his background to defend the clergy's right to the tithe. Chasset, deputy for Beaujolais, favoured simple abolition, and was supported by Mirabeau. No, he declared, the tithe was not property:

> It has never been anything but an annual perquisite for the clergy, a simple possession revocable at the wish of the sovereign; not even that, the tithe is a contribution destined for that branch of the public service concerned with ministers of altars; it is the subsidy with which the nation salaries its officers of morals and instruction.
>
> I hear many murmurs at the word 'salary' and it will be said that it offends the dignity of the priesthood; but it is time . . . to renounce the prejudice which makes one disdain the words 'salary' and 'salaried'. I only know of three ways of existing in society; one has to be either a beggar, a thief, or salaried. Apart from that, officers of morals and instruction should occupy a very distinguished place in the social hierarchy; they must be given consideration and respect in order that they should strive to merit it; they should have comfort in order that they should be recompensed in a manner conforming

with the dignity of their ministry and the importance of their functions; but they should not be able to claim a pernicious contribution as property.[14]

The tithe was declared not to count as property. At the same time Mirabeau's call for regular salaries for the clergy caused an outcry; he was accused of being an atheist, of trying to destroy religion. The events of 4 August brought him a letter from the bailli, horrified by the headlong renunciation. Mirabeau agreed that it would have been better if all questions of privilege had been fully discussed. He added:

> Not that I have the least regret over the abolition of the remains of the feudal system. I know your views about that: you think that a seigneur with fiefs is, first and last, the protector of his vassals. Judging others by yourself, and their attitude by your own, you fear that henceforth the peasants will have no defence against rapacious profiteers. But do remember, my dear uncle, that unfortunately for humanity seigneurs like you are excessively rare. If you recall the nobility's mad behaviour for over a year, in league with the *parlements* – which it should not defend – and the Court – which it should not serve – you will realise that it has been responsible for its own destruction. There was not a member of the third who was not extremely moderate on his arrival in the Assembly, but minds were heated by the obstacles that had to be overcome to establish a single assembly. The lunacy of the Court in the 14 July business turned all heads. After that it was no longer a matter of establishing liberty but of seizing it by force; and since then it has been clear that a revolution which began with the siege of the Bastille and decapitated heads would go to much greater lengths than had been expected.
>
> Having said that, my dear uncle, this revolution must be judged as a whole, and not by the anarchy and licence that reigns momentarily, and which is too violent to last. You know better than I that the intermediate stage in a revolution is always worse than what went before, however bad it was.[15]

Looking back at the opening of the Estates General, it was impossible not to notice how the early idealism had changed. Every step forward had resulted not so much from free will and public spirit but as a reaction to circumstance. As Duquesnoy remarked, fear had prompted all the concessions made by the privileged orders, and vengeance rather than real public spiritedness motivated the extreme left: the irony was that if the general good was indeed achieved it would have been brought about by fear and vengeance.[16] Marat, and after him Marx, said much the same thing from a different viewpoint, when they credited popular violence with all the achievements of the Revolution.

Mirabeau understood the violence, understood also that the Assembly, by its reaction to external violence, was sanctioning it as a weapon. Writing to his uncle he expressed optimism:

> It is as a whole that this revolution must be judged, not by the anarchy and licence which reigns momentarily . . . if the revolution progresses without

civil war we shall yet be able to say that many nations have not become free so easily.

But successful progress depended on two things, the people's confidence in their elected representatives, and cooperation between the Assembly and the king's ministers. Following 4 August he tried for a second time to establish a dialogue with Necker. La Marck sounded out the new Keeper of the Seals, Champion de Cicé, Archbishop of Bordeaux, whose progressive views were already known. He received a pessimistic reply: Necker understood nothing of the situation, he refused to approach the leaders of the Assembly, and he regarded Mirabeau as his personal enemy – more, as an incarnation of Satan. 'While M. Necker remains in the ministry', concluded Cicé, 'all approaches of this nature are hopeless.'[17]

It was perhaps too much to expect otherwise. Thanks to Mirabeau, Necker had seen his popular image slipping since his return, and his popularity with the people was his best defence against dismissal. Turning his critic into a monster of unprincipled ambition was the self-protective reaction of a man whose politician's egotism was matched by his moral self-esteem. It never occurred to Necker that by responding to Mirabeau not only would their common aim regarding the monarchy have benefited, but he himself would have been that much surer of staying in power.

The timetable of the Assembly was largely filled with debates on the constitution. The Constitution Committee (Mounier, Sieyès, the Bishop of Autun, Clermont-Tonnerre, Lally-Tollendal, Le Chapelier, Bergasse, and the Archbishop of Bordeaux) was formed on 7 July, but the Assembly insisted that a Declaration of Rights should be drawn up before any work commenced on the constitution itself. The first deputy to produce a Declaration of Rights for consideration was La Fayette, whose version, closely based on the American model, was loudly applauded when he read it on 11 July; but doubts being raised about whether the American experience was wholly relevant, it was passed to the Assembly's committees for further study. La Fayette's duties as commander of the Paris National Guard prevented him from taking any further part in framing the Declaration of Rights. Mounier, Sieyès, the Sixth Bureau, La Rochefoucauld, Target and others submitted their versions. Mounier's was slipshod, Duquesnoy thought, and that of Sieyès 'metaphysical and obscure'. Articles from these and La Fayette's version were put together in a draft which Mounier presented to the Assembly on 27 July. The events of the previous fortnight were already apparent in the tone of this Declaration which placed greater emphasis than La Fayette's on law and order – duties were mentioned along with rights; but realism had been gained at the expense of inspiration, and instead of accepting it the Assembly appointed a committee of five, headed by Mirabeau, to study the different versions and make a compilation.

He was drafted onto the committee against his will, regarding a Declaration of Rights as meaningless before they had a ratified constitution, a view shared by many deputies and by members of the Constitution Committee itself. Malouet feared that if natural rights were proclaimed and then restricted in the constitution it would lead to discontent and violence. Barnave and Duport argued that it was wrong to keep the people in ignorance of their rights; as the object of the constitution was to preserve the natural rights of man there should be a declaration of what those rights were.

In the second of two articles on the subject in the *Courrier de Provence*, he dismissed the Declaration of Rights as a vast and beautiful idea, warning his readers that it abounded in restrictions which belied its good intentions. It declared all men to be equal, but subordinated equality to what it called social utility; equality of taxation was accepted, the inequality arising from wealth remained. It was a Declaration of Rights for the propertied classes, not for the people.

> A simple declaration of the rights of man, applicable to all peoples and all ages, in every area, moral and geographical, of the globe, was no doubt a great and splendid concept; but before thinking in such generous terms of the code that should be applied to other nations, it might have been a good idea if the bases of our own had been laid down . . . Every step the Assembly takes in expounding the rights of man will result, we shall see, in its being struck by the abuses that could ensue if these rights were made available to the people; and prudence will often greatly exaggerate these abuses. Hence we find these numerous restrictions, these detailed precautions, these conditions carefully added to each article of the Declaration: restrictions, precautions, and conditions which in almost every instance replace rights with obligations and substitute fetters for liberty . . .[18]

These views did not endear him to his middle-class Assembly colleagues, who were as hostile to the idea of popular power as they were to royal authority.

Doubting the efficacy of declarations of rights, he did not forget that in his *Adresse aux Bataves* he had composed one for the Dutch patriots; he was writing then purely as a propagandist. Since then also he had read Bentham, but it cannot be concluded that when he spoke out against the Declaration he was merely parroting Bentham: in matters concerning his own country he needed no guidance from foreigners, neither Bentham nor Dumont, who decried the Declaration of Rights to him, and who may be suspected in this instance of passing off as his own some of Bentham's received wisdom. Despite their prejudice against it the Genevois helped him to prepare the preamble to the committee's Declaration of Rights – it was something they could boast about in the future. Dumont wrote:

> Mirabeau had the generosity to take this work upon himself and to give it to his friends. So there we were, Duroveray, Clavière, and myself, drafting, discussing, adding a word, taking out four, exhausting ourselves in this ridiculous task, and at last producing our bit of marquetry, our mosaic of pretended rights that had never existed.[19]

It was a case of too many cooks, for this version was rated by Duquesnoy as the feeblest of the lot. In the vote taken on all the versions on 19 August the most popular was the Sixth Bureau's, which received 605 votes; the Sieyès version came next with 245 votes, and La Fayette's only obtained 45, reflecting the growing unease over the power he now enjoyed and doubts about his ability to control popular unrest. The Sixth Bureau's draft eventually became the Declaration of the Rights of Man, though it owed some of its final language to La Fayette's version, enough for him to be able to claim forty years later that it was based more on his project than on any other. Long before then, however, he had realised that although a declaration of rights might keep 'the knowledge of liberty alive' in the midst of darkness, it could not ensure its practice.[20]

Article 3 of the Declaration of Rights proclaimed that 'The principle of all sovereignty resides essentially in the nation; no individual can exercise authority which does not emanate expressly from it'. In the light of this principle, what constitutional authority was the king to have? From the middle of August the deputies split into two camps over this question, and the related one of whether to have a single-chamber legislature, or an upper and a lower chamber. The *monarchiens*, headed by Malouet and Mounier and supported by Necker, wanted the king to have an absolute veto over the decisions of the legislature, and a hereditary upper chamber as in England; the centre and left sided with Sieyès, who insisted on no royal veto and no second chamber – no curb, in effect, on the absolute power of the Assembly. Mirabeau entered neither camp, believing that the *monarchiens* would cripple the Revolution and that the arrangement proposed by Sieyès would destroy the monarchy.

Conservative historians have criticised Mirabeau's failure to join forces from the beginning with Malouet and the *monarchiens*. Had he done so, it is argued, the moderates in the Assembly would have followed his example. Had he put himself at the head of a moderate party he would have gained the respect of all decent men and the king's cause would have benefited. This argument was favoured by earlier generations of English-speaking historians, who tended to assume that the establishment of a constitutional monarchy *à l'anglais* was all that the Revolution was about, or needed to be about, and that the only respectable place for Mirabeau was with Malouet and Mounier and other advocates of a British parliamentary system. Malouet's memoirs encouraged this view. It ignores the divisions which political parties would have emphasised at the start of the Revolution, before the system had even been created under which political parties would operate; as it does the fact that the monarchy would lose its hold on the nation's loyalty once it was identified with a political party – as happened after the Bourbon restoration. It fails to take into account the limited appeal of Malouet and Mounier, the drawbacks of their brand of constitutional monarchy, and, not least, the incompatibility between Mirabeau and his designated partners. A party of declared constitutional monarchists invited the resentment of the representatives of the nation, for 'monarchist' had a reactionary sound, suggestive of the Court. Constitutional monarchists would be trusted when they had proved their loyalty to the Revolution. Mirabeau was right not to join the Malouet–Mounier camp; ultimately it would not have helped the cause of monarchical government. Such errors of judgement were summed up in a favourite saying of his: *la petite morale tue la grande*.

One of those who expressed alarm over the division in the Assembly, though he did so only in private letters, was La Fayette. In his memoirs, written in old age, he liked to think that he had been a republican in 1789, but this is contradicted by his correspondence at the time. He was then, in so far as he understood the term, a constitutional monarchist, but he had the problem of reconciling his loyalty to the king with his popular 'American' image, and accordingly he avoided damaging political explicitness. As a constitutional technicality the veto did not interest him. He feared that the conflict would lead to the dissolution of the Assembly; and he wanted the veto to be rejected so that, as commander of the National Guard, he should not have to deal with the violent reaction in Paris which was otherwise inevitable, and which would force him to act a part which would destroy his popularity with the people. He therefore needed to persuade the advocates of the veto to back down. On 25 August, two days before the Constitution Committee was to report on the veto, he asked Jefferson to allow a group of deputies to dine at his house the following day. The reason he gave for meeting at Jefferson's was that his own house was always full, but it seems more likely, in keeping with his preferred neutral public image, that he did not want the world to know what he was doing. Those present at the meeting on 26 August were Duport, Alexandre de Lameth, Barnave, the comtes d'Agoult and Latour-Maubourg, the

marquis de Blacons, and Mounier. Mounier was the only representative of the Constitution Committee there, the others being La Fayette's supporters, and although La Fayette passed it off as a gathering of
patriots anxious to achieve solidarity in the Assembly, the meeting was
plainly organised with the intention of browbeating Mounier, and
through him the Constitution Committee, into accepting a populariste
solution, the one most convenient for the commander.

Their discussions went on for six hours. Jefferson did not join in; nor
did La Fayette, thus making sure that Mounier could not accuse him
of having personally used pressure against him. Duport and Lameth
began by arguing for a single-chamber legislature and a suspensive
veto, which would allow the king to withhold his sanction to a decree
for a limited period. The Sieyès no-veto option had already been
rejected by the Assembly; the suspensive veto was a compromise. But
Mounier was adamant: two chambers as in England, and an absolute
veto, because a suspensive veto would only create public resentment
over delays in legislation without contributing any real strength to the
executive. Mounier's stubbornness was a blow to La Fayette. The
next few days saw the permanent rupture in the Assembly between
the *monarchiens* and the moderates, who now fell under the radical
influence of Duport, Lameth, and Barnave, ironically dubbed the triumvirs. There was rioting in Paris, as rumours spread that the king
would use the veto to suppress the revolution, and that the Court was
conspiring to murder the most popular deputies. On Sunday 30 August
an impromptu force set off from the Palais-Royal to march to their
rescue, led by Saint-Huruge, an obscure member of the Orléanist
camp. It was turned back by the *garde municipale* of Paris, a mounted
contingent not connected with La Fayette's National Guard, but he
claimed it as another example of his peacekeeping efficiency. The
incident convinced him that Orléans and his supporters were taking
advantage of the disunity in the Assembly in order to foment trouble in
Paris; writing to his friends, he told them he was positive a plot existed
and determined to expose the ringleaders.[21] These letters, with their
stress on his dedication, give the reader the impression that his obses-
sion about an Orléans–Mirabeau conspiracy, unsupported as it was by
proof or plausibility, had its origin in the potential threat to his own
image as represented by the situation which he had the responsibility
of controlling.

In fact, although Saint-Huruge's march came to nothing, La Fayette
did not emerge unscathed from the occasion. The Assembly was angered by the constant attempts to influence its debates from outside,
and demanded that he and Bailly should resume their seats in order to
answer questions about their ability to prevent this sort of interference.

Clermont-Tonnerre moved that the Assembly should move elsewhere to escape the dictatorship of Paris, and Loustalot, editor of the *Révolutions de Paris*, came out strongly against the intimidation of deputies over the veto issue; in both cases there was implied criticism of La Fayette's performance.

On 1 September Mirabeau spoke in favour of an absolute veto. In doing so he had no royalist sympathies. It was a reasoned decision and entirely consistent with his choice of a single-chamber legislature. In his view the establishment of an upper chamber, even an elected one, so early in the Revolution could only perpetuate the people's deeply rooted hatred of the aristocracy; for the time being a single chamber was needed as an outward sign to the nation that the Assembly spoke for it and not just for privileged cliques. The left's ideological justification of a single chamber was as irrelevant as the English-precedent arguments of those who favoured a bicameral legislature.[22] What mattered was to have a system which attracted confidence. It was a foregone conclusion that the vote would be for a single chamber. In that event the absolute veto would become the only safeguard against unconstitutional moves by the legislature of the day.

By defending the absolute veto he risked being seriously misunderstood. The deputies who had declared in Article 3 of the Declaration of Rights that the principle of sovereignty resided in the nation, that is, in themselves as the representatives of the nation, would react furiously to the idea of allowing the king any direct authority. Wimpffen's phrase in the sovereignty debate about the government of France being a royal democracy had an attractive sound, but many patriot deputies could not reconcile it with their existing stock of ideas about systems of government. Words like 'democracy', 'nation', 'people', 'republic', had different connotations, both for the user and the receiver, depending on which authorities had influenced them individually. Thus, 'royal democracy' and 'constitutional monarchy' and 'republican monarchy' all meant, in theory, a system which retained a king while giving sovereign power to the representatives of the people. However, a typical constitutional monarchist would stiffen at the other terms because 'democracy' and 'republican' had current overtones of extremism; Montesquieurians and followers of Mably would differ over whether a republican form of government (one where all or some of the people exercised the sovereign power) could exist under a king; and Rousseauists, though fond of talking about the sovereignty of the people and democracy, really meant the sovereignty of the bourgeoisie. The one thing they shared was their hatred of despotism, especially royal despotism, and for Mirabeau – leader of the fight against aristocratic and royal tyranny, and upholder of popular sovereignty – to propose giving the king a veto seemed like a betrayal of principles.

He had to persuade ears deafened by prejudice that he did not seek the return of royal despotism, and that the veto was necessary in the interests of sound government, and if they wanted to obtain genuine and not illusory stability. He began by stressing that the right of veto presupposed a constituted monarchy, when the king would use it solely to maintain the constitution; it could not be used to hinder the creation of the constitution. He agreed that the idea of an individual vetoing the wishes of the people's representatives was, at first glance, unacceptable, since presumably what the Assembly presented to the king for his approval was the result of free and enlightened discussion. Common sense objected to any individual having the right to frustrate this rational general will, and the thought that the constitution would give one man, 'armed with this terrible veto', such a right was even more shocking. But without any right of resistance the power of the public guardian (*dépositaire de la force publique*) could often be usurped, and used to enforce wishes contrary to the public will.

The case for a suspensive veto had been argued by Barnave and a chorus of other speakers. They recalled Cerutti's description of a monarch as a perpetual and hereditary dictator, and assumed that the king would try to oppose the will of the people (that is, themselves) in successive sessions of the Assembly, and that a suspensive veto would be the safeguard of the Assembly's sovereignty. In reply Mirabeau contended that a suspensive veto posed the same problems as no veto at all. If the king refused his sanction it could only be because he judged a law to be contrary to the nation's interests, or because he was guided by personal views. In either case, with only a suspensive veto, would not he and his ministers be tempted to use irregular means to enforce his wishes? And what violent extremes would the people then resort to in opposition? To Mirabeau it seemed obvious that the king, having the ultimate sanction of the nation to call on, would only do so when national interests were at stake, and would not risk seeing that great force of opinion turned against him. Summing up, he proposed a package of constitutional measures which together with the royal sanction ('without written restrictions but limited in fact') would prevent abuses by the executive: an annual assembly, annual army expenses, annual tax laws, responsibility of ministers – 'that will be the *palladium* of national liberty, and the most precious exercise of the liberty of the people'.[23]

To the Assembly the idea that the executive power could ultimately appeal to the nation at large, by calling fresh elections, was insupportable. Mirabeau's definition of the king as the perpetual representative of the people caused particular alarm: the emerging bourgeoisie regarded it as the monarch's function to protect it against the people; a royal alliance with the people posed a double threat. The Assembly retaliated on 9 September by voting to make itself permanent. At this point Necker sabotaged the position of the executive by informing the Assembly that the king himself favoured a suspensive veto. Perhaps the minister thought he was buying the king popularity; he only played into the hands of those who wanted to strip the executive of all effective power. On 10 September the Assembly voted overwhelmingly against an upper chamber, and the next day adopted the suspensive veto by 575 votes to 325. The *monarchiens* were destroyed. But the merit of a single, democratic chamber was lost with only the sham brake of a suspensive veto: 'The king will be in the same relation to the National Assembly as his *parlement* used to be towards him', Mirabeau commented. 'It, too, will deliver its *lettres de jussion*, he will be forced to accede to them.'[24] He was one of eleven who abstained in the vote on the veto. It was not loss of conviction, as his stand in coming debates on the royal authority would show, nor was it fear of unpopularity: on 10 September a Breton address had been delivered to the Assembly which urged that deputies voting for the veto should be declared traitors to the nation. Scornful of that kind of intimidation, he abstained in order to preserve his usefulness. He had to assess how best to pursue his overall strategy for the constitutional stabilisation of the monarchy. The apparently obvious step of siding with the *monarchiens* would have been a fatal error. Their understanding of the subject was too narrow to be of any help to the monarchy. Apart from that there was the negative value of voting with them, for by doing so he would apparently have been supporting their entire political dogma.

Following their defeat in the voting on 10 and 11 September Mounier, Bergasse, the deputy for Lyon, the liberal nobles Lally-Tollendal and Clermont-Tonnerre, and the Archbishop of Bordeaux resigned from the Constitution Committee. Mounier was only prevented from resigning his seat in the Assembly altogether by his election as president on 28 September, but the gesture could not disguise the collapse of moderate influence. The Assembly from now on would be polarised in its ideology, with *monarchien* sympathisers turning towards the reactionary right and the moderate centre passively accepting the rule of the radical left. Mirabeau's independent position enabled him to continue his task of integrating the king's cause with that of the Revolution, uncompromised by factional allegiance to either the right or the left. A standing stone weathering the human elements, he appeared even more formidable in isolation.

In return for granting him a suspensive veto the Assembly expected the king to accept the decrees of 4–11 August, but this he would not do. 'I shall never consent to the despoilation of my clergy, my nobility', he had written privately on 5 August. The majority of the Assembly regarded these decrees as constitutional acts which therefore only required promulgation. They had been 'drafted by the constituent power; consequently they cannot be submitted to sanction', Mirabeau stated.[25] When the president, Clermont-Tonnerre, went to ask for the king's sanction on 14 September, therefore, it was purely as a courtesy. Louis replied four days later that he was ready to sanction the articles voted between 4 and 11 August when they were 'drawn up in laws'. His prevarication angered the left, while the right took hope that the king would successfully thwart the Revolution even at this stage. This counter-revolutionary spirit within the Assembly itself was a major menace: it stiffened the king's resistance, alienated the public, and made pre-emptive violence a certainty.

'We did not need to ask the king to sanction the decrees', Mirabeau declared on 18 September, as the right-wing clergy and nobility took this opportunity to challenge them. 'But having done so, public distrust and discontent will be greatly aggravated if we continue to argue.' In the circumstances it was useless to oppose them.

> The clergy, which would by the decree lose the right to any compensation for the tithes, would have lost the tithes anyway; the nobility, which might refuse to negotiate feudal rights, would still see themselves deprived of them by the pressure of opinion. We are all interested that the pure and simple sanction of these decrees, which our own attitude has hindered, should re-establish harmony and concord.

And the alternative? 'If we substitute self-esteem for patriotism, distrust for discussion, petty hatreds and bitter nostalgia for orderly debates, we are only treacherous egotists, and we are leading the monarchy to dissolution and not to constitution.'[26]

Louis and his ministers had still not learned that indecisiveness was fatal. On 21 September, playing for time, he deflected a final demand for his sanction by agreeing to publish the decrees, but refused to promulgate them. Two days later the Flanders regiment arrived in Versailles. There were demonstrations in Paris. On 25 September the *Chronique de Paris* proposed that the king and queen should be invited to come to Paris for the winter. It was still only an invitation. But the chain of circumstances which Mirabeau had warned against could only continue. 'A second onset of the revolution is needed', declared the *Révolutions de Paris* on 1 October. 'Everything is ready for it.'

# *NOTES*

1. See Gottschalk and Maddox (1969: 73f.), for the details of this incident. Writing of Mirabeau's political connections at this time, Gottschalk and Maddox (1969:73) appear to take press propaganda and La Fayette's biased view of him at face value, for they speak of him 'having recently aligned himself with another popular hero, the Duc d'Orléans'. The first popular hero, alluded to in this context, was Necker.
2. La Fayette (1837–38: II, 309–10).
3. *Discours*, 79.
4. Letter of 13 June 1789.
5. In his final years the marquis depended entirely on his brother and Mme de Pailly for financial support, and he died owing her considerable sums which were never repaid. What became of her is unknown; possibly she returned to her native Switzerland.
6. *Discours*, 84–6.
7. Rousseau (1968: Book IV ch. 2).
8. Mirabeau and Choderlos de Laclos, secretary to the duc d'Orléans, were the co-authors, supposedly, of two satirical works which were published in 1789: *La Galerie des Etats-généraux* and *La Galerie des dames françaises*. A piece on Necker in the first might seem suitable to lay at Mirabeau's door, but without factual proof it seems likely that his link with Laclos was a Court rumour. Sieyès, on the other hand, had close links with Laclos at this time.
9. Auguste-Marie-Raymond d'Aremberg, comte de La Marck (1753–1833) was the second son of the duc d'Aremberg, and a *maréchal de camp* in the French army. He possessed estates in Brabant and also in Alsace, his wife being the daughter of the marquis de Cernay. In 1793 he entered the service of Austria.
10. *Correspondance entre Mirabeau et La Marck*, I, 92–3.
11. *Mémoires biographiques*, X, 27f.
12. From 24 July Mirabeau's *Lettres à ses commettans* was replaced by the *Courrier de Provence*, directed by Mirabeau, with Dumont and Duroveray acting as editors.
13. Mirabeau's absence on 4 August is cited – together with his speech of 17 June on the Assembly's name, his criticism of the timing of the Declaration of Rights, his support for the veto, and the Tennis Court Oath, which he is alleged to have taken under duress – as evidence that he was covertly against the aims of the Revolution (Goodwin, 1970: 85). Such a list is misleading when his reasons for acting as he did are not mentioned. In the case of 4 August his endorsement of the results, in letters and in the *Courrier de Provence* refutes the suggestion that he opposed them privately. The Tennis Court Oath allegation was invented by the radical press in an attempt to destroy Mirabeau's popular support, by representing him as a calculating hypocrite who did not share the feelings of true patriots on that occasion.
14. *Discours*, 89–90.
15. *Mémoires biographiques*, (1834–36: IX, 47–50). Letter of 25 October 1789.
16. Duquesnoy (1894: I, 285).
17. *Correspondance entre Mirabeau et La Marck*, I, 98.
18. *Courrier de Provence*, XXVIII and XXXI.
19. Dumont (1951: 97).
20. La Fayette (1903: 207).

21. He did not hesitate to name Mirabeau as the man behind the plot. This may be deduced from a letter of Jefferson's, who echoed La Fayette's views, and who told Madison on 28 August 1789 that Mirabeau was the chief of those who were manipulating Orléans, and using Orléanist money for their own purpose (Boyd XV, 366).
22. Shortly afterwards Mounier changed his mind about the bicameral system (1789b, Chapter 3, p. 18). He said that he desired an upper chamber, but only after financial and other privileges had been destroyed, equality under the law established, and a constitution formed – Mirabeau's view expressed by one of his sourest critics.
23. *Discours*, 118. This speech was largely based on *Simplicité de l'idée d'une constitution*, by the Marquis de Casaux, a work 'which no one could either read or understand', according to Dumont. The Genevois, opposed to any veto, were furious that Mirabeau did not defer to their views. As usual, when they had not been consulted, Dumont denigrated the speech.
24. *Mémoires biographiques*, IX, 315.
25. *Moniteur*, no. 56, 12–14 September 1789.
26. *Discours*, 122–23.

# 9

## Conspiracies

## (September-November 1789)

In the Arcadia of 1789 the *ego* of hard reality waited unperceived. The finances, the reason for summoning the Estates General in the first place, the *ancien régime*'s only reason, had been swept aside by the priorities of the Revolution and the dreams of the revolution-makers. Emblem of the old order which was being dismantled, they had no place on an agenda devoted to the constitution of a new France. Unwelcome and ignored, they refused, nevertheless, to disappear.

On 7 August Necker came to the Assembly to remind them of the financial crisis, which made it necessary to raise a loan of 30 million livres. Although he did not say so in so many words, without it the country would draw even closer to bankruptcy and the loss of whatever credit it still retained abroad. One difficulty had to be overcome before the Assembly could give its assent: the deputies had been ordered in their *cahiers* not to allow any new taxes or loans until the constitution was completed. On principle each of them would have to get permission from his *bailliage* before he could vote, but the time it would take, even supposing the permission was forthcoming, made this procedure impracticable. Mirabeau's suggestion that the loan should be underwritten by the deputies themselves was a non-starter. The loan was finally agreed on, but the Assembly demonstrated its dislike of bankers and financiers by decreeing a lower rate of interest than had previously operated (4½ per cent instead of 5 per cent) with the result that it was effectively stillborn, only 2½ million of the 30 million livres being raised.

When Mirabeau next spoke on the subject on 19 August the failure of the loan was already apparent. He reminded the guardians of private interests who opposed it that 'the constitution cannot progress without the finances, nor the finances without the constitution', warning them that the minister would probably hold the Assembly responsible for the nation's bankruptcy, and would certainly blame it for the cessation of payments.[1] Another loan, of 80 million livres, was announced, but this time Necker made his approach more tactfully, allowing ten years for its repayment, and coupling it with a plan for reducing the tax on salt. On 27 August Mirabeau urged its immediate adoption, supported by the Bishop of Autun who also called for a renewal of the declaration of 17 June, honouring the national debt, as a vital step towards the revival of public credit. Necker's own favourite plan for raising money was by means of a national bank, along the lines of the Bank of England, but his suggestion that the Caisse d'Escompte should be used for this purpose was rejected by the Assembly after Mirabeau made a devastating attack on the Caisse on 16 September. Necker's next idea was for a patriotic contribution or voluntary tax. In his financial report of 24 September – a report which, he declared, it 'tore his soul to have to present' – he revealed that by October only 3 or 4 million livres would remain in the treasury, against the 30 million needed for that month alone and 60 million for the rest of the year. He proposed a contribution of up to a quarter of the contributor's revenues, with the mint paying above the current price for gold and silver thus donated, but the Assembly objected to the idea of a further loan under any name. Some deputies, who thought that only capitalists would suffer, found the prospect of national bankruptcy morally attractive.

There was surprise when Mirabeau spoke in support of the patriotic contribution on 26 September. It could only be, his enemies said, because he expected to take credit for the loan if it succeeded, or because he could discredit Necker if it failed. He acknowledged that his stand was unusual – 'I have never had the honour of being the friend of the Minister of Finance' – but pointed out that there was no time to draw up a better plan, or to query the figures they had been given. The country's confidence in the minister, he added, should persuade the Assembly to trust him at this moment of danger. Answering the accusation of right-wingers that he was setting a trap for the minister, who would be left alone to face the consequences if his plan failed, he did not deny that he was more concerned for the Assembly's reputation than for that of an individual:

I do not believe that the credit of the National Assembly should be balanced against that of the Minister of Finance . . . I do not believe that the kingdom would be in peril if M. Necker were mistaken; I believe that public welfare would be seriously compromised if a truly national endeavour were aborted, if the Assembly lost its credit and failed in a decisive operation.

The Assembly was in a negative mood; it still wanted the project to be submitted to the Finance Committee. Mirabeau spoke four times during the debate. The fourth time, addressing those who rejected the loan as a disguised form of taxation, he demanded: 'What is bankruptcy, then, if it is not the cruellest, most unfair, most disastrous form of taxation?' The kingdom was at the edge of the abyss, they had to act. And then devastating irony took over:

So here is a list of French landowners. Choose from the richest so as to sacrifice fewer citizens, but choose; for should a few not perish to save the mass of the people? Come! These two thousand nobles possess the means to meet the deficit, to restore order to the finances, peace and prosperity to the kingdom. Strike, immolate these unhappy victims! Cast them into the abyss; it will close. You recoil with horror. Inconsistent, cowardly men! Do you not see that in voting for bankruptcy, or what is more odious, in making it inevitable without voting for it, you will sully yourselves with an act a thousand times more criminal?

That horrible sacrifice would at least make the deficit disappear. But do you think, because you have not paid, that you will not owe anything? Do you think the thousands, the millions of men who will lose all sources of comfort in their lives, perhaps their only means of support, as a result of the terrible explosion, do you think that they will leave you in peace to profit by your crime? Stoical witnesses of the evils which that disaster will bring upon France, impassive egotists who think that convulsions of despair and misery will pass like so many others, are you really sure that so many men without bread will leave you to the peaceful enjoyment of those dishes which you have been unwilling to reduce either in number or in delicacy?

I hear talk of patriotism, praise of patriotism, invocations to patriotism. It is very magnanimous to give part of one's possessions in order to save all one's possessions! He who hesitates must accept contempt for his stupidity. Yes, it is common prudence, your crudest interests that I invoke. I ask you once again: will you present the world with the spectacle of an assembly failing the nation's trust? I tell you, you will all be caught in the universal ruin. Those who are most closely interested in the sacrifice the government is asking of you are yourselves.

Vote then for this extraordinary subsidy, and may it suffice! Vote for it because the situation brooks no delay, and for any delay we would be responsible. Do not ask for time; misfortune never grants it.

At the end of his speech he referred pointedly to the cliques, royalist and patriot, in the Assembly which portrayed him as a self-motivated agitator:

Gentlemen, a short time ago, in connection with a ridiculous motion of Palais-Royal inspiration, about an insurrection which has never seemed important except to feeble minds and in the perverse designs of certain men, you heard these frenzied words: 'Catilina is at the gates of Rome, and they are deliberating'. Certainly, there was neither Catilina, nor perils, nor plots, nor Rome.[2] But today bankruptcy, hideous bankruptcy, is here threatening to destroy you, your possessions, your honour. And you deliberate![3]

When he finished, said Ferrières, a single feeling seemed to grip the Assembly, as though each member was fleeing from the heavy responsibility with which Mirabeau had threatened him, only to see in front of him the deficit calling for its victim. The Assembly rose, called for a vote, and unanimously passed the decree.

Even his most implacable critics were enthralled by his performance. 'The effect was prodigious', said Mme de Staël. 'Although I could not believe in his good intentions, for two hours he captured my whole admiration.'[4] 'From this day Mirabeau was considered a unique being, he had no rival', wrote Dumont, his usual urge to belittle Mirabeau's ability temporarily overcome. 'There were other orators; he alone was eloquent, and the impression was all the stronger as this speech was an impromptu response which could not have been prepared.'[5]

But some sections of the Assembly were suspicious of his motives. Alexandre de Lameth said that in the matter of the patriotic contribution he had 'malignly' taken on trust the Director-General's proposal. Lameth represented the wealthy interests that might be expected to set the patriotic example. The speech did not go down well with the extreme left either, which objected to Necker's solution on the grounds that it was for the Assembly to take the initiative in rehabilitating the economy. In the debate on the address to the nation,[6] which was to inform the public of the need to support the patriotic contribution, Mirabeau assured the Assembly that its authority was not in peril – 'one man's strength of character [Necker's] can never rival the power of a national assembly' – and called on it to show a sense of unity: 'What is needed above all for the regeneration of the nation is a nation'.

The campaign being waged against him, which he alluded to in his speech on 26 September, was ugly and disturbing, not so much because of the resemblance to a kangaroo court as because of the way it was utilised by those with personal, as well as political, axes to grind. There were two campaigns in fact: the one he mentioned, orchestrated by Palais-Royal agitators, which stigmatised him as a counter-revolutionary following his speech on the veto; the other pursued by the Court, which hoped to kill two birds with one stone by linking him with the duc d'Orléans, patron of political radicals and rumoured usurper in waiting.

There was, besides, a running feud in the Assembly between him and 'the triumvirate' – Duport, Lameth, Barnave – and their followers, which led to confrontations in debates which were out of proportion to the issues involved, and promoted the very factionalism which both sides regularly condemned.

The feud went back to November 1788 and the founding of the *Société des trente*, which met thrice weekly at the house of the wealthy magistrate in the Paris *parlement*, Adrien Duport. The *Société* brought together liberal nobles (La Fayette, La Rochefoucauld-Liancourt, d'Aiguillon, Lauzun), members of the clergy (the future Talleyrand, Sieyès), Duport's fellow magistrates (Le Peletier, Sémonville), lawyers (Target, Le Chapelier), as well as the philosopher, Condorcet – all looking to the future and the political and social changes which would have to be made. Mirabeau was a founder member. But he was soon complaining to his friend Lauzun that the '*tyrannie parlementaire*' of Duport and his *parlement* colleagues at the meetings was frustrating the efforts of what was supposed to be a club of 'patriotic citizens', and he proposed an independent venue. He was always very aware that the Paris *parlement*'s historical record of defending the rights of the people went hand in hand with a regard for its own vested interests. The same *parlement* which prided itself on resisting royal despotism was also determined to keep the 1614 rules for the Estates General which denied the third estate equal influence. Judging by his remarks to Lauzun at the time, Mirabeau feared that Duport, particularly, in a future assembly, would follow the *parlementaire* practice of rallying popular support by denouncing royal despotism, cementing his personal power with promises to the people that realistically could not be fulfilled. There may have been an element of the Mirabeau family hostility to the *parlements* here, but Duport was a man of complex motives. As a political radical he had joined the party of the duc d'Orléans; his pet plan was to make Orléans a constitutional king, with himself as his prime minister. (Another man would have been arrested on suspicion of conspiracy.)

Duport was elected to the Estates General by the nobility of Paris. In the Assembly the members of the *Société des trente* formed the core of the powerful, well-organised party which gathered round Duport and the Lameth brothers, Liberal, radical in its proclaimed aims, it was still a party of wealthy vested interests, in defiance of Rousseau's teaching on the pernicious effect of 'particular' interests. After 14 July Duport was joined by the talented and ambitious orator from Grenoble, Antoine Barnave – another lawyer – who had previously followed the moderate Mounier. Barnave (who was still only twenty-eight) became the mouthpiece for Duport's ideas. The decision to draw up a Declaration of Rights ahead of a constitution was one of his early victories over Mirabeau. As the months passed, Mirabeau's proposals, his views, became the signal for automatic attack by Duport and Barnave, when reasoned discussion, not rhetoric, was needed to serve the national interest. The purpose of the triumvirate's tactics regarding Mirabeau was to remove him as a rival 'friend of the people'. They represented every attempt by him to defend the king in his executive role as a denial of the people's rights. Their own determination to remove all power from the king's executive role became proof of their patriotism. The triumvirate increasingly dominated the Assembly's proceedings. In some quarters they were increasingly resented.[7]

Palais-Royal propagandists denounced Mirabeau as a counter-revolutionary; the Court regarded him as an anarchist. Much as the Court wanted to get rid of him, however, his popularity and strength in the Assembly made it dangerous to attack him over political issues alone. Hence the movement to reduce him by alternative means. His ambition was known. The royalist press spread the rumour that he was bent on seizing power, either with Orléans or through Orléans. If the mud stuck he would be doubly damned: the great patriot who used the Revolution to further his own ends, the defender of the monarchy who sought to overthrow the king.

The *lieutenant civil* at the Châtelet, Antoine Talon,[8] was well placed to know everything that was going on. The Court and La Fayette both used him as an agent and ferreter of information. Shortly after the debate on the veto Talon asked La Marck when Mirabeau was going to declare openly his support for the monarchists. La Marck said that he did not think he was committed to any particular party. Behind the guarded reply was the doubt which La Marck still had about his political aims. He had also heard rumours in La Fayette's circle about Mirabeau's being in the pay of Orléans. So when Mirabeau, one day in September, asked if he could borrow some money as he was desperate, La Marck was relieved: if the rumours were true he would not have been reduced to the humiliation of scrounging from a friend.

La Marck lent him fifty louis (1,000 francs). 'The slight service I had rendered him gave me some right to discuss his financial position', he wrote in his memoirs. 'I thus became convinced that this man, represented as venal by everyone, had never sacrificed any principle for money.' At the end of the month he told the queen, whose displeasure he had incurred by this friendship, that he was certain Mirabeau would be 'useful to the king when the ministers found themselves compelled to work with him, as I foresaw would inevitably be the case'. Her reply put an end to further discussion: 'We will never be so unfortunate as to be reduced to the painful extremity of turning to Mirabeau'.[9]

La Marck arranged to lend Mirabeau fifty louis a month, and advised him to postpone the liquidation of his debts until he had time to attend to his father's estate. In their conversations he noticed that Mirabeau had little regard for either Orléans or La Fayette; when Orléans and Mirabeau dined with him at the beginning of October there was a reserve between them which he decided could not have been faked since neither of them had any reason to deceive him. One conversation in particular stayed in his memory. Mirabeau, who had been raging at the blindness of the Court, suddenly burst out: 'All is lost. The king and queen will perish, and you will see the people trampling on their bodies. Yes, they will trample on their bodies', he repeated, seeing La Marck's horror. 'You don't understand the danger of their position. They must be made to realise it.'[10]

How little they realised it was demonstrated on 1 October when the officers of the king's bodyguard entertained the regiments garrisoned at Versailles to a banquet in the palace. The *Courrier de Provence* reported that the queen had been present, and that, at the height of the celebrations, the National Assembly had been mocked and 'the national cockade, that emblem of the defenders of liberty, was torn to pieces and stamped on'. The *Courrier* forbore to mention that the king was also present. Guessing how the occasion would be seized on by agitators, Mirabeau wanted to keep the king out of it, so that he would not be branded along with the queen of crimes against the nation.

In Paris the news that the national emblem had been insulted exacerbated the tension already created by rumours that the king was planning to flee to Metz. On 4 October, the call went out to march on Versailles. The next day in the Assembly Pétion denounced the events of 1 October and Mirabeau proposed that such occasions should be banned for fear of the consequences. However, in reply to a deputy who called for signatures to Pétion's denunciation, he said that he regarded this as a highly impolitic step, but one he would comply with if the Assembly first declared that the person of the king alone was inviolable, and that all other individuals, whoever they might be, were equally subject to the law. By other individuals he meant the king's brothers and the queen. His motion, which scandalised the royalists, was another attempt to make a distinction between the king and the detested Marie-Antoinette and Artois, in preparation for that foreseeable moment when the monarchy would be called to account by the French people.

The sitting of 5 October had begun with the reading of the king's statement on the decrees of 4 August. He would sanction them, he said, only if the executive power remained entirely in the hands of the monarch. He refused to discuss the Declaration of Rights, as 'principles susceptible of differences in application and even interpretation cannot be properly appreciated until their true meaning is fixed by the laws to which they are to serve as a basis'. This was only what he had said before, and Mirabeau reflected the general frustration when he observed that it was vitally important to public tranquillity that the Assembly's decisions should be accepted, and accepted willingly.'If the king persists in his refusals the germ of patriotism would soon be stifled, and anarchy will begin the moment the people realise their power sufficiently to notice that it is desired to restrain it.'

Every word uttered by Mirabeau in the Assembly this day was to be remembered and pondered over and variously interpreted. The deputies were still considering their reply to the king when reports arrived[11] of major disorders in Paris: a mob was already on its way to Versailles to take revenge on the king's bodyguard and the Flanders regiment for insulting the national cockade. Mirabeau went up to Mounier in the president's chair. 'Paris is marching on us', he told him. Mounier, who believed the Orléans–Mirabeau conspiracy stories, assumed that he spoke so positively because he had prior knowledge of the march. 'So, Paris is marching on us', he replied sarcastically. 'So much the better; we shall be a republic all the sooner.'

Previous attempts to march on Versailles had been halted by the National Guard, and on those occasions La Fayette had stationed units at Sèvres to defend the road. This time the road from Paris was unbarred. The crowd of women and political agitators, which had gathered outside the *hôtel de ville* early in the day, demanding bread, set off for Versailles at 10 a.m.; they had already been gone an hour when La Fayette responded to the news of a disturbance. It was 5 p.m. before he decided to follow them with an army of 20,000 National Guard soldiers and four companies of grenadiers. For six hours he had waited in Paris, certain that his fixed personal belief in an Orléanist plot was correct, that a *coup d'état* was at hand, that the capital would be seized the moment he left it. Much of the time he had been trying to reassert his authority with his own men, who wanted to go to Versailles to destroy the Flanders regiment, and who declared that if the king was too feeble to wear the crown the dauphin should reign in his place. To La Fayette it sounded like further proof of an Orléanist conspiracy, since what his troops were asking for – the removal of the king – would lead to a regency, and who else but Orléans would become regent?[12]

Between 9 p.m. and 10 p.m. a message reached Versailles that La Fayette was on his way. When the horde of women invaded the Assembly hall Mounier had gone to the palace, to demand the king's 'pure and simple' sanction to the Declaration of Rights and the decrees of 4 August; he was outraged that La Fayette should be coming with an army to pressurise the king and Assembly. Saint-Priest advised the king either to resist or to flee, and orders were given for the royal travelling carriages to be made ready, but Necker warned him that confrontation or flight would be equally disastrous for the monarchy; it was essential to show the people that he was well disposed towards them and trusted their loyalty. Louis was still uncertain what to do when shots were heard outside: the crowd of marchers camped in the Place d'Armes had seen the carriages, and the cry went up that the king must not be allowed to leave. As men of the local National Guard turned the carriages back the crowd became quieter, but the moment showed the king the impotence of his position. Cynical as well as stoical, it is unlikely that he put much faith in Necker's advice when his subjects, armed with pikes and scythes, were besieging his palace, or that he derived any sense of security from the presence of the Versailles National Guard. Knowing only that La Fayette's army was bearing down on him he had no choice but to comply with the Assembly's demands. He sanctioned the Declaration of Rights and the decrees of 4 August; and Mounier returned to the Assembly to collect a body of deputies and bring them to the palace, ready to face La Fayette when he arrived. Only a few deputies remained in the Assembly hall, which had been taken over by a noisy armed mob. Mirabeau was one of those who had gone home, refusing to carry on amid the uproar. After the morning session he had dined with La Marck, who had escorted him back to the Assembly at 6 p.m. Dumont was in the Assembly hall when Mounier returned from the palace. When he went to Mirabeau's apartment he found him in bed, but he got up and they went back to the Assembly together.

Soon after 11 p.m. La Fayette reached Versailles and entered the Assembly hall. He told Mounier that his army had sworn allegiance to the king and to the National Assembly; there would be no violence; 'the factious' had taken advantage of the unrest and had whipped up popular feeling; his own troops had demanded this advance on Versailles. Then why had they come, asked Mounier logically, if their intentions were not hostile? To calm public indignation, La Fayette replied. He then went off to the palace. At 3 a.m. he returned to the Assembly hall to assure Mounier that everything was peaceful in the town. The session was adjourned and the exhausted deputies went home to sleep.

When they met again on the morning of 6 October the drama of the history books had already taken place. The palace had been invaded by the mob while La Fayette slept, the queen had narrowly escaped with her life, and the king and queen had appeared on the balcony to face the people, along with Necker, the Keeper of the Seals, and La Fayette. In the Assembly a motion was immediately put to transfer the session to the palace as a mark of solidarity with the king. It was opposed by Mirabeau – whose motives were to be generally impugned, though it is fair to assume that what he was questioning was the wisdom of exposing the Assembly to the possible wrath of the people, or of making it appear to acquiesce in the turn of events, the details of which were still confused and uncertain. Instead, he moved a declaration that the National Assembly was inseparable from the king, which was duly carried. In token of this a hundred deputies joined the procession which left Versailles that afternoon when the king and queen were carried back to Paris by their triumphant captors. After a reception at the *hôtel de ville* the royal couple were conducted to the Tuileries palace. La Fayette and a troupe of National Guardsmen saw them to the door.

Miraculously La Fayette had emerged from the previous thirty-six hours as the saviour of the day, certainly as the master of ceremonies of the final scene. Any other military commander would not have survived a similar performance in a crisis which sealed the fate of the king, but his reputation was so enshrined that legitimate criticism was reduced to the level of snide political malice by the visible and unparalleled power which he now enjoyed. Hero of Paris, chief of police, supreme commander of the National Guard since early September, mayor of the palace, he could afford to ignore the other title bestowed on him in the days that followed: General Morpheus.

With the king in Paris, brought there by him, thus consolidating his popularity with the people, La Fayette set to work to uncover the conspiracy which he believed lay behind the events of 5–6 October. Undoubtedly the march on Versailles had been premeditated to some extent, and political agitators were there among the women who set off to demand bread, but no evidence then or since has lent weight to the idea that the march was the opening act of a planned *coup d'état*, which would have ended with Orléans ruling the kingdom. An investigation to discover the instigators of the events of 5–6 October was ordered by the *procureur-syndic* of the commune of Paris. No names were mentioned when the charges were formally laid at the Châtelet on 1 December, but Orléans and Mirabeau were already considered guilty. The Châtelet enquiry, or witch-hunt, went on for ten months. Four hundred depositions were collected, from everyone who had been a participant or an eye-witness of what happened on the fatal days, and from others who had no connection with them at all. A Demoiselle Poitevin, for instance, deposition number 54, said that she had made Mirabeau's wedding clothes, for which she had never been paid; instead he had 'paid her with hopes, saying that he would become a minister, that this was certain'.[13] A lieutenant-colonel in the Flanders regiment said that on 5 October Mirabeau was seen passing through the regiment with a naked sabre in his hand, telling the men that their officers were conspiring against them. La Fayette remarked in his *Mémoires* that the preposterousness of some of the allegations had detracted from the value of the rest, that is, those depositions which sought to establish that Mirabeau had been plotting to depose the king and put Orléans in his place.

The depositions in this category relied heavily on remarks made by him in the course of conversations, or accounts of conversations heard at second or third hand. Le Peletier quoted Mounier and Bergasse as saying that Mirabeau had declared it did not matter whether the king was Louis XVI or Louis XVII. Bergasse in his deposition recalled Mirabeau talking to him and Mounier about Orléans being made regent. Mounier himself made no mention of these remarks in his deposition which he made in Geneva in July 1790. Only when Mirabeau and Orléans had been cleared of any complicity in the events of 5–6 October did he corroborate Bergasse's statement, possibly prompted to do so after raking over old stories with Bergasse and others: Mounier, Bergasse, Dumont, and Duroveray were all in London at the end of 1790 when Mounier completed his *Appel au tribunal de l'opinion publique*, the querulous defence of his own conduct in the Assembly.[14]

When La Fayette made his deposition on 27 April 1790 he concentrated on clearing himself of the suspicion that he had been negligent on 5–6 October. His deposition contained an apparently watertight account of his movements; gaps in timings were smoothed over, and encounters which had taken place at the wrong moment for his account were omitted.[15] Mirabeau's ultimate acquittal was a disappointment for him, but he admitted that the evidence was inconclusive. Regarding Mirabeau's remark to Mounier about making Orléans regent – to Mounier the incontrovertible proof of his guilt – he eventually recognised it for what it was, an instance of Mirabeau playing a game with the humourless Mounier: 'he could have been amusing himself by alarming Mounier', he conceded in his memoirs. But he never acknowledged in so many words that the suspicions he had harboured against him were wrong. While the investigation continued Mirabeau said nothing publicly in his own defence, choosing to wait until he had been acquitted, and his judges had become the judged. Perhaps, however, he did break his silence once. Among the many anonymous pamphlets which circulated at the time there is one, *Défense du comte de Mirabeau et le duc l'Orléans*, the style of which, unlike the shrill crudeness of the others, is so restrained and well ordered that the identity of the author is scarcely in doubt.

So much for the evidence. Some sort of plot to force the king's abdication could have existed, linked somehow to the events of 5–6

October, but Mirabeau's connection with either is only conjecture. The removal of the king and Assembly to Paris, where they were subject to direct intimidation, is one of the strongest reasons for absolving him from any complicity in the October days, for he constantly warned against the threat to liberty and good government from illegitimate pressure groups. It has been said that what he could have envisaged happening next, and what he certainly hoped for, was a change of dynasty.[16] Disillusioned with Louis XVI, realising that the king would never cease to resist the Revolution, thwarted in his efforts to advise the administration, he rested his hopes – according to this theory – on Orléans, a prince committed to the Revolution, whose installation would benefit the cause and also open the way to advancement for himself. This plausible idea, however, ignores both Mirabeau's historical sense of the monarchy and his concern for stabilisation. The value of the monarchy lay in its continuity, in a mystical significance that was both profound and fragile. The historic bond between the French kings and their people was the legacy from the past which would help to stabilise a society in upheaval; but Mirabeau was well aware that the office of monarch would lose its meaning if it were seen to have become the prize in a political game. Apart from that, Orléans's elevation would be illegitimate, an absolutist act by an arrogant Paris-based minority without regard for the will of the French people. Only someone blindly ambitious and politically naive could have imagined it succeeding.[17] Far from stabilising the country and helping the Revolution, putting Orléans on the throne would involve the Assembly in conflict and perhaps destroy it, would intensify counter-revolutionary movements, bring Austrian armies to the aid of the deposed Louis, and plunge the country into civil war. Envisaging all this, as he must have done, Mirabeau would not have hoped for a change of dynasty. The simple solution would have proved self-defeating.

The king's removal to Paris, followed by the Assembly, signalled a new stage in the Revolution. Superficially the prospect looked good. The king had been brought physically close to his people, rescued – though forcibly – from the symbolic remoteness of Versailles which estranged their loyalty and belied his assertion that he cared for them. His presence among them was the proof to them that all would be well. The Assembly could now continue with its major task, the completion of the constitution which would enshrine the social and political objectives of the Declaration of Rights. The ground had already been partly cleared by the decrees arising out of 4 August and constructive reforms were in progress. They were safe from enforced dissolution. The king could no longer initiate legislation, and his suspensive veto could only delay it. Secure from executive interference, the Assembly was also assured of the capital's goodwill: the day it met for the first time in Paris La Fayette and Bailly came to promise their support in its future work.

Looking more closely there was less cause for optimism. The king, confined to the Tuileries, was no longer an authoritative figure, able to protect his people: the change in his historical role would alter their perception of him, and eventually their view of monarchy itself. His residence in Paris was right in theory; in effect he was a hostage, and this would have widespread repercussions. Apart from political consequences, there was the perennial matter of Paris versus the provinces. Increasingly Paris would be seen as managing the Revolution to suit itself, regardless of what the rest of the country wanted.

The Assembly's early battles to exist and to survive were behind it; in its relations with the executive it was now invincible. It had gained experience, it was organised. In the coming months it would reform local government and the judicial system, sweeping away old inefficiencies and abuses, and creating the modern administrative structure which would be the Constituent Assembly's lasting monument. But the coming months would also show its shortcomings: its inability to solve the problems of state funding and the annual deficit (finance was not its *métier*), and its failure to learn the right lessons from events. The fall of the Bastille symbolised the defeat of despotism; but the wave of attacks on property, riots, civil disobedience, and, finally, the king's surrender to mob force, alarmed a property-owning, middle-class Assembly, and froze its members' egalitarian words on their lips. The people had always been present at their debates, a noisy pressure group in the galleries. (After the Assembly moved into the Manège, its Paris quarters, admission to the galleries was restricted to ticket holders.) They, 'the people', figured grandly in the speeches of patriot deputies. However, that 'the people', unenfranchised and outside the political framework, could dictate the political course of events as they did when they captured the king, was something they had not foreseen.

Political activity had been defined implicitly from the classical age onwards as the prerogative of males in the property-owning class, educated and with time to devote to public duties. This was the ineradicable assumption of the nation's legislators in 1789. The Declaration of Rights and the constitution would reflect their views as members (largely) of the property-owning middle class, and their desire to protect middle-class interests. The decree of 22 December, which created 'active' and 'passive' citizens, was the natural outcome of this philosophy. Only 'active' citizens could exercise the right of franchise; only

taxpayers at a certain level were eligible to vote in primary and municipal elections, to vote in electoral colleges, to hold municipal office.
Another decree restricted eligibility for election as a deputy to those
who paid taxes equivalent to a mark's weight in silver. Only a minority
of deputies objected.

The Assembly that spoke of equality of rights thus decided that the
great majority of Frenchmen would have no part in the administrative
or political life of the country. It was a decision which had long-term
implications. In the months that followed the move to Paris it sealed
the growing belief among the poorest citizens that the Assembly was
not on their side, that they would have to act for themselves.

When Mirabeau moved to Paris with the Assembly he had already
discussed what the king's next move should be with La Marck. They
agreed that his enforced submission had struck a blow at his authority
from which he could only recover by demonstrating to his people that
he was still a free agent, and that the longer he stayed passively in Paris
under La Fayette's protection the more irrelevant he, and the monarchy itself, would become.[18] According to La Marck, Mirabeau wanted him to move to Rouen, a city distant from frontiers with their
connotation of impending flight, but strategically placed in a region
loyal to the Crown. Before going, he said, Louis would need to make a
declaration to the provinces, telling them that he wished to be inseparable from his people, that he had been brought to Paris by malcontents, and that in this situation the progress of the revolution could be
compromised. He would also have to address the Assembly in similar
terms, and summon it to follow him and continue its work.

La Marck agreed with this plan and showed it to the comte de
Provence, the one man who might be able to persuade the king to act
on it. (Provence, after agreeing that it was the only sensible course of
action, said that it would never be accepted; he had no influence
himself, and the king only listened to the queen.)

La Marck also agreed on the need to expose the ministry's responsibility for the present crisis. Necker's unsuccessful attempts to rescue
the finances guaranteed his eventual dismissal, but La Marck sagely
advised that a direct attack on him would damage Mirabeau's chances
of ever being in a position to influence this, or any future, ministry; that
it would be better to concentrate on his record in the Assembly, as it
was on his performance as '*un homme publique*' that the fulfilment of his
higher ambitions depended.

Mirabeau's desire to become a minister is always regarded as naked
ambition pure and simple. It grew out of his commitment to a balance
of power between the executive and the legislature. The lack of any
understanding between the government and the Assembly convinced

him of the need to appoint deputies to ministerial rank, whose job would be to explain the Assembly's views in the cabinet. The Assembly would benefit, the king would learn. He had recommended such appointments several times in the Assembly and in the *Courrier de Provence*, initially in the issue of 14 September, following the vote on the veto. This article, and another which appeared on 15 October, were preparation for the motion on the subject which he intended to launch in the Assembly at the earliest opportunity. To him it seemed that the opportunity to become the Assembly's public relations man was rapidly approaching. There were rumours that a new ministry was about to be formed, headed by Provence. From the daily letters that passed between him and La Marck at this time it is apparent that negotiations of some sort, involving himself, La Marck, and Provence, were in progress, and although the details can only be guessed at the mood of Mirabeau's letters was confident and optimistic.

Too optimistic. Necker, Saint-Priest, the Minister for the Interior, and La Fayette were all afraid of the influence he already exercised, and determined to prevent him from extending it. La Fayette's first concern, following the king's move to Paris, was to eliminate the leaders of the supposed plot behind the march on Versailles, and in so doing rid himself of his greatest rivals in power and popularity. Summoning Orléans to Montmorin's office, he gave him the choice of being arrested or of going to London, ostensibly on a mission from the king. Lauzun, given the same choice, refused to go, but Orléans, timid by nature, put up little resistance.[19] Mirabeau exhorted him to stay, if only because his departure would seem to confirm his guilt, and told Lauzun that the duke must attend the Assembly the next day, and he would then attack La Fayette on his behalf. The next morning he heard that Orléans had already left for London. 'The poor prince has taken the bait', he told La Marck. 'There is no proof against him. This impudence is too much. I shall never bend my head to the despotism of the presiding genius.'[20]

His declaration that he would attack the commander-general over his treatment of Orléans brought an instant reaction from La Fayette. La Marck was visited by Talon, offering to mediate between La Fayette and Mirabeau, whose career, he gave La Marck to understand, would gain infinitely from this alliance. The discovery that Mirabeau was already negotiating with Provence gave added urgency to his mission. 'Matters are on the boil', he told La Marck. 'Your redoubtable *comte* does not know everything, and has knocked at a door which is not the best.'[21]

The immediate result of La Fayette's overture was a meeting on 15 or 16 October at the house of Mirabeau's niece, Mme d'Arragon, at

Passy, which was attended by La Fayette, his friend Latour-Maubourg, Alexandre Lameth, Laborde de Méréville (inculpated a week later in a pamphlet attacking Mirabeau and Orléans), and a few others. Their reason for being there, Mirabeau's threatened attack, was diplomatically ignored. The discussions turned mainly on the need for a new ministry, and various deputies were mentioned who might be included in it. Lameth explained in his history of the Constituent Assembly:

> The incompatibility of the functions of minister and deputy not yet having been pronounced on, it was among the members of the Assembly that we looked for the men best able to form a ministry . . . Mirabeau was then far from aspiring to the ministry since he said on this occasion, 'I cannot have the honour of making a sacrifice in this respect, for I know that I have erected a mole of prejudice against me which will take time to destroy'.[22]

While he spoke disarmingly Mirabeau remained on his guard, aware that if La Fayette made any promises it would only be in the hope of neutralising him. La Fayette for his part was not taken in by Mirabeau's renunciation of ministerial ambitions. He was the last man he wished to promote; nevertheless, he had to appear willing so long as Mirabeau constituted a danger to his own position, and accordingly on 17 October he conducted him to Montmorin, after which Mirabeau had a long interview with Necker.

At Passy the commander-general had implied that he had only to tell the king for the ministry to be dismissed and a new one of his own choosing to be appointed. In view of this Mirabeau may have thought that Necker would be ready to enter into discussions of policy, but no. 'My strength rests in morality', Necker told him. 'You have too much intelligence not to realise, eventually, the necessity of this support; until that moment arrives it may suit the king to have you in the ministry, but we cannot be in it together.'[23] 'They have insulted me', Mirabeau reported in fury. 'They have misrepresented my ambition.' La Fayette had probably made his own calculations as to how the interview would go, guessing that Mirabeau would be carried away by the heat of the moment, and that Necker would see him as an ambitious schemer and would be irrevocably set against him. This made it all the more certain that he would help La Fayette to pursue his own plan, which was for Mirabeau to be eliminated.

Direct action, as with Orléans, was out of the question; he would suffer if the public saw him victimising the great defender of liberty. Mirabeau's chronic lack of money seemed to offer the best weapon to use against him. Tending to regard integrity as a quality unique to himself, La Fayette assumed that Mirabeau could be bribed with money and an ambassadorship; this would get him out of the country and at the same time destroy his public reputation as a patriot. On 17

October, while Mirabeau was seeing Necker, he called on La Marck: Mirabeau would have 50,000 francs and the guarantee of an embassy, Holland or England, or, in eight months, Constantinople. 'Ah, *quel homme!*' exclaimed La Marck, who had rejected everything. The next day La Fayette approached Mirabeau himself: 'He made all sorts of conciliatory propositions; was discreet at first, and when I answered coldly ended by conceding that I was indispensable.'[24]

*Quel homme* indeed! Having made the propositions La Fayette gave others to understand that Mirabeau had demanded the money and the embassy, as can be deduced from Talon's letter to La Marck on 18 October:

> We have seen La Fayette. Everyone is revolted by Mirabeau's self-interest. La Fayette's friendship is unaltered. If the comte de Mirabeau prefers to live but a single day in history, and that the public should judge him severely, he will propose the Turkish embassy for him and the remuneration he desires. If, on the contrary, he decides as he should, then the arrangements we have discussed still stand.[25]

La Fayette was gambling on the hope that Mirabeau's circumstances would force him to accept the money; but he remained adamant: he would only take money given in earnest of an immediate appointment. Inasmuch as an embassy was a device enabling him to 'dip into the king's coffers', as he put it, without compromising himself, until he obtained a ministerial post, it did not matter where the embassy was. He had no intention of actually entering into residence. What did matter was that promises should not be broken. He would only believe in his appointment to an embassy, he told La Marck, when he had it in writing, preferably in a letter to himself, not one to La Fayette. Although he spoke of changing the ministry in the interests of the Revolution, the commander-general would be in a stronger position himself if he united with the ministers, and frustrated attempts to topple them. Suspecting that this was his real intention, Mirabeau determined to call his bluff.

Necker was even more anxious than La Fayette to destroy Mirabeau politically. The Director-General had endured much humiliation from his attacks in the past, attacks which had been easy for him to make since he did not have the responsibility of managing the economy, attacks mounted for political purposes, however valid the economic arguments which provided the ammunition. Necker's resentment ran deep. Whether he believed that Mirabeau was involved in recent events or not, he was not averse to seeing him incriminated, since that would forestall the attack which he was threatening to make in the Assembly on the minister's handling of the finances, an attack which could lead to popular demands for his dismissal.

Requiring evidence against him, Necker turned to Duroveray, who had grudges of his own to pursue. He was tired of serving as editor of the *Courrier de Provence*, particularly since the profits from the sale of the journal, which should have gone partly to him, were kept by Mme Le Jay, the publisher's wife. Rows between him and Mirabeau over her rapacious conduct were frequent. Exiled by the Geneva edict of 10 February 1789, he had counted on the French government's refusing to recognise it, instead of which it had guaranteed the edict on 14 September. He may have blamed Mirabeau for failing to prevent this happening. At any rate, Mirabeau's feud with Necker rendered him useless as a political patron, and Duroveray had no compunction about furthering his own interests by courting the still powerful minister. It was an added insurance against the possibility that he might himself be apprehended in connection with his suspected activities as an English spy.

Lucas de Montigny (Mirabeau's son) stated that Duroveray offered to compromise Mirabeau for Necker, but failed to do so. There is little factual evidence to go on, but Dumont, who knew nothing of Duroveray's secret occupations, unwittingly supplies the clues. Several days after the king's move to Paris, Duroveray told Dumont that a group of bankers had offered him a sum of money – 'In recognition', says Dumont, 'of the service we had rendered in supporting the minister's plan, for they knew the influence we had over Mirabeau, and at least suspected the part I played in the composition of some speeches and the address to the nation'.[26] The address to the nation was first suggested by Mirabeau in the course of his speech on the patriotic contribution; Dumont's part in writing the address was limited. It was therefore very flattering for him to hear from Duroveray that his contribution merited the gratitude of the banking world, even though he virtuously refused to accept a reward. While Dumont never questioned Duroveray's explanation for the proferred money others might be more sceptical. It was offered at the moment when La Fayette and the minister wanted to incriminate Mirabeau in the supposed conspiracy of 5–6 October; and it was offered to Duroveray, not directly to Dumont, the obvious recipient if it was indeed a reward for his labours. It would appear that the money was a *pourboire* offered to Duroveray at Necker's request, in return for some service. From what happened subsequently it appears that he was to supply evidence that Mirabeau was willing to overthrow the king.

On Sunday 18 October, Duroveray and Dumont went to Mirabeau's apartment at Versailles, now vacated by him, the Assembly having transferred to Paris where it was to commence work on Monday. Their reason for going to the apartment, says the unsuspecting Dumont, was to collect some papers of theirs. At the same moment Le Jay arrived, his carriage loaded with copies of a work, secretly printed, which should have reached him a fortnight earlier, he said, and which he was now afraid to bring into Paris. 'What work? What is it about?', Dumont quoted Duroveray as asking. 'Against royalty.' Dumont could not remember the title; he thought it was *De la royauté, extrait des écrits de Milton*, a collection of 'all Milton's republican writings', which he recalled Mirabeau had been working on with his friend Servan, 'an enemy of the Court'.[27] Dumont adds that the publication of such a book after the events of 5–6 October amounted to high treason: 'We were even more annoyed because the first people in Mirabeau's entourage to be suspected would be us, natural republicans, and familiar with the English language'. Alarmed by the thought that they and Mirabeau might be apprehended, Dumont helped Duroveray to burn the entire edition in Mirabeau's fireplace, apart from twelve copies which Le Jay took back to Paris. Afterwards he heard (doubtless from Duroveray) that Mme Le Jay was furious at the thought of all that incinerated profit, and that she had denounced Duroveray to Mirabeau; but he concluded that Mirabeau had enough trouble defending himself to worry about the loss of a few thousand francs. Dumont writes:

> Thinking about it since, I am tempted to think that there was some profound intention in the composition of this work . . . I suppose that if the king had fled Mirabeau would have proposed or supported the duc d'Orléans as lieutenant-general of the kingdom, and that he would have been his first minister. Such a fantasy could easily emerge from a head like his. And his fury against the duc d'Orléans makes one suppose that he was thwarted in his expectations. M. de La Fayette was perhaps informed of the secret of these events.[28]

There is, however, no indication in Mirabeau's correspondence that he was ever aware of Duroveray's bonfire. As for the work cited by Dumont, this was published in 1789 without any intervention by the authorities. As often happened, his memory was at fault. Years later he realised that it was not the *Théorie de la royauté, d'après la doctrine de Milton* (the correct title) which had been burned, but a different work, the title of which he pencilled in the margin of his manuscript: *Killing no Murder*. This work by Edward Sexby was a defence of regicide written during the Commonwealth. Duroveray confirmed to a friend that it was a translation of this work which he had burned, taking a whole Sunday to dispose of it. This being so, Mirabeau's failure to allude to its disappearance is not surprising: he was not the author of the translation which went up in flames.[29]

Then who was? In all probability Duroveray himself. In England at this time the Revolution Society was busy printing and disseminating political propaganda, including such works as Sexby's, and Duroveray could well have brought a copy of Sexby back from London. The translation of this work, if he were discovered to have prepared it, would have led to his instant arrest. It had to be destroyed but not at his own address, in order to avoid any hint of personal connection. By burning it in Mirabeau's apartment he incriminated him and saved himself. The twelve copies brought back to Paris were to prove Mirabeau's guilt: Duroveray could say that he found them when he went there, and also the ashes of those already burned. As it would have been easy to lose all the books in some out of the way place their deliberate introduction into Mirabeau's apartment takes on even more the appearance of a frame-up. Le Jay's arrival was no coincidence, for, though clearly not in collusion with Duroveray, he was nevertheless obeying his instructions when he delivered his load of books. Similarly Duroveray's horror on discovering their seditious content was, one suspects, put on for the benefit of Le Jay and Dumont. It all came to nothing. The conspirators never confronted Mirabeau with their planted evidence.

The next day, 19 October, the Assembly met for the first time in Paris. In a personal letter to La Fayette, dated that same day, Mirabeau went out of his way to reassure the Commander-General:

> Whatever happens I am yours to the end, because I am drawn by your great qualities, and I cannot cease to take a strong interest in a destiny so closely linked with the revolution which is leading the nation to liberty.

But following his interview with Necker there could be no more talk of conciliation:

> If you have reflected on the perfidious collusion of the ministers with the despicable charlatan who has brought the throne of France within a hair's breadth of destruction, and who is determined to finish it off rather than admit his own incapacity, you will no longer believe I could assist them. Do not expect me to show them any consideration.[30]

Before despatching this letter he discovered that Duroveray had also written to La Fayette, and he promptly let the commander-general know that he was aware of it. Was Duroveray's letter about the 'discovery' of seditious books? As far as Mirabeau was concerned, knowing nothing about the events of Sunday, there was no reason for him to write, and he may have suspected him of making mischief now that their relationship had soured. Dumont's memoirs reveal that the Genevois were suspicious of Mirabeau's friendship at this time with Desmoulins, who had made him his idol. Then there was Laclos, in the service of Orléans, whose encounters with Mirabeau they also noted. But La Fayette certainly knew about these acquaintances already, and

Mirabeau would not have been uneasy about Duroveray's letter for this reason. A greater fear was that Duroveray had found out from Mirabeau's secretary, Comps, about the Provence *mémoire* and the plan for the king to leave Paris. (It emerged soon afterwards that Comps had been persuaded to confide the contents of the *mémoire*.) He would have been anxious to find out if this was the subject of Duroveray's letter, but La Fayette was reticent in his reply, also dated 19 October, merely confirming that Dumont had brought him a letter from Duroveray. Was it the memory of this letter that led Dumont to wonder if La Fayette 'was perhaps informed of the secret of these events'?

Two days later Mirabeau told La Marck that he needed 1,000 louis to keep the services of Dumont and Duroveray, 'first-rate men'. La Marck had never met the Genevois, and wanted to judge for himself whether Mirabeau's confidence in them was justified. A dinner followed at his house, memorable for a violent row which broke out between the guests after La Marck left the room. It began, recalled Dumont, with Clavière remarking, in answer to a dig of Mirabeau's, that he did not go in for amusements, and certainly not the sort pursued by Mirabeau. Mirabeau retorted:

> You have your own. Don't you get Bourges to write libels against me? Don't you have Brissot's little effusions, and Mme Le Jay's shop, where you declare to all who wish to listen that I enjoy a usurped reputation, that I live on the work of my friends, and would be nothing by myself?

After this, said Dumont, the shouting reached such a pitch that a servant came in to ask if they had called.[31] If La Marck overheard the altercation it told him enough to doubt the wisdom of relying on the Genevois. The subject of a pecuniary reward for them is not mentioned again.

Only a week later Duroveray left for England, Paris having suddenly become too dangerous for him. He may have thought that the information he had lodged would lead to Mirabeau's arrest, in which case it was better for him not to be there. He told Dumont that his trip would last a week; it was December before he judged it safe to return.[32]

The harvest of 1789 was good but because of delays in threshing and distribution there were still severe shortages of grain. On 21 October a baker named François was murdered in Paris on suspicion of hoarding grain and the municipality, fearing more violence, sent a deputation to the Assembly to ask for the introduction of martial law. A week earlier, in the punitive mood bred by fear, deputies had called for martial law as the only way of dealing with public disorder. On that occasion Mirabeau described the imposition of martial law regardless of circumstance as provocative stupidity. Only in cases of organised 'seditious gatherings', where property was under attack, should it be considered: he suggested the possible adoption of the English Riot Act, with the proviso that citizens arrested under a similar act in France should have the right to a formal hearing of their grievances. The Assembly rejected this idea, but called for martial law in all its rigour when the municipality demanded it a week later. Observing that the Assembly was more willing to punish hunger than sedition, Mirabeau asked: 'What can martial law do if the crowd shouts "There is no bread in the shops"? What monster would reply with gunfire?' Instead they should ask the minister to inform the Assembly what measures were necessary to ensure bread supplies; the Assembly would then pass a decree giving ministers full power to put those measures into effect. His motion was adopted.

By making the ministers responsible for supplies he struck a blow at Necker, who had broken off communications with the municipality over provisions, and Saint-Priest, the minister said to have spurned the Paris marchers' demands for bread, and they took prompt revenge. In the following days, while Desmoulins in his *Lanterne aux parisiens* cried that La Fayette was imposing martial law in order to muzzle the people, journals of the right tried to stir up feeling against Mirabeau by accusing him of instigating the current disturbances. La Fayette, in his new jackbooted role, was vulnerable to press propaganda; he needed to shift the focus of popular anger elsewhere, and accordingly told La Marck that if Mirabeau attacked Necker he would support him. Like his other promises this was not one which Mirabeau took seriously. Their relations, studiedly amicable on the surface, continued to be mutually suspicious.

La Fayette still hoped to compromise, or at least fetter, Mirabeau with cash from the public funds. The danger he presented as an independent force was shown at the moment of the Assembly's move to Paris, when the commander-general learned that the Keeper of the Seals, Cicé, had started negotiations for his services. The prospect of Mirabeau forming an alliance with the Keeper of the Seals was far more alarming to him than the nebulous pact with Provence, for it would reduce his own political influence drastically. A renewed offer of the embassy at Constantinople on 21 October (which Mirabeau refused) and a promise of money, the first instalment to come in two days, coincided with the rumour that Mirabeau's future was already settled.

La Marck reported on 22 October that only the unexpected could now upset the plan for him to enter the ministry. Dumont's next letter to Romilly dwelled on the same subject:

Mirabeau is on the point of becoming a minister; first, they say, for Paris affairs, then for the interior, then for finance . . . The decree suggested by Mirabeau, making the ministers responsible for executing provision laws, seems malicious, and the ministers have responded with a *mémoire*, in which there is much spite and slander, intended to damage the Assembly in public opinion, and indirectly aimed at Mirabeau. N[ecker] is furious at his loss of popularity; he does not want to admit his incompetence, and never stops telling us about his morality.[33]

A list in Mirabeau's handwriting of likely ministers in a new ministry has Necker as prime minister, the Archbishop of Bordeaux, La Marck, La Rochefoucauld, and Ségur. The Bishop of Autun is finance minister, and Mirabeau has a seat on the council but no department. Autun (Périgord) had long had his eye on the finance post: it was his blatant ambition to enter the ministry, rather than Mirabeau's, which caused the Assembly to be so antagonistic to the idea of deputies as ministers. 'Everyone knows of his close connection with Calonne, and the pronounced immorality of the abbé de Périgord makes one think that he would not be minister for long without calling his worthy friend to his side', reported Duquesnoy, who asserted that Mirabeau also would get his friends into the ministry, and would be paid 'a large sum of money for what he had done for them'.[34] That was written in September, and shows that Duquesnoy, an admirer of Necker and La Fayette, was ready to listen to the stories fabricated in their circles about Mirabeau's venality. Since then, though still believing smears that came from respectable sources, he was shocked by the anti-Mirabeau campaign building up in the Assembly in answer to his stand on the veto and on questions of liberty versus licence. On 27 October a motion to exclude those who had been convicted in the courts from public office was deliberately aimed, said Duquesnoy, at Mirabeau, whose enemies said he had not yet purged the charge of contumacy brought by the Dijon *parlement*. Duquesnoy reported to the prince de Salm on 28 October:

Mirabeau . . . has changed completely. His former friends are today his most ardent enemies, and a truth is now iniquitous in the eyes of MM. Duport, Barnave, Lameth, etc., when it is uttered by Mirabeau. What is this giant doing in the midst of these pygmies? What I am saying now is the absolute truth: he alone has the genius, the talents, the force of character necessary to save us from the horrible chaos into which we have plunged. The circumstances are such that it is necessary he enters the ministry, but there must be a brief delay perhaps, in order that public opinion should be solidly fixed on him, and should finally understand that private immorality is not an obstacle to public virtue.[35]

The projected alliance between Mirabeau and the Archbishop of Bordeaux concentrated La Fayette's mind wonderfully. On 26 October he let Mirabeau know that his nomination to an embassy would be made immediately, while the king promised that he would be a minister in six months. After speaking with La Fayette, La Marck wrote the same day: 'La Fayette will send you 50,000 francs and will show you a draft of the king's letter. Accept everything. There is no difficulty in treating it as a compensation, you being at this moment unable to enter the ministry.'

Something happened at that interview to cause La Marck's volte-face. As he went on to say that he was seeing the Keeper of the Seals that evening, it seems likely that La Fayette and Cicé had joined forces, a manoeuvre which allowed La Fayette to retain the appearance of being Mirabeau's benefactor while gaining a place for himself in ministerial cabals. La Marck was swayed by the credibility of proposals which had, or would have, royal approval, though he had not actually seen the draft of the king's letter; and subsequent events proved that it never received his signature, if indeed it had ever existed. The minister's sudden positive stand was prompted by the fact that in four days Mirabeau was to speak on the nationalisation of Church property. Nothing the Assembly had done so far had aroused greater resistance than that mounted by the Church's hierarchy at the prospect of losing their enormous revenues, and among them no one was more anxious to hold on to his wealth than the Archbishop/Keeper of the Seals. Hence the last minute rush to placate Mirabeau, in the hope that he would withdraw his support for the nationalisation plan and defeat the motion.

On 28 October there were rumours of a new ministry with the commander-general's choice of La Coste as finance minister. No vacancies in six months in this ministry. La Fayette's advance on the promised 50,000 francs was now tainted. 'I hope you've returned the 23,000 francs', wrote La Marck.

Having persuaded himself that he was in the ministers' confidence, La Fayette found that he had been duped. Cicé, with his revenues in jeopardy, and Necker, trying to salvage his position, had joined together to defeat their common enemy, Mirabeau. 'What would you say if M. Necker threatened to resign because of Mirabeau?' La Fayette asked pointedly, alarmed by the thought that the unscrupulous Cicé would accuse him of encouraging Mirabeau to rock the boat at a critical moment. But no sooner had that prospect left its effect on his mind than he was assailed by doubts as to whether he would not gain more in the future by backing Mirabeau today; doubts sown by Talon, who told La Marck on 29 October: 'This morning I impressed on him and the Keeper of the Seals that they must finally decide, and open the door to the only man who can save their jobs for them.' Talon's transition, from lofty critic of Mirabeau when La

Fayette seemed omnipotent, to enthusiastic supporter, suggests either that he was hedging his bets or that he now genuinely believed that Mirabeau was their only hope.

The day after Talon spoke out Mirabeau entered the debate on the revenues of the Church. The attempts to muzzle him had failed.

The decision to nationalise Church property was a last attempt to stave off bankruptcy. The attention of the Assembly had first been drawn to the untapped revenues of the Church at the beginning of August, but apart from the Archbishop of Aix the hierarchy ignored the warning signals, and learned too late the truth of Mirabeau's dictum, that it was wiser to give voluntarily today what would inevitably be taken by force tomorrow. On 10 October the Bishop of Autun brought the subject up again, justifying the nation's right to the revenues from Church property on the grounds that the clergy were not proprietors but simply life tenants, and that their practice of borrowing to meet payments had left them with debts equal to the value of their properties, which therefore could be confiscated by their creditor, the state. Mirabeau supported this proposal on 14 October, and further proposed that parish priests, whose poverty contrasted starkly with the wealth of the higher clergy, should have an annual salary of 1,200 livres and a house. A formidable group had gathered behind him, including Barnave, Duport, Dupont de Nemours, Le Chapelier, Garat, Thouret, and La Rochefoucauld. The hierarchy of the French Church had lost many of its natural supporters with the second wave of emigrants which followed the October days, and when the debate on Church property reopened on 23 October they were left isolated. Passionate speeches by the abbé Maury, the orator of the right, were of no avail. On 2 November the Assembly decreed that the proprietorship of Church properties resided in the nation. In return the Assembly undertook to pay the clerical debt, to maintain public education and poor relief, and to pay salaries to the clergy. The devout Louis, who had agonised over the loss of the nobility's privileges, sanctioned the decree without a murmur.

It brought Mirabeau a torrent of hatred from the right wing of the Assembly. (He had harshly criticised the opulence of the hierarchy of the Church. This was taken to be an attack on religion itself.) The day of the decree a vicious piece on him appeared in the *Actes des Apôtres*. His brother was one of the wittier contributors to this, the most scurrilous of the royalist journals, but he was not responsible for this attack, which turned out to be the work of the editor, Peltier, who had been paid by the Keeper of the Seals. Hard on the heels of this attack came another piece, a savage denunciation of the *parlements*, which purported to be the work of Mirabeau himself – the author's name was given as 'the Comte de M——, author of *La Gazette Infernale*'.[36] This misrepresentation served the ministers by bringing together all parties with vested interests to fight Mirabeau. 'They are forming a terrible cabal against him in the Assembly', warned Talon on 5 November. 'They' also included Cicé, Saint-Priest, and Necker. The Director-General was due to ask the Assembly for an emergency subsidy of 170 million livres which he hoped to conjure up by converting the Caisse d'Escompte into a national bank; he knew that Mirabeau would seize this opportunity to demand his resignation, and was working desperately to isolate him in advance.

In this situation La Fayette played safe, holding parleys with La Marck while making sure that his lines of communication with the ministry remained open. La Marck and Talon met him on 5 November, their mission 'to do the impossible, to make him decide'; but he was as ambiguous as ever, 'equally incapable', said Mirabeau, 'of lacking faith, or of keeping his word for any length of time'. Once again there was the promise of an embassy. The next day the Assembly was to hear his proposal that ministers should have the right to sit in the Assembly. He had warned Necker that if he prevented the motion from succeeding he would not hesitate to expose his mismanagement of the finances. There had been no response. That evening La Fayette had a meeting with the ministers which had not ended by midnight. Early on 6 November Mirabeau sent him a final message: his only help in the future would be a minister of great strength; he would have the power, thanks to Mirabeau's 'personal fidelity', to form a new ministry, but he must not forget that this ministry could easily be formed without consulting him.

Since 6 November was a Friday, Mirabeau calculated that when the Bourse opened the following Monday there would be no specie to back transactions, and that in the resulting chaos he would be called by the government. On Friday it seemed a certainty. With this in mind the speech he made to the Assembly that day dealt, first of all, with the dearth of specie, and then with the national debt and the proposed establishment of a national bank. After analysing the reasons for the lack of specie he lamented that the nation's efforts to restore prosperity were fruitless, and concluded that the cause lay in the absence of collaboration between the king's ministers and the Assembly. And so he came to his main theme. Why was there this rule that the executive and legislative branches of the government should be enemies? Look at England. Had the king's ministers there ever been excluded from Parliament, and was not each member of Parliament able to question the ministers, making evasions and lies impossible? Where would the errors, prejudices, and ambition of ministers be more quickly exposed than in the National Assembly? The members of the Constitutional Committee, he went on, proposed that ministers should automatically be ineligible to sit in the Assembly:

> Do they say that a minister will have more influence in the Assembly if he has no right to sit there? They would find it hard to prove. The influence of ministers, unrelated to their talents and virtue, is in the realm of manoeuvres and secret corruption, and if anything could reduce the effect of that it is membership of the Assembly, being constantly under the eyes of an opposition which has no cause to flatter them.[37]

As he knew before asking the question, it was not the prospect of ministers sitting in the Assembly that agitated his listeners, but of deputies also being ministers, and one deputy above all. Autun, Le Chapelier, Target, Duport, all craved to become ministers; in Mirabeau alone was it a crime. Their prejudice was as much a reflection of ignorance as of malice. Apart from the right wing, bent on revenge, and the ambitious left, jealous of his ascendancy, there were many idealists who viewed all those who criticised the Assembly as recusants from the revolutionary faith, and who were readily persuaded that in opposing him they were defending the pure spirit of the Revolution. Lanjuinais, the deputy for Rennes, who spoke against Mirabeau's motion the next day, was one of these. Mirabeau alleged that he acted under influence, either from Necker or the Keeper of the Seals, but if he did it was because he had been led to believe that he was serving the public weal; he was not conscious of being manipulated. He took his cue from Montlosier, who warned the Assembly that Mirabeau's proposal had a hidden purpose. Lanjuinais rose.

> We wished to separate the powers, and in ministers we would reunite them, and would risk creating a plaything for ambitious men, if such existed in this Assembly. An eloquent genius is leading you on, captivated. What would he not do if he became minister?

Riding the crest of the Assembly's response to his words, Lanjuinais proposed that for the duration of the present Assembly, and for three years after, deputies would not be eligible for any executive position, or any office, pension, or advancement. Blin, deputy for Nantes, moved an amendment which was even more explicit: no member of the National Assembly could enter the ministry during the current session. His motion, clearly aimed at Mirabeau alone, drew wild applause.

In his reply Mirabeau gave vent to irony, a final lunge before defeat, Marius defiant *in extremis*. He could not believe, he said, that the author of the motion seriously wished to reject any means which might lead to greater trust or better policy planning between the Assembly

and the ministry; or that, while declaring that all citizens had equal
rights to all forms of employment for which they were qualified, he
wished to deny this right to twelve hundred deputies. The idea was
absurd. He did not think, he continued, that the Assembly regarded a
man as suspect simply because he was a minister – that would calumni-
ate three ministers (Cicé, La Tour du Pin, Le Franc de Pompignan)
who had come from the Assembly. Nor was it a constitutional point
since they had not yet discussed whether the functions of minister and
deputy were incompatible. He was forced to conclude that there was
some secret motive behind the motion. It could only apply to two
people in the Assembly:

> Who are these members? You have already guessed, gentlemen; the author of
> the motion or myself.
> I said first, the author of the motion because it is possible he anticipates
> some great mark of trust, embarrassing to his modesty, and wishes to seek a
> means of refusing it by excluding everybody.
> I said next, myself, because popular rumours about me have created fear in
> certain persons, and perhaps raised the hopes of several others. It is possible
> that the author of the motion believes these rumours; it is quite possible that
> he has the same opinion of me that I have myself; and in that case I am not
> astonished that he thinks me incapable of fulfilling a mission that I regard as
> far above my talents, especially if it must deprive me of the lessons and
> counsel that I have never ceased to receive in this Assembly.
> Therefore, gentlemen, I propose that you should limit the exclusion in
> question to M. de Mirabeau, deputy for the commons of the *sénéchaussée* of
> Aix.
> I should be very happy if, as the price of my exclusion, I could preserve for
> this Assembly the hope of seeing several of its members becoming close
> councillors of the nation and the king, for I shall not cease to consider these as
> indivisible.[38]

The Assembly passed Blin's amendment. On this occasion La
Fayette supported Mirabeau. The opposition produced strange al-
liances, Robespierre voting with Maury, and the liberal Grégoire with
the reactionary Cazalès. Lanjuinais himself, at any other time, would
not have supported Montlosier. Mirabeau's first reaction to his defeat
was one of bitterness, especially because it had been brought about, as
he put it, by 'little men'; but then he recovered his detachment. 'I am
more angry for the cause than for myself', he told his sister.

As he saw, and as those responsible for it did not see, the decree of 7
November set back the realisation of political democracy, by denying
the legislature the means of working constructively with the executive,
and ensuring, by extension, that policies would lack the stamp of
common consent on which their effectiveness depended.

Nearly fifty years later, in the Chamber of Deputies, Lamartine
recalled 'that fatal law' against Mirabeau:

He understood its evil and absurd implications, and he combated it on behalf of others. What happened? The law was passed, Mirabeau was not a minister, and France was deprived of the assistance of the greatest political genius born in modern times. That is the result of laws based on envy; they cut down capable men, console the mediocre, and ruin the country.[39]

## *NOTES*

1. *Mémoires biographiques*, IX, 160.
2. The remark about Catilina was an allusion to Goupil de Préfeln's attack on him on 31 August during the veto debate, when that deputy had warned the Assembly that Catilina (Mirabeau) was already at the gates of Rome.
3. Ibid., IX, 166–69.
4. Staël (1820–21: XII, 299).
5. Dumont (1951: 119).
6. Dumont claimed that he wrote the address to the nation which Mirabeau read to the Assembly on 2 October. He gave a revised version on the next day. Dumont's editor, Bénétruy, notes (in Dumont, 1951) that in the Bibliothèque Publique et Universitaire at Geneva there is a 'draft' which 'corresponds partially' to some of the first part of this address, and assumes that this is Dumont's original. Montigny had a draft in Mirabeau's hand and thought it possible that Dumont paraphrased ideas fixed on by Mirabeau in preparatory conferences. The Geneva draft may be Dumont's revised version.
7. Duquesnoy (1894: I, 491) was contemptuous of the lawyers who presumed to direct the Assembly, and particularly of the triumvirs: 'M. Duport, the demagogue Duport, who burns with desire to be Keeper of the Seals and would overturn the government to get there, M. Duport and his friends the two Lameths, Barnave, etc., are convinced that they are destined to save France. To such men, great gods, do you deliver the universe!'
8. Antoine-Omer Talon (1760–1811) was acting deputy for the nobility of Chartres, replaced in December 1789. Compromised by the discovery of the king's private papers in 1792, he went to America, but returned during the Directory. He was arrested during the Consulate and sent to the Iles St Marguerite.
9. *Correspondance entre le comte de Mirabeau et le comte de La Marck* (1851) I, 107. (Hereafter referred to as La Marck, *Correspondance*.)
10. Ibid., 108–12.
11. The first unofficial report was brought to Versailles by the queen's friend, the comte de Fersen.
12. This was the conclusion he drew in his account written soon afterwards. Strangely he never considered that in the event of a regency the king's brothers would be the automatic candidates for the role of regent, not Orléans. By the time he wrote his *Mémoires*, forty years later, he had forgotten that when his men mentioned a regency he had concluded that Orléans was behind it: with the *folie de grandeur* of old age he decided that they had naturally been thinking of himself as regent (La Fayette 1837–38: II. 336–7).
13. *Tableau des Témoins et Receuil des faits les plus intéressans contenus dans les dépositions de la procédure instruite au Châtelet de Paris sur les faits arrivés à Versailles les 5 et 6 octobre 1789* (1790).

14. Mounier's *Appel* was published in London in 1791. In a footnote he said that Mirabeau made his remark about Orléans becoming regent on 7 July. Bergasse, in his deposition, quoted incriminating words which Mirabeau, he said, had spoken in his presence – Mounier said that Bergasse had only heard them at second hand.

15. See *Suite de la procédure criminelle instruite au Châtelet de Paris sur la dénonciation des faits arrivés à Versailles, 6 octobre 1789*, 36–8, for La Fayette's deposition. In his *Mémoires* he left two versions of his movements on 5–6 October. They may be compared with La Marck's account of those movements.

16. Chaussinand-Nogaret (1982: 184).

17. It has already been noted that Duport favoured a change of dynasty. La Fayette's suspicions never rested on him as they did on Mirabeau, but then he and Duport were political allies.

18. *The Times*, 10 October 1789, printed Louis XVI's message of 5 October to the Assembly, and went on to report that Mirabeau had demanded a better answer from the king, and that after the arrival of the mob the king was forced to withdraw. It was this report, surely, which led Burke the same day to bewail to his son the 'portentous State of France . . . where Mirabeau presides as the Grand Anarch, and the late Grand Monarch makes a figure as ridiculous as pitiable'.

19. Camille Desmoulins, who thought Orléans lacked the qualities necessary for a successful conspirator, said that in the event of a plot he would have behaved as he did in 1784, when he went up in a balloon and demanded to be brought down to earth again within a few minutes.

20. La Marck, *Correspondance*, I, 363.

21. Ibid., I, 359.

22. Lameth (1828–29: I, 180–86).

23. Stael (1820–21: XII, 380).

24. La Marck, *Correspondance*, I, 392.

25. Ibid., I, 387.

26. Dumont (1951: 120). The bankers were headed by Delessert, whose daughter later married Duroveray's son.

27. J.-M.-A. Servan (1737–1807) was a former member of the Grenoble *parlement* and author of *Essai sur la formation des assemblées nationales, provinciales et municipales.*

28. Dumont (1951: 112). Yet, two pages earlier, he wrote: 'Despite my intimacy at this time with Mirabeau, if he had been linked with the duc d'Orléans he never took me into his confidence. Recalling those minor circumstances, which could not fail to betray a man as trusting and imprudent as Mirabeau, I find nothing which reveals his complicity in a plot against the Court.'

29. Bénétruy (Dumont, 1951) records that Duroveray's friend was M.-T. Coutau. Coutau told Dumont's original editor, Duval, what Duroveray had told him, and thus verified Dumont's marginal note. Bénétruy fails to comment on the fact that this evidence makes nonsense of Dumont's assertion that the work they burned was by Mirabeau.

30. La Marck, *Correspondance*, I, 389.

31. Dumont (1951: 137).

32. On 4 November 1789 the Revolution Society approved an address of congratulation, to be forwarded to the National Assembly. The Genevois gave out that it was in order to collect this address that Duroveray went to London; but he went in October, and it was fortuitous that the Revolution

Society subsequently produced an address which could be used to impart an air of legitimacy to his trip. Dard (1936) suggests without supporting evidence that Duroveray was acting as a go-between for Mirabeau and Calonne, who was then in London.

33. Bibliothèque Publique et Universitaire, Geneva, MSS, Dumont, no. 17, invo. 1473.
34. Duquesnoy (1894: I, 355).
35. Ibid., I, 493.
36. This work appeared just before the Assembly passed the decree of 3 November which prorogued the *parlements*, apart from the *chambres des vacations* then in session.
37. *Discours*, 176.
38. Ibid., 183.
39. *Moniteur*, 4 April 1835.

# 10

## The Shifting of Power

### (Winter 1789-Spring 1790)

The difference between the great and the might-have-been-great leaders of the Assembly was as much a matter of temperament as of intellect. If Sieyès had been less self-contained, less adamant, less reluctant to communicate or to argue his ideas, he would have been what his intellectual talents equipped him to be, the sage of the Assembly. His writings contained some of the concepts which had the profoundest influence on the course of the Revolution: he argued that the third estate, by itself, constituted the nation, from which came the idea that the third estate could claim national sovereignty; and he ruled that the representatives should have unfettered legislative authority when drawing up the constitution. The idea of 'active' and 'passive' citizens was his, as was that of converting the old provinces of France into equal departments, rationalising the administrative system. But when his theories were contested he immediately withdrew into an egotistical shell. He was not interested in any view but his own and remained a solitary figure.

Mounier was another might-have-been. He had the verbal skill, the authority, which made for leadership. It was he who proposed the Tennis Court Oath, the first formal act of disobedience to the king. His admiration for the English constitution attracted a large early following. At first he seemed to combine revolutionary enthusiasm and conservative wisdom; he turned out to be a narrow theorist, self-important, petulant. He was deeply jealous of his fellow lawyer from Grenoble, Barnave, the rising star of the Assembly. Following the defeat of the *monarchiens* he still had sufficient prestige to be elected president of the Assembly, and he could have thrown his weight behind the moderates and continued his work as a deputy. He chose instead to leave the scene altogether and retreat with his injured pride to Dauphiné, having first published a book in praise of himself. The Assembly was disgusted that a deputy could abandon his oath of service and vilify his colleagues in print. The news of his retirement was received with loud applause.

Baulked of his ministerial aspirations Mirabeau could have behaved like Mounier, but this setback served to show the conscious distinction he made between personal and transcendental objectives. 'I am growing too old to use the remainder of my strength in wars; I want to put it to the assistance of those who assist', he told Mauvillon. 'What matters the glory which should only be used as a tool?'[1] His aims regarding the Revolution remained the same: constitutional government based on a balance of powers; the achievement of a just, tolerant, compassionate society; security for the poorest against the pressures of the wealthy; the avoidance of war. To persuade the king to rule with the Revolution instead of against it, to be the king of the Revolution.

Asked by his sister what he would do now, he said that he looked forward to retiring 'with honour and security' but only when the Revolution and his work in it was complete.

> There are three enemies to national liberty: the clergy, the nobility, and the *parlements*. The first no longer counts in this age, and the sad state of our finances justifies our sacrificing it. The nobility are with us for ever; we have to get on with them. One can only do so by keeping them in check; one can only do that by forming a coalition of the people with the Crown. The Crown will never truly ally itself with the people while the *parlements* survive. Like the nobility they keep alive the Crown's fatal hope of bringing back the old order of things. Therefore scrapping is necessary . . . What has to be done next? Revive the power of the executive; regenerate the royal authority and reconcile it with national liberty. That will not be achieved without a new ministry, which will always be badly composed so long as the ministers are not members of the legislature; so the decree on ministers will have to be revoked, or the revolution will never be consolidated.[2]

Mirabeau's phrase 'regenerate the royal authority' neatly labels him for Marxist historians as a monarchist who wanted to halt the proper course of the Revolution. But this phrase must not be separated from the rest of the sentence, 'and reconcile it with national liberty'. National liberty came first. The sovereignty of the people – as he repeatedly said and wrote – was 'imprescriptible'.

So what did he mean by 'regenerating the royal authority'? It was not a euphemism for royal despotism. It did not mean restoring powers to the king which could be used against the people, or to halt or reverse the Revolution. (When he wanted the king to have the veto, for

instance, he stressed that it could never be used in the case of constitutional decrees, such as those of 4 August; the constituent power of the
legislature was absolute, he said, echoing Sieyès and Rousseau.) The
royal authority was not to be personal power but simply the authority
vested in the king in his executive role. The executive power no
longer balanced the power of the legislature. Mirabeau felt that it was
important in the interests of the nation that it should.

It could be argued that if Louis had more effective executive power
he would not necessarily have used it in the interests of the nation.
Also, that as the general will was supreme, investing the king with
greater executive power, or any executive power at all, amounted to a
threat to the general will and was inherently wrong. Mirabeau's answer
was that the general will was not infallible. Even Rousseau said the
general will could be misled.

Mirabeau's wish for more royal authority would be criticised by
radicals as an attempt to go against the democratic intentions of the
constitution. Having declared that France was a monarchy the constitution makers were confronted by a dilemma, how to frame a monarchical constitution that, at the same time, guarded the sovereignty of
the people. It ended with neither monarchists nor radicals being satisfied. France was described as a monarchy with a republican constitution. When Mirabeau spoke of increasing the royal authority he was
thinking of the prerogatives granted to the king under the constitution,
which in practice were ineffective. An effective executive under the
constitution was his aim.

It was a forlorn hope, for the Assembly would not countenance any
revision of its decrees. This also disposed of his hope that the decree
on ministers would be revoked. Meanwhile there was the immediate
problem of a ministry opposed to, or suspicious of, the Assembly. Now
that he could never take a direct part in shaping ministerial policies
himself he hoped to find a substitute, a spokesman for the Revolution
who could head a new ministry and work constructively with the Assembly. Before the end of November he renewed negotiations with
the comte de Provence.

It can be assumed too easily that he was mainly seeking a role for
himself, in which case being Provence's puppeteer would have enabled him to experience, if only in secret, the excitement of being at
the centre of action; but if he is to be believed – and he did not
disguise his attitudes – his concern had always been with the uses of
power, not the sensation of it:

> I have never been ambitious for administrative posts, or marks of prestige. I
> wanted to prepare, hasten, perhaps to induce, a great revolution in human
> affairs for the betterment of the species . . . I have succeeded up to a point,

and more than an ordinary mortal could have hoped, faced with so many obstacles due to his own faults and those of others.[3]

Whether Provence would prove capable of sharing this vision of revolution remained to be seen. His progressive instincts alarmed the queen, who treated him 'like a chicken that one strokes through the bars of a cage, but takes care not to let loose'. Mirabeau's rueful description was well chosen. Marie-Antoinette feared that her brother-in-law might become another Orléans; Provence feared that he might be regarded as another Orléans. Freed from his cage the chicken was unlikely to turn into a fighting cock.

La Fayette soon got wind of the negotiations with Provence, and told others. In these conversations he also repeated stories about Mirabeau's private life, for which he received a not unmerited letter from Mirabeau on 1 December, denying any political liaison – 'men are petty and less than ever do I see any with whom I would care to venture' – and dismissing the prurient gossip about his personal affairs. The last paragraph in the letter reveals how La Fayette's spies were employed:

> Allow me this opportunity to beg you to return – at long last – a trunk. They have doubtless had sufficient time to make an inventory of the contents, which will prove no more against me than the countless empty rumours with which you have been burdened for several months.[4]

Early in December, soon after he renewed contact with Provence, Mirabeau showed Dumont the papers of a plan which, he said, could save France and assure her liberty. Describing the occasion in his *Souvenirs*, Dumont wrote: 'I regret my imperfect memory and the lapse of time which has effaced the greater part of the details of this project'; but, faulty memory notwithstanding, he proceeded to make a categorical list of Mirabeau's proposals, which were apparently that the king should retreat to Metz, declare the Assembly's decrees null and void, dissolve the Assembly and order fresh elections, call on the *parlements* to resume their former functions, and summon the nobility to the support of the throne. The list was a complete contradiction of Mirabeau's views. According to Dumont, he argued strenuously with him for three hours, pointing out that the plan was likely to abort because of the king's irresolute character, and that even if it succeeded at first it would lead to civil war. Had he been consulted, he asked, was he sure they trusted him? Mirabeau, said Dumont, told him that the Court was determined on the plan, and that it was important for him to be associated with it, 'in order to make it succeed and to conduct it in the spirit of liberty'. To which Dumont replied:

> You are bitter about the decree excluding you from the ministry and your resentment leads you astray . . . It is in the Assembly that you have credit and

power; outside you would not have it any longer, and if the Court wishes to trust you you can serve it better as a deputy than as a minister.[5]

In the end, said Dumont, Mirabeau promised to resign from the plan, and also to tell Provence to encourage the Court to turn its thinking instead towards the Assembly. A few days later, he added, Mirabeau told him that the plan had been abandoned.

Dumont's account of this conversation has an air of truth, but the details he gives of the plan itself have to be treated with caution. They contradict everything in Mirabeau's October *mémoire* to Provence, in which he stressed that the king should not go to Metz or take any counter-revolutionary action, and that he should order the Assembly to continue its work and ally himself with the people. It is inconceivable that two months later he would have proposed the measures listed by Dumont, including the restoration of his *bête noire*, the *parlements*. Secondly, Dumont recorded the scene at least ten years later, with the hindsight gained from hearing countless stories of secret manoeuvres which did or did not take place in December 1789.[6] Because of them this meeting with Mirabeau doubtless took on a belated significance, and it would have been easy for details he had read about to be transferred in his memory to the plan presented by Mirabeau. Evidence that there was a plan for the king to flee came to light in the middle of December. Duly reported in the press, it called for an escape to Metz, the summoning of the nobility, and the dissolving of the Assembly, the same details Dumont allocated to Mirabeau's plan. The putative author, a tax-farmer named Augeard, was arrested but later released. At any rate, the plan Mirabeau showed Dumont was not the one Dumont describes, complete with his own reconstructed comments, which he may well have made when Augeard's plan was published. Possibly, before Mirabeau talked to Dumont, Provence showed the October *mémoire*, recommending a move to Rouen, to the queen, and the Court then drew up its own stupid plan for a flight to Metz. When Mirabeau heard that the king was indeed planning to leave Paris he assumed that the advice he had given was being taken seriously at last, that the Court intended to follow his *mémoire* to the letter, but, as he admitted to Dumont, he had not been consulted directly and did not know who the leaders of the Court plan were. At this point he must have realised that something underhand was going on, and that whatever it was he and Provence should not get involved.

Then, on 25 December, the marquis de Favras was arrested and charged with bringing armed men into Paris, as part of a plot whereby La Fayette, Necker, and Bailly would be assassinated, the king placed at the head of a waiting army, and the city reduced by starvation. Provence was named as the leader of the conspiracy. Favras had at one time been in his service, and had obtained a large loan in his name, for what purpose was never established, but the prosecution needed no further proof of guilt, and he was hanged on 19 February, protesting his innocence to the last.

The implication of Provence was the most alarming aspect of the affair for Mirabeau. Although the comte was well received when he defended himself before the Assembly, the press continued to revile him. The Favras affair had been utilised by interested parties to eliminate Provence politically. No one was better placed to know this than the baron de Staël, the Swedish ambassador and Necker's son-in-law, who reported to Gustavus III that Monsieur,

> who had engaged in a little intrigue with M. de Mirabeau in order to enter the Council . . . has been cleverly pushed aside. M. Necker and M. de La Fayette, now closely associated, may thus be regarded as the two sole departments of the government.[7]

It is not surprising to find Necker and La Fayette colluding to frustrate a Mirabeau–Provence coalition; had it been successful it would have signalled the political eclipse of the one and reduced the other to the role of a patrolling constable in Paris. The counter-revolutionary plot, in which Favras played the part of the fall guy, came at an opportune moment, providing Provence's accusers with the means to blacken him, and to benefit politically from the scandal, without exposing their personal motivation. Their main target was Mirabeau, but even if it had not been possible to connect him with the Favras plot, the investigations into the events of 5–6 October, which were already in progress, raised hopes that his destruction was imminent. In his memoirs – written in the third person, which gives them an air of Olympian detachment – La Fayette consoled himself for history's failure to convict Mirabeau, by depicting him as an indefatigable and cynical conspirator who moved from Orléans to Provence, and then, after the Favras affair, 'wasted no time in attaching himself to La Fayette, with whom he had conferences'.[8]

By the end of January it was plain that Provence would not be entering the ministry and that the royal family, rather than taking action, would wait fatalistically on events. Mirabeau's impatience boiled over:

> What balls of cotton wool! what ditherers! what cowardice! what unconcern! . . . And having failed to follow any of my advice they complain that I have not changed their position at all, and that they cannot count on me very strongly.[9]

Among his papers is a piece, written at this time, which speaks for itself:

If I were to write a treatise on politics I should deal at length with the *art of daring* . . . In reading history I note that almost all the mistakes made by leaders of parties come from uncertainty of principles and irregular actions. Revolt is half-hearted, loyalty is half-hearted; men dare neither to abandon their duties nor to sacrifice their whole passion to them. The first steps are hesitating and diffident, whereas they should be the firmest; men leave a retreat open, try different ways of achieving their ends. These very subter- fuges, so favoured by average politicians, are a result of timidity of mind or heart; they intrigue to cover themselves, to attract followers, to make a show of moderation; whereas they should act and press towards their goal by the shortest route. What always happens? The one who intends to deceive is deceived; the critical moment is missed, and no one has been persuaded. Just as extremes are unreasonable in the ordinary conduct of life, so half-measures are insufficient in crises, and the most dangerous as well as the most inconsi- stent course is to divest oneself of only half one's prejudices. But there are almost as few resolute evildoers as positively honest men. Most men lack strength of character.[10]

In mid-November the Assembly debated Necker's renewed sugges- tion to convert the Caisse d'Escompte into a national bank. The ma- chinery for receiving the revenues from Church property had not yet been set up, and 170 million livres was required immediately. Necker argued that by turning the Caisse into a national bank, and backing its operations with the credit of the state itself, the crisis could be averted and confidence in the money market restored.

The Caisse's record did not seem to justify his faith in it. Four times in recent years it had been saved from collapse by court judge- ments allowing it to limit, and then to postpone, repayments on its promissory bills. Commercial transactions had been severely affected, foreigners refusing to accept bills which were not payable on demand, while outside Paris the Caisse's banknotes were worth only a fraction of their face value. The depreciation of paper money encouraged people to hoard specie and to send it abroad for safe- keeping; and this was now happening at such a rate that despite the quantities of gold and silver sent to the mint by patriotic citizens – to which had just been added the deputies' silver buckles – Paris was denuded of specie. Silver plate despatched to the mint one day turn- ed up the next as French coins in London or Amsterdam, and so the cycle of national impoverishment continued. Speaking on 20 No- vember, Mirabeau blamed the Caisse for the current panic. Yet this 'soiled and discredited virgin' was to receive a certificate of respect- ability countersigned by the National Assembly itself. Its debas- ed notes would circulate throughout the kingdom, and, what was potentially the greatest danger, the executive power would be able to evade the Assembly's decrees, and obtain financial assistance by means that did not accord with its policies. (The revived executive power which Mirabeau wanted was never to be exercised illegitimately.)

A commission was appointed to investigate the affairs of the Caisse d'Escompte. Necker's star was waning, but he and the Caisse had powerful supporters in the Assembly, and on 19 December, when the commission's report was debated, his proposal to utilise the Caisse was approved, though the spectre Mirabeau had raised, of Paris financiers extending their grip over the whole country, led the provincial majority in the Assembly to reject the idea of converting it into a national bank. A decree was passed that day for the sale of Church property, and for *assignats* to the value of 400 million francs to be issued on the security; of this sum 170 million francs was earmarked for the Caisse d'Escompte. Mirabeau called it unspeakable stupidity.

December saw him successful in his efforts to win civil rights for Jews, Protestants, and actors; unsuccessful in the debate on the creation of departments in place of the old provinces of France. Necessary for the establishment of a homogeneous administrative system, the proposed departments would also extend the democratising process already begun in the municipalities, by opening up higher levels of administration to the middle classes, which had previously been barred from them. As things were all the administrative power of any province was concentrated in the hands of a few families, an entrenched caste of office-holders, automatically opposed to the aims of the Revolution. For Mirabeau the unclenching of this privileged grip, and the public education in affairs engendered by the creation of departments, were all-important factors; he welcomed the change, but criticised the way it was being treated as an exercise in pure logic. Sieyès, whose idea it was, wanted to graticulate the map of France into eighty identical squares: natural boundaries, differences of language and culture, the economic balance of the regions, were all to be ignored, and to remove any evocative reminders of the past the departments were to given numbers instead of names.

Surely numerical labels would lead to the very elitism they sought to avoid, Mirabeau suggested, since department one would be bound to think itself more important than department seventy-nine.[11] This was on 3 November, when his bid for the ministry had made elitism the sin of the day. On 8 December, when the Assembly was discussing the organisation of the departments, he made another barbed reference to the pretensions of the anti-elitists, at the start of a speech in which he proposed that all administrators, municipal and departmental, and deputies also, should have to work their way up through the administrative grades before assuming high positions: 'If we had not made equality a fundamental law one might perhaps say that it conflicts with the prejudice of certain individuals against commencing a career in public affairs with minor duties.'[12]

Rousseau had advocated a system of gradual elections in the *Contrat social*, but deputies disagreed with his suggestion that potential deputies should give proof of their ability and integrity before entering the National Assembly. Barnave declared that gradual elections were an aristocratic trick to deny citizens their right to serve in the Assembly. (The vicomte de Mirabeau joined in, but was cut short when his brother asked him, amid laughter, if he had expected to hold his present rank of colonel from the moment he entered the army.) There was considerable support for the idea of gradual elections, but the opposition was whipped up by Duport, Lameth, and Barnave, who had been using every available occasion since 7 November to isolate Mirabeau politically. This time they played on the prejudice of deputies who resented his displays of superior knowledge, and who readily believed that in some obscure way gradual elections were his revenge for their obstruction of his bid to enter the ministry. The verbal battle between him and Barnave was still unresolved on 15 December when the debate was postponed indefinitely: the Assembly thought the matter lacked urgency.

Elitism, in another guise, came to the fore in January when the Assembly had to deal with the intransigent *parlement* of Rennes. On 3 November the *parlements* had been suspended indefinitely; they had reacted to the termination of their hitherto inviolable power with predictable anger, and the *chambre des vacations* of the Rennes *parlement* had refused to register the Assembly's decree of suspension. The president of the *chambre des vacations* was called to the bar of the Assembly where he insisted that the decree contravened the privileges of *parlement* and the ancient rights of Brittany. Not only was this a direct challenge to the Assembly's authority to speak for the nation, it gave encouragement to all factions that were opposed to the Revolution.

One of the lawyers of the Rennes *parlement* was Lanjuinais, who had proposed the decree barring deputies from the ministry. Mirabeau had a personal reason, therefore, when he spoke on 9 January, for denouncing their arrogance. Who were these men, he asked? Were they – as might be thought – dethroned sovereigns communicating with usurpers? No, they belonged to a corps which had betrayed both monarch and people in the pursuit of their ambitions, and their plan was to bring back the social, political, feudal and judicial oppression which France had experienced for two centuries:

> Eleven Breton judges cannot *consent* that you should be the benefactors of their country . . . it is them, and their type, that you are overruling when you affirm the royal authority on the indestructible base of public liberty and the national will.[13]

As always when he defended the authority of the Assembly, he placed it in the context of a constitutional monarchy, and, as always, he recognised that the royal authority could only come from the general will. The next day Maury charged to the defence of the Rennes rebels, but the Assembly decreed that the members of the *chambre des vacations* at Rennes were disqualified from all the functions of active citizens until they had taken an oath of fidelity to the constitution. The defeat of the *parlements* was complete, and the authority of the Assembly had been reinforced.

Mirabeau spoke fifteen times in January and February. To the right he always seemed to side with the left. He denounced the right-wing press which labelled left-wing deputies as mad dogs: because insults 'provoke sedition and revolt, while decently motivated criticism prompts only useful controversy and moderate protests'.[14] In a wider sense this was also a call for the Assembly and its work to be treated with respect.

January brought another opportunity to confront the forces of reaction: the subject was the recurrent disturbances at Marseille, and again his opponent was Maury. Just as his ancestral province held a special place in his heart – 'I live for France, I would die for Provence' – so did Marseille, his speeches on the affairs of the city eventually filling nearly 200 pages in the Assembly records. The latest business arose out of a riot in November which led to several Marseillais being imprisoned. Under the Assembly's law on criminal procedure they had a right to see the documents in the case but the provost of Marseille rejected their application. He had been denounced by Mirabeau for flouting the law, and the Assembly had ordered the proceedings to be taken before the *sénéchaussée* of Marseille. In January Maury made a report which sought to prove that the unrest was the work of extremists, instigated by Mirabeau himself, but after Mirabeau refuted his twisted evidence the Assembly ordered a new report and dismissed the provost. It was a necessary victory if the Assembly was to be seen to be capable of defending its constitutional principles.

'We have to show all these myrmidons that despite their combined efforts, and La Fayette's cabal, and the rage of the right, and the corrupt activity of ministers, that the National Assembly does its duty on important occasions', Mirabeau commented somewhat floridly after his successful speech.[15] Like Robespierre and Marat he was constantly alert to the possibility of counter-revolution. Provence, with its reactionary nobility and with plotting *émigré* colonies close by in Savoy and Piedmont, was in a particularly vulnerable position. Hence his anxious monitoring of every incident at Marseille which could become the excuse for action by counter-revolutionary forces.

His fear of counter-revolution struck La Marck as unnecessary, and
all the more irrational in view of a move by the king, which seemed to
be a decisive sign of the Revolution's progress. On 4 February Louis
went to the Assembly to pledge his support for the constitution. This
conversion was the work of Necker and La Fayette, who realised that a
conciliatory attitude by the king would not only strengthen his position
but their own as well, since the public would put it down to their
patriotic influence. Neither of them liked the possibility of Louis falling under the patriotic influence of someone else, and of that particular
person's popularity rising in consequence.

The deputies responded to the king's apparent change of heart with
a new oath of fidelity to the nation, the law, the king, and the constitution, and the next day he and they attended a Te Deum in Paris.
'Everyone is trying to be the best actor in the comedy', said Mirabeau,
watching these celebrations in honour of a non-existent victory. He
saw the king's truce with the Assembly for what it was, a ministerial
gambit, and did not believe that his outlook had really changed. 'For
my part,' he told La Marck, 'I maintain that we are at the most critical
moment of the revolution, the one at which we have to guard against
both the impatience and lassitude of the nation and ourselves.'[16]

Taken one after another, Mirabeau's political acts from the moment
he was debarred from the ministry until the early spring of 1790 seem
unconnected, a series of secret manoeuvres and deliberate confrontations indulged in by a disappointed man. But they were more than
scuffles for attention. Every move and every intervention was part of
his policy to carry the Revolution forward, to build up respect for the
Assembly, and realise the paper ideals of the constitution. It was easy
for his critics to think that he no longer counted. Easy for the spokesmen of the right, Cazalès and Maury, to accuse him of encouraging
violence when he defended the insurgents of Marseille, or of having
subversive intentions when he opposed their proposal to give the king
unlimited power to quell unrest in the provinces. Unlimited power, he
replied, meant dictatorship. Their job was to finish the constitution:
that would provide the sovereign with all the authority necessary for
his function. And to that end he cited the necessity of having the king
as head of the army. The dictatorial role sought by the right was an
abuse of power; making the king head of the army was a defence
against abuses by others. He wrote:

> We have affirmed that the king is the supreme executive in a monarchical
> government. Now, if the military force is not in his hands he is no longer the
> supreme executive: there are two, ten, a hundred, several thousand executive
> heads, and soon the state is at the mercy of a military government, the most
> intolerable form of brigandage.[17]

On 21 March the Assembly decreed that the king should be head of the army and that higher military ranks were henceforth open to all applicants. The first was strongly opposed by the left; the second ended another of the *ancien régime*'s restrictive practices.

Mirabeau was a member of the Jacobin Club and also of the *Société de 89*, which was set up by moderate members of the Jacobin Club after a schism in April 1790, and attended by Sieyès, Bailly, La Fayette, Talleyrand, La Rochefoucauld and Le Chapelier. He was thus able to gather at first hand what both the left and the centre were thinking, what tactics they planned, what pressure groups were forming. The *Société de 89* never had the political potency of the Jacobins. Mirabeau was elected its president in July 1790, but it was in the Jacobin Club, rapidly becoming the intellectual and political powerhouse of the Revolution, that he felt his presence was needed.

He was also a founder member of the *Société des amis des noirs* which Brissot formed in May 1788 as a counterpart to Wilberforce's Society for the Abolition of Slavery. His hatred of the slave trade and of those who profited from it went back to his childhood and the bailli's descriptions of Guadaloupe. At the opening of the Estates General he had challenged the number of representatives sent by the colonists of the French Antilles, pointing out that they had been elected by the 23,000 white inhabitants of the islands, while the much larger coloured (as distinct from black) population was unrepresented, though free and property-owning and as eligible to vote as citizens of metropolitan France. His speech on that occasion, in which he also attacked slavery, led to the number of colonial representatives being halved, but the colonial influence remained strong in the Assembly, and his call for a decision on the slave trade was conveniently forgotten.

The scale of the trade in which France was engaged was colossal: in a single year, 1788, nearly 30,000 slaves were shipped over from Africa to San Domingo alone, representing a market figure of something like 174 million livres. With an investment of that magnitude to protect, the colonial nabobs were determined to block any move by abolitionists in the Assembly; the slave trade, they argued, was indispensable to the maintenance of commerce and the prosperity of the West Indies. But the Caribbean could not be kept immune from the spirit of the Revolution. The Declaration of Rights started a ground swell of protest in the colonies, which ended the following year in the bloody uprisings in San Domingo and Martinique. As the *amis des noirs* pursued their campaign to end slavery, and powerful commercial and mercantile groups like the traders of Bordeaux protested at the threat to their interests, the Assembly had to choose between its ideals and

economic realism. Maury bluntly declared that if they voted for abolition they would have to blame themselves for the destruction of France's commercial empire, and if they voted to maintain the slave trade
they would be guilty of denying other human beings that liberty which
they took to be a fundamental right: the furious reaction of deputies
such as Dequesnoy to these words was a measure of the embarrassment felt by anti-abolitionists, who did not like to think that they had
compromised their principles.

Mirabeau had prepared a long, deeply felt speech on the slave trade,
in which he offered solutions to the practical problems which the *amis
des noirs*, in their evangelical zeal, did not consider. Opponents of
abolition feared the consequences of giving freedom overnight to vast
numbers of slaves – 400,000 in San Domingo; he proposed instead a
gradual transition from slavery to freedom, following a Spanish system
under which a slave worked for himself on one, then two or more days
a week, until he had earned enough money to buy his freedom. By this
method he acquired confidence and a means of livelihood, and could
command respect from society. It was not enough to liberate subjugated people, Mirabeau warned, if they remained subjugated by the
attitudes and prejudices of their former masters: 'Freedom without
dignity is not freedom'.[18]

On 2 March he failed to read his speech in the Assembly when
Maury's call for an immediate debate on the slave trade was rejected.
Lameth, with family interests in San Domingo, gained time by proposing that all colonial and commercial questions should be studied by a
committee. As the strongest argument for retaining the slave trade was
based on the commercial advantage which England would gain if
France abandoned it unilaterally, Mirabeau had written to Wilberforce,
asking him to enlist Pitt's co-operation. It would have been a victory
for the abolitionists if he had been able to tell the Assembly of Parliament's readiness to match it in philanthropy, with both nations laying
aside their rivalry in the name of humanity, but as yet there was no
reply from Wilberforce, and meanwhile frantic efforts were being
made to prevent his speech from getting a hearing. Rumours that Pitt
had secretly engaged him to bring about abolition in France, and that
the British government was paying him for the purpose, had the intended effect of making him into something worse than any abolition-
ist: a traitor to his country. Refusing to be silenced, he outmanoeuvred
the colonial lobby in the Assembly by reading his speech at the Jacobin
Club. The sensation it created there made his opponents all the more
anxious to prevent a rereading in the Assembly. On 8 March Barnave
presented the Colonial Committee's report, recommending that no
changes should be made which would affect French trade, and that

anyone inciting rebellion against the planters should be found guilty of *lèse-nation*. The hand of the Lameths was clearly visible, with their desire to trap Mirabeau if he brought the subject of the slave trade up again. In vain he demanded a debate on the committee's report. The Assembly voted at once to accept it.

Several times after this organised defeat he tried to open a debate on abolition; always without success. The first move in this direction did not come until May 1791, after his death, when the Assembly voted to give civil rights to blacks born of free parents. Slavery itself was abolished by a decree of 4 February 1794.

It would soon be a full year since the Assembly began work. In the spring of 1789 few would have predicted that twelve months later the country would still be in a state of crisis, the constitution still unfinished, and that the king would no longer be living at Versailles. Those who had wanted the greatest changes were angered by the slow progress that was being made and now advocated more extreme measures; moderates had been turned by fear into conservatives. Deputies who had voted conscientiously according to their mandates were disillusioned and wondered how they could justify the results to their constituents; many of them had a clause in their mandates limiting their presence in the Assembly to one year, and the call for dismissal and fresh elections had strong support. But besides the loss of goodwill which such an admission of defeat would bring, it was probable that another election would produce a more radical body of deputies, contemptuous of their predecessors' approach, who would sweep aside the achievements of the first assembly and start all over again, imposing their own theories; the unfinished constitution would suffer a fatal setback and the country's state of vulnerability would be further prolonged. The Assembly decided that fresh elections could not take place until the constitution was completed, and the instructions in individual mandates were overruled.

At the end of its first year the Assembly had a great sense of its own power. Acting on the view that the monarch was the natural enemy of public liberty, it had reduced the king's actual power to a level where his constitutional role was meaningless. In its determination to subjugate the executive it had disregarded Montesquieu's basic rule, that in order to prevent abuses of power it was necessary to arrange things so that power checked power; or rather, it had gone half-way with Montesquieu, eagerly checking power in the executive, extending its possession by the legislature. Any criticism of its own growing despotism could sound, or be made to sound, like a threat to the sovereign power of the people – Montesquieu again – as represented by the Assembly.

Mirabeau's efforts to retain some functional strength for the king under the constitution were attacked on these grounds, and always the
rhetoric about the Assembly defending the people drew loud applause.
Yet when he spoke in the veto debate of the king being the 'perpetual
representative of the people' – meaning the unenfranchised – he
alarmed many of his hearers. Defenders of property-owning, middle-
class interests, they looked to the king to defend them against democracy, and the idea of the king and the people coming together was
seen by them as a threat to the future of their own class. They themselves had challenged the established order; now they were concerned
to prevent similar challenges from below. The constitution they were
drawing up was as much a guard against the unenfranchised as against
royal tyranny.

Debates on the constitution still occupied half of each working day.
Food shortages, unemployment, and other urgent issues were relegated to the afternoon and evening and had to compete for space on an
overcrowded agenda, while countless hours were still wasted in ab-
stract arguments. At the popular level the Assembly's achievements
made less impression than the price of bread. Its image had changed;
more and more it was perceived as the ally of the despotic powers
which it had been charged to destroy. The point had been reached in
the Revolution when the pupils were taking over from their instructor,
and putting what they had learned to their own use. The Assembly's
committee system had taught the street politicians how to organise
themselves, and the rhetoric of the revolutionaries of the Enlightenment had been borrowed by agitators, or paraphrased physically: 'Châ-
teaux were burned, putting into execution the epigrams pronounced
by the orators of the Assembly'.[19] In the spring of 1790 the sequence
Mirabeau had predicted, of inaction aggravating frustration, of frustration leading to civil disorder, disorder to anarchy, anarchy to repression
and the return of despotism, seemed more likely than ever.

Relations between the Assembly and the ministry remained hostile.
The emotions stirred up by the king's speech had quickly subsided
when it became apparent that nothing had changed, that the ministers
were merely playing for time. For Necker the speech had been a
desperate last attempt to restore his own image. His popularity with
the public and his influence at Court had been slipping steadily, until
he was now – in Mirabeau's cruel words – 'nothing any more than an
old idol in his niche, without worshippers and without a cult'. Since
authorising the first issue of paper money in December, Necker had
kept very quiet about the state of the finances. At the end of every
month he sent a terse statement to the Assembly: This is what I have,
this is what I need. This formula was received with growing suspicion

by the deputies, and gave Mirabeau an excuse to launch another attack on ministerial despotism:

> The Assembly does not have the right, but is it not its duty to ask the minister: Why is this what you have? Why is this what you need? Our knowledge of the finances is limited to trusting the minister, albeit uneasily. We are sleeping only because one can sleep at the foot of Mount Vesuvius . . . No matter how much trust one has in a minister the nation should not leave the dictatorship of the finances to him, because he is but mortal. Avoiding the duty of reporting on one's management, and failing to reveal one's resources, is a decided dictatorship, especially when one's tenure of office is marked not with a succession of miracles but with fatal calamities. It is important that the Minister of Finance should give us his account in order to end this deplorable situation.[20]

On 6 March Necker addressed the Assembly. Much as he regretted having to speak pessimistically, duty compelled him to do so, he said. In November he had announced that an advance of 80 million livres would suffice for the coming year; that was on the assumption that by the beginning of 1790 a balance would have been established between revenues and expenses, but in January there was already a shortfall of 40 million. Apprehension about the rest of the year was, therefore, only too justified. He went on to reproach the Assembly for its lack of confidence in his financial programme and ended metaphorically, recounting the stormy voyage of the ship of state and the efforts of the devoted pilot to bring it safely into harbour. The task had exhausted him. However, he said, he would never have sought assistants if the opportunity had not arisen for a treasury department to be formed: the king wished to accept its members from the Assembly; but before that could happen it would be necessary to repeal the decree forbidding deputies to accept any government post. As for himself the precarious state of his health would force him to retreat that coming summer in order to take the waters.

Necker had read the writing on the wall, and had prepared an excuse in advance to avoid the humiliation of his anticipated dismissal. The treasury department was his idea, a parting revenge on the Assembly, which would have the opportunity – if the decree were repealed – to demonstrate whether its financial skills were greater than his own. The obvious candidates for treasury jobs were Dupont de Nemours and Autun, but even if the bishop had not been detested for his ambition, the Assembly still insisted on the principle of separate powers. There was no repeal.

Ten days after Necker addressed the Assembly, La Marck returned to Paris from Belgium, and went at once to see Mirabeau, whom he found deeply depressed about the state of the country and his own situation. La Marck's position outside the factionalism of

French politics, and his close knowledge of the Court, gave his advice a unique value, and they had corresponded regularly during the three months of his absence. Mirabeau called him 'my Mentor'. For his part, and despite his aversion to Mirabeau's more inflammatory performances in the Assembly, his 'flair for dissonance' as he called it, La Marck's loyalty was unshakeable. At the new year he had written:

> The friendship which attaches me to you is dearer for being the means of doing justice to you, and my own self-esteem is flattered by the superiority I have gained over those who do not know enough to appreciate you, or who do not wish to, for envy exists everywhere, and is exercised most against men of outstanding worth.[21]

Since Mme de Nehra's departure La Marck was the only friend Mirabeau could fully confide in. His sister, Mme du Saillant, was fond and foolish – she had recently conceived the lunatic idea of bringing him and Emilie together again, refusing to believe, despite their assertions to the contrary, that they wanted to remain apart. His secretary, Pellenc, was devoted and intelligent, but still only an employee. Duroveray and Dumont were hangers-on rather than friends, and anyway they had now gone, Duroveray to Switzerland,[22] and Dumont back to England. The row between the Genevois and Mme Le Jay, over the way she used the profits from the *Courrier de Provence* to expand her husband's business, had come to a head in January when they announced that they would resign their editorship if they were not paid. Confident that this threat would put 'la Le Jay' in her place, they were furious when she promptly installed two new editors, Giraudet and Luchet.[23] The *Courrier* row gave Dumont an excuse to escape from Mirabeau's *atelier*, and a situation which had brought him little satisfaction. The modest pastor with secret ambitions, and a knack of inserting his foot into the doorways of more talented men, had assumed that working for Mirabeau would bring him a certain fame among the *cognoscenti* as the true author of his genius. Mirabeau, like Bentham after him, had had to engage with a character genial on the surface but with a core of resentful vanity, and it was this vanity, trampled on unknowingly by Mirabeau, which induced Dumont to leave. The last straw came when he found himself ridiculed in *Les Actes des Apôtres*. Dumont, it said,

> will no longer be confined to narrating M. de Mirabeau's operations; he will rectify the French state, after which he will do the same for Geneva, and his work will become the prototype on which all political articles, present and future, will be modelled.

The comment offended him all the more in its perception of his private ambitions. 'I felt a deep disgust at being mentioned publicly', he wrote in his *Souvenirs*. 'The reputation of a minor fabricator does not flatter one's self-esteem; that of being an influence on a man of impure celebrity alarmed my feelings.'[24]

Dumont returned in January 1791, having failed to find employment with his patron, Lord Lansdowne. The intervening months saw Mirabeau's public career reaching its peak, and he may have regretted his earlier decision to distance himself. When they met again Mirabeau's situation had changed in other ways as well, not publicly known. It was this imminent change which brought La Marck back to Paris in March 1790. The worsening crisis, loss of trust in Necker, and the failure of various proposed counter-revolutionary schemes, had combined to make the king and queen think again about Mirabeau. The queen's volte-face was the work of Mercy-Argenteau, the Austrian ambassador, who had negotiated her marriage in 1770 and acted as her adviser ever since. One of the few people in her circle who understood how important it was for the Crown to form an alliance with the National Assembly, he also believed that Mirabeau was the only man who could bring it about, but he needed to hear La Marck's opinion of his political views first: the queen had yet to be convinced that this man was not responsible for the traumatic October days.

La Marck having reassured him, Mercy revealed that the king had decided to call on Mirabeau's services. The greatest secrecy was to be maintained. Necker must know nothing about it. The impracticality, apart from anything else, of what was proposed alarmed La Marck: the insistence on secrecy in itself indicated that there was no serious intention of acting on Mirabeau's advice, since nothing could be done without ministerial involvement; and besides, with the situation now so critical it was unrealistic to believe that one individual could put things right.

He said as much during a private interview with the king and queen which took place a few days later, but Louis had already made up his mind. The queen told him that they had made their decision two months previously, but that her horror of Mirabeau had caused the delay in approaching him. La Marck went home from this meeting 'in a state of terror' at the realisation that Mirabeau was to be given the responsibility of saving the monarchy on his recommendation. Plainly the royal couple's present attitude was dictated by the fear that he could prove dangerous if steps were not taken to neutralise him; at any moment they might withdraw their tentative trust, and follow a course that was the very opposite of the one he advised. La Marck's doubts regarding their commitment were well founded, for even as they professed their willingness to listen to Mirabeau they were considering a plan of Artois', who wanted to invade France from Turin and carry the king off by force. As late as 15 May Mercy was warning the queen that such a venture would lead to the entire royal family being seized and placed at the mercy of a furious populace.

Breaking the news to Mirabeau that the king wished to employ him, La Marck was astonished by his spellbound reaction. This was the man who had written: 'I have never understood how one could give one's personal affection to a king',[25] whose contempt for Louis's irresolute character had been constantly expressed; yet he still succumbed, said La Marck, to 'that sort of magic which royalty exercises in acting benevolently'. He recovered quickly. In his preparatory *mémoire* for the king, dated 10 May, he pledged himself to serve the king's 'true interests', and declared in this respect that a counterrevolution was both dangerous and criminal – he had doubtless heard about Artois' project. His aim, he continued, would be to give the executive power its proper place in the constitution; progress would be slow; they must not judge his conduct on the basis of one act or speech, nor expect too much: 'I promise the king loyalty, zeal, energy, and a courage of which he is perhaps unaware; everything except the success which can never depend on a single man'.[26]

Before the balance between the executive and legislative powers could be rectified it had to become a matter of general concern, and to that end Mirabeau's own position had to be strong, in the Assembly and in Paris. He needed a body of supporters in the Assembly, and, at least, to be spared the government-paid attacks on him in the press; and he needed the public support of La Fayette, whose aim so far had been to nullify his influence. Twice before he had sought his co-operation. Following his appointment he made another attempt:

> When the public weal is in peril, *monsieur le marquis*, when it cannot be saved except by shared effort, to isolate oneself, even with pure intentions, from a means of achieving that end would be the act of a bad citizen, and to consider the petty conventions which link or separate men would be a base weakness.
>
> I have distanced myself from you because your political liaisons were unworthy of you or myself; because you misplaced your confidence – I do not say your personal confidence: why examine hearts? – but your public confidence, your means, your hopes, and those of the state.
>
> These reasons for separation no longer exist; the Barnaves, Duports and Lameths no longer weary you with their active inaction; one can put on a good show with machines, even imitating the sound of thunder, but one cannot replace it.
>
> So there you are, *monsieur le marquis*, not necessarily isolated, and faced above all by the state of the nation. What are you going to do, and what shall I do? I ask these questions simply in order to tell you my own feelings. The true perils which menace the state are anarchy, the loss of respect for the law, divisions of public opinion, the wrangles in the new administrative bodies, and, above all, the judgement which Europe will pass on the edifice of this constitution, which for want of adequate scaffolding will soon disappear.

What was he to do? the letter continued. Inactivity would be too difficult for a man known for his 'impatient talent, strength and courage'. Act without La Fayette? The effort might be useless. Therefore he sought an alliance, not in order to combat the commander-general, but so that he could pursue his career more courageously, and because, wishing the well-being of the state, he knew that this could not be achieved without La Fayette's assistance. Should this union be refused he knew that a man of honour would 'remain silent and return my letter'.

So far in this accomplished letter he had appealed both to La Fayette's patriotism and his ambition – his political position had weakened of late with a cooling in his relations with the triumvirate. The problem was that the true reason for an alliance could not be revealed. La Fayette's own strength depended on the king's remaining impotent as Paris demanded; if he guessed that Mirabeau was advising the king he would denounce him; the aim of that advice, and its relevance to the future stability of the state, being beyond his own understanding. To counteract possible rumours about his activities Mirabeau created a red herring for his benefit, by referring in his letter to the old promise of an embassy:

If thoughts of antique Greece, Asia, and the Bosphorus were not sufficient to seduce me before, I now see at Constantinople the means of exerting an entirely fresh influence. When one thinks of the work involved in such a career one must pardon those with proofs of talent who wish to embark on it.[27]

The embassy ploy succeeded in throwing La Fayette off the scent, but Mirabeau ruined any hopes of gaining his support by mentioning the remuneration which had originally been offered as a pledge of an ambassadorship. 'I do not regard the renewal of the retainer given me by the king for the first major embassy as a new demand', he wrote. He could not deny that his debts were pressing, La Fayette could not deny that he had tried to buy him off in the past. There is an indication that he had repeated these attempts more recently, for Mirabeau insists in his letter that only if La Fayette supported him politically would he 'desire to have my debts paid'. By mentioning the subject of money, however, he confirmed the disdainful opinon which La Fayette – an immensely wealthy man – always had of him. The partnership which could have overcome all obstacles was lost through the commander-general's inability to see beyond his prejudices, and his own indelicacy.

The letter to La Fayette was dated 28 April. Either he genuinely did not expect any financial reward for his services from the king, or he had been told that he would be rewarded, and was assisting the secrets game by giving La Fayette an opportunity to authorise the transaction, which would otherwise rouse his suspicions should he come to hear of it. As it was, by the second week of May the conditions of his appointment had been arranged. The Archbishop of Toulouse, let into the secret in order to act as go-between, arranged that he should receive 6,000 francs a month, and that 80,000 should be paid towards liquidating his debts which totalled 208,000 francs. (It was later wrongly said that the king paid all his debts.) Four bonds, for 250,000 francs each, were deposited with La Marck, to be paid to Mirabeau at the close of the Assembly if the king was satisfied with the progress he had made. In the event these were returned to the king after his death. Though it appears crude and demeaning, this arrangement between the monarch and his subject, the crudity was Louis', who thought that Mirabeau's loyalty needed to be bought, and not Mirabeau's, who regarded the money as a salary for valuable services, honestly undertaken. Money, not medals, was indeed the normal form of recognition for services of any sort to the king, and not even that most scrupulous of men, La Marck, considered it in any way dishonourable for Mirabeau to benefit financially.

Nevertheless, this commitment to serve the king's interests would become the great ineradicable stain on his record for future historians of the left. Albert Soboul states that after being barred from the ministry 'he had gone over to the service of the Crown which had, in fact, bought him'. Without any further evidence the uninformed reader would conclude from this that Mirabeau, for money, was now helping destroy the Revolution. The distortion continues when Soboul, after saying that his first *mémoire* to the king was dated 10 May 1790, describes his advice as a 'comprehensive plan for a network of propaganda and corruption'.[28] Again the reader would think that this plan was already there in the first *mémoire*, when the desperate measures in question were only considered the following year, when the situation had deteriorated critically. There is no mention of the dozens of *mémoires* in the interval, in which he tried to lecture and coax the king into actively supporting the Revolution and the nation.

The mythology relating to the fortunes Mirabeau received from the king and others is endless, and the rumours which inspired it had been circulating well before April 1790. It was a fact that at the beginning of the year he had moved from his shabby lodging in the hôtel de Malte, rue Traversière. 'The great man', Dumont told Romilly, now had an apartment in the chaussée d'Antin,

> previously occupied by a *fille*, from whom he has bought the furniture; in effect the tribune of the people, lodged in a boudoir, softens his republican severity with emblems of voluptuousness, and allows luxury to caress him in his austere labours.[29]

The *fille* was Mlle Carreau,[30] whose salon was frequented by Chamfort, Narbonne, Ségur, and David. Lucas de Montigny pointed out that the opulence of these new surroundings was exaggerated, the house at 42 chaussée d'Antin being quite small and the rent for Mirabeau's apartment on the second floor being 2,400 francs a year; but he lived and entertained there in a style that caused comment. Speculating in his *Souvenirs* about the source of this apparent wealth, Dumont concluded that Provence had 'engaged to pay him 20,000 francs a month until his affairs were settled'. It could all be explained, he went on, by the king's decision to abandon counter-revolutionary activities and to side with the Assembly; it was necessary to provide Mirabeau with the means to entertain lavishly and so attract influential men. Factually and rationally Dumont was in error: the king did not seek a reconciliation with the Assembly until February; and the idea that Provence, terrified of active commitment, had promised Mirabeau nearly a quarter of a million francs a year in order to woo political clients, belongs to the realm of those propagandists whose fantasies Dumont had assimilated by the time he committed his own recollections to paper. This is not to reject his evidence. 'The pension of 20,000 francs was only paid for a short time', he states. At the moment when Mirabeau was most confident of seeing Provence in the ministry, in mid-December, the subject of a retainer may have been mentioned, but this would have needed to go through government channels, and it is possible that Montmorin was induced to guarantee some sum, albeit far short of Dumont's figure. Indirect evidence that Montmorin may have been involved can be deduced from Peuchet, one of the myth scatterers whom Dumont read, who asserted that Montmorin received a *mémoire* suggesting that Provence should be made lieutenant-general of the kingdom, an idea that apparently delighted the king so much that he promised Mirabeau an embassy and gave him an allowance of 50,000 francs a month.[31] It must be said that anyone who believes Peuchet would believe anything.

A similar caution is needed for the *Livre rouge*, a record of alleged payments made over the previous ten years by the government, which was published in the spring of 1790 by an Assembly committee set up to investigate government pensions. Mirabeau is listed in it as receiving 195,000 livres. (Talon gets 200,000.) The payments recorded in the *Livre rouge* were those known as *ordonnances de comptant*, which by custom were not audited, as ordinary payments were, by the government accounts department; instead the receipts were kept in the Louvre archives. In publishing selections from the *Livre rouge*, with a foreword suggesting that these payments were secret and nefarious, the Assembly committee hoped to embarrass Necker by proving that he had not kept a sufficiently tight rein on the finances. (Necker published a reply explaining that although *ordonnances de comptant* used to be secret, the practice arose of letting a minor official process them separately, for speed and convenience; they were not secret but available for inspection.) The Assembly committee did not say who had been snooping in the archives on its behalf. However, Laborde de Méréville, friend of Duport, administrator of the royal treasury, unscrupulous intriguer, and already inculpated in publications against Mirabeau, was in a position to provide facts as well as 'facts'.

If the figures cited from various sources were apocryphal the fact remains that Mirabeau's financial state improved sufficiently at the start of the year for him to acquire a carriage and horses, and to indulge his taste for fine books and an elegant table. Following his appointment by the king, La Marck cautioned him – in vain – about his style of living, for besides the need to avoid all cause for speculation there was the damage to his public reputation to consider. The revelations of wanton government expenditure in the *Livre rouge* had scandalised the public, and the inclusion of Mirabeau's name provided his enemies with a potent weapon. The ideologues of the left could now proclaim that he was sold to the Court, though they knew perfectly well that he led them all in his hatred of what the Court stood for. 'I am as profoundly averse to a counter-revolution as to the excesses to which the revolution, in the hands of incompetent and wrong-minded men, has led the people', he declared in his *mémoire* for the king. He stood, as he had always stood, for the same liberty within a framework of order as his detractors believed in. The same ideals, the same revolution. But in his case his labours to that end were to be construed as treachery.

## NOTES

1. *Lettres amicales*, 416.
2. Mme du Saillant to the comtesse de Mirabeau, quoting Mirabeau verbatim. La Marck, *Correspondance*, I, 427–30.
3. Ibid., I, 427.
4. Ibid., I, 425.
5. Dumont (1951: 125–29).
6. Authors who wrote later about a planned flight to Metz, and whose works Dumont mentions, include Bouillé (1820–28), Peuchet (1824), and Bertrand de Moleville (1800–1803).
7. Quoted by Vallentin (1948: 407).
8. La Fayette (1837–38: I, 363).
9. La Marck, *Correspondance*, I, 456.
10. *Mémoires biographiques*, X, 216f.

11. Mirabeau wanted 120 departments in order to create as many opportunities for public service as possible. This was an unwieldy number and it was finally reduced to eighty-three.

12. Ibid., X, 38–40.

13. Ibid., X, 56.

14. Ibid., X, 59. Brissot, staunch defender of press freedom at the start of the Revolution, wrote in 1792 that 'the free circulation of writings does not justify the free circulation of those journals openly sold to the enemies of the revolution.' This idea of selective censorship would have appalled Mirabeau, who, in his time, condemned all political writing, left or right, that spread lies and incited violence, but who saw suppression as a denial of a fundamental liberty.

15. La Marck, *Correspondance*, I, 457. 27 January 1790.

16. Ibid., I, 465. 11 February 1790.

17. *Mémoires biographiques*, X, 99.

18. See ibid., X, 122–208, for whole speech.

19. Staël (1820–21: XII, 255).

20. Ferrières (1932: I, 407–8).

21. La Marck, *Correspondance*, I, 444. 6 January 1790.

22. On 18 December the ruling oligarchy in Geneva had authorised Necker to offer the Assembly 900,000 francs. Suspecting that the aristocratic party was making the gift in return for French government sanctions against the popular party, Mirabeau got the Assembly to reject it, and as a result the General Council of Geneva had to bow to popular pressure, and recall the leaders of 1782 from exile, Duroveray amongst them.

23. Giraudet, the deputy for Alès, was reader to the wife of the comte de Provence. The marquis de Luchet was a friend of Mirabeau's from his days in Berlin.

24. Dumont (1951: 141) and *Actes des Apôtres*, no. 19, 4–7.

25. *Mémoires biographiques*, VI, 110f. Letter to Van Kussel, 30 October 1787.

26. La Marck, *Correspondance*, II, 11–13.

27. Ibid., II, 1–6. In his *Mémoires*, La Fayette (1837–38: IV, 150) said that several people had seen the letter from Mirabeau, in which he spoke of taking the embassy at Constantinople and expressed the desire for money to pay his creditors. This letter, with its declaration of fidelity, was burned during the Terror, he explained; adding that it did not prevent Mirabeau from becoming his enemy. Unaware that Mirabeau's original copy of the letter still existed, La Fayette presented his edited version, omitting all reference to the proferred political alliance: the evidence that Mirabeau wanted one at this date was something he did not wish to reveal. Nor, naturally, did he record that the original retainer in connection with an embassy had been a bribe devised by him to get Mirabeau out of the way, and that it had been refused.

28. Soboul (1974: 214).

29. Bibliothèque Municipale et Universitaire de Genève, MSS. Dumont, no. 17, inv. 1473. Letter of 18 January 1790. In issue 31 of *La Lanterne magique* the vicomte de Mirabeau wrote: 'How does the debauched host come by this palace? Who in Paris does not know that he has passed his life in prisons or furnished apartments? . . . And this wretch has had mansions and carriages since being a deputy: the profession must be a very lucrative one'.

30. Louise-Julie Carreau was born *c*.1756. She married the actor Talma on 19 April 1791, a fortnight after Mirabeau's death.

31. Assertions of this sort (the more defamatory, the more welcome) were typical of the royalist memoirs which were either published in England, or in France after the restoration of the monarchy. Peuchet declared that as early as May 1789 Mirabeau had offered his services to the king and demanded to be made ambassador at Constantinople. Mme de Campan said that he had been given a large sum of money in early November 1789 and promised a place in the ministry. In May 1790 he had received 200,000 francs from Montmorin, according to Peuchet; and Lacretelle, Mérilhou, Peuchet and Bouillé all repeated the story that in February 1791 he received 600,000 francs as a bonus to his monthly 50,000 (*sic*). Talleyrand, who liked to deal in large figures, told Dumont in 1792 that Mirabeau had received a full million.

# 11

## The Revolution
## and the Monarchy

### (May-December 1790)

Mirabeau found himself defending the king's constitutional role within days of his secret appointment. In the middle of May an aspect of royal prerogative which had not needed previous consideration suddenly demanded the Assembly's attention. Spain and England were disputing each other's fishing rights in Nootka Sound off Vancouver Island. Spain, claiming that she had established the first colony there, had seized an English vessel, thereby provoking a bellicose reaction in England, where Pitt ordered a fleet to be prepared. Under the Pacte de Famille France had obligations to support Spain in any war she entered, and accordingly on 15 May Montmorin asked the Assembly to sanction the fitting out of fourteen ships to fight alongside the Spanish. A week of furious debates ensued. Spain was not in a position to fight England without French support; France did not want the expense of a war in which she was not concerned; and half the Assembly was opposed to war on grounds of principle. England was less disposed to fight if she knew that France was going to support Spain in the conflict. Alleyne Fitzherbert, the British ambassador in Madrid, went to Paris to ascertain French feeling, and on 17 May he dined with La Marck, the only other guests being Ségur, the former war minister, and Mirabeau, there in his capacity as *rapporteur* of the Assembly's Diplomatic Committee. It would have been part of Fitzherbert's purpose to gauge the strength of French commitment to the Pacte de Famille: if France were not to renege on her pledge she must support Spain now, at the risk of being drawn into a war not only against England, but against other powers, should Pitt proceed from the point of vantage he already had and engage England's allies under the Triple Alliance. Fitzherbert may also have been curious to meet Mirabeau, in view of the fact that the Assembly was now the seat of power in France.

Montmorin's demand for fourteen ships had raised a separate question, the king's right to take the nation to war without consultation: how this issue was decided was crucial for the standing of the executive power, but besides its constitutional importance it affected the whole sphere of France's international relations. In the Assembly it became a battle of ideologies as the left and the right disputed whether the right of peace and war belonged to the Assembly or to the king. After five days it seemed that the triumvirate, backed by the Jacobins, would win the right for the Assembly. Everyone was wondering how Mirabeau would speak. Already it was rumoured that he was sold to the king, but when he went to the tribune on 20 May it was still not known which side he would support.

He began by saying that if he addressed them on a subject which had already been debated for five days it was because he felt it had not been presented in the right way. So many important matters were involved – liberty and the safeguarding of the constitution – that an attempt must be made to conciliate 'cold reason' with 'the excusable emotion that the fears surrounding us are bound to inspire'. The question was whether the exercise of the right of making peace and war should be delegated to the king or attributed to the legislature. It was with this alternative that the question had so far been posed, and this in his opinion rendered it insolvable.

> I do not believe that the right of making peace and war could be delegated to the king without destroying the constitution; nor do I believe that it could be attributed exclusively to the legislative corps without producing other dangers, no less serious. But are we forced to make a choice? Can we not, for a function of government which involves both action and will, combine the two powers which constitute the strength of the nation, without one excluding the other?

The idea of an offensive war (which had outraged the left in the debate) was unthinkable. But in a defensive war one could not wait to react until the Assembly had deliberated. On the other hand, the Assembly would have all the time to decide whether the war should be pursued or not. If they judged that the ministers were taking France into an unjust war they could always constrain the king by refusing the necessary funds to pursue it. 'These are the true rights of the legislative corps. The powers are not confounded, the forms of government are not violated, and national interest is preserved.'[1]

Already in this impromptu speech he had shown adroitness, by placing both the right and the left on the defensive. He himself wanted the right of peace and war to be part of the royal prerogative but to have said so would have placed him with Maury and Cazalès, and so he asked instead what these men were thinking of who wished to erect another authority beside the constitution. But the left wanted to deprive the king even of the right to concur in a decision: were they not seeking something unconstitutional, since the Assembly's decrees had accorded the king a form of concurrence, even in purely legislative acts? He was well aware, he said, of the danger in confiding the means of ruining the state to a single man, but in avoiding that danger they risked a greater:

> Will we be assured of having only just wars if we delegate the right of making peace and war to an assembly of 700 persons? Have you not seen the lengths to which passionate feelings can carry imprudence? We have heard one of our orators propose that if England made an unjust war against Spain we should cross the sea and fight to the last man against these arrogant English. And we all applauded. And to my surprise I applauded too. A flight of oratory sufficed in a moment to cheat your wisdom.

If the Assembly had the exclusive right of making peace and war it would be tempted to substitute for the executive in the direction of the war, thus creating a rival power and undermining the principles consecrated by the constitution. His own proposal was that the king should have the initiative in making war, the Assembly the right of confirming or refusing: this would conform with the principles of all those who, regarding the Assembly as 'the only barrier against despotism, also regard royalty as a useful barrier against the aristocracy'.

At this point he played a master stroke. He called on the Assembly to improve his proposed decree; one man, above all, was capable of doing so:

> I do not conceal my profound regret that the man who set the bases for the constitution, who has contributed the most to our great work, condemns himself to a silence I deplore . . . that the abbé Sieyès – I beg his pardon, I have named him – does not himself find in his constitution one of the greatest resorts of the social order.

By challenging Sieyès to declare himself, Mirabeau was bidding for a supporter who would be invaluable to the development of his strategy for securing the constitutional power of the executive. If he did not respond that was also a point gained, for Sieyès followers were disappointed by their guru's performance and ready for more positive leadership. He remained silent;[2] and Mirabeau proceeded to read his decree.

The following day Barnave set out to demolish Mirabeau's decree which he described as constitutional anarchy. He finished his speech

amid loud applause from the left, which thought that victory was theirs
and wanted the vote to be taken immediately. Mirabeau demanded to
reply the next day, however, and the Assembly agreed, fascinated by
the contest between the older and younger orator. The Jacobins were
determined that Mirabeau should not win. That night Alexandre de
Lameth denounced him at the Jacobin Club as a traitor to the Revolution, and the next morning a mob, 50,000 strong, surrounded the Manège, yelling for his blood, persuaded that the constitution's very
survival depended on the rejection of the decree. A pamphlet entitled
*Trahison découverte du comte de Mirabeau* had appeared overnight,
manipulative propaganda at its most virulent:

> So your crimes have been found out at last. We only suspected your conduct
> in the National Assembly; today these suspicions are confirmed. You only
> wanted the National Assembly to be constituted an assembly of the repres-
> entatives of the people in order to gain support for your entry into the minis-
> try; you declared yourself a supporter of the absolute veto only because you
> wanted gold and honours. You wanted the abolition of the negro slave trade,
> an abolition that might ruin the National Assembly; you wanted it only be-
> cause you had been promised gold. Finally, you have carried your crimes and
> your treachery to the last extreme, by making the specious pretext of the good
> of the people the pretext for giving the legislative power a derisory share in
> that terrible prerogative of making war. Beware lest the people parade your
> head as they carried that of Foulon. The people are slow to rouse, but are
> terrible when the day of vengeance arrives. Your name will be an embodi-
> ment of all crimes to future generations; your shameful existence will cause
> nature, your country, your century, to blush for having given birth to such a
> monster as you.[3]

Inside the Assembly hall the atmosphere resembled that at a Roman
circus. A right-wing deputy called out, 'Yesterday the Capitol, Mirabeau, today the Tarpeian rock!' For three-quarters of an hour, according
to witnesses, he stood at the tribune, arms folded, waiting for the
uproar to die down. When he was able to speak he began by observing
that reasonable discussions were more worth listening to than malev-
olent ranting and unfounded accusations: for a week those who wanted
the king's concurrence in the question of peace and war had been
accused of murdering public liberty; rumours had been spread abroad
of perfidy and corruption, and popular vengeance invoked to support
the tyranny of opinion. Fixing his eyes on Barnave, he said:

> A few days ago they wanted to bear me in triumph, and now they cry in the
> streets: the great treachery of the comte de Mirabeau. I do not need this lesson
> to know how short the distance is from the Capitol to the Tarpeian rock, but the
> man who fights for reason, for the *patrie*, does not accept defeat so easily.

Then, moving to the attack, he let loose the full diapason of his
oratory against the Lameths, courtiers by upbringing, demagogues by

calculation, and their associates. Let them denounce as the enemy of the revolution the man who looked to it alone for the safety of the commonweal; let them abandon to the misled fury of the people the man who for twenty years had resisted oppression of every sort, who had been speaking to Frenchmen of liberty and the constitution while they, 'vile calumniators, sucked the milk of the Court and enjoyed every ruling privilege'. M. Barnave, he continued, had done him the honour of addressing him alone; he would treat his talent with the same regard. He had ascribed action to the king and will to the legislative body, and concluded that war, as an act of will, could be decided solely by the legislature. His conclusion would be inarguable, Mirabeau allowed, if the legislative body were synonymous with the legislative power; but it was not, the constitution stating that part of this power should reside in the king.

> If you wish to substitute the words, 'the legislative power' for 'the legislative body', and define this expression in an Assembly decree sanctioned by the king, we shall be in agreement on principles. But you will then return to my decree because it accords less to the king. You do not answer me . . . I shall continue.

He proceeded to ask the Assembly to consider what a declaration of war would involve if the king did not have the veto, and if he did. If the legislative body had the decision the constitution would be 'denatured'; from monarchical it would become aristocratic. On the other hand, the principles of the constitution would be complied with if, leaving the initiative to the king, the Assembly had the right to consent or refuse; only that way could the respective control of the two powers, envisaged by the constitution, be achieved. The solution had already been reached, he said, as was proved by Barnave's resort to sophisms:

> Despite having so much applause directed at him in this chamber and outside it, M. Barnave has not tackled the question . . . he has not shown the slightest knowledge either of statesmanship or of human affairs. He has declaimed against the evils which kings could commit, and has avoided drawing notice to the fact that under the constitution the king can no longer act despotically; above all, he has avoided speaking of popular movements, although he himself has demonstrated the ease with which the friends of a foreign power could influence the opinion of a national assembly, by inciting the people outside it, and by procuring applause from their agents in the public galleries.

Take instead his own decree. His enemies saw a trap in it. All he asked was that the right of peace and war should be delegated concurrently to the executive and legislative powers. Where was the trap in that?[4]

His decree was adopted with minor amendments. Although the right of peace and war belonged to the nation, war could only be decided upon following a formal proposition by the king; he alone could conduct international relations; he had the supreme command of the army. For Mirabeau it was a satisfying outcome, for he had repulsed the faction opposed to him on an issue of their own choosing. The popular press tried to cover up the left's partial defeat by dwelling wishfully on what would have happened had the king been accorded the right of peace and war unconditionally: 'Paris today would have been flowing with blood, the Tuileries would have been burned', wrote Fréron in the *Orateur du peuple*. 'Mirabeau! Mirabeau! less talent and more virtue, or watch out for the lamppost!'

Virtue here meant civic virtue, not personal morality. Although Montesquieu's definition of civic virtue, as love of country and love of equality, still held, at street level and in the popular press virtue was now politicised, synonymous with deference to the Jacobin Club and obedience to the voice of organised street protest, a voice with an increasingly republican accent. Mirabeau had won a constitutional victory for the king in the peace and war debate, but the public hysteria over it showed how deep-rooted was the conviction that any trace of royal authority meant a resurgence of despotism. The prospect for the monarchy was doubly bleak, for the king's executive function was meaningful only to the extent that its implementation was sanctioned by decree, yet every attempt to consolidate his position via the statute book would stir up old fears, and lend weight to the arguments of those who wanted to abolish the monarchy altogether.

Mirabeau wrote his first Note for the Court on 1 June. From now on he led, in effect, a double life, but he did not act a double role; his aims were what they had always been, to keep the Revolution on a straight course, to save it from being sabotaged by extremists, and to construct the monarchy anew, so that it became, and was seen to have become, an integral part of the new order, a monarchy of the Revolution. He pursued these aims in the Assembly, and in his Notes to the Court he explained to the king and queen what was happening, what needed to be done, what would happen if the wrong action were taken, or if – as was usual in their world of illusion – they did nothing at all. With hindsight these Notes make poignant reading. Here was a guide to their survival if the royal pair had only been able to recognise it. Political developments, the future role of the monarchy, ways of establishing good relations with the people, the actualities which governed the lives and reactions of these people: subjects which they understood little or nothing about were expounded in lucid detail.

The first Note dealt with the imminent appointment of new ministers. It seemed likely that the choice would be left to La Fayette, but as he might propose weak or incompetent men Mirabeau felt it might be a mistake to consult him when forming a new ministry. He explained:

> M. de La Fayette's strength lies in the trust he inspires in his army. He only inspires this trust because he seems to share the opinions of the masses. But since it is not he who has dictated these opinions but the city of Paris, where public opinion, directed by writers of the enlightenment, has been his means to power, it follows that he will always have to defer to the masses in order to conserve it. It is easy to guess how he will act: flattering the people, supporting rightly or wrongly the most powerful party, alarming the Court with popular demonstrations instigated by himself. This man will be a threat to royal power so long as public opinion in Paris imposes the law. He is therefore of all citizens the one on whom the King can rely the least, since even in recognising the principles of monarchical government he will be the last to profess them.[5]

This was a harsh but perceptive analysis of the commander-general, who continued to reject all offers of a political alliance. Mirabeau's latest attempt in that direction was dated 1 June; when it was spurned the queen herself, acting on his advice, asked La Fayette to co-operate with him. La Fayette later wrote:

> This proposition implied a union on a totally different footing from their previous relations; it was doubtless a trap, for La Fayette could only disapprove of their new projects. Whatever it was, he rejected this idea, and they did not speak of it to him again.[6]

Mirabeau had deliberately asked that the queen should be the one to write to La Fayette. If the proposed alliance resulted from her initiative, he explained in his Note, it would link her to a popular movement and so help to modify her hated reputation, which by itself was capable of losing her husband his throne. 'I like to believe that she would not wish for life without her crown, but I am sure that she will not conserve her life if she does not conserve her crown', he commented in one of the Sibylline statements which adorned the Notes, and which the Queen found gratuitously offensive. Warned not to express his opinion when it had not been sought, he turned in his next Notes to international affairs, and wrote at length about the situation created by the peace and war debate in relation to Nootka Sound, and the risk of France becoming involved in a war by the Pacte de Famille.

It was the sort of analysis which showed that the king was employing the wrong man as Foreign Minister. But it brought Mirabeau up against the difficulties which Louis' rule of secrecy had engendered: no matter how sound his advice it could not be acted on without discussions with ministers. At best the king might pass on an isolated suggestion which, modified or applied inappropriately, would prove useless. The third and fourth Notes, dated 23 and 26 June, outlined the problems inherent in the Pacte de Famille, which had been drawn up in 1761 when the government of Spain was in safe hands, unlike now when the king, Charles IV, was dominated by his Parma queen and her lover, Godoy. In view of this, Mirabeau said, France could run into trouble if she were bound by the original terms of the Pacte; a fresh compact was essential, and an agent should be sent to Madrid to negotiate it. He himself, as *rapporteur* of the Diplomatic Committee, could present the new terms to the Assembly as already agreed upon, terms free from the military commitments of the Pacte to which the Assembly objected, and which had to be eliminated before it would consent to its continuation.

Thought had to be given to the level at which these prior negotiations were to be conducted. An ambassadorial mission was ruled out by the king's insistence that his Foreign Minister should be kept in the dark. Was Montmorin to know or not to know what was going on? asked La Marck. If not, the number of possible agents who were both obscure and diplomatically talented was limited. Mirabeau thought that Ségur would be the best choice, though he might not be welcomed in Madrid where he was believed to be an ally of La Fayette's; on the other hand he had diplomatic experience and it would be better to send him than to offend Spanish susceptibilities by expecting them to negotiate with an errand boy. Time, however, was running out. For its fullest effect the new compact, presented as the king's personal achievement, had to be ready before 14 July, for the anniversary of the fall of the Bastille would see an upsurge in anti-monarchical feeling, which could only be offset by visible proof that the king was working in the interests of the nation through the Assembly. Knowing that La Fayette planned to stage a personal triumph on 14 July, the Day of Federation, Mirabeau was anxious that he should not hear of the negotiations until their completion was assured, and with it the king's psychological victory; but Louis hesitated, alarmed by the prospect of a rift with his Spanish cousin and by the fact that he would have to explain his action to his ministers, unconvinced also that his image needed to be carefully defended in the coming weeks.

Mirabeau's speech on peace and war, and its effect on the Assembly, had created consternation in England, where it was feared that France would encourage Spain to go to war over the issue of Nootka Sound. In July Pitt sent his spy, William Augustus Miles, to Paris to discover whether the new national compact recommended to the Assembly was likely to become fact. Nothing is known about Miles's contacts; he knew La Fayette, and was a member of the Jacobin Club where he would have formed an idea of the opposition which would be mounted in the Assembly to any continuation of the Pacte de Famille. He may or may not have known that a French agent had been sent to Madrid; Mirabeau learned on 27 June that one had gone, but without the all-important letter to the minister, Florida Blanca, which he was to have provided. He was incensed by the way his advice had been bungled. The king had apparently passed on his ideas to Montmorin without telling him where they came from, probably thinking that the minister, a former ambassador to Madrid, would have the skill to handle the affair. As a result the poorly instructed agent returned in the middle of July without accomplishing anything, and France was left in the same position, morally bound to observe the Pacte, and with her relations with Spain soured by what was seen as her attempt to default.

While the king and queen allowed Mirabeau to think that they were listening to him they were simultaneously accepting advice from other quarters. One of these advisers was Duquesnoy, whose journal comes to a stop at the end of March 1790 in consequence of his new commitment. On 22 May Barnave had darkly announced that certain deputies – by implication Duquesnoy – were communicating with ministers; it was evident that there were informers everywhere. Mirabeau learned that Talon had resigned his post at the Châtelet as he was to become the king's privy Keeper of Seals, in charge of the civil list. That the snooping Talon should be placed where he would have access to the king's most confidential papers was incredible, and it seemed probable that La Fayette had recommended him in order that he should know everything that was secretly going on at the Tuileries. If such a man were appointed, Mirabeau wrote furiously in his fifth Note, they would have to do without useful and trustworthy servants. The futility of only being able to submit written advice, the feeling that the queen still mistrusted him, made a personal interview an urgent necessity, and a meeting was duly arranged for 3 July at Saint-Cloud, where the royal family had been allowed to go for a holiday.

In preparation he summarised the current situation in Paris (Note 6, 1 July), where political tensions had been concentrated by the Assembly's decision on 21 May to replace the sixty districts by forty-eight sections, in an attempt to end the districts' organised opposition to the official municipality, and with it the incessant agitation which threatened to make the city ungovernable. The provokers of unrest were not all left-wing. Mirabeau took this opportunity of condemning the tactics employed by the Club Monarchique, which had set up a fund to enable the poor to buy bread at reduced cost. The poor would have been glad of it, but the cry of political bribery which went up from the Jacobins led to such a storm of feeling against the Club Monarchique that Bailly had to ban it. The lesson for the Court was that the lavish use of money, whether to feed the poor, or to bribe the troops, or to promote counter-revolutionary movements, would have the opposite effect from the one desired, especially since the money was known to come from wealthy bankers, the group most loathed by the people.

Following this comfortless Note, Mirabeau met the queen at 8 a.m. on 3 July, in a remote corner of the park at Saint-Cloud. Time and place were chosen to avoid witnesses; despite this, rumours of their meeting were soon circulating. The queen told La Marck later that on meeting Mirabeau for the first time she felt a certain horror, remembering the events at Versailles, even though she knew that her fears were groundless. Mirabeau came away enthusing over her charm – persuading himself, perhaps, that it signified a capacity for enlightenment. Even so, that he was so carried away, as Mme Campan says, that he exclaimed 'The monarchy is saved!' is unlikely – the monarchy was far from being saved. When Michelet was writing his history of the French Revolution in the 1840s he asked two questions about Mirabeau's relations with the Court. Was he guilty of treason? No, said the republican Michelet, he was the very voice of liberty. Guilty of corruption? Yes. Not because he had received money but because of that meeting with the queen, because he was motivated by a desire to play the part of Mazarin, to be 'a sort of political husband' to Marie-Antoinette.[7] Ignoring the queen's determined character and influence over the king, which made her goodwill a strategical necessity, Michelet came to the idiosyncratic conclusion that Mirabeau weakly put a woman and his own greatness before the country. Had he been intent on the woman and indifferent to his country he would not have consistently affronted her with the content of his Notes, nor continued to force an awareness of political reality on the king.

Note 8, written on his return from Saint-Cloud, reminded Louis that although he was the sole administrator under the constitution, the Assembly could yet take over that power, without which the royal authority was simply a phantom. The king must therefore act positively, at the same time remembering the monarchy's debt to the Assembly, for in abolishing the *parlements*, the corps of clergy, and the privileges of the nobility, the Assembly had done much for liberty while also liberating the royal authority. True, the proliferation of administrative bodies created by the constitution favoured neither the monarch nor the people, but these would correct themselves in time. And some Assembly decrees contradicted the authority given to the king by the constitution; but the majority of them deserved his assent and he should approve them. In the case of those which displeased him the solution would be found in the pressure of public opinion, 'the sovereign of legislators'. Public opinion would be the king's most powerful weapon against legislative excesses, especially if anarchy continued; therefore he should do everything to gain popular backing and his ministers should devote their energies to this end. A warning followed. Attempts to influence public opinon could have an exacerbating effect if, despite it, opinion remained divided: prolonged anarchy could result in civil war. It would be essential then for the king to give himself to the provinces, not for the provinces to surrender to him, and public force would have to be deployed only in the name of the nation. By maintaining a wise balance the national party would soon be that of the king.[8] (By national party he meant the majority of people throughout the country.)

The immediate opportunity for the king to influence public opinion lay less than a week ahead. On the Day of Federation the whole nation would affirm allegiance to the constitution, and whoever emerged as the leading figure on this occasion would have an immeasurable psychological advantage. That the king should be that figure was an important part of Mirabeau's strategy. La Fayette had supplied a form of oath for the king to take: 'I, the first citizen, king of the French, swear to maintain the constitution with all the power that the constitution delegates to me'; Mirabeau wanted him to address the nation in person as well. Louis prepared a speech – it was, marvelled La Marck, his own work – but would only agree to address a deputation of citizens in private and to have his speech printed. His decision was no doubt determined, at least in part, by the Assembly's decree of 12 July on the civil constitution of the clergy, which obliged the clergy to take an oath of loyalty to the constitution. Having undertaken at his coronation to uphold the Catholic Church in France he could not accept that the clergy should be expected to put sworn allegiance to the state before their other vows. As a result of his decision, however, the Day of Federation became a day of triumph for La Fayette, mounted on his symbolic white horse before the altar in the Champs-de-Mars where the oaths of allegiance were taken. For Mirabeau the anniversary marked a personal defeat: he had hoped to be elected president of the Assembly for the fortnight in which the Day of Federation fell. With La Fayette's support he might have succeeded, but the commander-general refused, telling Mirabeau's friend, Frochot: 'I have conquered the power of the king of England, the authority of the king of France, the fury of the people; I shall certainly not give way to M. de Mirabeau'.[9]

In his twelfth Note, dated 17 July, Mirabeau did not conceal his fury at the way the occasion had been bungled by the king's advisers. La Marck, Mercy, and the Archbishop of Toulouse were equally perturbed by the myopia which had handed the oriflamme to the commander of the National Guard on such a historic day, and agreed on the need for countermeasures to restore the balance. Mirabeau advised an immediate move to Fontainebleau on the pretext of taking a holiday, the journey to be made quite openly and with the sanction of the Assembly. Once there the king would be in a stronger bargaining position, no longer the hostage of Parisian factions, free to act as king of all France, to which end even the few miles separating Paris from Fontainebleau would serve as confirmation. He did not think that the Assembly would raise any objections. The king should write to the president, he said, and La Fayette should be charged with the task of addressing the Assembly when the king's message had been read, in order to explain his intentions.

> The advantages of this precaution are easy to conceive: M. de La Fayette will be forced by his commitment to the King's plan to maintain public order; on the other hand, if he fails to carry the Assembly he will lose his popularity; if the journey is attended with difficulties he will be blamed for them. Now the result of all this is that M. de La Fayette will either be more strongly attached to the King's cause or his power will diminish.

The journey to Fontainebleau did not take place. The queen thought it nonsense that he should want them to leave Paris when La Fayette was always saying that they were safe there with him to protect them. Three weeks after the meeting at Saint-Cloud she was as prejudiced against him as she had ever been, citing the unsuccessful mission to Madrid, mismanaged by Montmorin, as an example of the unreliability of his advice. It was with relief, therefore, that the Archbishop of Toulouse read his fifteenth Note, written on 30 July, which contained questions and observations on European politics, to be used by the king in discussions with Montmorin. The Archbishop told La Marck:

> I am well pleased with the comte de Mirabeau's Note. I believe they know very little at Saint-Cloud about foreign affairs; and how could they know anything with a minister like M. de Montmorin? It would be very useful if the comte, who in my opinion is brilliant in this respect, could provide sound and accurate ideas on this subject.[10]

The following day Mirabeau was seen by the Foreign Minister, who took copious notes which he promised to pass to the king, but the advantage of gaining Montmorin's ear was discounted by the hostility of the other ministers. Saint-Priest, the Minister of the Household, whose dismissal he had called for and who was behind the attacks on him in the right-wing press, worked skilfully on the queen's prejudices: Mirabeau's plan for the king to leave Paris was a ruse to seize power; his lust for power was revealed in his attention to Provence; he intended to profit by the upheavals there and to seize control of the province if he failed to achieve his aims in Paris. Mirabeau's passionate concern for Provence, which often gave the impression that he felt he had an inborn monopoly of interest in its affairs, lent plausibility to conjectures about his motives. (Duroveray must have been thinking along the same lines as Saint-Priest on the occasion when Mirabeau, disappointed by his early failures in the Assembly, said that he could always fall back on Provence, for he had remarked: 'He already sees himself as comte de Provence'. Spoken in jest, the words were perceptive.) But if vanity and ambition contributed to his attitude to Provence they did not induce subversive fantasies. Saint-Priest, however, saw the continuous ferment at Marseille as an opportunity to incriminate him, and set his spies to work. In the middle of July Mirabeau reported that letters of his had been intercepted on the road from Provence. Fearing arrest on some trumped up charge, he sent La Marck his confidential papers, requesting somewhat melodramatically that if he should die his friend would tell the world what he had hoped to achieve.

Incidents like this all helped to close the queen's mind, and his credibility was further undermined by the delivery to the Assembly on 7 August of the Châtelet's report on the events of 5–6 October, its production a piece of deliberate timing by the ministers. Although its findings were still unknown – the report rested with the Reports Committee for the next two months – Mirabeau's enemies acted as though his guilt were already proven. Right-wing deputies blocked proposals that the report should be printed, on the grounds that the accused would try to escape. To cheers from the left Mirabeau retorted that the witnesses had more need to escape than the accused, and he called for the speedy publication of the report. But partisan support could not dispel the miasma which hung over his reputation so long as the Châtelet's findings remained hidden, a mine of slander and speculation. The question arises as to why the king allowed his ministers to pursue the man whose public strength he needed. Louis' inertia in this respect is the clearest proof that he still refused to treat him, or his own situation, seriously.

When Mirabeau drew up his plan for the king's move to Fontainebleau he dealt in detail with the military escort that would be needed on the journey. If it were chosen from regiments supporting the Revolution the king's safety would be compromised, if from royalist regiments he would be suspected of trying to flee, and the consequences might be fatal. Mirabeau advised that the National Guard should provide the only escort as far as the border of the department of Paris, and that there they should be joined by twelve soldiers and one officer from the loyal Bourgogne cavalry regiment. The small number, he thought, would not arouse hostility. This concern with loyalty reflected the deterioration in the situation since the beginning of the year. The king and queen believed that the devotion of the regiments that guarded the royal palaces was typical of the whole army. On looking closer, however, the loyal forces mainly turned out to be proprietory regiments or ones composed of foreign troops; standards were higher in these, and as the language barrier prevented the soldiers in the foreign regiments from following French politics they did not identify with the civilian population, and were less likely to desert. On the other hand, the loyalty of the special regiments had to be weighed against the mood of revolt in the rest of the army, caused by bad administration, irregular pay, and harsh discipline. The Assembly had decreed various reforms, and soldiers could now appeal against their officers and be tried in civil courts, but these measures only increased the restlessness: the summer of 1790 brought daily news of soldiers arresting their colonels and refusing to obey orders, culminating at the beginning of August with a major insurrection at Nancy. The regiments involved were all ones Mirabeau had classified as trustworthy when planning the king's move. This fact, and the help given to the rebels by the citizens of Nancy, cast grave doubts on his plan of letting the king appeal to the innate love of his subjects. It now seemed that they would be more likely to denounce than to defend him.

The royal couple, already wary of following his advice, could hardly have been encouraged to learn that he was now a marked man in the radical press. On 10 August Marat wrote in the *Ami du peuple*:

> We have all noted the versatility of Riquetti's (*sic*) political manoeuvres. I watched in terror as he flailed around like a madman to get himself elected to the Estates and I said to myself then: if he is reduced to prostituting himself in that way in order to live, then he will sell his vote to the highest bidder. He started out against the king, yet today he has sold himself to him, and it is to his venality that we owe all these baneful decrees, from that on the royal veto to that giving the king the right to initiate war. But what are we to expect from a man utterly devoid of principles, morals, or honour?

It was against a background of crumbling security that he wrote his sixteenth Note on 13 August. Four enemies were approaching at speed, he declared: taxation, bankruptcy, the army, and winter. Civil war was certain, perhaps necessary. In saying this he was not, as historians often assume, suggesting that they should actually provoke civil war, but simply taking into account its frequency in French history, and noting that chaos sometimes had to intervene before order could be established. Anticipating the worst, he proposed preventative action. The Swiss and German regiments should be isolated and their loyalty encouraged by the appointment of their own inspector-general; he recommended La Marck, who would leave the king and queen 'only on the scaffold'. At all costs they must decide on a plan of action: 'What I do not yet see is a will to act', he concluded bluntly. 'Without it there will be no rescue.' The queen found this Note offensive, particularly the reference to scaffolds. The project was absurd, she told Mercy, and Mirabeau must be mad to think of civil war. He had been misunderstood. In subsequent Notes he repeated his proposals, remarking that although they had 'given rise to unease bordering on fright', this would be a salutary alarm if it replaced terror with activity. It was a bizarre situation, he added, when his loyalty was in doubt because he warned of danger.

> But if fidelity consists in knowing when to displease in order to serve, it also consists in braving the very perils one has foreseen, and which would have been averted if one had been listened to. I shall therefore continue to serve, as much as the nature of things permits, even in the passive role to which I have been condemned.[11]

Someone must have told him that personal digressions would further annoy the queen, for after the middle of August his Notes concentrate on three themes, the need to avoid war, to sustain the king's authority, and to achieve a working partnership with the Assembly. In the Assembly he pursued the same ends. On 25 and 26 August he presented the report of the Foreign Affairs Committee on the Pacte de Famille question, which in a larger context was the question of what sort of role France intended to play in international politics. Nootka Sound became the test of her integrity. He expressed the hope that France would not be implicated in a war. One day other nations might follow her example and renounce war, but meanwhile she must honour her existing treaties. True, he said, the Pacte de Famille contained clauses which did not conform with 'our new political religion'; the Foreign Affairs Committee therefore intended to modify the alliance when the time came for its renewal. The next matter, obtaining ships to send to Spain's assistance, had to be well camouflaged in order to get the Assembly to agree to it. The Spanish alliance would be illusory, he said, if France did not match her neighbours in armaments. French commerce and colonies had to be protected. All because of this execrable suspicion that made neighbouring people regard each other as enemies. 'Why is it', he asked, 'that the need to guarantee peace forces nations to ruin themselves in preparations for defence?'[12]

He got what he wanted by playing on French distrust of England. They must not think that a free and enlightened people would wish to profit by France's troubles; even so, they should be prudent. France could only match the English navy in size if Spain came to her aid; therefore it was in her own interest to preserve their alliance. He suggested thirty ships. The Assembly insisted on raising the number to forty-five.

He said afterwards that he had succeeded in the Spanish affair better than he had dared to hope. His performance caused even more of a stir in London than in Paris, for it was realised that Spain would refuse to back down over Nootka Sound so long as she had French support. Pitt decided to make an unofficial approach to the man who effectively controlled France's foreign policies, and sent Hugh Elliot, Mirabeau's former school friend, as his agent. His task was to obtain an understanding that the Assembly would withhold support if Spain refused the conditions offered her by England. Elliot arrived in September. The British ambassador, Lord Gower, reported that his meeting with Mirabeau went well and held out the prospect of good relations with the popular party in the Assembly. In this he may have been led astray by Elliot's own impressions. With memories of the voluble, dramatising boy he had known at school Elliot thought that to gain Mirabeau he only had to lay on the rhetoric. 'The Speech I made was in every sense a *French Speech* and therefore the term *Glorious revolution* and others of a similar nature are applicable to *their* notions and not to my own opinion', he reported.[13] He found, as he put it, that nothing got done in France without an oratorical debate, and was content that this should be so since it meant that a month after Mirabeau's speech in the Assembly a decree had still not been formulated. Time played into England's hands. On 10 October the Assembly finally voted to maintain the alliance with Spain, but retracted French commitment to any action not conforming with the Assembly's principles. A month earlier, said Mirabeau, the decree would probably have upset England's plans and assured peace; now it was too late.

In a *mémoire* to Montmorin he said:

> We must assume the worst. Spain, detached from us by our shilly-shallying, prejudiced against our constitution, seduced by England, will refuse to make a national pact with us, and will ally herself with Great Britain by a treaty of friendship and commerce.[14]

(Florida Blanca, in fact, capitulated to England's conditions, and signed the Treaty of Escurial with the bitter remark that he did not do so because they were just but because he had been forced to without French help.) This *mémoire*, a cool, penetrating analysis of France's vulnerable position in the European power game, demonstrated how mistaken Elliot was to think that he could outwit Mirabeau, or, as British historians have suggested he did, bribe him into compromising France's wider interests by hinting unofficially at an Anglo-French alliance.[15] No one could subvert Mirabeau's patriotism or cloud his judgement in matters of statesmanship. He put little faith in the assurances he had had from Elliot that England only wanted peaceful coexistence. If war should come France would be without allies, he warned Montmorin. Add to that the state of the army, her ruined credit, the breakdown in law and order, and it was impossible not to be filled with dread. All the more reason to act at once to build up good relations with Vienna and The Hague, Berlin and the princes of the Empire. The king must come to a decision quickly. And Montmorin? 'The King's minister may remember that in the event of war and misfortunes the nation will demand an account from him of everything that has not been done, and of every minute that has not been employed.'

After international affairs and the Pacte de Famille the Assembly turned to another unwelcome legacy from the past, the financial crisis. The first issue of *assignats* was exhausted, a further 200 million livres was needed. Necker was opposed to a second issue, as were economists of every political hue – all, that is, except Clavière, their inventor. Mirabeau had stated his views unequivocally at the time of the first issue, when he denounced paper money as 'a culpable deception, a very great physical and moral evil';[16] but no feasible alternative solution was forthcoming, and against the argument that *assignats* were inflationary there were weighty counterarguments: they would speed up the sale of Church land, restore stability, avert anarchy and a return to despotism. Mirabeau himself did not share Clavière's faith in their soundness. At best they were the least controversial policy to adopt, he told the Court in his twenty-first Note; and as Necker would undoubtedly go because of them Clavière should be appointed in his place, the one man who could make them work. In the Assembly he accepted that *assignats* were risky but stressed that they were politically necessary in order to create a climate of optimism. Speaking on 27 August, at the start of the month-long debate on *assignats*,[17] he countered the prejudice against them as something favouring the esoteric world of high finance, by linking them to the survival of the emerging class of small proprietors, the corner-stones of the stable, bourgeois society envisaged by the Assembly: *assignats* were essential, therefore, to the Revolution, to the maintenance of law and order, and to the reshaping of society. The statistics of the financial experts were no match for the human approach. At the end of September, following his second speech, the Assembly voted a further issue of 800 million livres worth of *assignats*. Mirabeau's service to his country, in getting the decree passed, 'cannot be put high enough' in the opinion of Jean Jaurès. '*Assignats* saved the Revolution.'[18]

They saved it in a way unforeseen by Mirabeau. He saw *assignats* as politically useful since they would benefit the small proprietors, the class he had in mind when he said, Physiocratically: 'Interest links egotists through their private fortunes to the public fortune, to the advantage of the revolution'.[19] This interest, once satisfied, he counted on to provide future support for the monarchy. Instead, because they were issued initially in high denominations, *assignats* became the currency of the wealthier bourgeois, and poorer citizens remained outside the revived prosperity. *Assignats* held the Revolution together long enough for the monarchy to fall, and the loyalty of those who had benefited by the sale of Church property went not to the monarchy but to the Republic.

Necker did not wait for the decree. On 4 September he tendered his resignation and left for Switzerland. His previous departure had produced the attack on the Bastille; this time he went unregretted, unnoticed, save at Arcis-sur-Aube where the National Guard held him under arrest until the Assembly sent an order for his release. He spent the remainder of his life brooding over the ingratitude of the French, absolving himself from all responsibility for the disasters of the Revolution. His contempt for Mirabeau was never tempered by comprehension: 'He was a tribune by calculation and an aristocrat by taste'. Experience had given him little respect for either tribunes or aristocrats.

Although Necker had gone the rest of the ministry hung on. Mirabeau continued to warn the king and queen against appointing La Fayette's men to a new ministry. The thought occurred to him that the imminent collapse of the ministry would be a good time to bring up the question of appointing ministers from the Assembly again, which, of course, would entail changing the existing decree. He believed that La Fayette would help in this, for they had discussed the problems arising from the Assembly's insistence that its decrees were untouchable, and La Fayette had agreed to speak on the need to make provision for repealing existing decrees in the public interest. But when he made his speech on 28 September the vital points they had discussed were omitted: La Fayette was well aware that had he presented the argument as outlined by Mirabeau he would have been preparing the ground for an attack on the decree banning deputies from the ministry.

Two days later the committee studying the Châtelet's investigations reported to the Assembly. It cleared Mirabeau and Orléans of any complicity in the events of 5–6 October, and the Assembly formally acquitted them.[20] On 2 October, vindicated, Mirabeau had the satisfaction of replying at last to all those who had intrigued to destroy him. After dealing lightly with the preposterous depositions which had been laid against him, and offering his sympathy to the man who was now officially hideous since a witness had mistaken him for himself, he continued more gravely:

> I am not speaking here in order to stir up hatred and create new divisions. Nobody knows better than I that the salvation of everything and everyone lies in social harmony and the subduing of factious feelings; but I cannot prevent myself from adding that it is a sad way of obtaining this reunion of minds, to institute infamous proceedings, to transform the law into an offensive weapon, and to justify this form of combat by principles which would horrify slaves.[21]

After this speech, said Ferrières, the nobles and bishops sat silent and embarrassed. La Fayette had promised Mirabeau his support on this occasion. He was not there.

Mirabeau's position in the Assembly was strengthened by his acquittal but it brought no improvement in his standing with the queen. Mercy was no longer there to reason with her, having gone to The Hague, and La Marck was left to answer for the fidelity of a man whose approach to problems often alarmed him because he was unable himself to appreciate all the nuances and complexities. He thought that Mirabeau should defend the king's corner at every opportunity: he failed to understand that this could be self-defeating, and he ignored the essential fact that the man he was dealing with was not a royalist and courtier like himself, but a revolutionary, whose cause was the Revolution, and who could not neglect that for a king.

At the Tuileries there was no sign of growing awareness from the king and queen. 'The house they are sleeping in could be reduced to ashes without them even waking up', Mirabeau remarked, tired of hammering at the door with warnings that were never heeded. Notes 23–34, written between 7 September and 23 October, were a sustained attempt to make them comprehend the finality of the Revolution; why their future depended on the constitution, how it could still be overturned. The greatest threat to the constitution, he wrote on 7 September, lay in the discontent provoked by some of its rulings;[22] what would happen when the discontent exploded? A torrent had overturned the *ancien régime*; public opinion, badly directed, could become a second torrent, which would sweep aside solid achievments along with mistakes. In all his political writings he had hailed public opinion as the ultimate weapon in a just cause. Seeing the influence of newspapers, posters, and the leading voices in the sections and political clubs, on ordinary apolitical citizens, this view now seemed simplistic. People allowed themselves to be led. This inexorable force, public opinion, was a fabrication.

> Public opinion is not always dictated by the understanding of the people. Certain men forestall it. Their contemporaries simply echo them and after

that the crowd blindly adopts errors as truths. This problem is even more evident in a revolution. The employment of all the forces of the people demands their individual consent, and so public opinion is formed almost by chance. It is not so much enlightened as it is universal, and all the more dangerous in that it assumes the guise of the general will and of the law.[23]

An explosion was inevitable because the French people were 'incapable of moderation'. It was inevitable because they had been given hopes which were impossible to realise. 'In the last analysis the people will judge the revolution by one thing only: Will it put more or less money in their pocket? Will there be more work available? Will it be better paid?' Mirabeau's autumn reflections on the mood of the people echoed earlier speeches in the Assembly, in which he had spoken of a chain of circumstances being set in motion which would end by imposing its own desperate logic.

To the queen his latest Notes seemed to be preoccupied with things that were irrelevant to her personal situation. Her priorities did not include the preservation of the constitution which stood as a monument to the defeat of the monarchy, and Mirabeau's regard for it underlined his identity as a revolutionary. Fresh doubts about his motives were triggered by his recommendation that the king should include Jacobins in the ministry in the event of the decree being repealed which banned deputies from becoming ministers. With cynical wisdom he observed:

> Jacobin ministers would not be Jacobins, for promotion to senior rank cures a man's existing faults and bestows others he does not have. The most violent demagogue, placed at the helm, will recognise the inadequacy of the executive power and will strive to improve it. Why not choose some ministers from the Jacobins and some from a different section of the popular party? Equality of power is a strong instrument of reconciliation. This union would be mutually corrective and the different parties acting together would benefit the royal authority. I have often thought about the effect on the provinces of any change of temperature in the National Assembly, and I am convinced that if the malcontents [the reactionary nobles] laid aside their mad hopes, and the extremists felt abandoned, moderate citizens who have remained silent up till now would come into the open, and would soon dominate public opinion.[24]

Note 31, dated 15 October, expanded on this theme. Discontent would increase with the approach of winter. While patching each crisis temporarily the Assembly would blame the ministry for disasters which really stemmed from its own procrastination, and would make the situation an excuse to encroach more and more on the royal authority. The disunity of ministers and legislators, and the detachment of central government from the rest of the country, could only be overcome when deputies entered the ministry. The decree must be attacked by the king at once; he would write the necessary letter for the Assembly. If it failed the ministry would still fall.

There was a reason for his sudden urgency. In October a naval squadron had mutinied at Brest, and the trouble spread to the army garrison still smouldering at Nancy; it was the signal for the ministry to come under renewed attack in the Assembly. Writing his Note on 15 October, a Friday, he was so certain that the attack would succeed, and that by the following Monday there would be a new ministry, that he submitted a list of suitable candidates: Rochambeau, Moustiers, La Prévalaye, La Millière, Lambert. The jotted form of Note 31 suggests that it was only a preliminary draft, or that he lacked the time to write at length. The next day he assured the Tuileries that if the new ministry strengthened the executive, discouraged La Fayette, and forced the Jacobins into moderation, great advantages would have been gained. He could write no more, he said, as he was 'very ill'.

On Monday, however, he was perfectly well again, though by his own account he had barely escaped death over the weekend. Monday also brought La Marck a letter headed dramatically 'For you alone!', in which Mirabeau announced that he had discovered that the former deputy, Bergasse, was advising the Court. (The lawyer Nicolas Bergasse, deputy for Lyon, resigned with Mounier.) He even enclosed a copy of the letter which Bergasse allegedly had written for the king to send to the Assembly. In it the king agreed to dismiss the ministers, but refused to name their successors; he told the deputies that this was their job alone and that he would abide by their choice. A fatal plan of action. Mirabeau fulminated at the stupidity of 'the royal cattle' who listened to this sort of thing. 'So they expect to find the solution to their problems in the mesmeric tub! Good God! What reasoning! what insanity!'[25]

La Marck commented later that Mirabeau's language could only be explained by the shock of learning that the mediocre Bergasse was his rival adviser. Bergasse's letter, he noted, was never produced in the Assembly, where it would have had a cataclysmic effect; and as for Mirabeau's copy, he had 'no other proof of its origin than the assertion of the comte de Mirabeau'.

He was right to be suspicious. Although it has always been accepted that Bergasse wrote the alleged letter, all the evidence points to its having been imaginary, and Mirabeau's 'copy' of it a concoction prepared by him during the weekend when he was supposed to be ill. He gave no explanation as to how he came by it. The copy in his own handwriting was all anyone saw. It materialised three days after he himself offered to write a letter for the king to send to the Assembly – which suggests that as he drafted Note 31 he had a better idea: to produce documentary 'proof' of disastrous advice given to the king by Bergasse, in the knowledge that La Marck would pass it on to Montmorin. Even the most politically naive of the king's advisers knew that if he refused to fulfil his constitutional duties by appointing new ministers the monarchy would become redundant. Montmorin and the queen would be appalled by Bergasse's counsel, and the sagacity of the comte de Mirabeau would shine by comparison like a light in darkness. An imaginary letter was not an inconceivable ploy for him to use at a crucial moment; almost certainly he resorted to it at the time of his sudden return from Berlin. Since Bergasse was advising the Court, a man whose judgement was negated in Mirabeau's eyes by his credulity regarding occult manifestations ('the mesmeric tub'), a man who had tried, moreover, to destroy him through the Châtelet investigation, the opportunity to take revenge by making him look a dangerous fool was irresistible. And to complete the lesson there was his own Note of 16 October, in which, after hinting that he knew about the other advice the king had received, he analysed with brilliant acumen the consequences of following that advice. His own was that the king should take the wind out of the Assembly's sails by dismissing his ministers before they passed a decree demanding it. Instant action was necessary. It was not forthcoming.

On 19 October a motion to demand the dismissal of the ministers (apart from Montmorin) was narrowly defeated in the Assembly. Mirabeau abstained, not out of respect for Montmorin, as La Marck thought, but because the decree subtracted from the authority of the Crown. For this reason he had been anxious that the king should avoid the challenge by dismissing the ministry before the Assembly acted. The significance of his silence on 19 October, however, was lost in the uproar which attended his performance two days later during a debate on events at Brest, where the revolutionary flag had been hoisted on ships in imitation of the army, which had already adopted the tricolour. A Jacobin deputy proposed that the tricolour should replace the royalist white flag still used by the navy. A right-winger replied by dismissing the tricolour as a *hochet*, a plaything. Seizing his cue, Mirabeau observed that the Assembly was being asked to regard as a bagatelle the language of symbols, the most potent language in existence. What the right was saying in effect was: we believe ourselves strong enough to retain the white flag, the colour of counter-revolution, in place of the odious colours of liberty. They should not sleep in such a perilous security, he warned the right, for their awakening would be terrible.

Cries that he was nothing but a factionary rang out. He retorted:

The real factionaries are those who speak of preserving prejudices, hankering after our former errors and the misery of our slavery. No, their stupid presumption, their sinister prophecies, their blasphemous cries will prove vain: the national colours will fly at sea, not as a symbol of battles and victory, but as that of the holy fraternity of the friends of liberty throughout the world, and as the terror of conspirators and tyrants.[26]

La Marck accused him afterwards of being an irresponsible demagogue. He denied it: 'I am for the re-establishment of order, not for the re-establishment of the old order.'[27] His outburst had been consistent with this statement. To have insisted on the royalist flag being flown by the navy, when the army had replaced it, would only have increased mutinous feelings and made the royal symbol the focus of resentment. He refused to change his attitude in his next Note as well, declaring that he was quite prepared to be regarded as a demagogue by the ministers if they, not being demagogues, proved to be better defenders of the royal authority than he was.

Two of those ministers, Lambert and Luzerne, had already resigned in the wake of the debate attacking the ministry. La Tour du Pin followed on 8 November; Saint-Priest and Cicé hung on. In the Paris sections, calls for a petition to the Assembly to demand their dismissal were accompanied by riots, and on 10 November Bailly escorted a deputation to the bar of the Assembly, where its leader, whose pockmarked face had earned him the nickname of the people's Mirabeau, read out their demands. Danton's manner was like a battering ram. In the sound of his voice as he indicted the ministers, referring to them only by name as though they were convicted criminals, and in its assent to this naked external pressure, the Assembly could well hear its own doom. Cicé resigned a few days later, Saint-Priest in January. Only Montmorin survived. Despite everything Mirabeau had said about the danger of letting La Fayette extend his tentacles still further, the new ministry included two of his men: Fleurieu became Minister for the Navy and Colonies, Duportail the Minister for War. The new Finance Minister was neither Mirabeau's choice, Clavière, nor La Fayette's, Condorcet, but a former colleague of Necker's, Valdec de Lessart. A ministry influenced by the deviant *Club de 89* and Necker's ghost could never win public confidence.

The victory of the Paris sections in precipitating the exit of the ministers determined Mirabeau's tactics in the following weeks. Once more the king had failed to act, signalling his lack of common purpose with his subjects and his hostility to the popular party in the Assembly. The ever growing power of the Jacobins, which could have been working on the side of legitimate authority if they had entered the ministry, would now instead be directed against it. The Jacobin ascendancy in the Assembly and Jacobin monopoly of the public mind had to be contained; but a frontal assault would simply reinforce the accepted image of the king as the enemy of popular movements. Mirabeau's reputation as the defender of liberty was the king's only asset, which could either be wasted in confrontation with the extremists, or used to appease and convert them. November saw him doing just that, pre-empting the rhetoric of the Jacobin faction, justifying the actions of the Paris crowds, taking up popular causes such as the one to have the Jeu-de-Paume made into a national monument. In the middle of the month the wounding by the duc de Castries of the triumvir Charles de Lameth in a duel, and the sacking afterwards of the Hôtel de Castries, roused partisan feelings to fresh heights. Mirabeau outraged the right on this occasion by his failure to denounce the mob. The evidence, in fact, showed that the destruction was instigated by Lameth's suppor-ters and that La Fayette, though called to the scene, failed to inter-vene. They were the real culprits, and Mirabeau warned the Assembly against popular idols who led the people astray. His speech succeeded in antagonising both the left and the right, and confirmed the general view that he was nothing but an unprincipled intriguer. Uncontrite, he went to a performance of Voltaire's *Brutus* at the Théâtre de la Nation, where he received a standing ovation from the audience which hailed him as the apostle of liberty. This, though the Court would not under-stand it, was the sort of victory he needed to gain in order to be able to defend the monarchy.

On 30 November, in reward for his defence of popular causes, he was elected president of the Jacobin Club. Even more than when he delivered his speech on the abolition of slavery here, the club regarded itself, and was regarded, as the guardian of liberty, of pure principles, of revolutionary virtue. It, and not the elected legislature, was now the national forum. The transfer of perceived political power from the Assembly to the Jacobins was apparent in the attitude of speakers at the club, the left-wing deputies with an eye to the future, who made a point of dissociating themselves from the body to which they had been elected. Thus, on 5 December, when the Assembly decreed that only active citizens could enter the National Guard, Robespierre made a speech at the Jacobin Club criticising the decree and denouncing the legislators who insulted the people by presenting them as unworthy to enjoy their rights. Mirabeau had also voted against the creation of 'active' and 'passive' citizens; he agreed with what Robespierre was saying, but could not admire the self-popularising motive that promp-ted him to speak to the Jacobins, where he gained easy applause, rather than in the Assembly. As a parliamentarian he also deplored public attacks on the legislative body: although often bitterly critical himself, he never insulted the dignity of the Assembly by attacking it either in print or in a public place. After a full hour he intervened in his presidential capacity to say that no one could speak against a given decree. This citing of rules prompted a near riot; Mirabeau had to stand on his chair and summon his supporters, who included Charles de Lameth on this occasion, while another group, 'the true Jacobins' as Desmoulins called them, rallied round Robespierre. After further uproar Mirabeau allowed him to continue. It may or may not have been at this meeting of the Jacobins that he made his apocryphal remark about Robespierre: 'He will go far, he believes all he says'; but the words reflect his long-held view that ambitious men who were also self-righteous had to be watched, for they were the greatest threat to *la chose publique*, to the common good.

His election as president of the Jacobin Club confirmed the queen's worst suspicions regarding him. He was about to embark on his most hazardous undertaking and his credibility with the Court was at its lowest.

In the new ministry Montmorin was the only man whose loyalty was known to the king and who could be depended on to guide him wisely. Mercy's recommendation and personal interviews had enabled Mirabeau to gain his confidence. That, however, was all. Timid and unassertive – 'one has to lead him like a child' – Montmorin was not the ideal colleague in a crisis, and Mirabeau would never have chosen him normally, but there was no one else.

On 4 December his forty-fifth Note opened with the sombre comment: 'The state of our evils is daily becoming so much more complex that soon it will be impossible to find any remedy. Henceforth one can expect help only from a systematic plan that has been constructed very skilfully.' Later in the Note he revealed that an opportunity to save the situation had just arisen: Montmorin had proposed a suitable plan and a coalition with himself. Duquesnoy and Talon were involved, and so 'I must be on my guard', but apparently Barnave had also approached the minister, 'and in this case the coalition could be a very important one'. The idea of the sluggish Montmorin initiating anything seems odd, of him approaching the out-of-favour Mirabeau still odder. However, the next evening they had a long interview, after which Mirabeau wrote an account of their conversation to be sent to the queen. As there were no witnesses it is not certain that Montmorin was quite so obligingly talkative as he made out. According to him the minister, whose views seem uncannily like his own, began by condemning La Fayette's ambition and fatal influence, recommending that he should be excluded from the government. Montmorin went on to regret the lack of confidence in him shown by the queen and king, but added that the arrival of the new ministers, 'La Fayette's men', altered everything: 'I am not suspect in the eyes of the Assembly or of the public. I have some right to the Court's confidence. I could be a useful intermediary between the nation and the monarchy.' Montmorin continued in this reported conversation:

> It is evident that we will perish, all of us, royalty, authority, the entire nation. Even universal discontent is insufficient to restore order; the Assembly is killing itself and us, and yet, however important it is to prorogue it, one must not be precipitate or the result will be an even greater extreme of rage. If the king popularised himself this would be the quickest way of reducing the Assembly. His action alone would not suffice, and the queen's unpopularity still detracts from the king's popularity. So what must be done? Temporise, but govern; wait for a favourable wind, but prepare the sails and do not let go of the rudder for an instant. I wish to restore authority, I wish to consecrate all my strength to this end.
>
> As for you ('It is still the minister talking', explained Mirabeau), I cannot compare you with anyone. It is not that the Assembly does not include some men of a certain strength, but they are rare. You alone have been able to make yourself unpopular through courage, and popular again through prudence.[28]

At this point Montmorin asked Mirabeau to help him with a plan of action he had in mind, whereby they would devise ways of bringing the present Assembly to an end, of influencing public opinion, and of making the queen more popular. Mirabeau wrote in his Note:

> After thinking deeply about this conversation, I have no reason to doubt M. de Montmorin's wish to serve the Queen. For my part I shall follow the instructions I am given. I shall write nothing to M. de Montmorin that the Queen has not seen; but I ask for it to be kept a secret from the King for fear that an indiscretion, by destroying the minister's trust, creates an obstacle in the way of a coalition.[29]

This ingenious document was conveyed to the queen by La Marck; he asked her whether Montmorin was acting on her orders, but she knew nothing about it. He was worried about the involvement of Duquesnoy and Talon, and relieved when Montmorin told him that they would no longer be used as intermediaries. Like a well-drilled child Montmorin added that he would only act after consultation with Mirabeau. La Marck undoubtedly guessed who had really initiated the proceedings, and kept the knowledge to himself. No one of his shrewdness could have been taken in by Mirabeau's account of his conversation with the minister. All the details were selected with the effect they would have on the queen in mind: Montmorin's protestations of loyalty, his disavowal of La Fayette, his praise of Mirabeau. Montmorin's plan was Mirabeau's plan. How little the minister was really in charge is shown by La Marck's remark in a letter to Mercy:

M. de Mirabeau and I have agreed to leave M. de Montmorin in ignorance for the time being of the full extent of our relations with the queen. Mirabeau will only tell him that he has been indirectly consulted by her on several occasions, and that his advice has hardly been followed.[30]

Mirabeau began work on his plan to save the monarchy at the end of the first week in December. His only distraction was the fresh outbreak of violence in Provence, one of the victims of which was his old adversary, Pascalis, who was lynched at Aix. Certain that his presence was needed if Marseille were not to be 'lost to France', he arranged to go there on a short visit. He had not anticipated the storm that broke when it was learned that he had been given leave to visit Provence: the right accused him of wanting to stir up civil war, Marat announced that 'the infamous Riqueti' was planning to join the counter-revolutionaries at Turin, deputations from the Paris sections begged him to stay, and the *Chronique de Paris* urged its readers to oppose the departure of the man who was 'as necessary to the National Assembly as a king is to monarchical government'. He had no option but to remain.

No one was more relieved than Montmorin, who had staked his future on Mirabeau's success. Despite their faith in him and knowledge that the coalition gave him the strongest incentive to stay, Montmorin and La Marck could never have been completely sure that in Provence he would not have found another role. Without going there he could not have been certain himself. La Marck, taking note of his attitude to the proposed coalition, had told Mercy: 'M. de Mirabeau will calculate the future chances; he will always want to keep in with the party in power'. It would have been stupid of him to ignore the probability that the proposals in his plan would never be acted on; in which case the best hope for himself and the monarchy might lie in his retreat to Provence, whence he could return after the deluge to guide the work of reconstruction. The need for chaos to intervene before the nation would accept the necessity for order was an idea long held by him. On the other hand, if he went Montmorin would collapse and it would never be known whether the last gamble to save the monarchy would have succeeded. Glory in Paris or in Provence? Or in neither?

His plan was ready by Christmas. It carried the heading, *Aperçu de la situation en France et des moyens de concilier la liberté publique avec l'autorité royale*, the significant word being 'conciliate'. Its stated aim was the restoration of the king's authority in order that he should be better able to defend public liberty, not in order to enable him to threaten it. This project, said Mirabeau, was so in keeping with his own principles that he would have been tempted to undertake it without assistants, had he not realised that a systematic plan and a great pooling of means was needed, 'that mere theoretical ideas would no longer suffice, and that action was necessary as well'. The one person whom he deemed capable of positive thinking was the queen, and the lines of argument that he followed in the *Aperçu* were aimed, in effect, at her.

He began with the obstacles that would have to be surmounted. The indecisiveness of the king came first, along with the queen's deep unpopularity. Next to these he listed the demagoguery of Paris, the mood of the National Guard and the Assembly, and the discredit into which the nobility and clergy, the natural defenders of the monarchy, had fallen, interacting factors which had to be studied together if they were to be properly understood. If the king's indecisiveness persisted, he said, and affected the government as a whole, the people would get accustomed to another form of government, and royalty would become a phantom, without power or substance; the queen must use her influence, and the ministers must be seen by the country to be doing their job. As for the queen's unpopularity, it was the result of rumours, inevitable in revolutions, which could only be countered by reassurances on her part as to her intentions, and by a change of conduct; an enlightened benevolence was necessary, which would endear her to the public.

He conceded that one obstacle, the demagoguery of Paris, was invincible – 'the concentration of ability, ambition, and discontent generates a fire too intense to be doused' – but it would be possible to make use of this extremism in order to separate the capital from the provinces. The influence of Paris was one of the most dangerous threats to the Crown's authority.

> This city is aware of her strength; she exerts it on the army, the king, the ministers, the Assembly; she exerts it on individual deputies, depriving some of the power to act, others of the courage to speak out, and a mass of decrees are the fruit simply of her influence . . . Paris will be the last city in the kingdom where peace is restored; it is necessary, therefore, to demolish her influence in the provinces, and to promote a desire for the next legislature to be placed in a city where its independence and the king's liberty are better assured.

The Assembly, with its arrogance, its refusal to correct its mistakes, and its own infectious demagoguery, posed the most serious problems for the future. He felt that the best way of dealing with it, as with Paris, was to let its excesses speak for themselves, and so create a build-up of public opinion against it which must eventually lead to an election and a fresh legislature. But open attacks on it must be avoided; counter-revolutionary tracts of the sort being written by Calonne only intensified hatred. In seeking to reduce the influence of the present Assembly the people's anger and fear must not be allowed to get out of hand:

Great masses of humanity are difficult to move, but their strength deceives those that use them. Above all it is necessary to save the kingdom in order to save the king. Therefore one power must imperceptibly replace another, and the royal influence must gradually increase as that of the Assembly diminishes.

The royal authority, he went on, could not be re-established with the constitution in its present shape, a mixture of democracy, aristocracy, and monarchy. They had adopted from aristocracy what was most dangerous, the influence of wealth, and from democracy what was most baneful, the domination of the towns over the rural areas (an echo of Physiocracy here). As to the monarchy, the king no longer had sufficient influence or power, or the means to exercise the inadequate power delegated to him. He had no part in the making of the law or in the administration of the kingdom. The actual instruments of the executive power were the departments, the districts, the municipalities, but these were deliberating bodies, possessing all the means to resist higher authority: it was folly to expect that they could fulfil their executive role efficiently. The makers of the constitution had wished to distinguish between executive and deliberating power, but had given the deliberating power too much executive power, to the end that the total disorganisation of the kingdom could not have been better provided for. (The decentralisation resulting from the new system of local government, which Mirabeau is talking about here, posed a serious threat to the unity of the nation as the political situation worsened. In 1793 the revolutionary government enforced centralisation again.)

The fundamental flaws in the constitution would have to be corrected, either by the present Assembly or its successor. Mirabeau believed a fresh Assembly was necessary. Why? Because anyone in office is loath to criticise himself or to revise enactments. A second Assembly would have less compunction about correcting the work of its predecessor and every incentive to prove itself more capable. He wished to make it clear, however, that while insisting on the need for corrections, he recognised 'both the benefits of the revolution and the basic principles of the constitution'. Many advantages had been gained: the laws to prevent tax evasion, the freedom of the press, religious freedom, ministerial responsibility, accessibility to all forms of employment by all citizens, properly supervised administration of public money; these fundamental benefits would survive whether the Assembly which had obtained them for the nation lost its popularity or not. An improved constitution would retain all those decrees which gave sufficient power to the executive and established the legislative power of the Assembly; but those which shackled the proper function of the

executive, and contributed to disunity or a return to despotism, must
be repealed. Could changes to the constitution be made by royal pro-
clamation? No. That would be despotic. Their aim must be to restore
the royal authority, but never to attack the revolution,

> for the movement which leads a great people to obtain the best laws for itself
> deserves support rather than obstruction. By halting the revolution one would
> obliterate an entire generation, banish the memory of 25 million people.
> Respecting the revolution, while returning the people to the point they were
> at on 27 April 1789, would be yet another chimerical plan, impossible to carry
> out with a nation naturally impatient, which wants a constitution, thinks it has
> obtained it, and will not have its hopes deceived.[31]

Continuing his question and answer method, he now asked whether
petitions from the people might persuade the present Assembly to
correct the constitution. Again the answer was no. Before there could
be petitions public opinion must change, a process which could not be
completed within the lifetime of the present Assembly, and meanwhile the Assembly had only to sound the alarm for the public to
believe that any modification of the constitution was the last desperate
gambit of the counter-revolutionary party. The nation would be less
frightened, he said, if the next Assembly were specifically one with
ratifying powers. But how was the present Assembly to be brought
down? Well, if it completed its course in triumph the thermometer of
public opinion would leave no hope; if, on the contrary, it failed to
complete it that part of its handiwork which needed reforming would
necessarily fall as well. The only way to ensure that this happened was
by encouraging the Assembly to behave in such a way that it lost the
nation's confidence. Mirabeau listed the ways in which they could help
the Assembly to prepare its own death warrant: by letting it pass
decrees that would increase the number of malcontents; by encouraging it to favour the capital at the expense of the provinces; by introducing unimportant subjects, thus creating boredom and impatience; by
pushing it into usurping all legislative, executive, and judicial powers.
Admittedly, the kingdom would become more and more disorganised,
but for that very reason a crisis would be created, and as the troubles
continued the royal authority alone would soon be the only resort left.

The Assembly's disarray, he said, would help bring about a reform
of the constitution, and it could prepare the way for that reform by
the type of decrees it passed, decrees which would make it easier to
influence the composition of the next legislature. He proposed two in
particular, not without embarrassment: 'the kingdom has to be reduced to its last extremity for me to suggest such means'. The first of
these decrees would render all deputies in the current Assembly
ineligible to serve in the next. (This decree, proposed by

Robespierre, was passed on 10 May 1791.) The demagogues of the present Assembly would be kept out, he explained, while the continuing crisis would encourage the election of moderates, determined to bring order out of chaos and to rectify the existing constitution. The other decree which he hoped would be passed was also intended to ensure that the next Assembly would not be ruled by factionaries: candidates would only be able to stand for election in their own departments, thus preventing the growing army of Paris-trained politicians from mopping up seats right across the country. He regarded both decrees as a safeguard for the survival of real democracy in future Assemblies; in passing them the Assembly would therefore be performing a public service. He thought they would have no difficulty in getting them adopted as a great many deputies knew that they stood no chance of being re-elected, and they 'would be happy to hide their failings behind a legal ineligibility'.

Summing up ways in which the Assembly could become unpopular, he proposed that its leaders should be encouraged to alter their attitudes. For instance, it would be easy to persuade them that if the decree on ministers were reversed new careers of the sort they hankered for would open up for them; public opinon would turn against party leaders who defected in this way. (Including himself, presumably.) Finally, there was loss of credit. He had already outlined how this would come about: if the Assembly favoured Paris over the provinces, if it rejected projects proposed by the departments, if it destroyed rural municipalities and changed the organisation of urban ones. (Given the autocratic tendencies of municipal administrations and their suspicion of the Assembly, his plan of increasing the existing friction to the point where departments and municipalities denounced the Assembly's policies was quite likely to succeed.) The ministers were to play their part by drawing public attention to the numerous enactments by which the Assembly had usurped all power and rendered the country ungovernable.[32] In suggesting these methods he felt compelled to add: 'If it were not a matter of saving a great people my character would make me reject all these intrigues and subterfuges'.

He guessed the sceptical questions that would be raised by his arguments so far. How could they influence the next legislature if it were as powerful as the first? How could they correct the constitution if it and its authors were enshrined in the public imagination? What did it matter in an age of factions if the faction currently in power passed inconvenient laws? The answer was simple. If they did nothing they were lost. If changes had to wait until the climate was rational enough to demand them it would take more than twenty years. Where would the monarchy be then?

'So here we are then, with the second legislature', he announced. 'But how can one ensure that it will have both the power and the will to correct the constitution? How can one influence public opinion and the electoral assemblies?' In the remaining part of the *Aperçu* he explained what he called the mechanics of his plan. Action was needed in three areas: the Assembly, Paris, and the provinces. A number of deputies must be recruited to influence opinion in the Assembly; he suggested Montesquiou and Cazalès from the right, Duquesnoy, Autun, Le Chapelier, Barnave and himself from the left. None of them was to know that anyone else was involved, a safety factor which would also reassure the deputies, each of whom would think that he was the sole recipient of Montmorin's confidence. In Paris assistants 'of another sort' would be needed to report what was happening in the sections, the National Guard, and the political clubs. He proposed Talon and Sémonville as two men whose characters suited them to this sort of undercover work, adding that with Sémonville money would be required, and with Talon the promise of an important post. For the provinces two offices would be needed, an *atelier de correspondance* and an *atelier d'ouvrages*. The first would employ forty agents who would assess public opinion in different parts of the country, filling in questionnaires which would be returned to Montmorin. The second would process the information obtained by the first, and be responsible for producing speeches, *mémoires* for ministers, broadsheets for Paris, and 'dissertations' for the provinces.

The distribution of information in the provinces he regarded as being of primary importance. As the left knew already, the press was the most powerful moulder of public opinion: he cited the situation in Paris, where public demonstrations had become a weapon of intimidation which the mayor and municipality were powerless to resist. In the provinces, which had not yet been so affected by extremist influences, it was necessary to educate the people, taking care, however, that all works written for this purpose 'were sufficiently dosed with patriotism' in order not to antagonise their readers. The worse thing that could happen, he observed, was that public opinion might polarise, being either violently for the revolution or violently against it: how did one direct citizens who refused to listen or to be enlightened?

This, then, was the broad outline of his plan. The *Aperçu* was completed three months before his death. The first response to it is one of incredulity – that he ever thought they would read it at the Tuileries, let alone learn anything from it. It was not so much a guide for the royal couple as a great soliloquy. The queen, especially, would not have wanted a lecture on the constitution. As far as she was concerned the constitution attempted to legitimise the destruction of the monarchy, and it is doubtful if Mercy had convinced her that it and the Assembly could not simply be expunged by royal command, which was what the Court nobility wanted the king to do.

La Marck agreed with Mercy that the plan was 'perfect in theory' but would be 'very difficult to execute'. Indeed, it would have been impossible, if only because people would have talked. They tried to get the plan into action. The opinion-gathering network never really got off the ground. The surveillance network headed by Talon and Sémonville worked (at great expense) for a while and then closed down: the idea that Talon was in the same division as Fouché, Napoleon's police minister, exaggerates his activities. The pressure groups within the Assembly failed to exert much pressure. As for the plan to subvert the deputies and force an election, Mirabeau seems to have abandoned it as unworkable – and perhaps also as unthinkable – almost as soon as he described it; he never did anything to implement it.

Machiavellian is the adjective used for the proposals to disrupt the Assembly, the *Aperçu* being described as the *Il Principe* of its age. However, these tactics reluctantly suggested by Mirabeau were a response to the circumstances of the moment: the nation-wide unrest, the crisis over food and inflation, the Assembly's perceived failure to control the situation, and the threat which all this posed to the Revolution itself. They were never put forward as acceptable, normal practice. His hope that the election of a fresh Assembly would lead to stability and moderation, and the reconciliation of all sections of society, seems far-fetched, for under the system of suffrage stipulated by the constituents any future Assembly would be composed of deputies drawn from a narrow band of property-owners; and their interests would continue to prevail, and the unenfranchised would continue to have cause for resentment. It was unlikely that a new Assembly would succeed where the present one had failed, but that is what he hoped, and an election was the only legitimate way of trying to bring about change.

The *Aperçu* was not a discourse on the philosophy of government but a practical manual; it has to be read as such. Alphonse Aulard, the first occupant of the chair in revolutionary history at the Sorbonne, condemned it as an attempt 'to divert a popular movement from its proper end',[33] judging it in the light of nineteenth-century neo-Jacobinism. Aulard's 'popular movement' was that of the 'people' who were determined to have a voice, a share of political power. He takes Mirabeau's remarks about the inflammatory atmosphere in the Paris sections to mean that he wanted to silence that voice, and sees his wish for a working executive as a step in that direction, despite the evidence of his expressed views to the contrary. The danger in the sections, to Mirabeau, was not the people but the agitators who incited them to violence, exposing them to legal reprisals and creating propitious conditions for a swing towards counter-revolution. He never blamed the people for their actions. He supported them, and the 'popular movement' (which he recognised as the rightful wish of those who were not part of the nation to be part of the nation) but he deplored the language of agitation as irresponsible. Aulard justifiably describes the campaign to destabilise the Assembly as 'a plan for government by corruption'; Mirabeau knew it was and that was why he thought better of it. Though it is a far cry from his plan (to hasten the election of a fresh Assembly) to the Revolutionary Commune of 1792, seizing power when the legally elected legislature got in its way. Where Aulard shows a certain myopia, however, is in his identification of Mirabeau as the opponent of the 'proper end' of the popular movement. The instinctive opponents of popular power were the middle-class representatives in the Assembly who modified the Declaration of Rights to maintain their own social and political advantage.

Where the *Aperçu* really falls down is on grounds of feasibility. The eight months which elapsed between the adoption of the plan and the completion of the constitution would not have allowed the full effect of the policy towards the Assembly to be felt, had such a policy indeed been adopted, and it could have backfired seriously. The idea that popular measures should be rejected, for instance: the Jacobins would never have done anything so destructive to their own interests, and would have publicly denounced those who backed such a policy. And again, confusion and frustration were such a regular part of the Assembly's proceedings that an increase in the level would have been scarcely noticed. Even if national disillusionment with the Assembly had come about it would not have been allowed to retire before the constitution was completed. Later events also proved that Mirabeau's hope of amending the constitution would have been dashed. After his death the constitutionalists and the royalists in the Assembly formed an alliance with the aim of getting it revised, but after a fatally misplaced speech by Malouet on 29 August 1791 any thought of revision was rejected, and the alliance itself did not survive.

If Mirabeau had lived would his plan have achieved anything, or would it have remained the dark flower of his virtuoso imagination? Malouet described it afterwards as the last important attempt to prevent the total collapse of the monarchy,[34] but those who knew about it at the time were sceptical. Mercy pointed out that the difficulty would be to find able collaborators; Montmorin was a fragile reed, the queen too capricious for her co-operation to be counted on. Sooner or later, too, the auxiliaries entrusted with the execution of the plan would either lose interest or begin to talk about their activities: Mirabeau failed to appreciate that subordinates would not have his own driving commitment. In practice everything would have depended on him. In his own words he had set up 'a sort of political pharmacy in which the sole director, furnished with both wholesome medicines and poisonous plants, prepares his mixtures as his genius dictates and with the complete trust of the patient'.

But he never had the patient's trust and time was not on his side. The irony is that so much of what he advised became the policy of the next Assembly, when instead of benefiting the monarchy it paved the way for the Republic.

## NOTES

1. *Discours*, 199f.
2. Sieyès aloofness to Mirabeau in the Assembly did not affect their personal relations. In 1790 they dined together regularly once a week.
3. The author of this pamphlet was a lawyer named Lacroix who admitted, when brought to court for it by Mirabeau, that Duport and Lameth had paid for its publication. Lameth also published a pamphlet, *Examen du discours du comte de Mirabeau sur la question du droit de paix et de guerre*, in which he claimed that discrepancies existed between Mirabeau's speech as he gave it in the Assembly and as it appeared in the *Moniteur*. The text printed in the *Moniteur* was the written proposal for a decree which Mirabeau read in the course of his otherwise unprepared speech. The differences, in fact, were trivial, and nowhere had his meaning been altered or disguised: Aulard's (1914: III, 14) assertion that he altered the printed version of his speech in order to gain popularity is without foundation.
4. *Discours*, 227f.
5. La Marck, *Correspondance*, II, 38.
6. La Fayette (1837–38: I, 366–7).
7. Michelet (1961–2: I, 562).
8. La Marck, *Correspondance*, I, 154.
9. Ibid., II, 118f.
10. Ibid., II, 124. Letter of 30 July 1789.
11. Ibid., II, 1136–9. Note 18. 17 August 1789.
12. *Mémoires biographiques*, XI, 59.
13. Public Record Office, 30/8/132, fol. 263.
14. *Mémoires biographiques*, XI, 62–7.
15. See Rose (1911: 578–81), who assumes that a man reputedly open to financial bribes would be susceptible to political bribery as well. Similarly, Lefebvre (1962–4: I, 198) refers to 'Pitt's agents Miles and Elliot, who had probably paid Mirabeau'.
16. *Lettres à Cerutti*, 38.
17. The speech on *assignats* was written by a Genevois newcomer to Mirabeau's *atelier*, Etienne-Salomon Reybaz, with additions (the political content) by

Mirabeau. The economical arguments were Clavière's, who had chosen to revive his friendship with Mirabeau at this opportune moment.

18. Jaurès (1901–08: II, 108).

19. Second speech on *assignats*, 29 September.

20. Mounier objected afterwards to Mirabeau's acquittal by the Assembly, on the grounds that the Châtelet, in its report, spoke of evidence which pointed to both him and Orléans being implicated. He thought there had been a miscarriage of justice, disregarding the fact that by accepting the evidence of patently false witnesses the Châtelet had itself connived at a miscarriage of justice in the making.

21. *Mémoires biographiques*, XI, 135. Speech of 2 October 1790.

22. The sort of rulings he had in mind included the Assembly's decision in December 1789 to create 'active' citizens,and its other act of electoral discrimination which made the *marc d'argent* the qualification for election as a deputy. He had joined Robespierre and Pétion to denounce this wealth barrier which was replacing that of social privilege.

23. La Marck, *Correspondance*, II, 162f, n. 23.

24. Ibid., II, 225f, n. 30. 14 October 1790.

25. Ibid., II, 237–43.

26. The patriotic rhetoric of this speech led Aulard to praise it as the expression of the true Mirabeau. No less than right-wing deputies, who were incensed by it, he was taken in by the language and mistook the purpose of Mirabeau's argument.

27. La Marck, *Correspondance*, II, 251. Letter of 22 October 1790.

28. Ibid., II, 387–95, n. 46. 6 December 1790.

29. There is a striking parallel between the circumstances in which this affidavit was written and those of the Bergasse letter. In both cases Mirabeau was trying to circumvent prejudice against himself, in one instance by putting irresponsible words into a rival's mouth, in the other by ascribing his own views to a loyal minister.

30. La Marck, *Correspondance*, II, 404. Letter of 14 December 1790.

31. Ibid., II, 428–9.

32. The ministers, he said, should also make a point of attributing to the king and queen those acts which were favourable to the public, and they in turn should improve their image by 'appearing often in public, walking in the most frequented public places, assisting at reviews of the National Guard, visiting hospitals and the workshops which have been established for the unemployed'. All this, he said, would be more useful than remaining in their impenetrable retreat.

33. Aulard (1905–07, 33f).

34. Malouet was one of the deputies chosen to use his influence in the Assembly. At his preliminary interview with Montmorin he was shown a letter from the king, approving of the plan, and also the bond for 200,000 livres which was to be paid to Mirabeau if the plan succeeded. Malouet asked in what circumstances this sum had been demanded. 'What we gave him he did not demand', Montmorin replied. 'The base motives you suspect do not exist' (Malouet, 1874: II, 97f).

# 12

## The Thread of Fate

### (January-April 1791)

The civil constitution of the clergy was later described by Talleyrand as the greatest political mistake the Assembly ever made. At the moment when France needed unity it created schism. When the Revolution needed to appear respectable to the rest of the world the Assembly made it synonymous with tyranny and persecution. It encouraged the spirit of counter-revolution. All this might have been avoided; having started well it went wrong because the Assembly, in its liking for logical progression, did not know when to stop. The constitution of the clergy was the answer to demands for reforms in the civil affairs of the Church. Its early clauses removed the glaring differences of income between the highest and lower members of the clergy; reduced the number of dioceses in order to bring them into line with the new departments; and improved the lot of parish priests by giving them a salary and adequate housing, basic requirements which Mirabeau had proposed in recognition of their responsible role as *curés* and teachers. These measures, passed in July 1790, were necessary on the grounds of social utility and justice, but instead of stopping there the Assembly unwisely pressed on into deeper waters. The Ecclesiastical Committee, which had a Jansenist vision of a national Church, proposed that bishops and *curés* should be elected, as they had been formerly in the French Roman Catholic Church, and that they should take an oath to the nation, the king, and the constitution before being consecrated. The Assembly adopted these proposals. For the clergy to accept them, however, they had to have the sanction of Rome. This essential gave the hostile French hierarchy the weapon it needed to nullify the Assembly's rulings. It called on Pius VI to exert his papal authority. The provocative appeal to another sovereign power was followed by a publication, signed by 139 bishops, urging resistance to the new regulations. The Assembly retaliated with a new decree, drawn up by the joint committee which had studied the bishops' manifesto. On 26 November the committee's spokesman, Voidel, read their report: it accused the Catholic clergy of sullying the purity of the primitive Church, and denounced priests who refused to take the oath as disturbers of the peace. The new decree ordered them to take the oath within eight days, two months if abroad, or to forfeit their offices; those who continued to resist were threatened with legal action and the loss of their civil rights.

The uproar over the civil oath of the clergy contrasted with what had happened in Austria, where the clergy had become salaried servants of the state, and Joseph II made the bishops take an oath of allegiance to the Emperor without papal objection. The Assembly, however, had already provoked Rome the previous June, when the left proposed the annexation of the papal territory of Avignon, and an international incident that could have started a war was narrowly averted. Voidel's coercive decree promised to precipitate another war situation, a religious civil war this time, if a compromise could not be reached. At first Mirabeau had abstained from the controversy, the oath and election of bishops not seeming to him to pose such dire threats to the survival of religion that he wished to ally himself with the reactionary leaders of the clergy by condemning them. Nor did he want to join in a game that was being played out solely in order that political and religious factions might score points. But the situation was so inflammatory that he prepared an alternative decree to Voidel's, with no time limit on taking the oath, and on 26 November he addressed the Assembly. 'If they want to push us into a religious war I must oppose them', he told La Marck that morning. 'If they don't they will not find a plan as pacific, negotiable, and conciliatory as mine.'

This should have warned those who were expecting him to place all the blame for approaching schism on the left. He made a violent, truthful speech, the opening salvos of which totally misled his indignant right-wing hearers. His oldest trick, Ciceronian, when speaking was to start by disarming those with whom he intended to disagree. On this occasion, therefore, he commenced by echoing Voidel's indictment of the bishops, playing on the anti-clerical, anti-corporatist feelings of his listeners until he had them running at his heels, at which moment he could turn the pack, without it realising, in the direction he had previously decided it should go. He intended at this point to consider Voidel's decree and the schism it would precipitate. Persecution would turn the faithful against the Revolution. The Assembly was creating a potent justification for counter-revolution which could only be avoided if the decree on the clergy left room for tolerance – which was, after all, required by the constitution.[1]

The pack would have obeyed this call to reason, had it not been for the right-wing clergy which misinterpreted his motives and over-reacted. The next day he was attacked by Maury, who thundered against the Assembly's challenge to the Church's authority in doctrinal matters, though there had been no interference with articles of faith. Maury's eloquence was self-defeating: the Assembly, anti-clerical but not anti-religious, saw in the counterattack not just resistance on grounds of conscience but resistance by enemies of the Revolution. Mirabeau's hope of arbitrating between conflicting passions vanished, and Voidel's decree was adopted in all its rigour.

The year 1791 opened with another round in the bitter fight over the oath of the clergy. The king had reluctantly sanctioned the decree, but the clergy continued to ignore it and only four bishops had taken the oath, Autun being one of them. On 4 January Barnave proposed that all the clergy deputies should be required to take the oath immediately. Mirabeau objected to this intimidation: the Assembly had neither the right nor the desire to force the clergy to take the oath, he said, but they did have the right to forbid non-jurors from continuing in their function; refusal consequently involved cessation of function but did not constitute a breach of the law. He said this, he added, because he had seen a poster in Paris which described all those who had not taken the oath as disturbers of the peace. This poster was 'unconstitutional, iniquitous, and reprehensible', but, at the same time, the opponents of the decree, 'if they have no counter-revolutionary intentions, must accept the Assembly's declaration, a thousand times repeated, that *it has not challenged spiritual matters*. All the difficulty, if it exists, lies in dissidents calling *spiritual* what the Assembly calls *temporal*.' He went on to consider the practical problems that would arise if thousands of priests chose to resign rather than submit to the decree. Foreseeing the protests that would be made in the Assembly itself if the religious life of the country were threatened, he commented: 'You will soon hear all sorts of fanatical prophecies about the suspension of instruction and of evangelical consolation being the death of Christianity, a step towards the desecration of sanctuaries; that an impious constitution will soon succeed in destroying the Church'. On the other hand, 'People have a constant, sacred right to receive all the consolations of religion'.[2] It was agreed that the number of years the clergy had to serve before appointment to a parish should be reduced temporarily, in order to provide replacements for the livings that would fall vacant.

Believing strongly in the need for a civil constitution of the clergy to reform the economic administration of the Church, disturbed by the way it was being used as a platform by different voices within the Church, and by the way schism was being exploited for counter-revolutionary ends, Mirabeau prepared an address on the subject for the Ecclesiastical Committee, which wanted it for distribution in the departments. His task was to explain the civil constitution to the general public, to correct misinformation, above all to dispel the idea that Catholic doctrine was under threat. The address that he read to the Assembly on 14 January was factual, moderating in intention, but too outspoken about the degenerate state of the Church in France to please its spokesmen on the right.[3] Four days later the election of the Jansenist Grégoire as president of the Assembly gave the right wing further cause for anger.

The split over the clergy oath seemed to Mirabeau to offer a chance of improving the king's image, in a roundabout sort of way. The time was right, he told the Court on 21 January, 'to increase the King's popularity at the expense of the Assembly'. What he did not say was that it might be increased at the expense of the right wing. As the king had already sanctioned the decree on the civil oath of the clergy its vehement critics in the Assembly, the right-wing and clergy deputies, were left isolated and, theoretically, could be presented as opposing the Revolution without also indicting the king. It was perhaps rather too clever, for if he himself won applause from the left, the king would not understand the attack on the right.

On 26 January the right-wing spokesman Cazalès demanded the repeal of Voidel's decree and was shouted down, whereupon his colleague Maury called out ironically: 'Let them go ahead, we have need of this decree. We love your decrees; give us more of them'. Mirabeau could read Maury's mind: schism, civil war, counter-revolution, the *ancien régime* restored. 'A profound remark', he retorted, 'but perhaps indiscreet. Perhaps those who make sinister prognostics base their views on their hopes.' In his own speech he attacked Cazalès (the front for deeper counter-revolutionary plots) at length, though he also deplored the divisive effect of Voidel's decree. 'M. de Mirabeau would like . . . to have the merit of success without straining his popularity too much', La Marck reported to Mercy. 'One must not be deceived. With his intelligence, his wariness, his finesse, he often escapes the closest surveillance.'[4] La Marck failed to appreciate that his ability to make progress depended on his popularity.

After 26 January Mirabeau took no real part in the debates on

Church affairs. A speech defending the marriage of priests – 'The Church has forced priests into celibacy; we do not propose, God forbid, to force them into marriage, only to give them the option' – remained unread.[5] He maintained that the oath of the clergy should not have been made an excuse for persecution. At the same time he defended the intention of it, which was to demonstrate that the clergy were no less citizens for being priests, and had the same right to protection under the law, as well as the same obligation to obey it. His own religious beliefs, or lack of them, always come up in connection with the civil constitution of the clergy. His speech on 26 November has been condemned as the product of an atheist. Rather it was the speech of a politician who left dogma to the theologians. The criticism has not been all one-sided. Aulard, for one, was surprised that he did not find Roman Catholicism incompatible with liberty, implying that he should have said as much in his speeches; the reason for his omission, Aulard concluded, was that 'fundamentally he is indifferent to religion'.[6] Fundamentally he was; but more to the point he did not confuse the issue. The civil constitution of the clergy showed him, unlike many of its promoters and opponents, avoiding the sectarian zeal which all too often benefited neither liberty nor religion.

The royal family still slumbered on. When Montmorin tried to discuss urgent matters with the king he was made to feel, he said, as though he were talking about the affairs of the Emperor of China. Louis passed his time reading histories, in particular the life of Charles I, and 'even this subject', wrote La Marck, 'did not give him any incentive to act vigorously'. After much urging Montmorin persuaded him to give serious consideration to Mirabeau's advice about leaving Paris. A safe retreat, however, was now harder to find: Fontainebleau was too exposed; only a fortified town near the northern or eastern frontier offered sufficient security. The army in the north was commanded by Rochambeau, a friend of La Fayette's and reputedly a republican; the king accordingly chose Metz where Bouillé had his headquarters. Neither Mirabeau nor La Marck knew that he had in fact been in touch with Bouillé since October. Behind these negotiations was the former minister Breteuil, now living in Switzerland, for whom the queen had an exaggerated regard, and to whom she had turned for a second opinion when Mirabeau advised them to leave Paris in the summer of 1790. Breteuil produced his own plan, in which Mirabeau's careful political strategy was brushed aside; instead the king and queen were to flee and surround themselves with troops, thus creating the very image of a fugitive, untrusting monarch which Mirabeau had warned against. Breteuil's plan was brought to the queen by Fersen, and the association of two names which influenced her mind and her emotions was enough to give it a fatal aura of credibility. Such was the secretiveness of the royal couple that La Marck, on being approached, believed they were now ready to follow Mirabeau's advice, unaware that another flight plan was already in preparation.

It was arranged that La Marck should have discussions with Bouillé at the beginning of February. He carried two letters of introduction, an open one from Montmorin, and a sealed one from the king in which Louis referred to Mirabeau and him in these terms:

> Although these persons are not estimable, and I have paid the first very heavily, I believe that they can be of service to me. In Mirabeau's plan you will perhaps find useful points; listen to it without committing yourself and let me know what you think.[7]

From what he had heard about him Bouillé took Mirabeau to be a republican, and his manner was guarded until La Marck explained his plan to strengthen the monarchy. He approved the idea that the king should move openly to Metz – unlike the secret flight recommended by Breteuil, whose plan he naturally did not mention to La Marck. He told La Marck of a letter he had just received from La Fayette (who was his cousin), warning him against La Marck, and assuring him that he would soon restore the situation to normal, a promise Bouillé had heard many times before. Years later he said that Mirabeau's ambition was appeasable, besides which 'he had too much intelligence not to realise that the gratitude of a king he had helped to reinstate was preferable to popular favour and a passing role as the leader of a party'. On the other hand 'La Fayette was a fool, drunk with self-esteem, whom one could neither get to know nor trust; the most dangerous sort of man, especially in a revolution'.[8]

La Fayette's letter to Bouillé revealed his awareness of his own declining influence. The Lameths had broken with him, he was distrusted by the Tuileries, and sensed that the mantle of popularity was slipping from his shoulders.[9] On 18 January Mirabeau was elected commander of the La Grange-Batalière battalion of the National Guard in the district where he lived. According to Marat the election was fixed by La Fayette's spies – an olive branch? The honour caused him much embarrassment as it obliged him to undertake guard duty at the Tuileries, and he could think of better ways to win the king's confidence than by parading under his windows in the uniform of the National Guard. After three days the new commander resigned, apparently because the queen had objected, although the jeering account in the *Orateur du peuple* of his arrival at the Jacobin Club, 'decked out in a blue coat, with two immense epaulettes, high collar, and all the trappings of a staff officer', may have had something to do with it.

More significant was his election to the administration of the Department of Paris, and in February to the directory of the Department, along with Autun, Danton, Sieyès, and Alexandre de Lameth. He was defeated in his bid to become *procureur-syndic*, the position which effectively would have made him, in Desmoulins's words, 'minister for Paris'; but election to the directory was proof of his popularity in the capital. It was too much for Brissot, savouring his dignity as a member of the Paris Commune, who now saw Mirabeau in the rarified ranks of departmental administration. He consoled himself by saying that it was only the efforts of the Jacobins that had brought him to the directory, and he failed to become *procureur-syndic* because none of the parties 'had any confidence, any esteem for him'.[10] La Marck reported at this date: 'His popularity has genuinely increased for some time, which worries me; if he ever despairs of government, and measures his glory by his popularity, he will be insatiable.'

The accolade he most coveted was the presidency of the Assembly. On 3 January he missed getting the necessary majority by only three votes. Forty-two deputies had already held the office when he was finally elected at the end of January. All ideas of promoting disorder in the Assembly were now laid aside, though not entirely as a result of the presidency: the Jacobins were also hoping to hasten the Assembly's end, so that a pro-Jacobin one could take its place, and for this reason, as Mirabeau told the Court at this time, it would be better to keep the present Assembly. The plan to force an early election, for which he has been condemned ever since, was abandoned a month after he first suggested it. The Jacobins did not attract a similar condemnation.

His performance in office led one deputy to remark that when the president's chair was eventually deposited in some museum the guide would point it out, not as the president's chair, but as that once occupied by Mirabeau. People remembered the tact and sincerity of his replies to the different deputations that came to the Assembly. When the Quakers petitioned to be exempted from military service, for instance, he succeeded in balancing respect for their pacifism with a sense of reality, telling them that while pacifism was a noble philosophical principle, it had to be remembered that defending oneself and others was also a religious duty. Would they surrender to tyrants? If their brothers in Pennsylvania had encountered savages would they have allowed them to murder their wives, children, and old people, rather than repulse violence? It was weakness which invited war. The Quakers' address and his reply were printed by the Assembly's order.

In his *Souvenirs sur Mirabeau*, Dumont wrote:

> His energy, impartiality, and presence of mind enhanced his reputation in a
> role which was the reef on which most of his predecessors had foundered. He
> had the art of fixing everyone's attention on himself, even when he seemed
> deprived of his greatest advantage by not being able to speak from the
> tribune. Several of his enemies who had thought to efface him by reducing
> him to silence, had the chagrin of having added to his glory.[11]

Dumont had returned to Paris, and had had a preview of Mirabeau's
now legendary reputation while travelling to the capital. On his remarking at one stage that the horses were terrible the postilion had
agreed that two of them were very poor, but added that the third was
excellent; '*mon Mirabeau*' he called it, and Dumont learned that this
was the name popularly given to the lead horse, the strong one in the
middle which worked the hardest.

'Mirabeau writes nothing', he reported to Romilly soon after his
arrival. Of his real activities he was, of course, ignorant; the unhealthy
look, intensified by overwork, he put down to debauchery, encouraged
in this view by his visits to the chaussée d'Antin where the evidence of
Sybaritic tastes both dazzled and repelled him. He was struck by the
sight of a jewel-case containing several precious stones: 'This proclaimed the civil list, and I was surprised that his popularity had not
suffered in consequence'. Patently it had not: the house was filled with
visitors from 7 a.m. every day, a kind of royal *lever* which continued
until he went to the Assembly, attended by the crowd which gathered
daily outside his door. He was still addressed as '*M. le comte*' and his
blue carriage was still emblazoned with his arms, despite the abolition
of titles and all marks of nobility the previous summer.[12] All this
astonished Dumont, who remarked to Clavière that people would say
that he was afraid of passing for an honest man. Partisan censure this –
Mirabeau's appreciation of luxury was shared by such honest revolutionaries as Danton and Desmoulins. Clavière had shrugged the
criticism aside: 'He is necessary to us; he alone can handle the Jacobins
and the Court, and if it costs the nation a million the money will be
well spent'.[13]

Dumont was also shocked by his physical state. Mirabeau's
opthalmia was agonising and he had alarming internal symptoms. 'If I
believed in slow poisons I should have no doubt that I have been
poisoned', he said, 'I feel myself wasting away, being consumed by a
slow fire'. While Mirabeau was president Dumont saw him have
leeches applied to himself in the interval between the afternoon and
evening sessions, and then return to the Assembly with his neck ban-
daged to stanch the blood. In private he was as warm and disarming as
ever. Guessing, perhaps, that Dumont would not have been averse to

working for him again (he had not been re-employed by Lansdowne) but having to make it plain that that door was closed, he invited him, by way of consolation, to contribute to a report on the political situation of foreign powers in relation to France, which he was to present on 28 January. He wanted it to include a condemnation of Burke's *Reflections on the Revolution in France* which had just appeared in a French translation. Dumont complied and reported complacently afterwards that the speech was very well received, 'especially the parts concerning England and Burke'.[14]

Mirabeau's term in the presidency ended on 10 February and Dumont left to join Duroveray in Geneva at about the same time. At their last meeting Mirabeau was full of foreboding that they would not see each other again, and seemed to be making a valedictory on his own passing as he said: 'When I am no more they will realise what I was worth.' The burden of work during his fortnight as president had taxed his system to the limit, and after handing over the presidency he went to his house near Argenteuil[15] to rest. He returned, feeling worse than when he left, because he had promised La Marck that he would speak in the debate on the ownership of mines on 17 February. In the Assembly the view was widely held that the income from coal-mines belonged by right to the owners of the land under which they ran and not to the mine owners; for La Marck, who derived his wealth from mines owned by his wife's family in Alsace, it was a crucial issue. However, Pellenc had not completed the technical details of the speech he was to give, and Mirabeau was relieved when the debate was postponed for there were other measures of greater general importance waiting for his attention. In the coming weeks he had to speak on education, the death penalty, and the extradition of criminals; and the clause in the constitution relating to a regency was soon to be debated, the shaping of which would affect the continuation of the monarchy. In addition he was anxious to get legislation passed on two questions which touched on his concern for the welfare of the weakest: state-assisted pensions for the old and needy, and equal rights of inheritance, regardless of sex or primogeniture. Both measures were profoundly revolutionary, the first rejecting the idea, as old as Christianity, that charity was an acceptable solution to the problem of poverty, the second rejecting a concept as outworn as any other relic of feudalism. Mirabeau was ahead of most of his fellow revolutionaries in his realisation, from the start, that political democracy was meaningless without social democracy. Jacobin leaders later in the Revolution came to share this view, but more out of political expediency than instinctive altruism; then, as earlier, professions of solidarity with the poor were negated by lack of economic understanding. This was the case on 3 March

1791 when the debate opened on pensions for the poor and aged. In his speech Mirabeau pointed out that nine livres a year, a mere six deniers a day, paid into a sinking fund would yield a pension of forty-five livres, nearly equal to the annual earnings of a labourer, or, as he put it, the difference between starving and eating, between a family's having a roof over its head and being evicted. He proposed that every deputy should have five days' pay deducted from his salary towards the formation of the fund. His motion was defeated after Robespierre declared that such deductions would be an infringement of public liberty. Mirabeau's ideas had to wait until the next Assembly – in which Robespierre did not serve – to be implemented.

The issue which created the most heat during Mirabeau's presidency was emigration, brought to a head by the departure of the king's aunts, Adélaïde and Victoire, for Rome. On 3 February he had warned the Court:

> Mesdames' journey is not only dangerous for them but may be the cause of a thousand dangers for their majesties. The malevolent will think their departure presages that of the King, and the factious will make it the excuse for fresh agitation. If they are arrested at the frontier the event will be used to embitter opinion still further against the Court; if they are brought back the outcry could engulf the Tuileries, and when one lives in a house of straw it is best to avoid fire. In any case the people of Paris will not be indifferent to a journey which robs the capital of a million livres a year.[16]

He advised the king to tell the Assembly that while personally objecting to his aunts' journey he had not dared to forbid it for fear of exceeding his powers; and to ask the Assembly, therefore, to decree what powers he possessed over members of his family. If it was decided that the royal family was answerable only to the law he would gain the advantage of no longer being responsible for the counter-revolutionary plots of his brother and Bourbon-Condé cousin.

The advice was ignored; the king's aunts departed, and were stopped at Arnay-le-Duc pending instructions from the Assembly. Paris was in an uproar. The king wrote to the Assembly, regretting his aunts' action but defending their right as citizens to go where they chose; to which Desmoulins retorted that other citizens were not given a million livres a year by the state and the king's aunts had no right to take public money abroad. Barnave's warning that another member of the royal family might also try to leave, was enough to send a crowd to seize the comte de Provence, who was confined in the Tuileries like his brother. Yet again it was noted that La Fayette and the National Guard did not intervene.

On 24 February the Assembly decided that the king's aunts could continue their journey but pressure to control emigration was strong.

Le Chapelier, *rapporteur* of the Constitution Committee, presented the draft of a decree governing where public officials lived: the king was designated as the first public official and therefore bound, while the Assembly was sitting, to reside close by. Barnave proposed an amendment forbidding him to leave the country. Mirabeau tried to avert the danger by proposing that the law on residence should be considered together with the laws on the eligibility of public officials and the regency; and reminded the Assembly that the inviolability of the king was upheld in the constitution. Barnave's amendment was postponed, but the storm over the emigration question continued to rage in the Assembly and the popular press.

On 28 February the Constitution Committee proposed that the right to emigrate should be decided by a council of three persons, nominated by the Assembly: they would have the sole authority, *un pouvoir dictatorial*, to grant or withhold permission to leave, and Frenchmen abroad who did not obey their order to return would be regarded as rebels. The reading of the proposed decree was punctuated by protests; even Le Chapelier, the presenter, acknowledged that it would infringe both the constitution and the rights of man. Mirabeau said that while it might sometimes be necessary for the police to prevent individuals leaving, there was an immense difference between that and having a law which forbade free movement. He himself would never obey such a law. Apart from anything else it would be inoperable; even the most tyrannical regimes had not succeeded in stopping people who wanted to leave a country. They had to decide whether it was desirable to keep people in France by other means than the attraction of liberty alone. It was a question of human freedom. He quoted a passage from his *Lettre à Frédéric-Guillaume II*, in which he had condemned the laws forbidding emigration, but his words were drowned by the fury of the left, and when he proposed that the Assembly should refuse to consider the decree and go on to the next item on the order for the day, the triumvirate and their followers from the *Société des trente* – eager enough for dictatorship over emigration – cried that he was dictating to the Assembly, and demanded an adjournment of the debate. The uproar continued until Mirabeau halted it with an imperious '*Silence aux trente voix!*'. The words temporarily deflated them. Although an adjournment of the debate was allowed[17] he had the backing of the majority, and the humiliated *trente voix* left the Assembly bent on revenge.

That same evening at the Jacobin Club they proceeded to hang, draw, and quarter him with their rhetoric. Desmoulins, who had dubbed him Saint Mirabeau only recently, recalled the scene delightedly: 'O the beautiful, the magnificent, the immortal meeting of the Jacobins on 28

February! How the National Assembly dishonoured the French people, and how the Jacobins avenged them the same day!'[18] Mirabeau had gone from the Assembly to a meeting of the directory of the Department of Paris, where they agreed to issue a public statement in connection with the latest organised disturbances in the city; apropos of which, and remembering the scene he had just left, he said: 'Those who wish to lead you into unlawful assemblies constantly tell you that the constitution is in danger, and that the enemies of liberty attack the new laws'. He had been invited to dine with the duc d'Aiguillon, a friend of Lameth's, but was refused admittance. At that he went on immediately to the Jacobin Club, to confront the triumvirate and force them into making their accusations to his face. His entrance was greeted with loud protests. Duport was in the middle of a speech denouncing La Fayette, who organised riots, he said, in order to fabricate evidence against the factious; seeing Mirabeau he continued:

> The men most dangerous to liberty are not far from us. Our most dangerous enemies are here: the men on whom we rest our greatest hopes, the men that you have elevated only – it appears – to have them attack you more advantageously, armed with your approval and assistance.

As the Jacobins turned on the isolated figure of Mirabeau Duport warmed to his theme: here was a despot, consumed with pride, a traitor, the man who had united the Assembly against his friends, his brother Jacobins. And yet, despite everything, if he mended his ways, he, Duport, would run to embrace him; he would proudly suffer his enmity if Mirabeau became once more the friend of *la chose publique*.[19]

Mirabeau began his reply by saying that in the Assembly he had sustained the doctrine of the philosophers and political writers; if his view was diametrically opposed to that of some of his colleagues perhaps it was not to the principles of liberty and the constitution. Some of the right had shared this view. It would be a cruel thing if one had to renounce those principles because men like Cazalès and Maury had supported them on this occasion. (This was the real reason for the orchestrated abuse against him in the Jacobin Club: his defence of the right to freedom of movement had been supported in the Assembly by the right.)

To the anger of the club he then defended La Fayette, before returning to himself and asking why they had not made their accusations against him in the proper place, the tribune of the Assembly. They presented differences of opinion as crimes. Did they understand the meaning of liberty?

Charles de Lameth spoke, disgorging all the bile he had been harbouring since his defeat in the Assembly. Yes, he told Mirabeau, they were no longer thirty voices as they had been that morning when he was so sure of victory; here they were 150, united to save the country, who realised that his real intention was to destroy the Jacobins. Had he not denounced the factious in the directory? They, the Jacobins, were the factious he wished to exterminate. Let him deny it if he could; they pronounced him guilty, a traitor. And so it went on. Lameth was beside himself. Did this verbose, ruined intriguer know who were the truly factious? They were those who joined the Jacobins and then moved to the *Club de 89* and back again; the factious would not be hanged if there was a counter-revolution because they made themselves popular with all parties; it was Mirabeau who was factious, who opposed the national interest, who had voted for the veto; and he for one did not believe that it was good politics to deal with him.

According to Desmoulins, Mirabeau sat through all this, suffering like Dante's damned. Another witness, Oelsner, the editor of the *Mercure universel*, noted his cool composure and the applause which greeted his closing speech, in which he praised the Jacobins and declared that he would remain with them 'to the point of ostracism'.[20] He was not deceived by the applause. The suspicion were still there, and the rancour of Duport and Lameth. 'I have pronounced my death sentence', he told Mme du Saillant that same evening. 'They will kill me.'[21]

That day, 28 February, was memorable for other reasons besides what happened in the Assembly and at the Jacobin Club. That morning a large crowd from the Saint-Antoine section set off for Vincennes, having heard that friends of the revolution were imprisoned there. In Paris the sight of the marchers started another rumour, that the Tuileries was under attack, and 300 royalists, armed mostly with daggers, rushed there to defend the king. La Fayette had gone to Vincennes, and the story went round that he had planned the march on the prison in order to leave the way clear for the *chevaliers du poignard*, as the press called them, to kill the guards at the Tuileries and allow the king to escape. When he got back to Paris he found the city gates shut against him, and had to threaten to use guns on them before he could gain admittance. At the Tuileries he had the royalists disarmed and arrested, to the fury of Marat, who said that they should have been massacred and that friends of liberty would always regret the loss of such a good opportunity. These events explained the attack on La Fayette at the Jacobin Club, and Mirabeau's words in his defence. It was not an act of philanthropy. He thought it possible that within hours La Fayette could have been publicly denounced, the National Guard could have joined forces with gangs in the sections, and the whole of Paris been under mob rule.

Neither Barnave nor Robespierre spoke against him that evening. It was Robespierre's policy to wait quietly in the wings, and Barnave was holding himself in reserve for the next stage in the triumvirate's campaign, which was to present themselves as the upholders of law and order. On 11 March Barnave read an address to the affiliated societies at the Jacobin Club, calling for an end to violence and agitation as it was now the time 'to desire peace and to end the revolution'. The Jacobins applauded. But Gorsas of the *Courrier de Versailles* condemned their response, and Brissot accused Barnave of harbouring aristocratic leanings, with the result that public opinion turned abruptly against the triumvirate.

Meanwhile, on 1 March Mirabeau addressed the Assembly in his new role as spokesman for the directory of the Department of Paris. The task of the new administrative departments, he explained, was to transmit the people's needs and wishes, and to execute the laws formed by the legislature; above all, their duty was to preserve public peace:

> Out of the debris of old institutions and abuses a corruptive leaven has been formed which perverse men stir unceasingly. These are the factious who, in order to overthrow the constitution, persuade the people that they must take action into their own hands, as if they were without laws, without magistrates. We will unmask these enemies of the peace, and we will teach the people that if our most important function is to watch over their security, their job is to get on peacefully with their work.[22]

Lameth and his followers tried and failed to have this passage omitted when the Assembly voted for the address to be printed to mark its solidarity with the administrative department. Its appearance, especially in juxtaposition with the diatribes against him in the extremist press, enhanced Mirabeau's image as a moderate; it drew attention, also, to the formidable power which he might exercise in the near future from his place in the directory. On 4 March Lord Gower reported:

> Whilst the person of the monarch is entirely in La Fayette's hands, the government seems to be passing rapidly into the hands of Mirabeau, whose conduct since his presidency and his election as one of the administrators of the department of Paris has been much and deservedly applauded.[23]

La Fayette apparently thought it prudent to make a conciliatory move, for he now honoured him with a sudden social call, clad in full regalia: '*in fiocchi*, with four aides-de-camp'. The hint of mockery as Mirabeau reported the visit was allowable; he knew on good authority that the commander-general had used all the means in his power to prevent him being elected *procureur-syndic* or president of the directory, and to appoint instead his own men, Pastoret and La Rochefoucauld. Either post would have enabled him to put his talents to worthier use than his current occupation as a secret adviser. In the event his defeat was irrelevant; time, as well as prejudice, was against him.

'What I have always foreseen has happened', Mirabeau told La Marck on 4 March. Duquesnoy had denounced the Lameths in a letter to the Jacobin Club; as a result the Jacobins were united solidly behind their leaders, instead of those leaders being isolated, which had been his aim when he addressed the club. Mirabeau was very conscious that 28 February had set the moderate cause back by several months. He had already told the Court that as the Jacobins were calling for the early dissolution of the Assembly, with the intention of forming the next one, it would be better to keep the present – more moderate – one. (In fact, the day after Mirabeau's funeral, the Jacobin Club voted that the Constituent Assembly should retire and new elections take place within six weeks.) He also rejected, now, the idea of civil war, even as a last resort. It would appear that he was reconsidering his own position. Were a civil war to end in victory for the monarchy the Court's royalist advisers would lose no time in ousting him. As it was, the mounting revolution was bringing ever more power to the Jacobins. Michelet fancied that he must have seen himself in the hopeless position of 'pitting himself against the Ocean'; and that therefore, at this time, he decided to swim with the tide. Michelet believed that, had Mirabeau lived, he would have been 'the first citizen of the Republic'. Mirabeau's logic and patriotism make this a convincing idea; on the other hand he was already damned in the eyes of republican zealots, and their attitude towards him would not have changed.

The alarm caused by Duquesnoy's letter and its consequences spread rapidly through the ranks of those who were supposed to be supporting the monarchy in the Assembly. Beaumetz, Le Chapelier, and d'André, singled out by Duquesnoy for their trustworthiness, suddenly had their careers to think of: they popularised themselves by proposing the demolition of Vincennes, and abstained when the left introduced a fresh law against *émigrés*. A week later Talon announced that he had to go to Brussels to attend to the affairs of his brother-in-law; at the same time Sémonville found that he had to leave for Genoa immediately. Montmorin felt his own position growing more and more precarious. Even La Marck caught the infection and began to wonder whether Mirabeau was still the best man to defend his interests in the mines debate, due to start on 20 March. He need not have worried: his speech on 21 March, with its wealth of technical detail on the workings of coal mines (provided by the industrious Pellenc) was well received by the Assembly, which ordered it to be printed. The mines debates was then adjourned for a week. But for Mirabeau there was no chance to rest. There were instructions to deliver to Montmorin; the queen's Easter communion promised a new crisis in the conflict over juring and non-juring priests; and the threat of schism had hardened with the Pope's unsympathetic letter to the Assembly on the civil oath of the clergy – there was no way he could retain his influence over the left without appearing to further schism and without alienating the king and queen.

The first hurdle to be surmounted was the regency debate which opened on 22 March. On this constitutional issue it was vital not to make mistakes. Three points had to be resolved: whether the post of regent should be hereditary or elective, what body should assume the power of regent during a king's minority if he had no relatives constitutionally eligible to act as regent, and the age at which a child king should attend meetings of the council. Mirabeau, who favoured the hereditary principle, spoke on 25 March. The day before he had sent La Marck a pessimistic note from the Assembly: 'We are in very great danger. They are determined to bring in elections, which will mean the destruction of heredity and the destruction of the monarchy. I have never been truly frightened until today.'

His speech of the morning of 25 May took masterly account of the Assembly's mood. Instead of recommending a hereditary regent, taking this to be the king's nearest relative, which was the natural choice of monarchists, he spoke lengthily in favour of an elected regent, in opposition – which was more extraordinary – to the views of the committee which had presented the regency report. He pointed out that the question of the continuation of the monarchy did not arise in the event of a regency, but only on the death of a king: therefore rules of precedence lost their importance. The closest relative of a child king could well be weak, treacherous, unpopular, yet all power would be in his hands for perhaps twenty years. Without naming them, he was plainly referring to the queen and Artois. If Louis XVI were to die, and the queen became regent, civil war would follow; the monarchy would certainly fall. Artois was as hated as the queen, the comte de Provence weak, the duc d'Orléans untrustworthy. With such a choice of natural candidates, he implied, the monarchy would be better served by an elected regent, answerable to the people and the law.

The Assembly was divided in its response. Those who failed to divine the reasoning behind his approach found it bizarre. Some had the idea that the real reason he argued for elections was because he saw himself becoming regent; this notion did not seem preposterous to those who had watched his growing power in recent months. He knew that the strongest argument against the hereditary principle was posed by the potential regents themselves: make it possible to disqualify the most unpopular and the hereditary principle might be salvaged. This is what happened. The Assembly decreed that, in the event, the regent should be the king's nearest male relative, provided he was of French birth, lived in France, had taken the civil oath, and was not heir presumptive to another crown. Effectively this excluded the queen, who was made the dauphin's guardian; Artois, who was abroad; Provence also if he emigrated or became heir to his father-in-law; and left the duc d'Orléans. For those who voted as they did in order to avoid the risks of an elected regent it was a disconcerting outcome. Mirabeau voted for a hereditary regent, ignoring his own speech, which, after all, had only been intended to demonstrate the risks the opposition would run. He had also been able to vote for the monarchy without assuming an overtly monarchical stand. He had the pleasure of seeing both those who suspected him personally, and those who suspected his politics, voting in accordance with his private views.

The vote was taken on Friday 25 March. That evening Mirabeau entertained two dancers from the Opéra to a late supper in the chaussée d'Antin. The next morning he went down to Argenteuil with Pellenc to prepare his notes for the resumption of the mines debate. Though he had only been able to visit it a few times, his house there, Le Marais, captivated him as much as Bignon had captivated his father, and, with the same enthusiasm he had shown at Mirabeau in the early days of his marriage, he had embarked on lavish schemes of improvement, embellishing the grounds with statuary and a temple of liberty. It was at Le Marais, in the middle of Saturday night, that he had an attack of colic, not severe, but made alarming by the fact that no doctor was available. Early on Sunday morning he insisted on returning to Paris for the winding up of the mines debate. He arrived at La Marck's house before nine o'clock; once indoors he fainted. La Marck begged him not to go to the Assembly but he was adamant, and after drinking two glasses of tokay he managed to walk to his carriage. About three o'clock, having intervened five times in the mines debate, he returned. Throwing himself on a sofa, he told the petrified La Marck: 'Your cause is won and I am dead'.

Mirabeau's doctor was Pierre Cabanis, an enthusiastic young revolutionary who was to have a distinguished career in medicine and as a senator under Napoleon. He succeeded Dr Bagnières, who had attended him during an attack of cholera in 1788; it was Bagnières' nearly lethal treatment then, when he took twenty-two basinsful of blood from his patient in two days, which led Mirabeau to seek a new medical adviser.

In his published account of Mirabeau's last illness Cabanis recorded that during the two years he had known him there had been signs of chronic ill health, with nephritis, recurrent swelling of the legs, rheumatic pain in the arms and chest, and gastric disturbances, quite apart from the opthalmia which was destroying his sight. Before the Assembly moved to Paris he had enjoyed walking, riding, and swimming, but since then there had been few opportunities for exercise, and the most robust of men, said Cabanis, had become susceptible to the slightest thing. Frustration brought on fits of depression, during which he brooded on death, and was shadowed by the presentiment he had had ever since he was in Vincennes, that he would not live to complete his work. In his last months 'the idea of imminent death had replaced the plans for great undertakings; even *la gloire*, the idol of this passionate imagination, no longer had the same attraction'.[24]

By Monday morning Mirabeau, resting at Le Marais, needed a doctor urgently. Once more he returned to Paris, passing Cabanis, who had been alerted by La Marck, on the way. In the chaussée d'Antin he took a hot bath, which eased his symptoms so completely that he decided to visit the Théâtre Italien where the singer Morichelli was performing; but as he entered his box the pain returned, the intensity of it forcing him to leave. As his carriage was nowhere to be found he insisted on walking, and although breathing with difficulty he refused to rest in a café until his carriage was brought, not wanting to create a spectacle. By the time he got to his house he was groaning with pain. Cabanis' treatment succeeded in reducing the most critical symptoms; on Tuesday evening he was able to remark on the pleasure of returning from the edge of the grave; but during the night the symptoms returned, and would not respond to the remedies Cabanis had previously used. He resorted to purgatives to clear the stomach and bowels, with some success according to his report, though the pulse continued to fluctuate, the shooting pain in the pericardium had increased, and the patient's breathing was still constricted. Apart from this, noted Cabanis with professional sang-froid, there were no untoward symptoms.

The news of Mirabeau's illness had spread like wildfire from the first day and the street outside his house was packed with people from every district of Paris and from every political party. There was a sudden awareness of the difficulty of finding another leader capable of reconciling all shades of opinion. The bulletins put up outside the house several times a day could not be seen by the crowds struggling to read them, and so they were printed and distributed. Nowhere was there more concern about his state than at Court: Montmorin and the Archbishop of Toulouse wrote daily to La Marck, and Louis frequently sent for reports. This anxiety of the king's, had it been generally known, would have done much to popularise the monarchy. 'Let us be thankful to Louis XVI for not turning up in person', wrote Desmoulins, 'for that would have made him idolised, and would have resulted in a serious setback for patriotism.'[25]

On Wednesday evening a deputation came from the Jacobin Club, led by Barnave. It was not affection that brought them to his deathbed, but prudence, respect for decencies, and – uncomfortable as it must have been for them to acknowledge it – the wish to redeem their own intellectual integrity, surrendered so often, with regard to Mirabeau, under the pressure of mass emotion. Alexandre de Lameth was the only member of the Jacobin Club who opposed the deputation's visit. 'I knew he was an agitator, I didn't know he was a fool', Mirabeau commented. In fact, Lameth's attitude did much to lessen his popularity.

Cabanis reported that on Wednesday evening his patient's condition was reasonable. The blistering agents he had applied had taken effect, all the passages were open, and the pulse was not alarming. But at midnight, when he left to get some sleep, he saw signs of an approaching crisis, a racing pulse and irregular breathing. At daybreak he returned to find that the pain was once more at its highest level, with suffocation, spasms, 'and all the terrifying side-effects which had accompanied them originally, now rapidly increasing and presaging a cruel day'.

At this point Cabanis panicked. Comparatively inexperienced, he felt the overwhelming responsibility of treating a national idol unassisted. None of his remedies had done more than temporarily alleviate the symptoms. What was causing them had not been touched; indeed, he had no idea what was causing them, though others were ready enough to tell him. Already rumours were circulating that Mirabeau had been poisoned, and if it proved to be true and Cabanis had failed to realise it, his career would be ruined. The pressure put on him to seek a second opinon only increased the nervousness of the young patriot, who had the choice of either killing his hero or of having his incompetence exposed by another doctor. The day before there had been a confrontation between him and Mirabeau's friends and family, in which he had shown that he would not tolerate criticism, especially from those whose political philosophy differed from his own. Within hours Mirabeau's condition had deteriorated. Cabanis's first instinct was to redouble his efforts, so that the world should not be able to accuse him of neglecting any possible remedy.

> I sent for M. Delarue [a surgeon] and the nearest apothecary, in order to place leeches on the chest. Both were still asleep but the latter sent me the leeches. I placed them myself. They did not work effectively. Meanwhile the spasms and

pain increased rapidly; they were so violent when M. Delarue arrived that we decided to repeat the bleeding from the foot, to apply plasters of Spanish fly, to renew the blisters on the legs, and to place very large blisters on the thighs. Immediately after this we administered a pill of six grains of musk every half hour, until the patient had taken between thirty and forty grains.

Musk was then used as a stimulant and antispasmodic. It is significant that Cabanis used the first person plural from then on, as a precaution against future blame. Later that day Montmorin told La Marck that when he wrote to Cabanis that morning he had received a 'detestable' reply, at which he had sent a demand for more information. He could not have been reassured by what he learned. Cabanis recorded that despite everything the patient's condition remained grave:

> The appearance took on an aspect which it never lost thereafter; it was that of death, but of a death full of life, if one can use that expression. Despite the improvement in the pulse, the lessening of the breathlessness and spasms, I found it impossible to think any more of Mirabeau as living. He himself felt that he no longer existed. And assistants remarked that from now on he and I spoke about his life in the past tense, and about him as one who had been but was no longer alive.

Panic was not confined to the sickroom. On Thursday morning Duquesnoy asked La Marck to transfer Mirabeau's papers to his own house without delay: 'Remember that if we lose him some creditor, genuine or false, will have seals affixed, and everything will be revealed.' Montmorin had the same thought. Comps was instructed to sort out Mirabeau's papers, and on Friday Pellenc took them to La Marck's house in a series of bundles. He and La Marck burned the less important papers the same day, spurred on by the report that secret agents of every description were mingling with the crowds outside Mirabeau's house, and that they were even in the house itself.

On Thursday evening Cabanis was at last persuaded to seek further opinion. By his own account he took it upon himself to do so. He chose Dr Antoine Petit and Delarue proposed Dr Jeanroi. When Petit arrived two hours later Mirabeau was unwilling to see him, and all Cabanis could do was to describe the symptoms and the treatment he had given, which, he said, met with Petit's approval. They agreed that he might be suffering from what Cabanis termed an intermittent malignant fever, and proceeded to administer quinine, 'at first in a weak dose, in combination with gentle laxatives; next in a very strong dose'. There was no improvement.

For four days Mirabeau had been constantly purged and bled, without being given anything to maintain his strength. When Petit called again Cabanis told him that for four hours he had been unable to feel any pulse. This time Mirabeau consented to see Petit, but the occasion was conducted more in the manner of a social call than a professional visit if Canabis' account is accurate. Mirabeau explained – in remarkably long sentences for a man who could hardly breathe – why he had only now agreed to receive him, and Petit replied that he had followed Mirabeau's immortal career, and cherished him as the incarnation of liberty and the constitution. After these courtesies Petit examined him. Mirabeau's arms and hands were icy but he could still move them, his breathing was becoming weaker every minute. He asked for a frank estimate of his chances. Petit said he thought they could save him but could not guarantee it.

Mirabeau accepted the death sentence philosophically. His mind remained calm and detached; he talked with Frochot, who was acting as nurse, about what was happening in the Assembly and foreign affairs. 'He was principally occupied with England's secret policies', recorded Cabanis. 'Pitt, he said, was the minister of preparations, he governed by menaces rather than by acts'. 'If I had lived', he told Frochot, '*Si j'eusse vécu*, I think I would have been able to annoy him'. Cabanis' conversations with him, on the other hand, seem to have been directed by the doctor with the aim of amassing posthumous propaganda. On Cabanis telling him of rumours that the king was about to flee he is supposed to have replied:

> I defended the monarchy to the end even when I thought it lost, because it depended on the king whether it were lost, and I believed he was still useful; but if he left I would mount the tribune, declare the throne vacant and proclaim the Republic.

The idea of furtive flight by the king he had always condemned; flight abroad, which Louis was suspected of contemplating, would certainly have lost him his throne and Mirabeau would have regarded it as an act of abdication. But 'proclaim the Republic'? The republican Cabanis would have welcomed such a move, and the words sound like an attempt on his part – once the Republic was a reality – to deny the rumour that the people's hero had gone over to the Court. What would Mirabeau have done after the flight to Varennes? Broken with the Court, certainly. Being a realist, he would also have accepted that the monarchy would shortly become inoperable, none of the hereditary candidates being capable of sustaining it. A republic, alien to French instincts, and a form of government that he knew would provide no lasting solutions, was inevitable; but he would not have been its sponsor. Ideologues and demagogues proclaimed republics; statesmen realised that change changes nothing.

Another remark recorded by Cabanis has the same apocryphal ring: 'I carry in my heart the death of the monarchy, the corpse of which will become the prey of the factious'. But even if he never uttered the actual words they expressed a truth which subsequent events only endorsed. When Cabanis was not gleaning seminal pronouncements he encouraged his patient with news of the popular reaction to his illness. Both ends of the chaussée d'Antin had been blocked to save him from being disturbed, but crowds still packed the streets outside. 'It was glorious to dedicate my life to them, it is good to die in their midst', he is recorded as saying. One completely genuine gesture survives amid the welter of sticky apocrypha – a letter written by someone called Mornais, who lived at 52 rue Neuve-Sainte-Eustache, contained an offer of blood:

> I have read in the papers that blood transfusions have been successfully carried out in England in cases of serious illness. If the doctors think it could help M. de Mirabeau I offer some of my blood, with all my heart. Both are pure.

Cabanis said he thought no more about this letter, which he decided must have come from some well-meaning crank.

It was now Friday 1 April. By the sick man's bed were Frochot, attending to his needs, and Cabanis, catching every line that could thrill posterity. Also in the room were La Marck, the little Lucas de Montigny, Mirabeau's faithful servant, Legrain, and his wife, Henriette, and Mme du Saillant, loudly declaring that her brother had been poisoned. A priest was announced, sent by Mirabeau's mother – the marquise was actually in the house – and the *curé* of Sainte-Eustache also came, but they were told that their services were not required as the Bishop of Autun was already expected. Talleyrand-Périgord arrived that afternoon. A worthy confessor for such a sinner, the watching crowds remarked. He stayed for one-and-a-half hours, and Mirabeau gave him the speech he had prepared on equality of inheritance, asking him to read it to the Assembly. He did not see any other cleric, nor his mother, and there is no mention of the occasion in Talleyrand's memoirs.

After Autun's departure he made his will. To 'Coco Lucas de Montigny' he left 24,000 livres, to Mme de Nehra 20,000 livres, to Pellenc a diamond worth 100 louis, to Le Jay's children his share of their father's business. His silver plate and rings were to be sold and the proceeds given to charity. He made his nephew Saillant his heir; La Marck and Frochot were the executors. In effect, his will was useless: his debts amounted to more than 300,000 livres. The estate proved unable to meet the claims on it in full; the specific bequests were paid by La Marck out of his own pocket. His greatest asset turned out to be his books, which were sold at auction for 139,719 livres and 16 sous. The auctioneer's commission was 7½ per cent.[26] His son, Lucas de Montigny, was left to the benevolence of his sister; this charge was ignored.

Several times in the course of the day he called for Comps, the young secretary who was passionately devoted to him. At 4 a.m. he asked for him again. Hearing the knock at his door, and thinking that Mirabeau had died, Comps stabbed himself in a frenzy of grief. When the door was forced he was found covered with blood, but still alive. The police came, Comps was revived and gave a distraught interview, which greatly alarmed Montmorin when he heard about it, for he was told that under cross-examination the secretary had blurted out the truth about Mirabeau's secret correspondence with the Court. This was untrue, but Comps did talk wildly about Mirabeau being poisoned, adding substance to the rumour that many people were now accepting as fact.

Dawn came while the drama was in progress. By now Mirabeau had lost the power of speech. He made a sign that he wanted to write, and, paper being brought, wrote one word, *dormir*.[27] Cabanis professed not to understand. Mirabeau wrote sarcastically: 'Don't you think that death, or its facsimile which is approaching me, might have dangerous effects?' Cabanis' conscience was placated by the question which, he said, Mirabeau then wrote: 'Can you leave one's friend to be broken on the wheel for three days?' As he was preparing a sedative Petit arrived. Mirabeau suddenly regained his speech and commanded him to say nothing about what he was going to do. In the next room the two doctors quibbled over whether syrup of poppies was to be given in plain or distilled water. By the time a messenger was sent to the apothecary Mirabeau was in agony. It was eight o'clock. He reproached Cabanis bitterly for not keeping his promise to spare him such pain. 'Ah, doctors, doctors', he commented to La Marck. At half past eight Petit, standing at the foot of the bed, said: 'His sufferings are over'.

Within hours of Mirabeau's death placards had appeared in the streets, accusing Barnave and the Lameths of murdering him. So loud was the outcry that he had not died naturally that the public prosecutor called for an autopsy, which took place the following day, 3 April, at Mirabeau's house. No less than forty-four doctors and surgeons were present, headed by the eminent anatomist, Vicq-d'Azyr, who had as his assistant Athanase Barbier, later to be one of the most celebrated surgeons in France. Also present were magistrates, delegates from the sections, and citizens who had been elected by the crowd outside to see that no deception took place. Seals had already been placed on everything in the house and National Guardsmen stationed to keep the public out. The autopsy began at 10 a.m. Cabanis described the proceedings:

The stomach, the duodenum, a large part of the liver, the right kidney, the diaphragm, and the pericardium showed signs of inflammation, or rather, in my opinion, of sanguineous congestion. The pericardium contained a considerable quantity of thick, yellowish, opaque matter. Lymphatic coagulations covered the entire exterior surface of the heart with the exception of its point. The chest cavity contained a small quantity of water.

Certainly the state of the heart, and the fluid in which this organ was swimming, could be regarded as mortal. But I believe, as did Lachèze, that death was directly due to the state of the diaphragm, and I always attribute this state, like that of the heart, to the rheumatic, gouty, vague condition that from the beginning we had regarded as the cause. I can say frankly that finding the same conditions again, I would form the same opinion, and employ the same treatment.[28]

From the symptoms described it is now believed that Mirabeau died as a result of pericarditis. Some of the symptoms point to the presence of gallstones. Before the discovery of penicillin his chance of survival was slight, and, though Cabanis' treatment was exaggerated, there is no reason to think that he would have fared better with any other medical practitioners of his day. Certainly not with those at Edinburgh and Geneva, who, when given Cabanis' diagnosis by Dumont, all declared that his death had been due to his 'excesses', evincing a deplorable readiness to let moral prejudice form their judgement. In talking with them Dumont may just have mentioned the stories circulating in Paris about the evening Mirabeau had spent with the two dancers from the Opéra. These stories – doubtless coloured by the girls themselves – gave the impression that his death was precipitated by a sexual orgy. Cabanis warned his readers sternly against believing them: 'He had none of those habits of which one has to be secretly ashamed. With passionate inclinations, he had none which were demeaning.' Lucas de Montigny, while rejecting with filial loyalty the orgy theory, noted one detail which Cabanis omitted from his account:

His passion for women was to some extent involuntary, or rather, entirely physical; the effect of a congenital form of satyriasis tormented him all his life and still showed several hours after his death – a strange fact, certainly, but true.

Mirabeau's family refused to accept the verdict of natural death. Mme du Saillant never ceased to declare that her brother had been murdered; there was no doubt in her mind that Barnave and the Lameths had planned his death to rid themselves of a political obstacle, and she hinted at aqua Tofana, this seventeenth-century Sicilian poison seeming to lend itself to the sinister circumstances in which he had died. Her son, who was present at the autopsy, was certain that the doctors had detected poison and suppressed the evidence. When Lucas de Montigny set out to interview everyone still living who had assisted at the autopsy, he found seven who thought that the evidence had pointed to poison. One of them remembered Professor Sue whispering to two junior assistants, who had mentioned erosions: 'He has not been poisoned, he could not have been poisoned, understand? Do you want the king and queen, and the Assembly, and all of us to be destroyed?'

This awareness of crisis was shared by everyone. When Vicq-d'Azyr saw the queen after the autopsy he said that the state of the intestines could have been caused as much by violent remedies as by poison, and that 'the prudent conclusion was a natural death, since with the present state of crisis anyone, though innocent of such a crime, could be the victim of public vengeance'.[29] Lord Gower, reporting Mirabeau's death from 'a putrid fever', commented that with his talents he might have been not only an ornament of the age but the saver of his country, and added: 'The Jacobins will no longer be curbed by Mirabeau and the friends of government will feel the loss of his abilities'.[30]

The government's loss was underlined by Marat's screech of joy in the *Ami du peuple*:

> People, give thanks to the gods! Your greatest enemy has been cut down by the scythe of fate; Riqueti is no more; he has fallen the victim of his numerous betrayals. But what do I see? Already clever cheats are trying to work on your feelings, and taken in by their propaganda you are mourning this traitor as your most zealous defender; they have represented his death as a public calamity, and you weep for him as a hero who has been sacrificed for you, as the saviour of the nation.[31]

Nowhere had there been a greater display of grief than in the shrine of liberty itself, the Jacobin Club, whose members had voted to attend the funeral as a body, to wear mourning every year on the anniversary of his death, and to have a marble bust installed in a place of honour. The shapers of popular opinion, Marat, Hébert, Fréron, Brissot, were disgusted by the panegyrics. How dared they speak of his patriotism when he had just prostituted it? Brissot demanded, unable to get over the fact that Mirabeau had opposed the restrictive law on emigration and denounced the triumvirate as factious; how dared they give him the title of virtuous when he had taken such a title for an epigram?[32] (He was referring to the epigram at the head of *Dénonciation de l'agiotage*.) Brissot and Marat might view his apotheosis as a black farce, but the public emotion which stirred their spleen was genuine: Mirabeau was seen as transcending politics, as the symbol of national purpose; his death touched the nation's consciousness at the deepest level and united it as nothing had done since the Day of Federation.[33]

Meanwhile Paris had become a city of mourning. All places of public entertainment were closed and royalist parties celebrating his departure from the scene were forcibly halted. The day after his death, in response to a deputation from the Department of Paris, the Assembly decreed that the new edifice of Sainte-Geneviève (Soufflot's church, begun in 1764 and still unfinished) should receive the ashes of great men of the era of liberty; that Honoré Riqueti Mirabeau should be thus honoured; that above the entrance should be inscribed *Aux grands hommes la patrie reconnaissante*; and that until the new edifice was ready Mirabeau should lie beside Descartes in the crypt of the old church of Sainte-Geneviève. The Assembly also voted for a public funeral. Robespierre, supporting the proposals 'with all the feelings of my heart', paid tribute to 'that illustrious man who, at the most critical moments of the revolution, confronted despotism so courageously'.

Silent crowds packed the route of the funeral procession on 4 April; the whole of Paris seemed to be there, at every window, on balconies and rooftops, in the trees. It was after 10 p.m. before the cortège reached Sainte-Geneviève. Nearly three miles long, it moved through streets lined with National Guardsmen, cavalry at the head, followed by detachments from each of the sixty Paris battalions of the National Guard, led by La Fayette and his staff. After them came the Cent-Suisses and guards from the *hôtel de ville*, a military band playing a march specially composed by Gossec, the clergy, and then the coffin, borne by twelve sergeants of La Grange-Batalière battalion, with six officers acting as pallbearers. Mirabeau's heart was carried in a lead casket, adorned with flowers.[34] The unused hearse followed, and behind it stretched a unique procession; the president and nearly all the members of the Assembly, government ministers, members of the directory of the Department of Paris, the municipality, the judiciary, the Jacobin Club, deputations from the forty-eight sections and the patriotic clubs; and, finally, six divisions of the National Guard and a great crowd of people. Nothing like it would, or could, be seen again. The conciliation of the funeral procession was illusory. Those who saw Mirabeau as being necessary to the Revolution feared what would happen without him.

In November 1792, following the deposing of the king and declaration of the French Republic, a concealed safe was found in the corridor behind the king's apartments in the Tuileries. It contained Louis' private papers, among them documentary evidence of Mirabeau's relations with the Court, though not the Notes he had written which had been returned to him as soon as read. (The Notes, reiterating the need for the monarchy to accept the Revolution and co-operate with the Assembly, would have provided evidence of his revolutionary integrity.) The promissory notes which he had received from the king were there, however; La Marck had returned them after his death.

The discovery caused a public outcry. Mirabeau was hanged in effigy in the place de Grève, his bust at the Jacobin Club was veiled, Robespierre denounced him as an intriguer and political charlatan, unworthy of the honour of lying in the Panthéon. Reminded by Prudhomme in the *Révolutions de Paris* that he had wanted him there in the first place, Robespierre replied that he had agreed because public opinion demanded it; he had been wrong to do so, but hoped that his fault would be expiated by his career as a whole and the persecutions he had endured in the name of freedom: 'I feel remorse today for the first time in my life, for I may have let it be thought that I shared the good opinion of Mirabeau held by the Assembly and the general public.'[35] Like Desmoulins, who also advertised his own political purity by denouncing Mirabeau at this time, Robespierre was now a deputy in the Convention. He had just proposed that the king should be sentenced to death, and with the living to punish there was no time to deal with the already dead; the Committee of Public Instruction called for a full report on Mirabeau, which was only completed a year later. On 27 November 1793, after hearing the report which found him guilty of seeking 'to reestablish despotism with constitutional material', the Convention ordered that his body should be removed from the Panthéon and the place given to Marat, who had died four months previously.

Another nine months passed without any move, but in September 1794, nearly two months after Robespierre's execution, his faithful supporters in the Jacobin Club called for the Convention's order to be carried out. On 21 September Mirabeau's wooden coffin was extracted from its outer one of lead and removed from the vaults of the Panthéon. The report of the police commissioner stated that it was then deposited in 'the ordinary burial ground' pending further orders. The ordinary, or paupers', burial ground was the Sainte-Catherine cemetery, adjoining the Clamart cemetery in the faubourg Saint-Marcel.[36] In July 1797, under the Directory, the Council of Five Hundred moved that the remains of Mirabeau, 'the glory of whose name belongs to posterity', should be restored to the Panthéon. A search was carried out, but no trace of them could be found.

## NOTES

1. Mirabeau was very aware of the implications in words. On 22 August 1789, when the Assembly was debating religious tolerance (Article 10 of the

Declaration of Rights), he said: 'To me religious liberty is a right so sacred that the word tolerance, which is intended to express it, seems itself to be tyrannical, for the existence of the authority which has the power to tolerate is oppressive to liberty of thought by the very fact that it *tolerates*, and therefore would be capable of not tolerating' (see Aulard, 1910: I. 155).

2. *Mémoires biographiques*, XI, 266–7.

3. Dumont ascribed Mirabeau's speeches on the civil constitution of the clergy (26 November and 14 January) to Lamourette, the constitutional Bishop of Lyon. He made his name on 7 July 1792 in the Legislative Assembly, when he urged all those who hated the idea of a republic, and who were opposed to anarchy as well as to feudalism, to declare themselves. In an extraordinary scene deputies of the right and left embraced and kissed – the *'baiser Lamourette'*. Lamourette may have been involved in the address of 14 January; his putative authorship could also have been a smear put out by the extreme right, which despised the bishops who had taken the civil oath.

4. La Marck, *Correspondance*, III, 28.

5. See *Mémoires biographiques*, XI, 208f, for this speech.

6. Aulard (1914: 20). Chaussinand-Nogaret (1982: 248) finds proof of Mirabeau's atheism in the words he wrote to Sophie de Monnier from Vincennes: *'Tout notre être finira avec nous'*; but this is surely a too literal interpretation of what, after all, was simply Mirabeau's sad recognition as a lover of the finite course of all human love.

7. Bouillé (1820–28: 197). The move to Metz which La Marck and Bouillé discussed is only known to us through their respective memoirs. The initiative came from La Marck, and there is no evidence that Mirabeau knew about it. The idea of an open move came from him originally, but the choice of Metz as a destination suggests strongly that the plan was made without his knowledge, since the psychological objections to going there, which he had pointed out, still existed.

8. Ibid., 198.

9. La Fayette (1837–38: I, 366–7) did not conceal his resentment: 'The acquaintance of Mirabeau and Montmorin was resumed on an intimate level and in conferences to which La Fayette was a total stranger. An aide-de-camp of La Fayette's named Julien was admitted, and he was the only one during the revolution regarding whom he had to make this reproach'.

10. Brissot (1911: II, 44).

11. Dumont (1951: 150).

12. When the decree abolishing titles was passed Mirabeau remarked ironically that his change of name to Riqueti would disorientate Europe for three days. True equality would not be accomplished by removing the outward marks of distinction. He continued to use his arms and livery, not out of pride, but out of impatience with the naive preoccupation with external symbols, when what mattered, and could not be changed, was character.

13. Dumont (1951: 148).

14. In his contribution, which amounted to a few lines, Dumont referred to Burke as 'a member of the Commons, whom all admirers of his great talents are distressed to include among the superstitious detractors of human reason'. These words, which did not originate with Mirabeau, sealed Burke's animosity towards him. In a letter of 11 February 1791 to Captain Emperor John Alexander Woodford, Burke (1976: 225) wrote: 'A friend of mine, just come from Paris, tells me, he was present, when the Comte de Mirabeau (I beg his

pardon) Mr Ricquetti, thought proper to entertain the Assembly with his opinion of me. I can only answer him, by referring him to the WORLD'S opinion of *him*. I have the happiness not to be disapproved by my Sovereign. I can bear the frowns of Ricquetti the first, who is Theirs'.

15. He had bought the house, Le Marais, from Beaumarchais. In fact it was never paid for; he agreed to buy the remainder of the lease but died before the first instalment was due.

16. La Marck, *Correspondance*, III, 38–9.

17. Robespierre supported Mirabeau in this debate. No law forbidding emigration was ever passed by the Assembly, though it continued to criticise the *émigrés* strongly. Two decrees of 9 July and 1 August 1791 imposed fines on those who did not return to France within one month, but these were cancelled by the decree of amnesty which was passed on 14 September 1791.

18. *Révolutions de France et de Brabant*, no. 67.

19. Ibid.

20. Oelsner's account was published by A. Stern in *Das leben Mirabeaus*, (1889).

21. *Mémoires biographiques*, XII, 29.

22. Ibid., XII, 33–6.

23. Gower (1885: 67).

24. Cabanis (244). All quotations regarding Mirabeau's illness are taken from this source.

25. *Révolutions de Paris et de Brabant*, no. 91.

26. An inventory of Mirabeau's wardrobe listed 45 coats, mostly velvet or embroidered satin, 34 fancy waistcoats, 17 pairs of breeches, 50 pairs of silk stockings, 3 National Guard uniforms, 8 pairs of buckles, and a silver toilet case. He also possessed a silver gilt table service for twenty-four and one in silver for forty-eight, 15 silver plates, and various pieces of gold plate.

27. According to Montigny. Staël (1820–21: XII, 382) said that he quoted Hamlet's words, '*Mourir, c'est dormir*'. Montigny was trying to save his father's memory from the slur that he had contemplated suicide.

28. Cabanis (315).

29. Campan (1849: II, 135).

30. Gower (1885: 76).

31. *Ami du peuple*, no. 419.

32. Brissot, *Le Patriote françois*, (newspaper) 4 April 1791. In February, when Brissot calumniated him in print, Mirabeau replied with a personal letter, containing this magisterial rebuke: 'Although the despotism of opinion and the monopoly of patriotism that he affects are completely unworthy of a friend of liberty such as he has often shown himself to be, I do not believe that a personal wrong diminishes the recognition due to public services, and I shall avenge myself on him by always trying to render justice to him' (Brissot, 1912: 263).

33. Recognising him as first and foremost a patriot, Staël (obituary on Mirabeau, cited by Montigny, XII, 239) wrote: 'This man, who often braved public opinion but who always supported the general will, was the leader of those friends of order and the monarchy, who were no less defenders of the French constitution, liberty, and equality, than were the republicans. He could have moderate principles, he who voiced them with passion; he could attack the factions, he who had so well earned the name of revolutionary . . . a man devoted enough to the success of the revolution for it to be possible for him to speak of order, without the people fearing that he wished for despotism, and of safety for all, without them suspecting that he had exceptions in mind'.

34. His heart was buried in the church of Saint-Eustache.
35. Thompson, *Robespierre* (1935: I, 295–6). The condemnation of Mirabeau was an expression of Jacobin, not general, feeling. According to Jaurès (1901–08: II, 344), the people, 'unblinkered by parties and feuds, reconciled all the forces of the Revolution in its revolutionary consciousness', and in its Popular Societies 'set side by side the bust of Robespierre the Incorruptible and the bust of Mirabeau accused of corruption'.
36. Montigny noted that it was bordered by the rues Fer-à-Moulin, des Francs-Bourgeois, des Fosses-Saint-Marcel, and place Scipion.

# 13

The Legacy of the
Constituent Assembly

Louis XVI accepted the completed constitution on 13 September 1791, and on 30 September the Constituent Assembly retired. The constitutional monarchy which the men of 1789 had created on paper lasted officially until the king's suspension on 10 August 1792, but the monarchy had entered a terminal state long before; the flight to Varennes in June 1791 signalled the inevitable end; the war hastened it; the efforts of political parties – the triumvirate and the constitutionalists in the summer of 1791, the Feuillants in the Legislative Assembly of 1791–92 – to shore up the monarchical framework were futile. The 'second revolution' of 10 August, the revolution of the 'passive' citizens, took over from the first revolution, that of the middle classes against the *ancien régime*. The constitution of 1791, designed for a middle-class, property-owning society, headed by a king, was obsolescent even while it was being drawn up.

The members of the third estate elected to the Assembly of 1789, whether they were labelled *monarchiens*, or constitutionalists, or patriots, or radicals, had all been exposed to the Enlightenment's curriculum of political ideas. Montesquieu and Rousseau, of course, were their admired masters, Montesquieu appealing more to those who instinctively liked the idea of constitutional pluralism and an English parliamentary system, Rousseau to those who instinctively liked the idea of an egalitarian society, devoid of invidious distinctions (though there was nothing fixed about their followers who drew from both sources, depending on the situation, and without any sense of contradiction or inconsistency).

279

But it was not all Montesquieu and Rousseau. Or even Turgot, Voltaire, and Mably. Many of the theories which the revolutionary generation picked up in the course of its political education had been around for a long time. Locke, discoursing on popular sovereignty and the right to revolution, had enthralled their grandfathers, and such ideas were old even then: popular sovereignty, and the Rousseauist proposal that a king should have the status of an elected official, went back to twelfth-century teachers at the University of Paris. Machiavelli was another source of radical ideas; not the stereotyped master of cunning, but the Machiavelli of the *Discorsi*, who was hostile to monarchical government and who defined liberty as the power of free people to govern themselves. Rousseau took many of his views in the *Contrat social* from him.

Treatises on government were not for everybody. In the Assembly it was the classical authors they had studied in their schooldays – Cicero, Tacitus, Plutarch, Livy – which supplied the language of ideas in daily use, the models for their rhetoric, and that vision of an ideal, virtuous world, the golden world of the Roman Republic, which many of them appeared to believe in literally. These were not political Republicans who did so.[1] They took ancient Rome as their moral model in their task of regenerating France. The Roman concept of civic virtue as being the foundation of good government, liberty, the state itself, became part of their own creed. France, struggling Laocoön-like in the coils of corruption and despotism, could not become the land of freedom and justice desired by its people unless, collectively and individually, they were morally transformed.

Liberty and virtue: these were the key words – both capable of wide interpretation – in the political vocabulary of the left. (Of course they were part of the right-wing's vocabulary, too; Montesquieu attached as much importance to liberty and virtue as Rousseau, but they did not acquire the same ideological overtones.) Liberty was not so much a word as an invocation, a promise, with all the hopefulness and fear of unattainability of promises. For many of the revolutionaries it was one of the formative words of their childhood; it did not take the American Revolution to give it emotive power. 'Every age has its dominant idea; that of our age seems to be Liberty', wrote Diderot in 1771. For nearly another twenty years liberty remained an idea, to be embraced in books or distant places: the young liberal nobles who came back from the American war retained an essentially romantic idea of what liberty consisted in. But so too did the young lawyers and journalists who looked back nostalgically to a mythified Rome.

In the Assembly that vanished Rome was as real as Paris. The

Romans, too: in expressing their ideals the left frequently summoned up Cincinnatus and Catiline, who together epitomised the revolutionaries' idea of good and evil. Cincinnatus was the virtuous patriot who chose quiet retirement in place of honours. Catiline was clever and corrupt, a dictator, the enemy of the people. In the *Contrat social* Rousseau warns against the appearance of 'one ambitious man, one hypocrite, one Catilina', who is 'cunning enough to master the art of imposing on others, and gains a part of the public authority'.[2] It was a passage which encouraged the practice of personal denunciation in the Assembly.

Virtue and liberty: as the Revolution evolved these concepts became more difficult to define, but in the innocent days of 1789 it seemed to the new Assembly that its good intentions must be crowned with success, that liberty could be legislated into existence. The record of the Constituent Assembly is one of extraordinary achievements in the face of daunting opposition. The establishment of a permanent legislature, the end of feudalism, the abolition of privileges, fiscal reform, the creation of new administrative and judicial systems, clerical reform, make this the most revolutionary period of the Revolution; but at the same time the Assembly created problems for itself and for the future by its own policies, particularly with regard to Church affairs, the franchise, money supply, and local government. These problems were as much the legacy of the Constituent Assembly as its achievement.

Fundamentally it was the inevitable conflict between sectional interest and the greater good, between ideals and reality. The legislators whose stated mission it was to regenerate France and bring liberty to the nation started with clear enough ideas about the broad issues, the ending of all forms of privilege and creation of equal rights under the law. The vision in their minds of a land guaranteeing freedom and a better life for all its citizens was one thing. The society they actually set out to create was one to suit themselves and their kind; in other words, one in which the aspirations and interests of the property-owning middle classes – the dominant, most articulate class in the Assembly – automatically prevailed. The Declaration of Rights was adamant: property rights were sacred. And so, after the relinquishing of feudal rights on 4 August 1789, they were faced with a dilemma: free the peasants from all their dues or oblige them to redeem those relating to property. As few peasants could afford to do so their situation remained, in effect, the same as before until the law on redemption was changed. The constituents saw no inconsistency between their rhetoric and the protectionism of their legislation. A Barnave could proclaim the right of all people to liberty, and defend slavery with an equal passion. 'Law and order' policies were wanted by all sections of the Assembly. They feared the destructiveness of the mob as much as royal despotism, moderates because of the threat to security, the left because of the risk of repressive reaction by those eager to stamp out the Revolution. There was a noticeable absence of empathy with the poorest people or those involved in disturbances, even among the radicals in the Assembly, though they paid lip service to the 'people'.

The difficulty of reconciling ideals and sectional interests was brought sharply into focus by the article in the Declaration of Rights which stated that all citizens had a right to contribute towards the making of the law. In principle this meant equal voting and electoral rights. When this right was incorporated in the constitution, however, the Assembly restricted it to property-owners of specified degrees of wealth; the great mass of the population had no political voice at all. By restricting decision-taking power to a propertied minority the Assembly was seeking to ensure the future stability of society; it succeeded in creating a class of resentful, excluded citizens. The imposition of the civil oath of the clergy, which created schism, alienated the faithful, and encouraged counter-revolution, would be rated its greatest error. The decision to withhold rights on grounds of poverty was equally unjust and unwise, for it was the support of the unenfranchised that would be needed to secure the power of the middle classes.

It was Sieyès who gave the word 'nation' the special meaning which it had for the revolutionaries. In his pamphlet *Qu'est-ce que le Tiers Etat?* he stated that the third estate formed in itself the whole nation (or body politic), that the clergy were not members of an order but a profession, and therefore part of the nation along with the third estate, but that the nobility were excluded by privilege, and by their insistence that they were distinct from the rest of the nation. Sieyès gave the third estate a sense of its own identity and awoke it to the importance of unity, while excommunicating the nobility politically. From being outside the nation it was a short step to being against it in the popular mind. Not deliberately, but effectively all the same, Sieyès with his intellectual analysis incited violence.

The bringing together of the three estates in one chamber was the third's first victory. That it brought unity was a myth. The lower clergy, the liberal nobles, and some others – mainly provincial and fiefless nobles – accepted the implications of joining with the third estate. The higher clergy, with few exceptions, and the rest of the nobles joined the third under duress, and remained in a state of alienation, opposing the Assembly's policies, hostile to the Revolution. Concessions by the king only intensified their hostility. As time went on many of them joined the *émigrés* abroad. Their contempt for democratic ideas and suspected encouragement of counter-revolutionary movements made them an insurmountable obstacle to any reconciliation between king and Assembly, for the idea that the king and the aristocracy were natural allies, or birds of a feather, remained firmly fixed. Every intemperate speech by a member of the first estate was a setback for Louis. Any attempt to improve the image of the monarchy had to include dissociating it from the aristocracy, which was impossible.

The *monarchiens*, led by Mounier and Malouet, discovered this when they advocated constitutional monarchy in exact imitation of England, with the nobility exercising an active political role. The formation of a single-chamber Assembly removed the threat of a nobles' veto, but the *monarchiens* lost all credibility and retired from the scene. The influence of the Court nobility on the government and the king continued unabated, creating permanent suspicion in the Assembly. La Fayette's attempts to form an understanding between the party of the triumvirate, which succeeded the *monarchiens*, and a section of the nobility, were doomed to failure. He underestimated the nobility's determination not to compromise, and naively failed to see that for the middle-class patriot party, bent on power, connections with the politically suspect nobility would be disadvantageous, leaving them open to attack by the radical left. (Hence the sometimes calculated speeches by the triumvirate, anxious to establish popular political credentials.)

Mirabeau's wish for the king to be part of the Revolution and to dissociate himself from the reactionary aristocracy, estranged conservative opinion which thought it could only weaken the monarchy. Equally, his efforts to strengthen the king's constitutional position appeared suspect and dangerous to the left. His ceaseless denunciation of royal despotism, his insistence that 'the power of the people must always be greater than that of the king', made no difference. His argument was always that the king would never wish to exceed his constitutional powers because that would lose him the affection of the people. A good king would always treat the people kindly and put their happiness first. Was this a disguised form of *despotisme éclairé*? A king being benevolent, not for any philanthropic reasons but in order to reinforce his own power? For Mirabeau that was not the point. The only thing that mattered was that a king should earn the love of the people. If he forfeited it he must accept the consequences.

On this question of kings having a natural incentive to be benevolent, Rousseau took a negative view: 'A political preacher may tell kings that since the people's strength is the king's strength, a king's best interest is to have his people flourish . . . but kings know that this is not true. Their personal interest is primarily that the people should

be weak, wretched, unable to oppose them.'[3] Former admirers of
Mirabeau, who thought of him as the man who had written against
despotism even in prison, could not understand the apparent loss of his
ideals in his defence of the royal prerogative. After his death
Desmoulins summed up his policies in a single sentence: 'Nearly all
the good that has been done in the National Assembly has been done
without him, and nearly all the bad has been done by him alone'.[4] By
bad he meant all the concessions in favour of the king's authority
which Mirabeau had been instrumental in winning. In the eyes of the
left his wish for the king to have restraining powers was also 'bad'
because it implicitly denied the infallibility of the Assembly. The
feeling that his revolutionary faith was uncertain was thus fostered
every time he criticised the Assembly's judgement. The growing influence of the Jacobins had much to do with the doctrinaire tone of
Desmoulins' verdict. As Jacobinism came to be regarded as the expression of national political consensus any disunity of thought was culpable. Mirabeau in the Jacobin Club, challenging with straight speaking
the notion that the general will revealed itself unerringly through the
mouths of Jacobin leaders, was guilty of cracking the postulated unity
of opinion on which Jacobin power was founded. Later in the Revolution Jacobin energy in the conduct of the war strengthened their emotional grip on the nation, and made it possible for Mirabeau's eviction
from the Panthéon to be seen as an act of exalted patriotism; which it
would not have been in less rhetorical times.

Even Chateaubriand – who detested their bigotry – acknowledged
the Jacobin achievement, and later generations of Frenchmen saw
Jacobinism as the great political and moral phenomenon of the Revolution. Nearly a century after Mirabeau's death the Jacobin view of the
Revolution was ratified by the appointment of Alphonse Aulard to the
chair of revolutionary history at the Sorbonne. The significant date was
now 1792 instead of 1789. The First Republic was thought of as pre-
destined. In the light of history the Constituent Assembly's monarchical constitution, and Mirabeau's aims in 1790 and 1791, were
irrelevant. He himself was the defender of liberty but also the defender of monarchy, and Aulard would speak of him with almost the
same high moral indignation as Desmoulins.

Mirabeau's efforts to make the king constitutionally significant were
all part of his strategy to involve him actively in the work of the
Revolution, and so to enhance his image with the people. Only by
strengthening that link could the monarchy survive. He had no illusions about Louis' character and recognised from the start that he was
unlikely to re-educate him; that did not make his aim any less valid in
itself. Lefebvre, an unsympathetic commentator, cited his trust in the

king – which he never had – as a sign that he lacked statesmanship. His wider aims, the idea of a king of the Revolution, he ignored, as have most historians, who assume that if it ever had any meaning it died with him. It took François Furet to point out anew that the idea of a king of the Revolution was rooted in the historical, mystically binding relationship between the kings of France and the people, a relationship older and deeper and quite different in nature from that between the king and the aristocracy. It was a relationship which Louis could have built on at the start of the Revolution and which was not entirely destroyed by later events. Paris claimed to speak for the whole country, but the revolutionary message had less effect in the provinces; the peasant derived little benefit from the brave new world that was now supposed to be his: he had not become a proprietor, his conditions of work were still harsh; he remained instinctively monarchical, and he was not alone. Many people in 1798, Furet reminds us, still held to the idea of a king of the Revolution. They were the people who had welcomed the Revolution in 1789; who had seen, however, that without the monarchy acting as its rallying point it would be identified increasingly with a narrow circle of Paris politicians, and not with the nation as a whole. Burke described the Revolution as an alien growth of rationality imposed on the native culture. There was a lesson here for those who wanted the Revolution to succeed. Mirabeau's year of urging Louis to identify the monarchy with the Revolution was a conscious attempt to make a rational growth organic, to create – for ordinary people – a reason for loyalty to the Revolution which theories alone could not provide.

Analysing his contribution to the Revolution, the socialist Jaurès dwelled at length on his vision of government based on an alliance between the monarchy and the people, 'this conciliation, this synthesis of democracy and royalty'. Such an alliance, he thought, would have been entirely possible. Conciliation with the monarchy was desired by most of the revolutionaries until, and even after, Varennes, and Mirabeau was seen as the only man able to bring it about. He wished that his idea of a king of the Revolution had succeeded. It would have saved France, he said, from Caesarism and military enslavement. 'It would have saved her also from a bourgeois oligarchy, and the electors' regime of Louis-Philippe would have been as impossible as the warring regime of Napoleon.'[5]

Jaurès added that the king had every incentive to inaugurate popular reforms since he depended on the people's sanction to stay in office; but the conclusion he drew from this, that he would have granted universal suffrage eventually in order to win the whole nation to his side, is too optimistic. Louis never really understood the importance of conciliation, that word which Mirabeau used so often when describing the basis for lasting revolutionary progress. Conciliation and progress were, indeed, what differentiated his plan for a king of the Revolution from all the many other plans put forward at the time. His was the only one which was not counter-revolutionary in intention, which sought to unite and not to divide, to build on the achievements of the Revolution and not to reverse them, which thought out policies for the future. The only thing that was lacking was a king to share the vision.

After Mirabeau's death the divisions of opinion within the Assembly became even sharper as violence caused by inflation and unemployment spread out of control, and invasion by foreign armies seemed daily more imminent. The schism over the civil oath of the clergy had been so inflated by royalists (as objective commentators feared it would be) that civil war seemed inevitable. *Emigré* groups in the Rhineland and Italy were plotting armed intervention. The activities of Artois, especially, in this direction ensured that his brother Louis had no chance of being allowed freedom of movement. At the other end of the political spectrum the popular societies like the Cordelier Club were organising street-level protests, and the radical newspapers were informing and influencing the public. Against this background the call was heard again that it was time to halt the revolution. On 17 May 1791 Duport, supported by Barnave, declared that the revolution must rest at the point it had reached, and that extremism had to be resisted: 'Equality must be restricted, liberty reduced, opinion steadied. The government must be strong, solid, stable.'

The triumvirate had changed their political attitude. The former liberal left recognised in the breakdown of law and order, and the growth of alternative political power in the streets, a threat to the interests of the property-owning classes, to one of the fundamental principles defined in the Declaration of Rights, the right to property. In an attempt to bring the situation under control they formed an alliance with the constitutionalists (followers of La Fayette) and surviving *monarchiens* such as Malouet. They used Court money to start a paper, *Le Logographe*, which was to combat the revolutionary propaganda of Gorsas's *Courrier* and Carra's *Annales patriotiques*. In June, panicked by the prospect of militant workers, the Assembly closed the public workshops which had been set up in 1789 to assist the unemployed: Mirabeau had urged the king and queen to support these *ateliers* which were desperately needed. Also in June, the Le Chapelier law was passed, unopposed by the democrats, which forbade all forms of association or strike action by workers. (It was not repealed until 1884.) The anxiety to contain any violence by the masses was matched by a misplaced attempt to placate the clergy who had refused to take the civil oath. They were now allowed to conduct religious services, which only created friction with the constitutional clergy. The Pope's condemnation of the civil constitution of the clergy encouraged the non-jurors to harden their opposition to the Revolution, which in turn prompted a wave of anti-clerical attacks in the radical press. Until June the Assembly had only succeeded in handing ammunition to both sides in the religious conflict, and in worsening the social crisis. On 21 June the royal family took flight for Varennes.

Four days later they were brought back. The intensifying of popular loyalty to the Revolution in the wake of the king's defection made the Assembly all the more anxious to play down the situation in order to preserve its own authority. Louis was merely suspended from his function. Barnave put the problem facing the Assembly in a nutshell when he declared on 15 July that any further step towards liberty would involve 'the destruction of the monarchy', and any further step towards equality would mean 'the destruction of property'. In other words, democracy would undermine the aims of the constitution. Two days later the Cordeliers who had gathered in the Champ-de-Mars to sign a petition for a republic were fired on by order of the Assembly, and martial law was imposed. The fiction of an assembly that spoke for the nation vanished in a fusillade.

In August the constitutionalist–triumvirate alliance obtained a revision of the constitution in favour of the ruling middle classes by means of yet stiffer monetary qualifications for electors. And, as one of its last acts, the Assembly decided that entry to the National Guard should be limited to active citizens, thus obviating, it hoped, the possibility of armed, disaffected bands seizing control of towns and cities. When the Assembly broke up at the end of September the retiring deputies believed that the constitution they had created would guard their world for generations, and to make sure they decreed that it should not be revised for thirty years. Accepting the constitution, the king declared that the Revolution was now over. The majority of deputies thought that it was.

Throughout the summer months of 1791 the political strength of the triumvirate seemed unassailable, especially with Mirabeau no longer there to challenge them. But within days of his death signs appeared that their position as popular leaders was beginning to crack. The new voice was Robespierre's. On 7 April it was Robespierre who moved that for four years after the dissolution of the Constituent Assembly none of its members could become ministers; who, on 29 April, tried unsuccessfully to extend the membership of the National Guard to passive citizens (which Mirabeau had also proposed on democratic grounds); who, on 9 May, defended the rights of citizens to petition; and who, on 10 May, proposed that no member of the present Assembly should be eligible for election to the next. On 10 June he was elected public prosecutor in Paris. Robespierre's career began when Mirabeau's ended. His speeches showed that he had noted carefully Mirabeau's line of reasoning,[6] and it was no coincidence that when he started his own journal he imitated Mirabeau's original title and called it *Lettres à ses commettans*. At the close of the Constituent Assembly he had established a popular reputation as the defender of citizens' rights – despite his silence over the repressive Le Chapelier law – which would carry his career forward; the constitutionalists, dismissively labelled the men of 1789, would end up being remembered by Republicans not as the defenders of liberty but as those who had tried to restrict it.

Mirabeau's early death prevents any equitable comparison of his aims with those of other revolutionary leaders, the evolution of whose ideas, and their translation into actions, can be followed through to the later stages of the Revolution. If Robespierre had also died in 1791 his surviving image would be different. Had Mirabeau lived it is fair to assume that, as someone who believed the right course of action depended on the circumstances, he would have reached a point at which he had to choose between the Revolution and the monarchy. He had tried to fuse them, to secure for Frenchmen the liberties they sought and the stability of government which he, like others, thought more likely under a monarchy. But when supporting the monarchy became tantamount to supporting a reactionary minority, which expressly wanted to undo the achievements of the Revolution, he would have had to decide where his loyalties lay.

Wondering what he might have done in the future, Etienne Dumont made the mysterious pronouncement in his *Souvenirs* that, 'had he lived, the destiny of France would have taken a different course'. This was not the sentimental dreaming of a monarchist who thought that Mirabeau could have prevented the downfall of the monarchy regardless of everything: Dumont was a Republican. The 'different course' he envisaged would still have involved a change of system from monarchy to Republic. The inference is that Mirabeau would have continued to exert a moderating influence, would have combated dictatorship, that his voice would have continued to be heard in the sections, with beneficial results. Perhaps Dumont thought that Mirabeau, who had warned from the start of the danger to the Revolution of a foreign war, would have joined with Robespierre, who stood out against war in 1792, and that together they might have defeated Brissot and the war party. Or perhaps he thought that Mirabeau's presence might have kept Robespierre in the shadows. However, Dumont, like Michelet (who believed he would have become a leading Republican), failed to consider the most likely outcome if Mirabeau had survived for another two years. Like the other deputies in the Constituent Assembly he would have been debarred from sitting in the Legislative Assembly of 1791–92. As a member of the directory of the Department of Paris he would have continued his public work. In September 1792, like his fellow director in the Department, Danton, he might have been elected to the Convention. In November 1792 he would have been denounced when the king's secret papers were discovered. After that, if he did not flee abroad, which was not in his character, and even if he defeated his accusers in the Jacobin Club, which he might well have done, his chances of surviving the Revolution would have been slight. He would have shared the same fate as Barnave, who was arrested when his letters to the queen were also found in the secret safe, and guillotined in 1793.

Mirabeau's particular contribution to the Assembly came from his breadth of vision and ability to rise above party, and his pragmatism. Some of his most useful speeches were on foreign affairs; he was always aware of the judging world and the need for France's international relations not to suffer. Aware, too, that makers of revolution could not ignore economics. He went to the heart of a question, said Cerutti in his funeral oration, he focused attention on the long-term consequences. Dumont wrote of 'his political sagacity, his anticipation of events', of how he 'understood so completely the views of the popular party in the Party sections'.[7]

That understanding, the willingness to listen to the people and their leaders, in Paris or in Provence, was the mark of the man. He realised the political folly of not listening; he also had compassion for the human condition. The aspirations of the peasant, the right of those in humble employment to be protected – in Soboul's phrase – from 'the omnipotence of the rich', were for him the essence of what the Revolution was about. His sharpest Notes for the King, and interventions in the Assembly, were in connection with poverty and the social unrest arising from it. The section of society he liked least was that of the wealthy bourgeoisie, especially those who had profited financially from the Revolution without contributing anything to it, 'this new aristocracy' which had, he said contemptuously, all the selfishness of the old. He was a Rousseauist in that he believed that 'private interests' were 'enemies of the general interest'. For that reason he did not join any particular group in the Assembly. He had been conditioned by his background to put service to his country and countrymen – and he saw service to the Revolution as that – before allegiance to a party or a regime. The only party he supported was the 'poor obscure little party called the nation, to which all sensible, honest men should belong'.

Mirabeau's public career lasted less than two years. He never held office, never led a party or directed policies. He was remembered less for what he achieved than for what he stood for. He remained for later generations the figure in David's drawing of *The Oath of the Jeu de Paume*, powerful, inspiring, a symbol of the Revolution as they preferred to recall it. Like other leaders of the Revolution his final rating is neither that of hero nor villain. They were all, as he himself said, constrained by circumstance. How they responded, to a great extent, was a matter of individual character.

## *NOTES*

1. In February 1791 Marat stated that a limited monarchy was the best form of government, that the danger with a republic was that it could lead to an oligarchy. (*Ami du peuple*, no. 315.) Even after Varennes a monarchy was still preferred by the Assembly and by the majority of people.
2. Rousseau (1968: Book IV, Chapter 8).
3. Ibid., Book III, chapter 6.
4. *Révolutions de France et de Brabant*, no. 72.
5. Jaurès (1901–08: I, 410).
6. Sometimes he borrowed directly from Mirabeau's speeches. See, for example, his speech on universal suffrage, made to the Jacobin Club on 20 April 1791, which contains words from Mirabeau's speech of 15 June 1789: 'The people only want what is necessary, they only wish for justice and peace'. Mirabeau's voice can be heard in Robespierre's declaration of July 1792 that 'despotism is still despotism whether it has one head or 700', and that 'a great assembly set above the law' should not be given unlimited authority. On 2 January 1792, addressing the Jacobins, Robespierre advised them to put France's internal affairs in order before trying to take liberty abroad, an echo of an article in the *Courrier de Provence* (XXXI). And in April 1793, in a speech on the right of property, he used the same words as Mirabeau had used in his speech on slavery to describe a slave ship: 'this long coffin'. Mathiez, thinking the image was Robespierre's, called it 'magnificent'.
7. Dumont (1951: 161).

# Postscript

The public reaction against Mirabeau, following the discovery of the king's secret papers, brought inevitable reprisals on his relatives. His mother was imprisoned but escaped the guillotine. She died in 1794. His sister, Caroline du Saillant, was also imprisoned with her husband and daughters; her son fled abroad. The Saillants survived the Revolution. Mme du Saillant died in 1821.

Mirabeau's other sister, Louise de Cabris, emigrated during the Revolution. She later returned to France and died in 1807.

Emilie de Mirabeau and her father, the marquis de Marignane, emigrated and their fortune was confiscated. After Mirabeau's death Mme de Mirabeau married a Sardinian army officer named Focardi della Roccasparviera by whom she had a son. Widowed a second time in 1798, she returned to France and was able as a foreign citizen to reclaim the family assets. She lived in Mirabeau's apartment in the chaussée d'Antin, and died on 6 March 1800, aged forty-six.

In 1789 the bailli de Mirabeau became grand prior of the Order of Malta in Provence, but when the situation became too dangerous he retired to Malta and died there in 1794.

The vicomte de Mirabeau left France in the summer of 1790. The Touraine regiment, of which he was colonel, mutinied, and to punish it he stole the regimental tassels and bows; he was arrested, but fled before his case was heard by the Assembly. *Le Voyage national de Mirabeau cadet* is his own humorous account of what happened. Joining the *émigrés* in Germany, he raised a troop of mercenaries, but died at

Freiburg in September 1792, supposedly in a duel with an *émigré* officer.

J.M. Thompson, in *Robespierre*, reproduces a letter written to Robespierre by a 'Mlle Riquetti', who was seeking the Convention's permission to give free reading, writing, and music lessons. 'No my dear Robespierre, have no fear, I shall never desert you', she wrote. 'Your watchword is the love of what is good; mine is that your life may long be spared.' Thompson remarked on this evidence of the fallen fortunes of a great house. The identity of Mlle Riquetti, however, is a mystery. Mirabeau left no unmarried sisters or aunts; his brother had no daughters. Possibly she belonged to the unrelated Riquettis who hailed originally from Languedoc.

# Select Bibliography

The Mirabeau archives at the Musée Arbaud, Aix-en-Provence, contain an extensive collection of family records, letters written by Mirabeau and other members of the family, and the correspondence between the marquis de Mirabeau and his brother, the bailli. This material is detailed in an appendix to Castries (1960) (see below).

## Works by Mirabeau

*Essai sur le despotisme.* London, 1775 (published anonymously).
*Avis aux Hessois et autres peuples de l'Allemagne vendus par leurs princes à l'Angleterre.* Cleves, 1777 (published anonymously).
*Des lettres de cachet et des prisons d'état,* 2 vols. Hamburg, 1782 (published anonymously).
*Ma conversion.* [London, 1783] (published anonymously).
*Errotika Biblion.* Rome, Imprimerie du Vatican [*sic*], 1783 (published anonymously).
*Considérations sur l'Ordre de Cincinnatus.* London, 1784.
*Doutes sur la liberté de l'Escaut, réclamée par l'Empereur.* London, [1784].
*De la Caisse d'Escompte.* [Paris?], 1785.
*Lettre du comte de Mirabeau à —— sur MM. de Cagliostro et Lavater.* Berlin, 1786.
*Sur Moses Mendelssohn, sur la réforme politique des Juifs, et en particulier sur la révolution tentée en leur faveur en 1753 dans la Grande Bretagne.* London, 1787, reprinted 1968 by Editions EDHIS.

*Dénonciation de l'agiotage au roi et à l'assemblée des notables.* [Paris], 1787.

*Lettre remise à Frédéric-Guillaume II,* Berlin, 1787.

*Aux Bataves sur le Stathoudérat.* [Amsterdam?], 1788.

*De la monarchie prussienne sous Frédéric le Grand,* 4 vols. London [Paris], 1788.

*Sur la liberté de la presse, imité de l'anglois de Milton.* London, 1788.

*Réponse aux alarmes des bons citoyens.* [Paris, 1788] (published anonymously).

*A la nation provençale* [Aix, 1789].

*Correspondance entre M.C —— et le comte de Mirabeau* [1789].

*Discours sur la représentation illégale de la nation provençale dans ses états actuels, et sur la nécessité de convoquer une Assemblée générale des trois ordres* [Aix, 1789].

*Histoire secrète de la Cour de Berlin, ou Correspondance d'un voyageur français, depuis le 5 juillet 1786, jusqu'au 19 janvier 1787,* 2 vols. [Alençon], 1789 (published anonymously).

*Réponse aux protestations faites au nom des prélats, et des possédans-fiefs de l'Assemblée des Etats actuels de Provence, contre le discours du comte de Mirabeau.* Aix, 1789.

*Théorie de la royauté, d'après la doctrine de Milton.* [Paris], 1789 (published anonymously).

*Collection complète des travaux de M. Mirabeau l'aîné à l'Assemblée nationale,* ed. E. Méjan, 5 vols. Paris, 1791–92.

*Lettres originales de Mirabeau écrites du donjon de Vincennes, pendant les années 1777, 78, 79 et 80,* collected by P. Manuel, 4 vols. Paris, 1792.

*Mémoires du ministère du Duc d'Aiguillon,* Paris, 1792.

*Lettres amicales du comte de Mirabeau à M. Mauvillon à Brunsuic.* Hamburg 1794.

*Lettres de Mirabeau à Chamfort.* Paris, [1797].

*Lettres inédites de Mirabeau. Mémoires et extraits de mémoires,* ed. J.-F. Vitry. Paris, 1806.

*Mémoires biographiques, littéraires et politiques de Mirabeau, écrits par lui-même, par son père, son oncle et son fils adoptif,* ed. J.-M.-N. Lucas de Montigny, 12 vols. Brussels, 1834–36.

*Correspondance entre le comte de Mirabeau et le comte de La Marck,* ed. A. de Bacourt, 3 vols. Paris, 1851.

*Discours de Mirabeau,* ed. François Furet, Paris, 1973.

## Newspapers, journals and reports

*Les Actes des Apôtres.* Paris, [1789–91].

*L'Ami du peuple.* [Paris], 1789–92.

*Archives parlementaires de 1787 à 1860.*

*Le Courrier de Provence.* Paris, 1789–91.

*Gazette Nationale, ou le Moniteur universel.* Paris, founded 1789.

*Journal des Etats-Généraux.* Paris, 1789–91.

*La Lanterne magique nationale.* [Paris, 1790].

*Lettres du comte de Mirabeau à ses commettans,* Paris, May–July 1789.

*Le Patriote françois.* [Paris], 1789–93.

*Procédure criminelle instruite au Châtelet de Paris sur la dénonciation des faits arrivés à Versailles dans la journée du 6 octobre 1789,* 3 vols. Paris, 1790.

*Révolutions de France et de Brabant.* Paris, [1789–91].

*Tableau des Témoins et Receuil des faits les plus intéressans contenus dans les dépositions de la procedure instruite au Châtelet de Paris sur les faits arrivés à Versailles les 5 et 6 octobre 1789.* [Paris], 1790.
*Suite de la procédure criminelle instruite au Châtelet de Paris sur la dénonciation des faits arrivés à Versailles, dans la journée du 6 octobre 1789.* Paris, 1790.

## Secondary literature

Acton, J.E.E.D., Baron (1910) *Lectures on the French Revolution.* London.
Aulard, F.-A. (1882–86) *L'Eloquence parlementaire pendant la Révolution française*, 3 vols. Paris.
Aulard, F.-A. (1901) *Histoire politique de la Révolution française . . . 1789–1804*, 4 vols. Paris.
Aulard, F.-A. (1905–07) *Les Orateurs de la Révolution*, 2 vols. Paris.
Aulard, F.-A. (1910) *The French Revolution: A Political History, 1789–1804*, trans. B. Miall, 4 vols. London.
Aulard, F.-A. (1914) *Les Grands Orateurs de la Révolution.* Paris.
Bailly, J.-S. (1820–28) *Mémoires*, Vols. 10–12 of St.-A. Berville and J.-F. Barrière, *Collection des mémoires rélatifs à la Révolution.* Paris.
Barnave, A.-P.-J. (1960) *Introduction à la Révolution française*, ed. F. Rude. Paris.
Barthou, L. (1913) *Mirabeau.* London.
Bastid, P. (1939) *Sieyès et sa pensée.* [Paris].
Bénétruy, J. (1962) *L'Atelier de Mirabeau.* Geneva.
Bernard, J.F. (1973) *Talleyrand.* London.
Biron, A.-L. de Gontaut, duc de (1865) *Lettres sur les Etats généraux*, ed. Maistre de Roger de La Lande. Paris.
Blanc, L. (1847–62) *Histoire de la Révolution française*, 12 vols. Paris.
Blount, C. (1952) 'Bentham, Dumont, and Mirabeau, an historical revision', *University of Birmingham Historical Journal*, 3, 153–67.
Blum, C. (1986) *Rousseau and the Republic of Virtue: The language of politics in the French Revolution.* New York.
Bosher, J.F. (1970) *French Finances 1770–1795. From Business to Bureaucracy.* Cambridge.
Bouillé, F.-C.-A. (1820–28) *Mémoires*, Vol. 7 of St.-A. Berville and J.-F. Barrière, *Collection des mémoires rélatifs à la Révolution.* Paris.
Boyd, J.P. (1950) *The Papers of Thomas Jefferson.* Princeton.
Brissot, J.-P. (1911) *Mémoires, 1754–1793*, ed. C. Perroud, 2 vols. Paris.
Brissot, J.-P. (1912) *Correspondance et papiers*, ed. C. Perroud. Paris.
Burke, E. (1967) *Correspondance*, vol. 6, ed. A. Cobban and R. A. Smith. Cambridge.
Cabanis, G. *Journal de la maladie et de la mort de H.-G. Riqueti Mirabeau.* Paris, Crapart, an XI.
Campan, J.-L.-H., Madam de (1849) *Mémoires sur la vie privée de Marie-Antoinette.* Paris.
Carré, H. (1920) *La Noblesse de France et l'opinion publique au XVIIIe siècle.* Paris.
Castries, René de la Croix, duc de (1960) *Mirabeau, ou l'échec du destin.* Paris.
Chamfort, S.-R.-N. (1852) *Oeuvres.* Paris.
Chaussinand-Nogaret, G. (1976) *La Noblesse au XVIIIe siècle. De la féodalité aux Lumières.* Paris.

Chaussinand-Nogaret, G. (1982) *Mirabeau*. Paris.
Chevallier, J.-J. (1947) *Mirabeau. Un grand destin manqué*. Paris.
Cottin, P. (1903) *Sophie de Monnier et Mirabeau d'après leur correspondance secrète inédite (1775–1789)*. Paris.
Cubells, M. (1984) *La Provence des Lumières: Les Parlementaires d'Aix au XVIIIe siècle*. Paris.
Dakin, D. (1939) *Turgot and the Ancien Régime in France*. London
Dard, E. (1936) *Le Général Choderlos de Laclos*. Paris.
Desmoulins, C. (1874) *Histoire secrète de la Révolution*, in *Oeuvres*, ed. J. Claretie, 2 vols. Paris.
Droz, J. (1839–42) *Histoire du régne de Louis XVI pendant les années où l'on pouvait prévenir ou diriger la Révolution française*, 3 vols. Paris.
Dumont, E. (1951) *Souvenirs sur Mirabeau et sur les deux premières Assemblées législatives*, ed. J. Bénétruy. Paris.
Dumouriez, C. (1820–28) *La Vie et les mémoires*, Vols. 16–19 of St.-A. Berville and J.-F. Barrière, *Collection des mémoires rélatifs à la Révolution*. Paris.
Duquesnoy, A. (1894) *Journal*, ed. R. de Crèvecoeur, 2 vols. Paris.
Egret, J. (1954) 'La Prérévolution en Provence, 1787–89', *Annales historiques de la Révolution française*, 26, 97–126.
Egret, J. (1950) *La Révolution des Notables: Mounier et les Monarchiens*. Paris.
Elias, N. (1974) *La Société de Cour*, Paris.
Ferrières, C.-E., marquis de (1820–28) *Mémoires*, Vols. 3–5 of St.-A. Berville and J.-F. Barrière, *Collection des mémoires rélatifs à la Révolution*. Paris.
Ferrières, C.-E., marquis de (1932) *Correspondance inédite (1789, 1790, 1791)*, ed. H. Carré. Paris.
Fitzmaurice, Lord E. (1912) *Life of William, Earl of Shelburne*, 2nd edn, 2 vols. London.
Fryer, W.R. (1966) 'Mirabeau in England, 1784–1785', *Renaissance and Modern Studies*, 10, 34–87.
Fox-Genovese, E. (1976) *The Origins of Physiocracy: Economic revolution and social order in eighteenth-century France*. Ithaca, New York.
Furet, F. (1981) *Interpreting the French Revolution*. Cambridge.
Furet, F. (1986) *Marx et la Révolution française*. Paris.
Furet, F. and Richet, D. (1965–66) *La Révolution*. 2 vols. Paris.
Gagnebin, B. (1948) 'Jeremy Bentham et Etienne Dumont', Jeremy Bentham Bicentenary lecture, University College, London.
Godechot, J. (1961) *La Contre-Révolution: doctrine et action 1789–1804*. Paris.
Goodwin, A. (1946) 'Calonne, the Assembly of French Notables of 1787 and the Origins of the *Révolte Nobilaire*', *English Historical Review*, 61, 202–34, 329–77.
Goodwin, A. (1970) *The French Revolution*, 5th edn. London.
Gottschalk, L. and M. Maddox (1969) *Lafayette in the French Revolution*. Chicago.
Gower, G.G.L., Duke of Sutherland (1885) *The Despatches of Earl Gower*, ed. O. Browning. Cambridge.
Greenlaw, R.W. (1958) *The Economic Origins of the French Revolution: Poverty or Prosperity?* Boston.
Guibal, G. (1889), *Mirabeau et la Provence en 1789*. Aix.
Hampson, N. (1978) *Danton*. Oxford.
Hampson, N. (1983) *Will and Circumstance: Montesquieu, Rousseau and the French Revolution*. London.
Harris, R.D. (1986) *Necker and the Revolution of 1789*. Lanham, Maryland.
Hazard, P. (1946) *La Pensée européenne au XVIIIe siècle: de Montesquieu à Lessing*. Paris.

Hervieu, G. (1925) *Les Idées économiques et financières du comte de Mirabeau*. La Rochelle.

Higgs, H. (1897) *The Physiocrats*. London.

Higonnet, P. (1982) *Class, Ideology, and the Rights of Nobles during the French Revolution*. Oxford.

Hugo, V. (1834) *Etude sur Mirabeau*. Paris.

Jaurès, J.-L., ed. (1901–08) *Histoire socialiste (1789–1900)*, 10 vols. Paris.

Jouvenel, H. de (1928) *La Vie orageuse de Mirabeau*. Paris.

Kafker, F.A. and Laux, J.M. (1968) *The French Revolution: Conflicting Interpretations*. New York.

Kynynmound, E., Countess of Minto (1874) *Life and Letters of Sir Gilbert Elliot*, 3 vols. London.

Lacour-Gayet, R. (1963) *Calonne*. Paris.

La Fayette, G. du Motier, marquis de (1837–38) *Mémoires, correspondance et manuscrits du général La Fayette*, 6 vols. Paris.

La Fayette, G. du Motier, marquis de (1903) *Correspondance inédite de La Fayette*, ed. J. Thomas. Paris.

Lameth, A., baron de (1828–29) *Histoire de l'Assemblée constituante*, 2 vols. Paris.

Lanzac de Laborie, L. de (1887) *Un Royaliste libéral en 1789. Jean-Joseph Mounier*. Paris.

Lefebvre, G. (1951) *La Révolution française*, new edn. Paris.

Lefebvre, G. (1962–64) *The French Revolution from its Origins to 1793*, 2 vols. London.

Lefebvre, G. (1970) *Quatre-vingt-neuf*. Paris.

Le Forestier, R. (1914) *Les Illuminés de Bavière et la Franc-Maçonnerie allemande*. Paris.

Léon, P. (1953) *Mémoires de Talleyrand*. Paris.

Loménie, L.-L. de (1870) *La comtesse de Rochefort et ses amis*. Paris.

Loménie, L.-L. de (1879–91) *Les Mirabeau*. Paris.

Lourde, C. (1838) *Histoire de la Révolution à Marseille et en Provence*, 3 vols. Marseille.

Mack, M.P. (1962) *Jeremy Bentham. An Odyssey of Ideas, 1748–1792*. London.

Malouet, P.-V. (1874) *Mémoires*, 2nd edn. Paris.

Marion, M. (1914–28) *Histoire financière de la France depuis 1715*, 5 vols. Paris.

Marmontel, J.-F. (1818) *Mémoires*, 2 vols. [Paris].

Mathiez, A. (1913) *Les Grandes journées de la Constituante*. Paris.

Mathiez, A. (1922–27) *La Révolution française*, 3 vols. Paris.

Meunier, Dauphin (1908) *La Comtesse de Mirabeau (1752–1800)*. Paris.

Meunier, Dauphin (1914) *Louise de Mirabeau, marquise de Cabris, 1752–1807*. Paris.

Meunier, Dauphin (1926) *Autour de Mirabeau*. Paris.

Michelet, J. (1961-2) *Histoire de la Révolution française*, ed. G. Walter, 2 vols. [Paris.]

Mirabeau, Victor Riqueti, marquis de (1750) *Mémoire sur les états provinciaux*. Reproduced in Part 4 of *L'Ami des hommes*, 2 vols. Avignon, 1756–58.

Mirabeau, Victor Riqueti, marquis de (1760) *Théorie de l'impôt*. [Paris.]

Mirabeau, Victor Riqueti, marquis de (1769) *Les Economiques*. Paris.

Mirabeau, Victor Riqueti, marquis de (1780) *Les devoirs*. Milan.

Moleville, A.-F. Bertrand de (1801–3) *Histoire de la Révolution de France* 14 vols. Paris.

Montlosier, F.-D. de Reynaud, comte de (1830) *Mémoires . . . sur la Révolution française le Consulat . . .* 2 vols. Paris.

Mornet, D. (1933) *Les Origines intellectuelles de la Révolution française, 1715–1787*. Paris.

Mounier, J.-J. (1789a) *Exposé de la conduite de M. Mounier dans l'Assemblée Nationale, et des motifs de son retour en Dauphiné*. Paris.

Mounier, J.-J. (1789b) *Nouvelles observations sur les Etats-Généraux*. [Paris?]
Necker, J. (1802) *Dernières Vues de Politique et de Finance, offertes à la Nation française*. Paris.
Peuchet, J. (1824) *Mémoires sur Mirabeau et son époque*, 4 vols. Paris.
Plan, Ph. (1874) *Un collaborateur de Mirabeau*. Paris.
Pons, J. (1938) *La Révolution française et l'avènement de la bourgeoisie*. Paris.
Portalis, J.-E.-M. (1848) 'Mes souvenirs politiques', *Séances et travaux de l'Académie des Sciences morales et politiques*, 365–7.
Reynald, H. (1872) *Mirabeau et la Constituante*. Paris.
Ripert, H. (1901) *Le Marquis de Mirabeau . . . ses théories politiques et économiques*. Paris.
Rivarol, A., comte de (1820–28) *Mémoires*, Vol. 48 of St.-A. Berville and J.-F. Barrière, *Collection des mémoires rélatifs à la Révolution*. Paris.
Robespierre, M. (1910–) *Oeuvres complètes*, ed. Société des Etudes Robespierristes. Paris.
Robespierre, M. (1950) *Discours 1789–90*, ed. M. Bouloiseau, G. Lefebvre and A. Soboul. Part I, Vol. 6 of *Oeuvres complètes*. Paris.
Rocquain, F. (1878) *L'Esprit révolutionnaire avant la Révolution, 1715–1789*. Paris.
Romilly, S. (1841) *Memoirs of the Life of Sir Samuel Romilly, written by himself, with a selection from his correspondence*, ed. by his sons, 2 vols, 3rd edn. London.
Rose, J.H. (1911) *William Pitt and National Revival*. London.
Rousseau, J.-J. (1762) *Du contrat social*. Amsterdam.
Rousseau, J.-J. (1924–34) *Correspondance générale*, ed. Th. Dufour. Paris.
Rousseau, J.-J. (1968) *The Social Contract*, trans. M. Cranston. Harmondsworth.
Rousseau, J.-J. (1978) *Correspondance complète de Jean-Jacques Rousseau*, ed. R.A. Leigh, vols. 31–32. Oxford.
Rudé, G. (1985) *Robespierre: Portrait of a Revolutionary Democrat*. New York.
Skinner, Q. (1978) *The Foundations of Modern Political Thought*, 2 vols. Cambridge.
Soboul, A. (1962) *Précis d'histoire de la Révolution française*. Paris.
Soboul, A. (1973) *1789, l'an I de la Liberté*. Paris.
Soboul, A. (1974) *The French Revolution 1787–1799*, trans. A. Forrest and C. Jones, 2 vols. London.
Staël-Holstein, A.-L.-G., baronne de (1820–21) *Considérations sur les principaux événemens de la Révolution française*. Vols. 12–14 of *Oeuvres complètes*. Paris.
Stern, A. (1895–6) *La Vie de Mirabeau*, 2 vols. Paris. Originally published in German in 1889 as *Das Leben Mirabeaus*.
Talleyrand-Périgord, C.-M., duc de (1891–92) *Mémoires*, ed. duc de Broglie, 5 vols. Paris.
Thiers, L.-A. (1823–27) *Histoire de la Révolution française*, 10 vols. Paris.
Thompson, Eric (1952) *Popular Sovereignty and the French Constituent Assembly, 1789–1791*. Manchester.
Thompson, James M. (1935) *Robespierre*, 2 vols. Oxford.
Vallentin, A. (1946–47) *Mirabeau*, 2 vols. Paris.
Vallentin, A. (1948) *Mirabeau*, trans. E.W. Dickes. New York.
Viguier, J. (1896) *La Convocation des Etats généraux en Provence*. Paris.
Voltaire, F.-M. Arouet (1962) *Correspondence*, Vol. 79, ed. T. Besterman. Geneva.
Welch, O.J.G. (1951) *Mirabeau: a Study of a Democratic Monarchist*. London.
Welschinger, H. (1900) *La Mission secrète de Mirabeau à Berlin, 1786–1787*. Paris.
Weulersse, G. (1910) *Le Mouvement Physiocratique en France de 1756 à 1770*, 2 vols. Paris.
Young, A. (1929) *Travels in France during the Years 1787, 1788 and 1789*, ed. C. Maxwell. Cambridge.

# Index